The Wealth of Britain 1085-1966

SIDNEY POLLARD and DAVID W. CROSSLEY

B. T. Batsford Ltd London

First published 1968

© Sidney Pollard and David W. Crossley 1968

Made and printed in Great Britain
by William Clowes and Sons, Ltd
London and Beccles, for the publishers
B. T. BATSFORD LTD
4 Fitzhardinge Street, Portman Square, London W.1

c

Ian Livingstone
7, Roman Way,
DUNBLANE.
Perthshire.

The Wealth of Britain 1085–1966

Contents

Preface

It is well known among those who study the movements of national incomes that comparisons, even across a number of years or between countries with different traditions, are dangerous. How much more foolhardy, then, must be the attempt to trace the changes in the wealth of a country for over eight centuries, the fastest-moving centuries known to history! If men always had the same group of material objects to choose from, and if they always chose them in the same order, and if these choices remained constant over the years and the centuries, then, perhaps, sensible accounts of the changes in the wealth of a community could be written. But things are not so simple. Even if offered the same choices, different men will choose in different order and quantities—even one man will change his options from time to time. The choice has not always been the same, but, on the contrary, has changed vastly between the native food and primitive manufactures available in the Middle Ages to the processed foods and synthetic products of today. Our way of life, our distance from the countryside, even our motivation, and our concepts of achievement, happiness or wealth have been transformed out of recognition, and no man could ever live fully in two periods, comprehend them both fully, and then judge between them.

What meaning, then, could there be in putting together societies of such varied characters, aims and value systems as the conquered feudal communities ruled by the Normans, the subjects of the Tudors, exploiting massive overseas trade and new technologies under a strong monarchy, and the complex democratic society of the twentieth century? What benefit could be derived from trailing a single concept of 'wealth' across them? And if it could be done, would a small volume be sufficient to encompass the results?

In entering upon this dangerous ground, the authors are aware of many, perhaps of most, of the pitfalls. Yet they feel that, suitably warned, the reader can be invited to negotiate them to some profit. The pages which follow are not to be read as an account of less or more, of simply richer or poorer. They should, in part, be seen as an attempt to describe what 'wealth' in each age consisted of, and how it was shared out, at least as much as presenting a continuous and comparative narrative. But beyond this there is some sense in which, in a given climate and in similar surroundings, the basic material needs of men remain alike: food, shelter, clothing, warmth and light, some form of recreation, and so on. With all the differences in values set upon these things, and in the choices available, and the influence on desires of what other men do, a comparison across the centuries of these matters is not entirely devoid of purpose. Apart from the statistics presented in the Appendix, for which we wish to make due acknowledgment to the authors, and which carry their own warnings, we do not, in fact, attempt any generalised juxtaposition of all the nine centuries. But we feel there is some meaning in tracing the change from one period to the next, or in trying to evaluate whether, over any given span of years, wealth increased or decreased, or how its composition changed, and there may even be some value in certain limited comparisons over longer time-spans. This belief is our justification for writing this book.

There are, of course, many concepts of income and wealth. Modern statisticians, basing themselves on the Keynsian model of the whole ('macro') economy, approach the annual flow along three main routes: incomes, expenditure and production. Suitably adjusted for such complications as imports and exports, they must all come to the same figure. It is therefore legitimate to check and correct the information available for each of them, that is to say, for actual concrete output, for total incomes, and for expenditure, i.e. consumption plus investment, by comparison with the others. For each of these concepts there are some variants, particularly the distinction between 'gross' and 'net', i.e. including or excluding such expenditure as capital replacement which must be termed a necessary cost rather than a part of the end product. Furthermore, for certain purposes the distribution of the annual flow— for example the share-out of incomes among different classes, or the division of expenditure between consumption and investment—may be as important as the size of the total.

Similarly, there are many concepts of 'wealth', though for more recent periods, as the whole of society has taken on a wholly capitalistic aspect and everything is measurable in similar terms, there has been a tendency to call it all 'capital'. All wealth may be converted, for statistical purposes, into income-yielding property, even in such cases as owner-occupied houses where the idea is somewhat far-fetched.

Normally, the particular concept or variant used depends on the purpose of the discussion. Each has its value for certain illustrations, and would be misleading for others. In this volume, however, we have not always been able to follow this counsel of perfection for the earlier centuries, and we have had to make use of whatever measure is available, even if it is not wholly apt, and adjust it accordingly.

This brings us to a second warning. The material available for such a study is very unevenly distributed over the centuries. For the more recent period, and the last few years in particular, there is a great surfeit of reasonably accurate data on all aspects of national and *per capita* income and wealth; but, generally, the further we push back into the earlier centuries of this study, the less information there is, and the less reliable does it become. This book bears eloquent witness to these difficulties. Virtually each chapter, covering a distinctive phase in national economic development, is also largely based on different kinds of material. What are at first only indirect and literary rather than statistical approaches to wealth and income gradually become, in the absence of any quantitative knowledge, more direct literary statements. These in turn give way to numerical estimates, and ultimately to chapters which are almost entirely, and perhaps tediously, based on well-authenticated calculations. Thus, as the book proceeds, words and unscientific impressions give way to undisputed facts and figures. It is not impossible that some of the apparent changes that we trace are illusory, and are based on nothing more than a different, and usually more reliable, source for the later period than for the earlier. The reader is hereby warned to be on the lookout for such false conclusions.

Finally, we wish to thank our typist, Miss Helen Trippett, for the cheerful skill with which she mastered two sets of scarcely legible handwriting.

S.P.
D.W.C.

Chapter one

Early Medieval England:
An Economy Under Pressure, 1085–1315

There is little purpose in trying to measure the wealth of Britain before the late seventeenth century in numerical terms. Before the Political Arithmetic of Petty, Davenant and Gregory King there are no trustworthy contemporary estimates on which to draw, and we have to adopt broader and less precise methods. However, the use of signposts has its attractions; we rely not on figures but on more human evidence, on the signs of initiative in land clearance and the improvement of agriculture; on the human results of the pressure of population on natural resources, or the tangible evidence of living standards provided by the archaeologist. In spite of the chance nature of the samples which have come down to us we can gain some impression of the dynamic pattern of change in the wealth both of the country and of groups within the population.

For the medieval period we have first to take stock of resources at Domesday and then in the succeeding two centuries of expansion; these we may attempt to relate to changes in the population, by indicating the evidence of the success or otherwise of particular groups in maintaining their income and living standards.

England in the late eleventh century

The pattern of English settlement in 1086 left many resources underutilised. The Domesday survey presents a picture which, compared with evidence from two centuries later, shows significant areas only thinly populated, valuable land and mineral deposits only partly exploited, and many potential trading centres underdeveloped. However, five centuries of Anglo-Saxon settlement had seen the clearance of much of the more accessible land of the lowland zone,[1] and the strong tradition of reclamation had spread to more difficult areas; for instance, ground had been won on Pevensey levels from the eighth century, and the monks of Glastonbury were draining the Somerset marshes in the tenth. But there were still great contrasts within

---

[1] The valley bottoms of Wiltshire are typical; see *Victoria County History* (henceforward referred to as *V.C.H.*), Wiltshire, IV, 7.

Eastern and Midland England. In East Anglia, whilst population was commonly 40–50 per square mile and settlements with 100 or more recorded inhabitants were thickly spread along the lower reaches of the Yare and the Waveney, in Breckland the few that there were rarely had more than 40 and frequently fewer than 20 inhabitants, the peat-lands of the Fens were virtually unoccupied, and even the potentially fertile woodlands of West Essex retained their natural forest cover. Similarly, in the Midlands, whilst much of Northamptonshire and Leicestershire, South-East Worcestershire and parts of North War-wickshire had been easily settled and had attracted large populations, in 1086 Shropshire and North Staffordshire were thinly occupied.[2] Domesday's fiscal preoccupations make direct references to clearance few; they appear in the Gloucestershire and Herefordshire surveys, but by implication they can be seen elsewhere. Outlying parts of estates often received scant attention from a survey whose major pur-pose was to assess the taxability of the whole, and in Sussex and Kent the denes of the Weald often seem to have been included with the older centres on the edge of the wood. Indeed in Kent, churches appear in the early twelfth-century *Domesday Monachorum* and *Textus Roffensis* at places of which Domesday makes no mention.[3] Similarly, the Leicestershire survey of 1124–9 mentions apparently well-estab-lished villages ignored by Domesday, and in Oxfordshire earlier eleventh-century sources show settlements not mentioned in 1086.[4] But even if Domesday may give a slightly pessimistic impression of the extent of clearance, it points to the contrast between highland and lowland, and particularly between north and south. North of the Trent few areas had reached a population density of 10 per square mile, and apart from the Wirral, Holderness, the Trent Valley and southern parts of the West Riding 2·5 or less was normal. Lancashire and all territory north of the Aire received scant attention and, apart perhaps from the coast lands of Durham and Northumberland, prob-

[2] W. G. Hoskins, *The Making of the English Landscape*, 1955, 61–3; *Cambridge Economic History of Europe* (henceforward referred to as *C.E.H.E.*), I (1966), 550; H. C. Darby (ed.), *The Domesday Geography of Eastern England*, 1952, 116, 354–60; H. C. Darby and I. B. Terrett (ed.), *The Domesday Geography of Midland England*, 1954, 424–33.
[3] H. C. Darby and E. M. Campbell (ed.), *The Domesday Geography of South-East England*, 1962, 577–81; G. Ward, 'The Lists of Saxon Churches in the Textus Roffensis', *Arch. Cantiana*, XLIV (1932), 39–59; 'The Lists of Saxon Churches in the Domesday Monachorum and White Book of St Augustine', *ibid.*, XLV (1933), 60–89.
[4] Darby and Terrett, 421, 436; R. Lennard, *Rural England 1086–1135*, 1959, 9–13; N. Neilson, *The Cartulary and Terrier of the Priory of Bilsington, Kent*, 1928, 8–10; J. S. Moore, *Laughton, a Study in the Evolution of the Wealden Landscape*, University of Leicester, Dept of English Local History, Occasional Paper 19, 1966, 23–4.

ably corresponded with what little is known of the pattern of settlement of Wales and of Scotland at this time: a small dispersed
population relying very largely on pastoral farming, where insecurity
and the emptiness of the land made settlement boundaries far from
exact.[5]

Together with evidence of population-density may be taken the
numbers of plough teams. The contrasts in the lowlands are thus
reinforced, between for instance Central Norfolk and West Essex,
between the Sussex coast and the Weald, or the upper Thames Valley
and the empty heaths of the Surrey-Berkshire border. Such broad
differences stand out, for despite the reservations which have been
made over Domesday plough-team figures as a guide to wealth, they
indicate the scale of production of the grains so important to the
bread-based diet of the lowlands. Similarly with Domesday's water
corn-mills; in Lincolnshire, Norfolk and Suffolk one mill for three
villages was common, but the frequency declined further west. These
may be measures of wealth in the lowlands, but they are less appropriate to the pastoral west, for here too, where plough-teams and corn
mills were far less common, settlement had been active: in Devon the
place-names of Domesday show that a large proportion of modern
farm-sites at less than 1,000 feet above sea level had been occupied.[6]
England, and in particular the highland zone, was at a stage when
uncleared land represented an appreciable proportion of wealth—
hence the importance attached in 1086 to waste, woodland, marsh
or fisheries. The amount of waste surrounding a village was of major
importance for grazing, and the amount of cleared meadow and
pasture seems low enough to suggest that assarted ground was mainly
used for arable. Only in river valleys, in particular those of the East
Midlands, the Trent, the Soar, the Welland, was meadow plentiful,
and unless differences in recording have given a distorted impression,
Norfolk and South Oxfordshire show sufficient lack of good meadow
for the waste to have been particularly valuable.[7] Similarly, woodland
was recorded not only for its timber but also for its pig capacity,[8] and
marshland was a valuable asset for rights of turbary, for fishing and
for sheep-grazing. Domesday information about demesne livestock
survives only for those counties covered by the Little and Exeter
Domesdays, but it is clear that the Essex marshes, the coastlands of

[5] H. C. Darby and I. S. Maxwell (ed.), *The Domesday Geography of Northern
England*, 1962, 429–37; T. B. Franklin, *A History of Scottish Farming*, 1958, 64.
[6] M. M. Postan, 'The Maps of Domesday', *Ec.H.R.*, 2nd ser., VII (1954–5),
98–100; W. G. Hoskins, *Provincial England*, 1963, 15 *seq.*; Lennard, 278–87;
Hoskins, *English Landscape*, 65.
[7] Darby, *Eastern England*, 365–6; Darby and Terrett, 440–1.
[8] H. C. Darby, 'Domesday Woodland', *Ec.H.R.*, 2nd ser., III (1950–1), 21–43.

Norfolk between Wells and the Wash, and the Fens carried large numbers of sheep supplying the textile towns of the East Midlands.[9]

Of industry, towns and trade at Domesday we can say rather less. The importance of salt-making is seen in the recording of salterns on the east and south coasts, the brine springs of Cheshire and the rights of neighbouring villages therein, and the Worcestershire springs, linked to surrounding settlements by the need for fuel.[10] Lead-mining in Derbyshire was recorded, but lead from the Mendips and tin from Cornwall were not. Similarly, although the iron ore deposits in Somerset and Gloucestershire were clearly being thoroughly worked, there is only one reference for Yorkshire and only one works mentioned in the Weald.[11]

Our knowledge of late eleventh-century urban life is distorted by the loss of the Domesday entries for London and Winchester, but there was obvious urban development elsewhere. Each lowland shire had a number of boroughs with some of the characteristics of urban communities such as markets, traders, and at least a partial outside food supply. In Kent, for instance, there were eight boroughs, two of which, Rochester and Canterbury, were accorded the description *civitas*, 'city' by Domesday. At Dover we are told of a guildhall, four churches, and tolls which had almost trebled between 1065 and 1086. There were, however, boroughs with little to distinguish them from other villages; in Kent Seasalter was in this category, and between this and the three prominent Kentish towns lay Hythe, Romney, Sandwich and Fordwich, all four scantily recorded but appearing to have populations ranging from 400 at Fordwich to 2,000 at Hythe. The pattern varied from shire to shire. Suffolk had seven obvious towns, Bury St Edmunds with perhaps 3,000 and Ipswich with 1,200 inhabitants contrasting with Eye, 700, and Beccles, Clare, Dunwich and Sudbury, each with perhaps 600. Yet here there were also settlements without the tenurial accoutrements of borough status: five other villages also had markets, and the trading network was clearly more complex than the Domesday total of boroughs suggests at first sight. All over Midland England a similar pattern can be seen: the shire towns Northampton, Oxford or Bedford; the smaller towns like Tutbury or Newark dependent on a castle, a market, or a river crossing; and those smaller still, some of which are not named as boroughs,

[9] Lennard, 260 *seq.*; P. Sawyer, 'The Wealth of England in the Eleventh Century', *Trans. Roy. Hist. Soc.*, 5th ser., XV (1965), 163.
[10] H. E. Hallam, *Settlement and Society*, 1965, 171; H. C. Darby, *An Historical Geography of England before 1800*, 1936, 225–6; J. Varley and J. Tait (ed.), *A Middlewich Chartulary*, Chetham Soc., Remains, 105 (1941), 35.
[11] H. R. Schubert, *A History of the British Iron and Steel Industry to 1775*, 1957, 80.

on the verge of specialisation and most easily identified by their markets—Bampton in Oxfordshire, for instance, or Cookham in Berkshire. It is true that some boroughs with Saxon military origins had never developed an urban character, but they were more than balanced by the developing villages.[12] Though London's Domesday record is lost, other sources show its established commercial links. In the eighth century, in Bede's time, trade had been active with continental ports, and by 1066 the town, though probably covering an area little larger than that enclosed by the Roman walls, clearly possessed many of the resources and contacts for future trade expansion. On the local level it drew its supplies from a growing area of Middlesex, Essex and Surrey, and even in the eleventh century it was clearly influencing the economy of a widening region.[13]

The Conquest itself and subsequent campaigns were a setback to development. In the south-east many of the settlements assessed in Domesday were stated to have been worth more in 1065. These correspond with the line of advance of the Norman army after Hastings, both in the battle area and along the route round the south of London to Berkhamsted, and in the immediate London region.[14] Reductions in value in the Midlands in 1086 compared with 1066 can be attributed to the 1067 campaign, whose effects are noticeable over a broad stretch of country from Bedfordshire to Staffordshire, and the 1069 campaign in the north had a noticeable effect on the prosperity of Yorkshire, as seen in Domesday valuations[15]:

	West Riding	North Riding	East Riding
1066	£1,123	924	1,432
1086	597	184	387

The list of places lying waste is correspondingly large. Of 1,900 villages, 850 were depopulated and a further 400 reduced as a result of a combination of Norman, Scots and Danish damage. These were very widespread and extended to the marginal uplands, implying perhaps secondary depopulation as people moved into the devastated lowlands. However, even if these setbacks may have been serious in the north, the picture in general is of an economy with an expanding

[12] Darby and Campbell, *South-East England*, 545 *seq.*; Darby, *Eastern England*, 192 *seq.*
[13] Darby and Campbell, 583–5.
[14] *ibid.*, 569–75.
[15] Darby, *Historical Geography*, 165 *seq.*; T. A. M. Bishop, 'The Norman Settlement of Yorkshire', *Studies in Medieval History Presented to F. M. Powicke*, ed. R. W. Hunt, W. A. Pantin and R. W. Southern, 1948, 1–14.

agricultural base which was to continue its growth over a further two centuries as population rose and land clearance was maintained.

The outward appearance of wealth of eleventh-century England has been stressed in recent comment on the attraction of the country to raiders—Vikings, Scots and the Norman Conquerors themselves.[16] Another hint of the surplus being created may perhaps come from the extent of church-building and monastic expansion. Domesday's picture of churches is not complete, but in Suffolk and Huntingdon, where the evidence is most trustworthy, churches had been built at a remarkable proportion of the recorded settlements which, of course, include hamlets. The progress of church-building continued in the twelfth century, and it is in this post-Conquest period that monastic expansion is particularly notable. Not only were Benedictine houses enlarged, but the newer orders, the Cluniacs from the 1070s and the Cistercians in the mid-twelfth century, were able to found numerous houses on the basis of donations from a landed class with an available surplus. Obviously much of the wealth thus diverted contributed to economic development. Without the efforts of monastic communities fewer lands would have been cleared and the building trades would have been expanded less, but some funds were syphoned off: late in the eleventh century it was fashionable to present property to French houses, and income from these lands became of some importance, for instance, to Saint Wandrille which in the thirteenth century relied on its English income to a considerable degree.[17]

Medieval agriculture: the extension of cultivation and the improvement of methods

Over the twelfth and thirteenth centuries land clearance produced a significant increase in national output. There is some evidence of diminishing returns late in the thirteenth century as less fertile lands were reached—for instance on the Chalk Downs of Wiltshire, the Cotswolds, the Weald or Sherwood—but in most areas there are abundant signs of clearance of new lands capable of cultivation.[18] The gaps in clearance seen in Domesday were gradually filled: evidence from Sussex suggests that assarting reached its peak in the first half of the thirteenth century[19]; in the Midlands village arable fields reached the parish boundaries, with even the poorest land in use by 1300.

[16] Sawyer, *art. cit.*, 145 *seq.*
[17] Lennard, 209–330; D. Matthews, *The Norman Monasteries and their English Possessions*, 1962, 28, 65.
[18] E. Miller, *The Abbey and Bishopric of Ely*, 1951, 96; *C.E.H.E.*, I (1966), 551.
[19] Moore, 36 *seq.*

The cultivated area of Wigston Magna, for example, at its north-east and south-east limits in the late eleventh century and the south-west by the mid-twelfth, covered almost all the parish by the 1290s. Leicestershire, apart from Charnwood, was by 1300 covered with villages and hamlets spaced every 1½–2 miles, having a total of almost 400 villages and hamlets in an acreage of half a million.[20] The process was even more spectacular in the coastal marshlands. Large areas of the Romney and North Kent marshes were reclaimed in the twelfth and thirteenth centuries, and in South Lincolnshire there was a complete reversal of relative prosperity between upland and fenland silts. As the uplands slowly advanced in wealth, the Fens, from being virtually unoccupied in the mid-eleventh century, were sufficiently reclaimed to surpass them by the time of the 1332 subsidy.[21] In inland Cambridgeshire land under cultivation had grown by the middle of the twelfth century to an area not to be surpassed until the middle of the sixteenth.[22]

Assarting was conducted both by estates and individuals. Monasteries were particularly active in the clearance of large tracts; contemporaries such as Walter Map and Giraldus Cambrensis commented on the scale of reclamation practised by the Cistercians, the growth of whose granges hastened the recovery of production in the devastated parts of Yorkshire. The Cistercians were not alone; the Augustinian Canons expanded production on granges frequently based on tithes and land gifts in established villages, and operated by lay brothers with an enthusiasm rare in a normal community.[23] Bilsdale, cleared by Byland and Rievaulx Abbeys, and Eskdale, cleared by the Canons of Guisborough, were typical of the northern expansion, and the Benedictine orders provide examples elsewhere, amongst them the reclamation of Kentish marshlands by Canterbury Cathedral Priory, of fenlands by Crowland, Thorney and Ramsey, and Mere Marsh by Glastonbury Abbey.[24] These extensions were carried out in a period when much was to be gained from investment; Canterbury's reclaimed marshlands in North Kent were let out at competitive leasehold rents

[20] M. W. Beresford and J. K. St Joseph, *Medieval England: an Aerial Survey*, 1958, 91–2; W. G. Hoskins, *The Midland Peasant*, 1957, 58–63.
[21] R. A. L. Smith, *Canterbury Cathedral Priory*, 1943, 166 *seq.*; Neilson, 38–54; H. C. Darby, *The Medieval Fenland*, 1940, 141.
[22] M. Spufford, *A Cambridgeshire Community*, University of Leicester, Dept of English Local History, Occasional Paper 20, 1965, 12–13.
[23] Walter Map—see *De Nugis Curialium*, Cymmrodorion Rec. Soc., IX (1923), 40 *seq.*; Giraldus Cambrensis—*Giraldus Cambrensis Opera*, ed. J. S. Brewer, *Rolls Series*, 1873, IV, 113; B. Waites, 'The Monastic Settlement of North-East Yorkshire', *Yorks. Arch. Jnl.*, XL (1959–62), 478–95; 'The Monastic Grange as a Factor in the Settlement of North-East Yorkshire', *ibid.*, 627–56.
[24] R. A. L. Smith, *Collected Papers*, 1947, 108–14; Darby, *Historical Geography*, 180.

in the late thirteenth century. But whilst local population-pressure late in the century might lead to leasing, for at least a century from 1150 demands of local markets generally favoured direct demesne operation. Thus Ely's assarts for the demesne contributed to a striking increase in the estate's income; William of Colerne, Abbot of Malmesbury, organised the ploughing of pasture for incorporation in the demesne arable, and Canterbury used much of its marshland reclamation for sheep pasture.[25]

These large assarts were not entirely trouble-free. In 1189 the men of Holland invaded the precinct of Crowland Abbey in protest against the clearance of the marshlands they had traditionally used as common for grazing, turf-cutting and fishing. Nor were the new lands always highly productive. The Canterbury manor of Ebony, much of which was reclaimed under Prior Henry of Eastry, enjoyed little increase in cultivable area between the 1280s and the 1330s due to the infertility of the new lands and the repeated sea floods over ground which sank as it dried out. However, it has been suggested that at a time of chronically unfavourable weather, reclamation in Kent must be looked on as maintaining rather than increasing output. Landowners, monastic and lay, were beset with certain problems when enclosing waste, for before the Statute of Merton of 1235 those tenants with rights on the waste could delay with a charge of novel disseisin; however, after 1235 the manor might assart waste that it claimed was surplus to commoners' needs, although the opportunities for argument were obviously immense, particularly as the lord's right did not apply when commoners who were not his tenants were involved.[26]

The area assarted by individuals or groups, though significant, is less easy to establish than that of the great estates. But there were communal clearances on a scale as large as those of monastic houses. In the Lincolnshire and Norfolk Fenlands townships built and repaired new seabanks; in the wapentake of Elloe 50 square miles were reclaimed between 1170 and 1241; and in Skirbeck wapentake the townships of Leake and Wrangle expanded to the limit imposed by the East Fen Deep early in the thirteenth century. These well-documented communal clearances were on potentially excellent land—the minute descriptions in thirteenth-century surveys testify to their value.[27] The assarts undertaken by individuals rather than estates ranged from such corporate efforts to the clearances by men farming in severalty in the uplands

[25] *C.E.H.E.*, I (1966), 585; Miller, *Ely*, 99; Smith, *Canterbury*, 118; *V.C.H.*, Wiltshire, IV, 11.

[26] Hallam, 25; R. A. L. Smith, 'Marsh Embankment and Sea Defence in Medieval Kent', *Ec.H.R.*, X (1939–40), 33–7; T. F. T. Plucknett, *The Legislation of Edward I*, 1949, 84–5.

[27] Hallam, 38, 91.

of Devon or Lancashire. In Yorkshire in the twelfth and thirteenth centuries numerous assarts were made around the open-field cores of existing villages and on the lands in the Vale of York laid waste in 1069, many of which appear to have lain uncultivated for as much as a century.[28] Here many new free tenancies sprang up, having only slight connection with overlords, and there was a fairly general pattern among highland zone clearance of small rents and fines paid by free tenants in *de facto* recognition of assarts of moor or wood; fines for encroachment on royal forest were frequent, providing a useful source of Crown income rather than having any penal aspect[29]; there were many encroachments on the waste, and typical are entries in the Colne Halmote Court Rolls of fourteenth-century tenants paying rents for the odd acres over which they had spread, the infilling of lands by small farmers on Tavistock Abbey estates or the numerous assarts taking place on the upland estates of the Bishop of Durham. The Charter of 1204 for the disafforestation of Devon gave added opportunities for local upland farmers' expansion, and the increasing wealth of the county and its free tenants is amply testified by church-building in the late twelfth and early thirteenth centuries. The remaining dense forest of the Arden area of Warwickshire, contrasting with the early-cleared Felden, shows a similar pattern of clearance by migrant younger sons of villeins creating holdings and adopting freeholder status under the lordship of the many small religious houses established in the area.[30] In the more thickly populated areas of lowland England rather greater seigneurial attention was paid to assarting, for the increasing scarcity of land made new clearances an important source of high rents. Some manorial regulations were geared to this, as at Swannington, on the edge of Charnwood Forest, Leicestershire, where it was permissible in the late thirteenth century for a free tenant to assart according to the size of his holding.[31] The Bishops of Worcester actively made land grants in the late twelfth century. Ramsey estates

[28] H. P. R. Finberg, *Tavistock Abbey*, 1951, 43 *seq.*; R. B. Smith, *Blackburnshire*, University of Leicester, Dept of Eng. Loc. Hist., Occ. Paper 15, 1961, 10–11; T. A. M. Bishop, 'Assarting and the Growth of the Open Fields', *Ec.H.R.*, VI (1935), 13 *seq.*; M. W. Beresford, 'Glebe Terriers and Open Fields', *Yorks. Arch. Jnl*, 37 (1951), 336–7.

[29] S. Painter, *Studies in the History of the English Feudal Barony*, Baltimore, 1943, 163; J. R. Birrell, 'The Forest Economy of the Honour of Tutbury in the 14th and 15th Centuries', *Univ. Birmingham Hist. Jnl*, VIII (1962), 114–134.

[30] R. H. Tawney, *The Agrarian Problem in the 16th Century*, 1912, 87–8; H. P. R. Finberg, 'The Making of the Agrarian Landscape', *Devonshire Studies*, ed. W. G. Hoskins and H. P. R. Finberg, 1952, 318–19; W. Greenwell (ed.), *Boldon Buke*, Surtees Soc., XXV (1852), 2 *seq.*; R. H. Hilton, *The Social Structure of Rural Warwickshire in the Middle Ages*, Dugdale Soc., Occ. Paper 9, 1950, 12–15; E. M. Carus-Wilson, 'The First Half-Century of the Borough of Stratford-upon-Avon', *Ec.H.R.*, 2nd ser., XVIII (1965), 46–63.

[31] *V.C.H.*, Leicestershire, II, 158.

showed a boom in new peasant holdings which came neither from existing demesne nor from old villein lands, particularly in the twelfth century and continuing right through the thirteenth. These examples are as typical of the Midlands as the numerous assarts on Malmesbury lands are of the south-west.[32]

It is more difficult to measure how far a need for the increased production of food, notably grain, the basis of medieval diets, was met by intensive improvement in agricultural practice, as distinct from extension of the area under cultivation. There was a clear interest in increasing estate income over the thirteenth century, shown by the alert management of men such as Henry of Eastry, William of Colerne or Thomas Marlborough, Abbot of Evesham, and by the group of manuals of husbandry and management which have survived from the period. But it is important to keep manuals' advice in perspective. Their circulation is in doubt; they show occasional lapses from realistic description—for example in some remarkably high grain-yields mentioned by the *Anonymous Husbandry*—and the concentration on securing a greater proportion of an estate's potential for the lord, by checking boundaries, dues and customs, particularly in *The Book of Robert Grosseteste* and the *Seneschaucie*, is at times as prominent as the advice on the improvement of husbandry itself. However, this said, Walter of Henley's *Husbandry* embodied a standard of farming practice from which there was to be little advance before the late sixteenth century. What is uncertain is how Walter's methods compared with those of his contemporaries, particularly those working tenant land. His advice was apparently regular practice on the demesne lands of larger estates, but writing perhaps from experience as a bailiff he drew attention to problems of the period which, though general, were acute on tenant holdings.[33]

The major concern was over the fertility of arable land. Local conditions might provide or demand particular dressings; on the lands of Canterbury Cathedral Priory liming and marling represented a major investment on newly drained ground, and crop yields on the manor of Ebony show a difference of one third between treated and untreated lands. Lime or marl were the normal dressings for acid soils, and marl-pits were dug on many estates in Southern England. In the south-west shell and sand dressings were used, typically by Tavistock Abbey, which drew on rights of collection on the coast. At Tavistock the practice of beat-burning, the ploughing-in of the ash of burnt stubble

---

[32] J. A. Raftis, *The Estates of Ramsey Abbey*, Toronto, 1957, 71–6, and *Tenure and Mobility*, Toronto, 1964, 28; *V.C.H.*, Wiltshire, IV, 10 *seq.*
[33] E. Lamond (ed.), *Walter of Henley's Husbandry*; H. G. Richardson and G. O. Sayles, *Fleta*, vol. II, Selden Soc. (1955), 239–40.

or scrub, is also well attested, and tenant-land thus treated had under the terms of leases also to receive a sand dressing.[34] However, the major weakness of medieval agriculture lay in inadequate supplies of manure. Its importance was generally accepted; cartage services involving manure, and tenants' obligation to fold stock on demesne were common, but animals were frequently too few for adequate fertility. In one South Wiltshire village it would have taken the equivalent of 125 sheep to manure a holding of one virgate to eighteenth-century standards, yet only perhaps 40 were available, and some communities were worse off still.[35] The amount of common for grazing was apt to decrease during the thirteenth century over lowland England and in the Midlands. In particular the proportion of meadow to arable was low. In a sample of 55 Leicestershire villages only 20 had a ratio of arable to meadow of 20:1. By contrast to rare cases of 10:1 or better is an example as poor as Knaptoft with 40:1. Such figures imposed a limit on lengths of rotation, and heavily populated villages would extend their cultivated area still further into the commons in order to increase immediate production, thereby prejudicing grazing and manure supply.[36]

Changes of seed were encouraged by Walter of Henley, who advised seasonal alteration and invited his readers to prove him correct by experiment. This practice was still being carried on in the sixteenth century, and if it was really necessary suggests that infected ground was common and that farmers were ready to risk buying new seed rather than replant a variety known to carry fungal infection. On Canterbury lands seed corn began to be brought in under Henry of Eastry; with wheat this appears to have made little difference to yields, which were rarely more than 3–3·5 : 1, although barley did improve slightly. More important here, perhaps, was the intensive sowing of seed—a rate of $6\frac{1}{2}$ bushels of oats to the acre was increased in 1302 to 7.[37] But beyond this there were experiments with different varieties of seed, several types of wheat being recognised in the thirteenth and fourteenth centuries. At Tavistock in 1332 successful experimental sowings of large oats are recorded, and mixed crops, drage (barley and oats) and *mastillio* (wheat and rye) were tried out at Crowland from 1283 onwards.[38] Types of crops and rotation varied with conditions

[34] Smith, *Canterbury*, 135–8; Finberg, *Tavistock*, 89–94.

[35] M. M. Postan, 'Village Livestock in the 13th Century', *Ec.H.R.*, 2nd ser., XV (1962), 219–49.

[36] *V.C.H.*, Leicestershire, II, 162–3; R. H. Hilton, 'Technical Determinism: the Stirrup and the Plough', *Past and Present*, 24 (1963), 99–100.

[37] Smith, *Canterbury*, 134–5; see also E. M. Halcrow, 'The Decline of Demesne Farming on the Estates of Durham Cathedral Priory', *Ec.H.R.*, 2nd ser., VII (1954–5), 346.

[38] Finberg, *Tavistock*, 96; F. M. Page, *The Estates of Crowland Abbey*, 1934, 118–19.

and markets, and experiment developed traditional methods. It was for example standard practice to cultivate peas and beans in quantity in Leicestershire, and on Leicester Abbey's lands this was to increase over the fourteenth century.[39]

The ill-effects of the classic open-field system on production have been frequently stated, and the major objections—the difficulties of experimenting in cropping and rotation, cross-infection of stock during common stubble-grazing, and the problems of selective stock-breeding—seem to have received some attention from contemporaries. Both demesne farmers and larger tenants made some effort to consolidate lands, and the success of results is shown in the greater values of enclosed grounds, for instance, at Wootton Bassett, whose enclosed demesne acres were rated in 1334 at double the value of those in the common field.[40] These changes are sometimes disguised, for open fields often survived but were not necessarily used as *common* fields. In the Fens many selions were capable of separate cultivation, and meadow and arable grounds were surrounded by ditches or temporary fences, though with the apparent survival of an open-field layout. In Leicestershire, although there might be two or three great fields around a village, this did not mean overall two- or three-course rotations, for cropping was increasingly by furlongs, with agreement over husbandry among fewer men or, with further consolidation, according to individual choice.[41] Indeed, many estates seem to have lacked overall organisation of cropping, and some only had a uniform system on their demesne strips. There were others, however, which did practise extensive common organisation. In the twelfth century cropping was frequently uniform over demesne and tenant lands, although it is not clear in how many places complete regulation survived the medieval period; agreements over stubble-grazing in the thirteenth and fourteenth centuries suggest that some aspects often lasted into the period of rapid yeoman consolidation in Midland England.[42] The preference

[39] Hoskins, *Midland Peasant*, 69; R. H. Hilton, *The Economic Development of Some Leicestershire Estates in the 14th and 15th Centuries*, 1947, 63–5.

[40] Finberg, *Tavistock*, 50–2; P. D. A. Harvey, *A Medieval Oxfordshire Village*, 1965, 30, 39. Hoskins (*Midland Peasant*, 65–6) provides good examples of the scattered nature of many peasant holdings: in 1300 in Wigston Magna a tenement of 6½ acres and 3½ roods was composed of 23 separate parcels. For values of enclosed grounds see *V.C.H.*, Wiltshire, IV, 13–14.

[41] Hallam, *Settlement*, 150–1; N. S. B. Gras, *The Economic and Social History of an English Village*, 1932, 31.

[42] For the debate on the origins and extent of the relation between open-field and common-field methods see Joan Thirsk, 'The Common Fields', *Past and Present*, 29 (1964), 3–25; J. Z. Titow, 'Medieval England and the Open-Field System', *ibid.*, 32 (1965), 86–102; Joan Thirsk, 'The Origin of the Common Fields', *ibid.*, 33 (1966), 142–7; also W. O. Ault, 'Open Field Husbandry and the Village Community: a Study of Agrarian Bye-laws in Medieval Eng-

of the small man seems to have been towards enclosed farming, and new clearances frequently took this form; in Arden, Warwickshire, immediate division of assarts into separate holdings was normal; in upland country, Devon or Northumberland, whilst the village infield might be cultivated in common, the outfields periodically tilled on the waste perimeter were normally operated in severalty.[43] However, certain open-field institutions could survive and disguise change. Stinting of common lands, common responsibility for harvest, stubble-grazing or the maintenance of drains, ditches or roads survived to the sixteenth century and beyond. Even where consolidation could not be achieved, the problems of intensive improvement were not insuperable: it was possible to grow large quantities of peas or beans as fodder, allowing more stock to be kept, when population-pressure did not force a less farsighted policy of concentration on food grains. The amount that could be done by agreement to improve a village's common-field techniques may well have been underestimated, but the favour with which consolidated holdings were regarded in the land market must speak for itself.[44]

Our information about thirteenth-century grain-yields is too fragmentary to measure the effects of improvement, for there are few long runs of figures from particular estates. But the information we have does little to promote optimism, and the figures assembled by Slicher van Bath give, if anything, an impression of declining yields. To them may be added the more recently published figures for Cuxham's wheat-yields, which fall from 8·3 : 1 in the 1290s to 4·3 : 1 in the 1350s. The figures we have are based almost entirely on demesne farming, and there is good reason to expect that peasants' performance would be worse. It has in fact been suggested that, whereas a fivefold return on wheat might be expected on West Midland demesnes late in the thirteenth century, peasant yields would be between 3 and 4 : 1. A striking example—taken, it is true, from the later fourteenth century—is that of Walter Shayl, a substantial peasant at Hampton Lucy, a manor of the Bishop of Worcester, whose yields were substantially less than those achieved on the demesne. A century earlier, when there was greater pressure on land, which lords could satisfy by leasing off their poorer ground, one can expect such differentials to have been common.[45] It underlines, moreover, the insistence of men such as Osbert

land', *Trans. American Phil. Soc.*, N.S. 55, p. 7 (1965), 6 *seq.*—review; G. C. Homans, *Speculum*, XLI (1966), 516–17.

[43] Finberg, *Tavistock*, 32–4; T. A. M. Bishop, 'The Rotation of Crops at Westerham', *Ec.H.R.*, X (1938–9), 40–1.

[44] W. O. Ault, 'Village Bye-laws by Common Consent', *Speculum*, XXIX (1959), 53; *C.E.H.E.*, I, 503; Raftis, *Ramsey*, 220.

[45] B. H. Slicher van Bath, *Yield Ratios, 810–1820*, A. A. G. Bijdragen, 10,

Foliot, Abbot of Malmesbury, on the necessity for improved tenant standards, such as more frequent ploughing of the fallow open field. There was a major temptation to crop more intensively and to change from a two- to a three-course rotation, but unless adequate manure was available declining yields could well result.[46]

In providing manure livestock was vital to grain output, and thus if 'the wool of England is almost half the value of the whole land' the keeping of stock, cattle as well as sheep, contributed to the major part of income from agriculture.[47] Although the common grazing of stubble in open-field villages meant that little improvement could take place among peasant stock, the conditions for breeding were increasingly present on larger estates. The lands of the Bishops of Winchester, of Canterbury Cathedral Priory, Pershore Abbey and Crowland Abbey were among those designating particular manors for sheep or dairying, and there are some indications (as in the use of good-quality Lindsey rams at Winchester) of perhaps some knowledge of the principles of breed improvement, although the manuals of husbandry give only rudimentary advice.[48]

The export of wool had increased from 25,600 sacks per year in the 1280s to 35,000 sacks by about 1310. Any earlier rate of increase is unknown, nor is it possible to compare the Domesday sheep population with that of 1300. But the surviving records of numbers in East Anglia in 1066 (about 300,000 on demesnes alone), together with the high estate-valuations in other areas later to be thought of as sheep-country, suggest that at the beginning of the period sheep were making a notable contribution to wealth. Over the intervening years, even though stock numbers may well have diminished where the pressure on arable was greatest, the reclamation of marshlands and the foundation of the northern Cistercian houses led to the development of flocks which Pegolotti regarded in the 1290s as the most important source of wool for export.[49] Nor was village production insignificant; in the south, thirteenth-century village peasant-flocks frequently exceeded those of demesnes in size and, as on the most pessimistic esti-

1963, *passim*; Harvey, *Cuxham*, 58 (table IV); R. H. Hilton, *A Medieval Society*, 1966, 123; 'Rent and Capital Formation in Feudal Society', *Internat. Econ. Hist. Conf. Aix, 1962*, 1965, II, 57.
    [46] *V.C.H.*, Wiltshire, IV, 11.
    [47] E. Miller, 'The English Economy of the Thirteenth Century', *Past and Present*, 20 (1964), 26.
    [48] *V.C.H.*, Wiltshire, IV, 19–20; Smith, *Canterbury*, 148–50; M. Wretts-Smith, 'The Organisation of Farming at Crowland Abbey', *Jnl of Econ. and Bus. Hist.*, IV (1932), 168; *C.E.H.E.*, II (1952), 236.
    [49] E. M. Carus-Wilson and O. Coleman, *England's Export Trade, 1275–1547*, 1963, 122; Sawyer, 162–3; R. A. Donkin, 'Cistercian Sheep Farming and Wool Sales in the 13th Century', *Ag. Hist. Rev.*, VI (1958), 2–3.

mate 50 sheep could produce wool worth 10 shillings per year, represented a sizeable increment to peasant income.[50] The big wool producers, however, operated on a vastly greater scale: the flocks of the Bishop of Winchester totalled 29,000 in the mid-thirteenth century; those of St Swithun's, Winchester 20,000 early in the fourteenth century; and those of Henry de Lacy 13,400 in 1303. In the north comparable numbers were owned by the Duchy of Lancaster, Isabella de Fortibus in East Yorkshire, and the Berkeleys and the Clares in the west.

Quality of wool varied by breed and area. The finest, according to Pegolotti, came from Tintern Abbey and Abbey Dore, probably from the Ryelands breed which made Herefordshire the best known of the short-staple wool areas. The poorer grades came from the northern uplands and the products of the north-west, Holme Cultram, Shap, Calder and Furness Abbeys, fetched the lowest prices of five marks per sack, compared with the 12 normal in Herefordshire. The lowland grasslands and the Fens produced the best fleece-weights from the long-staple wool of the Lincoln and Cotswold breeds which, while less highly valued than the Ryelands, were in demand by the Flemish and Italian industries. If, as seems likely, there was an increase in the sheep population during the twelfth and thirteenth centuries, it came as much from extension of grazing in the north and west as from intensive husbandry on specialised lowland manors.[51] This was certainly the case with cattle-rearing, which appears to have grown in scale between 1100 and 1300. In the Peak District, North-West Staffordshire, Lancashire, Exmoor, Dartmoor, the Fens and North and Mid-Wales cattle were run over large reserved tracts of moor and forest grazing. They were frequently used in the early stages of land reclamation to graze ground yet unfit for sheep—the Cistercians' cattle-farming activities, less well-known than their sheep-farming but on some houses' lands more important, were often designed to improve pastures. At Valle Crucis and Strata Marcella in Wales and in Nidderdale, cattle formed the main stock, and at Louth Park, Sawtry and Revesby Abbey in the Fens, Jervaulx and Kirkstall they were of comparable importance to sheep.[52]

[50] E. Power, *The Wool Trade in Medieval English History*, 1941, 30–1; Painter, 164; cf. N. Denholm-Young (*Seigneurial Administration in England*, 1937, 54) for a suggestion that 1,000 sheep would earn 50 mks per year.

[51] Power, *Wool Trade*, 21–35; C. M. L. Bouch and G. P. Jones, *The Lake Counties*, 1961, 27.

[52] *C.E.H.E.*, I (1966), 555; Smith, *Blackburnshire*, 8; R. A. Donkin, 'Cattle on the Estates of Medieval Cistercian Monasteries in England and Wales', *Ec.H.R.*, 2nd ser., XV (1962), 31–53; Franklin, 22.

The measurement and distribution of wealth

We have seen significant signs of an increase in total agricultural wealth in the 250 years after the Conquest. But evidence is necessarily impressionistic and resists any exact measurement. However, the rise in population may have some value as a scale, and it should be asked whether the pace of development of national resources kept up with population growth. Some guidance may come from rural standards of living, although at first sight the use of peasant evidence may seem dubious with the chance of an upward redistribution of income and wealth. This is perhaps less of a danger than it may seem, for an improvement in the bargaining position of the landowner could strengthen any argument for pressure on resources from a rising rural population.

Population-pressure and its effects on living standards and personal wealth

It has been suggested that the population of England almost trebled between Domesday and 1300, rising from about 1·5 to about 3·7 million. Absolute figures are subject to strong reservations over, for instance, methods of calculating population from material which refer only to the heads of households,[53] but local studies show increases on this scale. In some settled areas where few new lands remained increases were small. In the hundred of Kineton, Warwickshire, some drift may have occurred to the forest villages of the Coventry area, but on the Bishops of Winchester's estates, where comparatively little new ground remained in the thirteenth century, there was an average annual increase of 0·85 per cent at Taunton, doubling the population in a century. Where clearance could still take place figures were far higher. At Chippenham, Cambridgeshire, the population quadrupled between 1085 and 1279, and some Fenland townships grew at up to double this rate (Spalding by a factor of six and Pinchbeck by eight by 1260), a picture confirmed by examples of replacement rates such as 1·6 for Moulton and 2·34 for Weston in the third quarter of the thirteenth century. Migration can exaggerate the extreme cases, for the Warwickshire forest hundred of Stoneleigh, increasing by 7½ times, partially balances its neighbour Kineton, and rapid development of small Midland towns such as Ledbury in Herefordshire or Stratford-

---

[53] J. C. Russell, *British Medieval Population*, Albuquerque, 1940, 235 *seq.* (Russell inclines to a rather lower initial figure, which may underestimate Domesday's omissions); 'Recent Advances in Medieval Demography', *Speculum*, XL (1965), 88–9; *C.E.H.E.*, I, 561–2; J. Krause, 'The Medieval Household, Large or Small?', *Ec.H.R.*, 2nd ser., IX (1957), 42; H. E. Hallam, 'Some 13th-Century Censuses', *Ec.H.R.*, 2nd ser., X (1958), 340.

upon-Avon must have drawn off part of the local rural surplus.[54] This rise had several widely applicable causes. In the late eleventh and early twelfth centuries there were few recorded epidemics, thus life-expectation and fertility were probably high. In addition new lands were available, and there are some reports of labour shortage, both probably making for earlier marriages. In the thirteenth century, particularly after 1250, epidemics were also few, but population increase was governed much more severely by the amount of available land—both birth-rates and death-rates were high, and the margin of births over deaths could vary greatly with circumstances. The mid-thirteenth-century rise seems to have come to an end in southern England by perhaps the 1280s, with death-rates as high as a suggested crude figure of 70–75/1,000 on some Winchester estates.[55]

If population roughly trebled between 1085 and 1315, could extension and improvement of cultivation have raised output on a similar scale? The evidence of food prices suggests that they could not.

Wheat prices (in terms of silver):

1160–79 =	100	1260–79	262·9
1180–99	139·3	1280–99	279·2
1200–19	203·0	1300–19	324·7
1220–39	196·1	1320–39	289·7[56]
1240–59	214·2		

Some increase in the quantity of money in circulation may have affected prices, but *prima facie*, as prices of other products, particularly non-foodstuffs, rose less steeply, these figures suggest a pressure on resources which must lead to an examination of living standards in the absence of meaningful figures for wages.[57]

Living standards, particularly those of the peasantry, do indeed provide a broad suggestion of the swamping of resources of land and foodstuffs. At the peasant level incomes depended to a great extent on

[54] J. Z. Titow, 'Some Evidence of the 13th-Century Population Increase', *Ec.H.R.*, 2nd ser., XIV (1961–2), 218–24; Spufford, 5; Hallam, 197; S. L. Thrupp, 'The Problem of Replacement Rates in Late Medieval English Population', *Ec.H.R.*, 2nd ser., XVIII (1965), 101–7; J. B. Harley, 'Population Trends and Agricultural Developments from the Warwickshire Hundred Rolls of 1279', *Ec.H.R.*, 2nd ser., XI (1958–9), 8–18; A. T. Bannister (ed.), 'A Transcript of the Red Book of the Bishopric of Hereford (c. 1280)', *Camden Miscellany*, XV (1929), 17–20; E. M. Carus-Wilson, 'The First Half-Century of the Borough of Stratford-upon-Avon', *Ec.H.R.*, 2nd ser., XVIII (1965), 46–63.

[55] M. M. Postan and J. Z. Titow, 'Heriots and Prices on Winchester Manors', *Ec.H.R.*, 2nd ser., XI (1958–9), 392–410.

[56] B. H. Slicher van Bath, *The Agrarian History of Western Europe, 500–1800*, 1963, 133.

[57] Sawyer, 147 *seq.*; D. L. Farmer, 'Some Grain-Price Fluctuations in Angevin England', *Ec.H.R.* 2nd ser., IX (1956–7), 34–43; 'Grain-Price Movements in 13th-Century England', *ibid.*, 2nd ser., X (1957–8), 207 *seq.*

the sizes of holdings and the need to seek supplementary employment. A certain amount of confusion can be stripped from the eleventh- and twelfth-century record by playing down the significance of the legal classification of the peasantry as a guide to their holding-sizes. We could for instance find on Peterborough lands some sokemen (free peasants) with more, some with less lands than villeins, and in the Middlesex Domesday we see cottars, bordars and villeins as overlapping groups in terms of land. It is more helpful to take the pre-Conquest *Rectitudines Singularum Personarum*, which expected the more substantial peasant, the *gebur*, to have a yardland, 25–30 acres, the virgate of the thirteenth century, and the *kotsetla* to have a smallholding of about five acres. This could hardly have been universal, and by the time of Domesday great variations occurred. The Middlesex Domesday shows clearly the number of virtually landless tenants, 292 out of 464 having no more than gardens; but it does show a noticeable number of virgaters among the villeins, and five-acre men among the cottars, and particularly the bordars. We are in effect dealing with three broad classes. At one extreme the virgate-holders, farming lands above the subsistence minimum, at the other, the landless wage-workers, and, between, those who could gain a proportion of their living from a holding, supplemented by wages.[58]

In some communities it is probable that lands were already limited by 1150; this can be expected at villages such as Wigston Magna, Leicestershire, where population at Domesday had been high, but in the thirteenth century there are increasing signs of such scarcity, with holdings diminishing in size all over lowland England. At Taunton this can be seen very clearly; in 1248 there were 3·3 acres per person, but in 1311 the figure had fallen to 2·5. In the Fens, smallholdings of two acres or less proliferated, and Cambridgeshire had the largest total of holdings below the subsistence minimum of any county included in the Hundred Rolls. The study of Chippenham bears this out, for in the thirteenth century closes along the main street were being divided up and strips were reduced in size; at Ruislip in Middlesex a semi-landless group emerged with assarts below subsistence size; at Pyrford in Surrey, on Westminster Abbey lands, the picture was similar, with 70 out of 160–170 tenants having cottages and holdings of five acres or less.[59]

There are several estimates of the size of holding needed for sub-

[58] Lennard, *Rural England*, 341–4, 364–5.
[59] Titow, 'Some Evidence . . .', 222; Hallam, 215–16; E. A. Kosminsky, *Studies in the Agrarian History of England*, 1956, 214 *seq.*; Spufford, 13; M. Morgan, *The English Lands of the Abbey of Bec*, 1946, 92–3; B. F. Harvey, 'The Population Trend in England, 1300–1348', *Trans. Roy. Hist. Soc.*, 5th ser., XVI (1966), 27.

sistence without supplementation from other sources. Hilton cites a yardlander with 26 acres (13 under cultivation) in 1299 at Hampton Lucy who could cover his rent and subsistence by sales of grain, but by a margin which left little in hand for poor years. A half-yardlander at Kempsey in 1299 with eight acres under crop would have sufficient income to cover rent and dues only if he relied on a son's labour.[60] These examples involve a two-course rotation. Gras, in a remarkably optimistic estimate based on Crawley, Hampshire, where a three-course rotation operated, suggests that a farthing-lander with a total of $5\frac{1}{2}$ acres and grazing on the commons could just support a family of five in a good year (1257–8), but not when yields were poor (1306–7). Bennett, working on the basis of good harvests, sees a holder of a 30-acre virgate on a three-course rotation as producing some surplus, but that the holder of about 10 acres would be near the subsistence margin; Kosminsky suggests that even in good years a holding barely short of 10 acres was the minimum for subsistence and left very little in reserve. Although actual acreage was far from the only variable, there does seem to be agreement on 10–15 as a general minimum.[61]

With increasing fragmentation of holdings in the thirteenth century, ways of supplementing income from land became more important to the smallholder. At Swyncombe, Oxfordshire, 10 smallholders, each with eight acres of enclosed ground, could hardly maintain themselves, but their rights each to keep 50 sheep, six oxen and one horse on the commons raised their incomes almost to the equivalent of yard-landers.[62] However, it became increasingly difficult in arable country to maintain stock numbers. Disputes over encroachments by land-owners for their demesnes occurred regularly, and forcible removal of fences by tenants was common late in the century. Fenland assarts were a source of bitterness in an area where many smallholders relied on grazing, often provided by village inter-commoning, and on turbary and fishing rights.[63] The stock a smallholder could keep depended on the regulations for stinting. However, the low capital resources of peasant farmers often meant that they were unable to afford enough animals. Men such as Gras' farthing-lander had, in poor years, to sell stock without making replacement, leading to a holding with a low

---

[60] Hilton, 'Rent and Capital Formation', 33–68. A guide to the amount of food required for subsistence can be derived from agreements by heirs to holdings to provide food for their parents in retirement; for a Bedfordshire example of 1294, see G. C. Homans, *English Villagers of the 13th Century*, 1941, 144–5.

[61] H. S. Bennett, *Life on the English Manor*, 1937, 95; Kosminsky, 230–3; N. S. B. Gras, *The Economic and Social History of an English Village*, 70–2.

[62] Power, *Wool Trade*, 29–30; assuming that 50 sheep would produce 10 shillings per year, this may be compared with the saleable surplus from Hilton's Kempsey half-yardlander's holding.

[63] N. Neilson, *A Terrier of Fleet*, 1910, introduction.

level of fertility and a chronic inability to purchase new animals.[64] Added to this, requirements to fold sheep on demesne land were often enforced, diminishing the manure available for tenants' land. However, areas did remain where the problems were less severe, and in Devon, Sussex, Lincolnshire and the north-west, for example, inter-commoning by several townships on tracts of moor, marsh and woodland was continued without serious dispute. Even in lowland England there was a stratum of holders of one or more virgates, with 20–30 sheep, who had the resources to increase their lands further by purchase or lease, and extend their grazing activities with the stints which accompanied further acquisitions.[65]

Wage-labour formed the other major means of supplementing an inadequate holding. The labour-requirement on demesnes can be divided between the base-load of work over the year and the peak needs, at harvest and ploughing. Regular work could be covered by tenants' customary services, by *famuli* maintained on service-holdings once part of the demesne, or by paid cottager or villein labour. Similarly the peaks might call either for customary seasonal boon-works or for paid workers. The proportions varied between estates or between manors on the same estate. Where small free tenants were as much in the majority as in Cambridgeshire or Bedfordshire, shortage of villeins and their services would provide opportunities for wage-work—although clearly on a manor such as Kettering, where 40–50 smallholders were available to work on a 300-acre demesne, there must have been chronic underemployment. Where villeins' services were available an estate would be presented with a choice between customary or wage labour, one which could be governed by the point made by Walter of Henley that pressed labour was apt to be slack and troublesome. Even in those Midland counties where the proportion of villeins was highest, less than half the regular work on demesnes was covered by customary services, so leaving the opportunity for cottagers' employment. Money wages were accompanied by important payments in kind; a supplement of $4\frac{1}{2}$ quarters of grain in a year could provide the 6 lbs. of bread per day needed by a family of five; a 'Saturday plough' could be of great assistance to the smallholder without draught animals, and the 'sown acres' commonly used on Ramsey lands to pay *famuli* were of great importance with the decline in the real value of cash wages. Winchester, Westminster and Glastonbury material shows a drop of 25 per cent

[64] In 1283 in the Suffolk hundred of Blackbourne 75 per cent of *taxpayers* had none or one draught animal and 47 per cent none or one for milk. Those below the taxable level would be worse off—Hilton, 'Rent and Capital Formation', 54.

[65] Power, *Wool Trade*, 30; cf. V.C.H., Wiltshire, IV, 26–29; Raftis, *Tenure and Mobility*, 24–5; Gras, 70.

in real wages between 1208 and 1225, and a further 25 per cent decrease by 1348. Thus the late thirteenth-century trend towards leasing of demesnes brought hardships of redundancy not confined to the loss of cash wages. Larger peasants who employed cottagers to carry out customary services on their behalf no longer needed to do so after their works were commuted. The more prosperous peasants who took on newly-leased parcels of demesne might provide some extra employment, but if some demesne did remain the new peasant lessees could be troubled by manorial labour preemption rights and thus were apt not to lease more than their families could cultivate. Circumstances clearly varied widely, but at Ramsey redundancy can be seen to have caused concern late in the thirteenth century and the Abbots' employment policy seems to have taken on a welfare aspect.[66]

Heavy money rent reduced peasant living standards and accumulation of capital, and labour services restricted work on the holding. Despite local variations some trends are apparent in the balance between kinds of rent. In the twelfth century commutation of labour services for money rents was fairly common; early examples appear on Burton Abbey lands between 1114 and 1143. On Durham, St Pauls and Glastonbury lands reductions in demesne sizes led to commutation of services later in the twelfth century, and on their Cotswold land the Templars tended at this time to favour money payments.[67] This tendency to commutation slowed in the early thirteenth century, but it was still convenient, where the landless or cottager population was large, to use money rents from peasant landholders to pay regular demesne employees and to restrict customary labour to boon-works at harvest peaks or to miscellaneous services. This occurred on the estates of the East Midlands with their small demesnes, on the fragmented lands of the Fenlands, and on scattered ecclesiastical estates. The Abbey of Bec's outlying manors resumed fewer services than their concentrated estates in Wiltshire, and the outlying Gloucestershire estates of the Bishop of Worcester displayed the same tendency.

Where the tradition of labour-services was strong, there was considerable resumption in the thirteenth century, due to the rising requirements of expanding demesnes. Large ecclesiastical estates with access to food markets were particularly active in the definition and enforcement of services. At Ramsey Abbey the number of holdings *ad opus* grew throughout the middle part of the century; at Ely between 1200 and 1250 labour services grew as rapidly as the area of the demesne,

---

[66] Lamond, *Walter of Henley*, 11; Kosminsky, 294–5; Postan, *Famulus*, 18–20; *C.E.H.E.*, I, 566–7; Raftis, *Ramsey*, 52, 229.
[67] M. M. Postan, 'The Chronology of Labour Services', *Trans. Roy. Hist. Soc.*, 1937, 169–93.

for land hunger and fission of holdings allowed the extraction of more dues.[68] There are, however, qualifications to this picture. There were manors where the pressure on the tenant was less severe than it seems at first sight: week-work at times included tasks not taking the time allotted; food provided for customary workers should not be ignored; and there was a frequent tendency to do away with week-work and to concentrate customary dues on boon-works and miscellaneous services such as cartage. In some cases there was no tradition of labour services, and in the newly cleared upland assarts of Yorkshire and the West Midlands their use never developed.[69]

But liability to works was a major source of discontent among tenants on the older lowland estates. Withdrawals of services are well documented due to the legal action which followed, and the 146 convictions for refusal of services between 1279 and 1311 on Ramsey lands, or the disputes on the lands of Halesowen over definition of status and services, indicate an unrest which was to continue into the fourteenth century and involve a large proportion of the peasantry. In particular, services restricted the smallholders' time for wage-work, and the middling tenant from the half-virgater upwards was kept from his holding and was prepared either to risk action for neglect of services or to pay for their commutation. Only the more substantial peasant who could afford to employ labour to fulfil obligations or the man with a large family could tolerate the system. Thus estate officials frequently felt that week-work was too troublesome to be worthwhile, hence the tendency to concentrate upon boon-works. These, however, could be almost as serious for the peasant; coming at harvest time they could mean a neglected crop on the holding, particularly if the demesne were separate from tenant land.[70]

Money payments underwent a corresponding development during the thirteenth century, whether in the form of rents for holdings, payments instead of commuted labour services, or entry fines. Comparisons between the 1240s and 1270s show how common increases were, and by late in the century payments reached a point where they represented a brake on peasant capital accumulation, whether by improvement or further land-acquisition. Entry fines could make the difference between, perhaps, a tenant having sufficient stock to manure the holding, adequate fencing or buildings, or perhaps enough marling,

[68] Miller, *Ely*, 102-3; Morgan, 76-83.
[69] T. A. M. Bishop, 'The Distribution of Manorial Demesnes in the Vale of Yorkshire', *Eng.H.R.*, XLIX (1934), 406; R. H. Hilton, 'Gloucester Abbey Leases of the Late 13th Century', *Univ. Birm. Hist. Jnl*, 4 (1953-4), 2; Bouch and Jones, 10.
[70] Raftis, *Ramsey*, 227-8; Kosminsky, 339; R. H. Hilton, 'Peasant Movements before 1381', *Ec.H.R.*, 2nd ser., II (1949-50), 117-36; Homans, 276-84.

and a hand-to-mouth existence. They gradually grew in importance as a source of income in proportion to rents. On lands where no further ground existed for assarts they rose the fastest, a Winchester example providing an effective comparison; at Taunton, where no fresh land remained, fines averaged £5.9.2. per virgate (1283–1348) whereas at Witney the average was £1.18.10. Here new land was available. Not that all estates arranged their affairs to concentrate on fines—£1–£2 per virgate was a more normal figure, though at a value of perhaps 10–15 times the annual crop of a virgate these still represented a considerable risk to the long-term maintenance of the condition of a holding.[71]

A crucial point for the peasant was his status, free or unfree, which could materially affect his liabilities. In the twelfth century there were wide local variations in the implications of villein or free status; Domesday and early twelfth-century references suggest that villeins who paid money rent were not uncommon, and free tenants and sokemen could be found who were liable for some labour services. But late in the twelfth century many landowners attempted to clarify their relationships with their tenants. There was a growing number of cases in manorial courts which involved problems of status, and a close connection developed between villeinage and the liability to week-work. Those who could prove their ancestors' freedom from such labour services could more easily resist attempts to prove them of villein status, but those who could not became the more liable to the burdens thought appropriate to the unfree. In economic terms these were severe. Whereas a free tenant had considerable legal security of tenure and, until the passing of *Quia Emptores* in 1290, freedom to alienate his holding, the villein customary tenant had little security or, unless manorial custom had developed in his favour, scant right to dispose of his land without its reversion to the lord. Dues such as merchet, heriot and tallage accompanied villein status, and local custom could embody numerous seigneurial restrictions and monopolies of justice, mills, bakehouses or breweries. By themselves many of these were merely irksome, but on manors where all were assiduously catalogued and enforced and added to a burden of week-work the position of the villein was in great contrast to that of the free peasant, who was most unlikely to be liable to more than occasional boons and minor payments. In short, the free tenant's capital was usually safe, but the villein's was far less so, being subject to the depredations of unpredictable rents and fines, and dues fixed at the lord's will. Whilst

[71] J. Z. Titow, 'Some Differences between Manors and their Effects on the Condition of the Peasant in the Thirteenth Century', *Ag.H.R.*, X (1962), 1–13; Harvey, 23–42.

a free peasant and a villein might have holdings of similar size, their actual living standards could be very different.[72]

During the thirteenth century the range of peasant wealth widened, and there was an identifiable minority for whom the pressures of the period were less of a problem and could often be turned to good account. Those with holdings of over a virgate, a line obviously varied by the size of any particular family and the character of the soil, might have some surplus in good years which could be spent on leasing or buying more land. The land market operated most freely and provided the greatest opportunities in those parts of the Midlands and East Anglia where free lands and free peasants were most numerous. When there were no seigneurial checks on alienation the poor could sell or subdivide their lands; thus amongst the free peasantry there occur the most striking examples of fragmentation, giving the man with money to spare the most chance to buy. Patterns of regular-sized holdings broke up. In Rothley Soke, Leicestershire, the traditional oxgang (12-acre) or yardland (24-acre) holdings became indistinct in the thirteenth century; even by 1231 82 of 360 holdings were over 24 acres, 131 were between 12 and 24, and 153 were 12 or less. Opportunities for land-acquisition arose not only from subdivision. The tenancies of the aged or infirm became available, and demesne parcels were leased out. Nor were only free tenants involved; most manorial lords resisted the break-up of villein lands unless services could be satisfactorily maintained, but clandestine transfers seem to have been fairly common. Villeins could acquire free lands by charter as at Peterborough, or by seal as on the lands of Gloucester Abbey. It was more rare for there to be similar dealings in unfree tenancies, although certain Wakefield, Ramsey and Peterborough examples show that this could occur.[73]

Even so, only about one per cent of villeins and eight per cent of free tenants in Midland England were farming holdings of more than one virgate in 1274. Within the group were examples of sizeable farmers, ranging from those Ely tenants with 40–50 acres to men such as Henry de Bray, a Northamptonshire freeholder, with a demesne of 250–280 acres, 180 under crop. The Randall family of Wigston Magna began to accumulate property early in the thirteenth century and were to be affluent farmers by the mid-fourteenth, while in the same village the Balle family made 12 purchases of land between 1260 and 1304.[74]

[72] R. H. Hilton, 'Freedom and Villeinage in England', *Past and Present*, 31 (1965), 3–19; *C.E.H.E.*, I, 610–13; Bennett, 99–145; Hoskins, *Midland Peasant*, 29–30.
[73] Kosminsky, 208–28; *V.C.H.*, Leicestershire, II, 169–70; C. N. L. Brooke and M. M. Postan, *Carte Nativorum*, Northamptonshire Rec. Soc., 1960.
[74] Kosminsky, 216, 223; D. Wills (ed.), *The Estate Books of Henry de Bray*,

The main preference in their spending does seem to have been for land; contiguous purchases meant the ability to farm more efficiently, and new lands could bring common rights for stock-grazing. Syndicates of peasants on Ramsey lands took up leases on blocks of demesne and subdivided them in consolidated parcels. Men of Henry de Bray's wealth could go further: between 1289 and 1308 he spent over £4 annually out of an income of about £25 on building, excluding other improvements. When scattered lands were leased or purchased they were sublet. Henry de Bray gained almost half of his income from rents, and if labour was scarce subletting was advisable. Wider patterns of spending are less clear: improved housing, the replacement of timber-and-wattle by stone construction, and more utensils are seen on certain medieval house-sites. In Leicestershire there was a striking amount of church-building early in the fourteenth century in communities where the wealthiest element must, in the absence of large landowners, have been substantial peasants.[75]

Archaeological evidence has recently shown the wide range of housing standards of medieval peasants. Whilst it has not yet been possible to connect particular houses excavated on deserted medieval village sites with documented inhabitants it has been possible to see the range of wealth expressed in material forms. Three main types of house stand out in the period from the mid-twelfth to the mid-fourteenth century.[76] The smallest were single-roomed cottages with no accommodation for stock or storage. Some were particularly small, one early fourteenth-century example at Seacourt, Berkshire, being no more than 12 feet by 10 feet internally, although some ranged up to 30 feet by 15 feet— the Essex tax assessments of 1296 and 1301 show how common this type could be.[77] The typical peasant house was more complex; in 1304 all the villein houses at Cuxham had two or more rooms, and fourteenth- and fifteenth-century evidence from Worcestershire shows a high proportion of two- and three-bay peasant houses.[78] Many of the larger structures were long-houses, where one or two rooms provided

Camden Soc., 3rd ser., XXVII (1916), introduction; Hoskins, *Midland Peasant*, 41, 52.

[75] B. Dodwell, 'The Free Tenantry of the Hundred Rolls', *Ec.H.R.*, XIV (1944), 169.

[76] J. G. Hurst, 'The Medieval Peasant House', *Fourth Viking Congress, York, 1961*, 1965, 190–6; Hilton, *A Medieval Society*, 98.

[77] M. Biddle, 'The Deserted Medieval Village of Seacourt, Berkshire', *Oxoniensia*, XXVI–XXVII (1961–2), 92–6. See also Area 29, p. 116, for a larger example, and M. W. Barley, *The English Farmhouse and Cottage*, 1961, 87 *seq.*

[78] Harvey, *Cuxham*, 132; R. K. Field, 'Worcestershire Peasant Buildings, Household Goods and Farming Equipment in the Later Middle Ages', 1, *Med. Arch.*, IX (1965), 107–21.

family accommodation at one end of the building, and the other end, separated by a cross-passage, formed a byre or barn. It was once thought that the long-house was a highland plan-type, frequently built on platforms on hill-slopes. Examples survive in Wales and Devon, and a number have been excavated; those at Gelligaer Common, Glamorgan, Beere, Hound Tor and Hutholes in Devon, Garrow Tor, Lanyon and Treworld in Cornwall, West Hartburn in County Durham and West Whelpington in Northumberland[79] conform to this general type, but excavated examples at Holworth in Dorset, Hangleton in Sussex and Wharram Percy in East Yorkshire, with surface indications on Cotswold and on Lincolnshire clayland sites, suggest that the long-house was more general. It existed in Worcestershire, examples being described in the Court Rolls of Hallow in 1340 and Kempsey in 1408, where accommodation for stock was clearly under the same roof. Thirdly, farmsteads comprising houses and substantial outbuildings have appeared on lowland village sites; at Hangleton they were being built at the same period as adjacent long-houses, whilst at Seacourt several were of this type. The number of rooms vary, but the presence of well-built outhouses such as the five-bay byre or barn at Seacourt separates this as a group. The significance of these differences lies in the stock or storage space, and corresponds with the range of peasant wealth suggested by animals or land. The landless can be fitted to the small cottages which lack outhouses, and the wealthier villeins or freeholders to the long-houses and farms.[80]

The rebuilding of houses is an important guide to prosperity, not only in the alteration of plans to give extra accommodation but also in changes in materials. At Gomeldon, Wiltshire, a long-house byre was converted to provide further living accommodation during the thirteenth century and a barn built nearby. Many excavated sites of larger peasant houses have shown evidence of increased accommodation late in the thirteenth century.[81] The rebuilding of a timber-and-cob structure in stone was a priority use for the rising income of the larger peasant; fifteenth-century Devon accounts show the extensive demo-

[79] A. Fox, 'Gelligaer Common', *Arch. Cambrensis*, 1939, 169; E. M. Jope and R. I. Threlfall, '...Beere, North Tawton...', *Med. Arch.*, II (1958), 112–140; *ibid.*, IX (1968), 210–12; *ibid.*, 212; D. Dudley and E. M. Minter, '...Garrow Tor...', *ibid.*, VI–VII (1962–3), 272–94; *ibid.*, IX (1965), 208, and VIII (1964), 282; L. Still and A. Pallister, '...West Hartburn...', *Arch. Aeliana*, 4th ser., XLII (1964), 187–206; M. G. Jarrett, '...West Whelpington...', *ibid.*, XL (1962), 189–225.

[80] P. A. Rahtz, '...Holworth...', *Dorset Nat. Hist. and Arch. Soc.*, 81 (1959), 127–47; E. W. Holden, '...Hangleton, pt 1', *Sx Arch. Colls*, CI (1963), 54–181; J. G. and D. G. Hurst, '...Hangleton, pt 2', *ibid.*, CII (1964), 94–142; *Med. Arch.*, IX (1968), 215 (also brief reports in *Med. Arch.*, I–VIII).

[81] *Med. Arch.*, VIII (1964), 289; *ibid.*, IX (1965), 214–15.

lition needed to restore faulty cob-built walls,[82] and excavated thir-teenth-century timber houses at Wharram Percy had been rebuilt every 30 years during the thirteenth century. Thus a durable rebuilding in stone suggests a measure of prosperity, and is seen at Wharram Percy around 1300 and in most Seacourt house-sites in the late thirteenth and early fourteenth centuries. The change amounted to capital for-mation, freeing future income for purposes other than rebuilding. Declining fortunes may also be seen: at Wharram Percy, whilst House 6 was a stone structure from the late thirteenth century onwards, House 10 degenerated after its rebuilding in stone, being replaced by a timber house in the fourteenth century and in the fifteenth by poorly built cob. The contents of these houses provide a further check on wealth. The Essex tax assessments show how few possessions occu-pants of single-roomed cottages had. The lists of property taken over by peasants with holdings give some measure of wealth differentials but do not include personal possessions which the more prosperous might buy. Excavated evidence is of some value, for pottery, the most common surviving material, shows the quality-range which house-holders could afford. At Beere, Devon, the wares found were local, bought perhaps from the nearby North Tawton market. However, at Seacourt, there were some good-quality wares from the Brill kilns, Buckinghamshire, bought perhaps in Oxford, while at Upton, Glou-cestershire, although much of the pottery was of local Cotswold origin, some probably came from the Birmingham and Oxford areas.[83]

In thus stating the evidence for the wide range of peasant wealth our attention is constantly drawn to the large numbers at the lower end of the scale. Large holdings were rare; small cottages were com-mon, and in very many cases chattels were virtually non-existent. It was in this level of society, largely without property, that the effects of the inadequacy of resources were felt. Towards the end of the thirteenth century a relation has been suggested between poor harvests and death-rates; the continuing high birth-rate was beginning to be accompanied by high mortality, and it is clear from what is known about medieval diet why this should be so. The corrodies, or pensions in kind, paid by monasteries to the elderly, show how largely the normal diet was based on carbohydrates. Bread and beer were con-sumed in relatively large quantities and protein was short. These examples show an ample diet by the standards of the period; peasant households would be worse off and would largely be restricted to

---

[82] N. W. Alcock, 'The Medieval Cottages of Bishops Clyst, Devon', *Med. Arch.*, IX (1965), 147–8.
[83] *Field 1965*, 121–5, 137–45; R. H. Hilton and P. A. Rahtz, 'Upton, Gloucestershire, 1959–1964', *Trans. Bristol and Glos. Arch. Soc.*, 85 (1966), 70–146, esp. 113.

second-class protein from peas or beans, although perhaps not enough attention has been paid to the contribution of eggs or fish, for chickens and fish were common items in the customary seasonal food rents paid at Christmas, Easter or in Lent.[84] Probably eggs were the peasant's most important protein source, for milk and cheese would be scarce among families with few stock. The staple sources of food were barley and oats, the wheat being sold, and this bias suggests not only how vulnerable families would be to poor harvests, but that their resistance to disease would be low.[85]

The pressures which threatened the real incomes of all but the largest peasants seem to have provided an increasing proportion of the national product for their lords. From late in the twelfth century costs of management remained stable and labour costs tended to decline. With the steadily rising demand for demesne products and for tenancies, reflected in rising prices and rents, estate incomes were buoyant. This applied to a wide range of tenants-in-chief and sub-tenants, not only those 50 or more wealthiest barons whose combined incomes equalled that of Henry II but, to a rather lesser degree, smaller men down to the holders of fractions of knights fees or holders in sergeanty. The largest increases in income took place early in the thirteenth century. One estimate compares average increases of 60 per cent between Domesday and 1220 and about 30 per cent between 1250 and 1350 with well over 50 per cent between 1220 and 1250. The net income of the Bishopric of Ely rose from £920 in 1171–2 to £1,930 in 1256–7 and £2,550 in 1292–9. On the lands of the Bishops of Winchester revenues were between £2,000 and £3,000 about 1200, and in the range of £3,000–£5,350 between 1221 and 1270.[86]

The biggest increases coincided with the growth in enthusiasm for demesne farming. Late in the twelfth century Ramsey Abbey began to resume its tenancies, investigate previous alienations and purchase land; Ely took steps to define peasants' status and services at about the same time. In the thirteenth century the largest estates ensured that the greatest proportion of their demesne output was sold; 32 Winchester demesne manors marketed 82 per cent of their net grain output, and this explains the attempts to resume as much land as possible. On Ralph Camoys' 12 manors the demesnes accounted for half the total value, and at Ely also, in 1255–6, demesne agricultural profits amounted to 50 per cent of the Bishop's income at a time when probably little more than one third of his lands were in hand. This was the

[84] N. Nielson, *Customary Rents*, Oxford, 1910, 30–33; Homans, 268, 365.
[85] M. M. Postan and J. Z. Titow, 'Heriots and Prices on Winchester Manors', *Ec.H.R.*, 2nd ser., XI (1958–9), 392–417.
[86] Painter, 160–70; Miller, *Ely*, 94; Miller, 'English Economy of the Thirteenth Century', 25–6.

peak of high farming and, even though total income continued to grow, demesnes expanded less after 1280—a measure of the demand for tenancies. By 1298–9 Ely's profits from agriculture had fallen to 40 per cent of the whole; at Taunton, due to the letting of holdings, the area of demesne under seed declined (here there was a reduction of 640 acres between 1248 and 1311); and at Ramsey corn sales from demesne manors fell and demesne and mills were farmed out.[87]

The continuing increases in profits resulted from efficient diversion of wealth towards the estate rather than from high rates of capital investment. Indeed, the treatises on estate management laid great emphasis on keeping existing sources of income secure: Robert Grosseteste's advice to the Countess of Lincoln emphasised the sworn survey to be made on first taking over an estate, and the *Seneschaucie* concentrated on the duties of officials, stewards and bailiffs who increasingly needed legal education and experience, and amongst whom the texts of the treatises probably circulated. It was particularly important that surveys should be made after periods of vacancy and wardship; the surveys of the Sussex manors of the Archbishop of Canterbury in 1285 show how great could be the depredations of royal officials during a vacancy, and the amount of sales of rents, corn and stock from the lands of William de Stutville in 1203, the year after his death, shows the damage a wardship could do.[88] Techniques of supervision may be seen improving at all levels. At Petworth fourteenth-century Ministers' Accounts show the emphasis put on the Reeve's ability to check sharp practices; at St Swithun's Priory, Winchester, the Reeve was under obligation to make up crops which fell short of a predetermined yield; and at Ramsey in the 1290s, when demesne output was in decline, particular care was devoted to scrutiny for waste, and safeguards against dilapidation were incorporated in tenancy agreements.[89] Accounting also received attention. Whilst accounts at Ramsey seem to concentrate on the prevention of fraud by manorial officials, the monks of Canterbury Cathedral Priory were calculating the *profectus* of some manors in the 1220s, while at Norwich Cathedral Priory in 1265 not only manorial but demesne profits were shown, and in 1289 the demesne reckoning was itself subdivided in a way which suggests some scrutiny of the relative merits of different uses of land.[90]

[87] Raftis, *Ramsey*, 97–103, 217; Miller, *Ely*, 82; *C.E.H.E.*, I, 195; Titow, 'Population Increase', 223.

[88] D. Oschinsky, 'Medieval Treatises on Estate Management', *Ec.H.R.*, 2nd ser., VIII (1955–6), 296–307; B. C. Redwood and A. E. Wilson (ed.), 'Custumals of the Sussex Manors of the Archbishops of Canterbury', *Sussex Rec. Soc.*, LVII (1957), xxix; Painter, 153.

[89] J. L. Drew, 'Manorial Accounts of St Swithun's Priory, Winchester', *Ec.H.R.*, 62 (1947), 20–41; Raftis, 1957, 76.

[90] Raftis, *Ramsey*, 120 *seq.*; E. Stone, 'Profit and Loss Accounting at Norwich

Despite the apparent scale of much of the improvement carried out by thirteenth-century estates, only a low percentage of income was used for capital formation, as distinct from mere land purchase. The treatises devote only sporadic attention to improvement, concentrating on caution and using the extent as a yardstick of performance. This attitude can be explained to a degree; the object was seen as the building of cash reserves, and the need for large estates to do this shows how vulnerable even they were to natural disasters. The use of more than five per cent of total receipts for capital improvement was rare; on the lands of the earldom of Cornwall only Knaresborough reached 4·5 per cent and the honours of St Valery and Eye were as low as one per cent. Five per cent was barely reached on Peterborough estates at the beginning of the fourteenth century; the annual average spent by Henry of Eastry, Prior of Canterbury, between 1285 and 1322 was 4·4 per cent of the average annual receipt known for the 1320s. The comparatively high figure of 5·6 per cent was spent by Adam de Stratton at his Wiltshire manor of Sevenhampton. These figures should be compared with the investment of Henry de Bray, who probably spent almost 20 per cent of his receipts on improvements.[91]

Town rents and dues from thriving fairs and markets contributed to baronial incomes. In the twelfth century the Earl of Gloucester derived 19–26 per cent of his income from Bristol, and his income from Tewkesbury rose from £12 in 1201 to £169 in 1263, though this was an exceptionally large increase. The honour of Richmond's share of Boston's fair revenue grew, the highest figure for the twelfth century being £184 and for the thirteenth £289. Feudal revenue was of most importance to larger tenants-in-chief; incomes from franchises and tallages were potentially high; proceeds of pleas varied from £380 in the honour of Perche in 1212 (compared with manorial income of £335) to the more modest £9 of the Fitzherberts in 1185, when manorial income was £121. Tallages could make occasional contributions; in 1212 the proceeds of a tallage on the lands of the Constable of Chester brought in 42 per cent of their annual value. Military dues probably declined; castle-guard was seldom performed or was changed to payments in lieu which were rarely exacted by the late thirteenth century. The enfeoffing of knights above the Crown's assessed figures, a frequent source of profit to tenants-in-chief in the twelfth century, was less

Cathedral Priory', *Trans. Roy. Hist. Soc.*, 5th ser., XII (1962), 25–48; D. Oschinsky, 'Medieval Treatises on Estate Accounting', *Ec.H.R.*, XVII (1947), 570. For a concise description of the standard layout of medieval estate accounts, see R. H. Hilton (ed.) 'Ministers' Accounts of the Warwickshire Estates of the Dukes of Clarence, 1479–80', *Dugdale Soc.*, XXI (1952), xi–xv.
[91] Hilton, 'Rent and Capital Formation', 36–47.

profitable after the introduction of licences to exact scutage from vassals in the reign of John.[92]

Trends in incomes are very hard to determine. Late in the twelfth century 54 barons with an average income of £202 and a median of £115 included seven with £400 or more, the highest being Roger de Lacy with £800 in 1210 and William of Gloucester with £700 in the reign of Henry II. To these sums should be added feudal dues, in William's case about £2,000 per generation. At the end of the thirteenth century 27 holders of lands whose incomes are known averaged £668 (median £339), the wealthiest of them being Edmund, Earl of Cornwall, with £3,800 in 1301. Another estimate for the late thirteenth century puts the Lord Edward's annual income at about £10,000, with six or so others in the £3,000–£4,000 bracket. The annual income of the Clare estates can be estimated from Crown valuations in 1266–7 and 1312–20—they rose in the intervening years from about £3,700 to £6,000.[93]

In the absence of any marked tendency to invest capital in improvements the major incentive to raise income lay in the wide field for spending on consumption. The demands of building, almsgiving, hospitality and devotional expenditure are clear for ecclesiastical estates. The pressures on lay landowners also grew over the period, although in general baronial incomes probably amply covered the comparatively primitive standard of noble living. Some strain came late in the twelfth century from crusade expenditure, which required some borrowing, though not a catastrophic amount. The regular expenses of barons in the thirteenth century comprised the cost of retainers—a knight's annual upkeep being £10–£11 late in the twelfth century—and household costs, which could be up to £500 per year for prominent barons. Expenditure was further affected by social pressures towards hospitality, the purchase of those luxury imports which formed the return trade for exported wool, the costs of the administration of private justice, particularly in the north where franchises were more extensive, and the semi-official duties in the shire or on eyres. The cost of building also rose: the minimum cost of a serviceable thirteenth-century stone castle with domestic appurtenances, perhaps £350, would be far higher than for the earth-and-timber mottes of Stephen's reign or before and the timber halls in their baileys.[94]

[92] Painter, 125–7.
[93] Painter, 170 *seq.*; N. Denholm-Young, *Seigneurial Administration in England*, 1937, 22; M. Altschul, *A Baronial Family in Medieval England, The Clares, 1217–1314*, Baltimore, 1965, 203–4.
[94] Painter, 170 *seq.*; J. E. Baldwin, 'Household Accounts of Henry de Lacy and Thomas of Lancaster', *Eng.H.R.*, XLII (1927), 180–200. For a banquet of the period see J. C. Russell and J. P. Hieronimus, *The Shorter Latin Poems of Master Henry of Avranches Relating to England*, Medieval Academy of

Smaller landowners, however, appear to have been less able to maintain their position. Their expenditure was raised by social pressures dictated by the rising living standards of the greater lords; the costs of knighthood were burdensome, particularly of horses, retainers and equipment, and, although incomes from their estates were generally rising with product prices, many could not keep up. There are numerous references to sales of lands to monasteries, sometimes for pensions, and indebtedness to Jewish money-lenders, involving, it appears, men within the broad class of the knights.[95] It must, however, be said that the nature of the sources of this kind of evidence contains a bias towards stressing the unsuccessful, and it would be unwise in the thirteenth century as in the sixteenth to suggest that all or even a majority of this group were spending beyond their means. Because of this problem of sampling it is worth noting that the archaeological evidence from the excavation of smaller moated house-sites does provide examples of improving, static and of declining material standards. This evidence, however, is not foolproof, for a mid-thirteenth-century rebuilding in stone, far from signifying a securely rising family standard of living, might have been undertaken to follow fashion and be a step nearer financial disaster.[96]

Industry and Trade

Developments in industry and trade in the twelfth and thirteenth centuries provided only slight compensation in terms of added employment for the land shortage in agriculture. If anything, the manufacturing sector seems to have declined, although there is evidence for

America, Studies and Documents, I, Camb., Mass., 1935, 69; K. R. Potter (ed.), *Gesta Stephani*, 1955, 61; B. Hope-Taylor, 'The Excavation of a Motte at Abinger in Surrey', *Archaeol. Jnl*, CVII (1950), 15–43.

[95] *C.E.H.E.*, I, 593–5; H. G. Richardson, *The English Jewry under the Angevin Kings*, 1960, 83 *seq.*; Hilton, *A Medieval Society*, 50–2.

[96] The number of excavations producing conclusive evidence is not large, and many remain unpublished apart from brief notes in the 'Medieval Britain...' sections of *Medieval Archaeology*. However, Scredington Moat, Lincs (L. A. S. Butler, *Jnl Brit. Arch. Ass.*), built late in the thirteenth century, had a poor standard of construction and associated finds; Humberstone, Leicester (P. A. Rahtz, *Trans. Leic. Arch. & Hist. Soc.*, XXXV (1958), 1–32) was small and of a standard compatible with the political difficulties of its occupants early in the thirteenth century; Northolt, Middlesex (J. G. Hurst, *Med. Arch.*, V (1961), 211–99), owned by a minor family through the mid and late thirteenth century, was remarkably short of high-quality pottery (pp. 263–273, 276) before a stone rebuilding in 1300, after which better wares appeared; Hutton Colswain, Yorkshire (M. W. Thompson, *Arch. Jnl*, CXIV (1957), 69–91) was rebuilt in stone late in the thirteenth century; the Manor of the More, Middlesex (M. Biddle, *Arch. Jnl.* CXVI (1959), 136–99) was rebuilt and improved about 1300; Shareshill, Staffs (A. Oswald, *T. Birmingham Arch. Soc.*, LXXVII (1959), 43–58), was also improved on two occasions, probably within the thirteenth century.

expansion in the output of primary products. This applies particularly to mining. After wool, tin was the most valuable English export in the thirteenth century, and its production expanded over the period. Whilst its extraction before the Conquest is a commonplace, there are no eleventh-century references, but after 1156 growth of output and employment is well established.

	1160	1171	1198	1212	1337
Thousand Weight	133	640	c. 900	1000	1328

The gap in the figures in the mid-thirteenth century corresponds with the farming of the Stannaries by the Earls of Cornwall, but during this period the number of tinners rose, if unevenly.

1243	1295	1296	1300
149	453	199	436

Growth was not without problems, with the working-out of deposits in South-West Devon; but production in West Cornwall increased, and new methods of smelting improved the rate of extraction. The prosperity of the industry and its export trade may be gauged from that of the Stannary towns, Tavistock in particular, and the attractions of free miner's status ensured a level of employment which rose to the point of diminishing their output per head. The figures above, scattered as they are, support this suggestion. The importance of the export of tin is amply borne out by references to its source in continental markets such as Bruges, and England herself was clearly self-sufficient for her needs for pewter, bell-metal and solder.[97] The production of lead, although less well-documented, made a considerable contribution to mineral exports. It was mined in Derbyshire at the time of Domesday, and on Alston Moor, in the Mendips and in Shropshire by the late twelfth century. By 1200 there are references to mines in Weardale and in Flint, and before 1300 in Devon. By the thirteenth century English output rivalled that of Central Europe, and a considerable export trade built up, particularly through Boston. In the twelfth and thirteenth centuries lead was greatly in demand for building, both ecclesiastical and military, and the increasing size of castles was an important factor in the opening of new mines. Much of the lead shipped from Boston went either to South-East England or to the Continent for buildings on the scale of Clairvaux. Also, the silver content of certain lead deposits was an attraction, and was a major objective at Alston Moor from 1133, at the Bishop of Durham's Weardale Mines by 1196, and in Devon in the late thirteenth century.[98]

[97] G. R. Lewis, *The Stannaries*, 1907, 34–58; Finberg, *Tavistock*, 168–87.
[98] Lennard, 241; Bouch and Jones, 27; *C.E.H.E.*, II (1952), 439; L. F. Salz-

By contrast, English production of iron was on a small scale, and there was considerable reliance on imports. Smelting sites are hard to locate at this period, but after Domesday a good deal of expansion seems to have taken place. The Domesday evidence suggests there was small-scale working in most of the areas of known ore deposits, but that only the bloomeries in South-West Gloucestershire operated on any scale. During the twelfth century there are clear signs of growth in areas hitherto producing only for local demand. The Gloucester iron market increased its reputation as production from ore dug by privileged miners grew in the Forest of Dean, described by Giraldus Cambrensis in 1188 as 'abounding with iron and deer'. Similarly, Durham iron met the needs of a widening northern market. Monastic development of ore deposits was widespread: in Glamorgan, Neath and Margam Abbeys had forges in the west of the county, and the northern Cistercian houses were active, developing the Tankersley Ironstones in South Yorkshire, the deposits in Knaresborough Forest, Wensleydale, Bowland and Furness. Guisborough Priory had bloomeries in Pickering and Baysdale, and lay estates in Derbyshire, Staffordshire and Worcestershire developed bloomeries during the thirteenth century. The size of the Weald industry is obscure at this period; one site is mentioned in Domesday but no precise locations are known until the fourteenth century. However, orders placed in the area included one for 30,000 horseshoes and 60,000 nails in 1252, a Lewes murage grant of 1263 mentioned carts loaded with iron, and in 1300 London ironmongers were in dispute with Weald smiths over standards for cart tyres.[99] The number of bloomeries in the country increased perhaps fivefold between Domesday and 1300, and annual national output may have reached 1,000 tons. Such low figures suggest a high degree of reliance on imports. Accounts for the construction of siege machines in 1278-9 show that two per cent of the iron required was home-produced, and that 65 per cent came from Spain; imports also came from Normandy and Sweden late in the thirteenth century. Arms requirements were largely for high-quality iron, and for building and agricultural purposes a greater proportion was home-produced, though imported qualities were also used for structural applications such as window bars and ties.[100] The English industry was dependent

---

man, *English Industries of the Middle Ages*, 1923, 42 *seq.*; A. Raistrick and B. Jennings, *A History of Lead Mining in the Pennines*, 196, 24; E. M. Carus-Wilson, 'The Medieval Trade of the Ports of the Wash', *Medieval Archaeology*, VI-VII (1962-3), 188.

[99] Schubert, 80-111; C. E. Hart, *The Free Miners*, Gloucester, 1953, 5, 11-12, 158; R. F. Tylecote, *Metallurgy in Archaeology*, 1962, 284; E. Straker, *Wealden Iron*, 1931, 33 *seq.*

[100] Salzman, *Building in England*, 286-317. The quantity of iron required for

on ores poorer in quality than those of Northern Spain; this hindered any widening of the market which might have enabled a more rapid adoption of higher-output techniques using water power. Hand-powered bellows were in use in Kent after 1350 at bloomeries producing only two or three tons per year, against the 25–30 possible with power, and there also remained some small hand-operated bloomeries where slag was not even tapped from the hearth, leaving it all to be hammered out.

A primary product of importance was salt. Domesday recorded brine springs in Worcestershire and Cheshire, and there were salterns round the south and east coasts; those of Sussex, Norfolk and Lincolnshire were of approximately equal importance in the eleventh century, but by the late thirteenth production was concentrated upon Lincolnshire. In the first years of the fourteenth century there are signs of an important export trade to Norway and the Low Countries, which it seems safe to assume existed before the 1303 Petty Custom on alien trade, which is the sole source of information. Salt had its major market at home as a preservative for meat, dairy products, and in particular for the growing east-coast fisheries, but in the later Middle Ages production fell and England became a net importer of salt. The trend probably began around 1300, for in the Lincolnshire Fenlands the peat-pits upon which salters relied for fuel were being flooded, and later in the century, as fuel became a growing problem, high labour costs reduced the home industry's competitiveness.[101]

Of the remaining extractive industries coal was as yet insignificant. Where outcrops were accessible it was dug in small quantities, although by 1214 the Bishop of Durham's annual income from his mines had reached £534; in Leicestershire in the later thirteenth century assarting had reduced firewood supplies to a point where coal was being extensively used, and in parts of Wales and Scotland coal was in regular use as a domestic fuel.[102] Of far more widespread importance was the quarrying of stone. The increasing size of buildings, which fostered the lead industry, also resulted in expansion of quarries. The oolitic limestones from Yorkshire to Dorset were used for much Midland building, and the radius of use of high-quality stones such as both these and the Reigate

agricultural purposes may be seen from inventories of implements—see L. F. Salzman, 'The Possessions of the Earl of Arundel in 1397', *Sussex Arch. Colls*, XVI (1952), 41–2.

[101] A. R. Bridbury, *England and the Salt Trade in the Later Middle Ages*, Oxford, 1965, 16–21, 26–39; E. H. Rudkin and D. M. Owen, 'The Medieval Salt Industry in the Lindsey Marshland', *Lincolnshire Archit. and Archeol. Soc.*, 76–84; H. E. Hallam, 'Salt-making in the Lincolnshire Fenlands during the Middle Ages', *ibid.*, 85–112.

[102] Painter, 165; Hoskins, *Midland Peasant*, 57; I. F. Grant, *The Social and Economic Development of Scotland before 1603*, 1930, 116.

stone used at Rochester and Windsor tended to increase. Further, the organisation needed for large Crown and Church building projects developed over the period, to the point where Edward I was able to organise finance and labour for his castles in North Wales at the end of the thirteenth century.[103]

Although these extractive industries contributed to the economy with exports or improved materials for agriculture or building, none offered sufficient employment to make any great contribution towards redressing the thirteenth-century balance between population and resources.

The textile industry could best have fulfilled such a role, for about half the value of the cloth sold lay in its labour content. In the twelfth century England had a cloth industry of repute, built up with the benefit of Flemish immigrants, wool supplies of excellent quality, a measure of Crown encouragement and established, even if largely foreign, supplies of finishing materials. Weavers' Gilds were present in the larger textile towns before 1150, and the cloth of Lincoln, Stamford, York and Beverley had stable markets on the Continent and with the Crown. The lower-grade producers, Winchester or Oxford, had important textile-making communities, and cloth for home consumption was made in numerous small towns and villages.[104] Over the thirteenth century this situation changed. After 1200 some towns had intermittent lean periods; York's weavers' gild built up arrears in its farm in 1202 and 1214, as did Winchester's in 1198 and 1202. Many clothing towns prospered well into the thirteenth-century. Marlborough maintained its sales of medium-quality cloths and the products of Northampton and Lincoln sold well in John's reign, but there appear references to sales problems and to rural weavers who avoided gild restrictions and came to dominate the medium-quality market. York began to be threatened by West Riding competition and Canterbury craftsmen complained of rivals in rural Kent. This was at a time when competition in European markets from Flanders made finding means of cutting costs more necessary. The high-quality urban producers had little answer, and there was a general reduction in town craftsmen late in the century, only York proving an exception. Most other English cloths were of lower quality, and their production was maintained by the cost reductions which rural working allowed. Free-

[103] Beresford and St Joseph; D. Knoop and G. P. Jones, 'The English Medieval Quarry', *Ec.H.R.*, IX (1939), 17–37; Salzman, *Building in England*, 119–39; J. G. Edwards, 'Edward I's Castle-Building in Wales', *Proc. Brit. Acad.*, XXXII (1946), 15 *seq.*; A. J. Taylor, 'Castle-Building in Wales in the Late 13th Century: the Prelude to Construction', *Studies in Building History* (ed. E. M. Jope), 1961, 104–33.
[104] E. M. Carus-Wilson, 'The English Cloth Industry in the Late 12th and Early 13th Centuries', *Ec. H.R.*, XIV (1944), 32–50; *C.E.H.E.*, II (1952), 366–9.

dom from gild restrictions allowed more apprentices and an ability to experiment without running into regulations originally designed to control quality. As in the sixteenth century, the countryside provided the necessary labour force, and the water-powered fulling mills contributed to lower costs. Increasing numbers of them were built in the thirteenth century, and even if the advantage was sometimes as much to manorial profits as to fullers, they became more useful as the proportion of heavily fulled cloth grew in the following century.

However, although this shift in location was to prepare for the protected cloth industries of the fourteenth and fifteenth centuries, the problems of the years before 1300 were increased by the amount of imported Flemish cloth taking the place of the quality products of the towns. The Flemings, by specialisation, had built up a cost advantage backed up by marketing in bulk through the English fairs.[105] The problems of the English industry, falling back on lower-quality cloths, are partly explained by the coincidence of the rise in Flemish competition, but that it was unable to compete suggests that its particular forms of urban organisation militated against efficiency and experiment. Further, the industry could not expand its sales at the rate of population-increase; even its lower-quality branches suffered from stagnant purchasing-power as the real incomes of the majority failed to rise, and the only market of any buoyancy was among the top levels of the peasantry.

The prosperity of another industry making semi-durables, ceramics, may illustrate this latter point. It is now becoming clear that this period saw the fullest development of the potter's skill in England. Standards of finish and decoration improved, and whilst the products of specialist kilns such as Scarborough or Nottingham clearly served upper-class and export markets, the less highly-finished decorated wares of kilns such as Toynton, Rye, Laverstock or Brill had a wider distribution. Decorated pottery found its way to peasant communities to supplement plain domestic wares, but was found only on the more substantial house-sites in excavated deserted medieval villages such as Seacourt.[106] Such distribution, with the general wealth of the industry and its skills, must encourage the assumption that appreciable purchasing power lay amongst the upper reaches of the peasantry. This may in 1300 still have been providing a thriving market for medium-grade cloths when

[105] E. Miller, 'The Fortunes of the English Textile Industry in the 13th Century', *Ec.H.R.*, 2nd ser., XVIII (1965), 64–82; *V.C.H.*, Wiltshire, IV, 117 *seq.*; E. M. Carus-Wilson, 'An Industrial Revolution of the 13th Century', *Ec.H.R.*, XI (1941), 39–60.
[106] E. M. Jope, 'The Regional Cultures of Medieval Britain', *Culture and Environment* (ed. I. L. Foster and L. Alcock), 1963, 329–40; Biddle, esp. pp. 133–4.

the upper-class market, whether because of fashion or finish, had turned to Flanders cloth, just as those wealthy households still buying the pottery of Scarborough or Nottingham also patronised the producers of the unique polychrome wares of Western France. What we do not see, however, is any significant market for durables of any but the most utilitarian kind amongst the mass of the peasantry.

The purchasing power of the middle and upper ranges of society is reflected in the increasing numbers of artisans and the organisation of crafts in towns. This can be seen not only in the largest towns of the period, London, York and Bristol, but in numerous smaller centres. London really stood on its own, for the market was not only the region, but the city itself, which at least doubled its population during the thirteenth century from 20,000 to perhaps 40,000. To measure the number of craftsmen is difficult, for the development of their gilds was not always a sure guide. In the late thirteenth century occupations with a hazy division between craft and mercantile activities had their development hindered by the merchant gilds. But despite this numerous indications, not least the part played by craftsmen in the disturbances of 1263 and 1272, show the growth, amongst others, of the various workers with leather, furs, metal and wood.[107] Whilst York, with its institutional market, and Bristol, as a port, had some internal trade, their crafts and those of most other towns catered largely for their surroundings. Nevertheless some specialisation did occur. Coventry's metal trades became prominent during the thirteenth century, and Northampton became a centre for skinners. These specialities were not to the exclusion of other crafts, and Coventry had just as wide a range as other towns of its size, Gloucester, Norwich or Chester.[108]

The overseas trade of thirteenth-century England, with its development of raw wool exports, mirrors depression in the textile industry. But this was a period when foreign trade, although not providing the employment which a market for manufactured products could have brought, did succeed in developing a basis of routes, experience and facilities which were to be of subsequent value. From the ninth century and before, connections had been built up between South-East England and the Continent; traders from Imperial towns, Teil and Bremen in particular, were frequent visitors to London, and contacts with Flanders and Lorraine were active before the Conquest. The northern markets were important, English cloth having a high reputation in Scandinavia, and after 1066 this trade developed further. Before the Conquest Rouen wine had reached London in some quantity, and in the thir-

---

[107] G. A. Williams, *Medieval London, from Commune to Capital*, 1963, 19–20, 157–95, 315–17; E. M. Veale, *The English Fur Trade in the Later Middle Ages*, 1966, 39, 117.
[108] Hilton, *A Medieval Society*, 193–9.

teenth century the extent of this and other links with France grew.[109] The pattern of North Sea trade in the immediate pre- and post-Conquest period is suggested by the archaeological evidence. Pottery found in London and the south-east coastal ports suggests contacts with the Rhineland (illustrated by wares from Pingsdorf and Badorf) and with Flanders (shown by Limburg and Andenne wares), while trade with Normandy, particularly after the Conquest, is confirmed by the quantity of red-painted wares from the Rouen area.[110]

In the twelfth century this pattern developed; cloth and wool were exported to a widening range of European markets, including Spain and the Mediterranean, and imports, with wine retaining its importance, increasingly included Baltic goods, dyes and finishing materials for the cloth industry, and a widening range of luxury items.[111] The major feature, however, was the growing export of wool; purchased in increasing quantities by Flemish craftsmen from the early twelfth century onwards, it had become the major export by 1200. The effects on the English economy were mixed. It clearly provided a great incentive to estates of all sizes in Eastern and Northern England to make the greatest use of pastures, and the growth of both demesne and peasant flocks probably eased the problem of soil fertility to some degree. Also, for peasant farmers, the ready outlet for wool increased the value of stock as a supplement to incomes.[112] But the fact remains that England was increasingly an exporter of a primary product in whose processing she was unable to compete. The trend continued throughout the thirteenth century. English wool exports were rising over the last quarter, for which figures are available, and the import of cloth from Flanders increased after 1250; even in the Scandinavian market, the import of timber and fish was increasingly in exchange for dairy products and grain. The wool export trade enjoyed further prosperity from the growing interest in English supplies of Italian merchant-financier houses, purchasing on long-term contracts with cash collected as Papal dues, sending wool to Italy, and thus simplifying the problem of security in overland cash remittances.

[109] *C.E.H.E.*, II (1952), 366 *seq.*; P. Grierson, 'The Relations between England and Flanders before the Norman Conquest', *Trans. Roy. Hist. Soc.*, 4th ser., XXIII (1941), 93–5; F. M. Stenton, *Norman London*, Historical Assoc. Leaflet 93, 1934, 19–20; E. Sabbé, 'Les Relations Economiques entre l'Angleterre et le Continent au Haut Moyen Age', *Moyen Age*, LVI (1950), 186–9; Sawyer, 160–4.

[110] G. C. Dunning, 'Pottery of the Late Anglo-Saxon Period in England', *Medieval Archaeology*, III (1959), 31–78; 'A Norman Pit at Pevensey Castle and its Contents', *Antiq. Jnl*, XXXIII (1958), 208.

[111] *C.E.H.E.*, II (1952), 232 *seq.*; E. M. Carus-Wilson, 'La Guède Française en Angleterre: un Grand Commerce du Moyen Age', *Revue du Nord*, XXXV (1953), 89.

[112] Power, *Wool Trade*, 41–62.

In the late thirteenth century the volume of trade grew considerably. Not only did wool exports increase, but also imports of wine from Gascony, Eastern Mediterranean goods (in particular those brought by Italian merchants to their growing colony of Southampton) and French salt, Spanish leather, wool and wax, and the fruits and Malaga lustreware pottery of Southern Spain.[113]

Although the balance of benefit of the trades themselves is a matter for discussion, the commercial infrastructure, both external and internal, undoubtedly developed and was a major reason for the increasing scale of exchange later in the thirteenth century. Increased use of credit in trade, despite the expulsion of the Jews in 1290, helped to swell the volume, and it became commonplace for buyers of wool to make contracts for four, six, or 12 years in advance. Similarly in the London import trade, notably wine, credit became increasingly important, and in all these fields the example of Italian firms was of major importance. Their strength lay in their experience of such business, their techniques of accounting and their financial resources. They were able to lend on a large scale (the Frescobaldi provided £100,000 for Edward I in 1286–9), and to attract deposits in England, for despite notable bankruptcies—those, for instance, of the Ricardi of Lucca in 1301 and the Bonsignori of Siena in 1302—noblemen and ecclesiatics had regular deposits with Italian houses in the early fourteenth century.[114]

Development of an infrastructure is clear in internal trading, and aided the supply of English goods for export: an increasing amount of currency was in circulation; fairs and markets were granted in some numbers from the middle of the twelfth century; English roads, despite their inadequacies, were comparatively free from seigneurial tolls[115]; and the foundation and growth of towns was most rapid in this period. The progress of town foundation shows that the provision of facilities for trade was potentially profitable. The proportion of the population living in towns at Domesday appears to have been about 10 per cent, and in 1381 it remained at this level; in the 1340s it was probably higher, but the high urban incidence of plague appears to have reduced the figure.[116] The absolute increase in town population, corre-

---

[113] Ibid., 42–51; E. M. Carus-Wilson and O. Coleman, England's Export Trade, 1275–1547, 1963, 36–41; A. A. Ruddock, Italian Merchants and Shipping in Southampton, 1270–1600, 1951, 12–19; G. C. Dunning, 'A Group of English and Imported Medieval Pottery from Lesnes Abbey, Kent', Antiq. Jnl, XLI (1961), 1–12.

[114] M. M. Postan, 'Credit in Medieval Trade', Ec.H.R., I (1928), 61–87; Miller, 'The English Economy . . .', 28–9; E. B. Fryde, 'The Deposits of Hugh Despenser the Younger with Italian Bankers', Ec.H.R., 2nd ser., III (1950–1), 344–62.

[115] F. M. Stenton, 'The Road System in Medieval England', Ec. H.R., VII (1936), 1–21; C.E.H.E., III (1963), 308–9; Williams, 264–6.

[116] Russell, 45–54, 140–6.

sponding with or slightly below that of the country as a whole, was partly achieved by expansion of existing towns, but more striking is the number of villages which either aspired to or developed urban characteristics and institutions or were planted by landowners virtually from scratch.[117] These processes of urban development were taking place at the time of the Conquest, when a number of places, though not described as towns, were acquiring urban forms of tenure and developing market functions; the larger towns, York, Winchester and Norwich, had long outgrown their immediate food supplies, and others were to do so before 1200.[118] In the twelfth and thirteenth centuries the granting of charters according borough status and the rights to hold markets and organise gilds was a measure of actual or potential prosperity. In the reign of Henry II this was a fair guide, although under Richard and John some places overbid their interests to gain privileges, the Crown putting its fiscal needs before certainty that would-be boroughs could pay.[119]

Landed proprietors promoted towns, purpose-built to take advantage of sites suitable for trade. Hedon on the Humber was laid out as a small port; Portsmouth was a royal creation of the 1190s to replace the silting Portchester; others, such as Stratford-on-Avon or Eynsham, depended on river crossings. The towns of the Bishops of Winchester in Hampshire and Wiltshire, Salisbury, New Buckenham in Norfolk, or Chipping Camden were collecting-centres where proprietors might buy or sell in the markets. Some were successfully laid out on a large scale: Salisbury adjoined its cathedral, a ready market for craftsmen and traders. Others were less successful: New Buckenham never became more than a very small market town and the Bishop of Winchester's Newtown, designed as a centre for estate products, disappeared entirely.[120] Significant is the profit which landholders saw in founding towns, amply shown in Stratford-on-Avon's rent rolls by comparing a new town after 50 years of growth with the original manor. Their experience agrees with what we know of the profitability of selling demesne products in the early thirteenth century, and the developing towns and fairs provided the network by which the commodities of foreign trade could be collected and distributed, for not only were town

[117] M. W. Beresford, *New Towns of the Middle Ages*, 1967, *passim*.

[118] H. R. Loyn, *Anglo-Saxon England and the Norman Conquest*, 1962, 368–375.

[119] J. Tait, *The Medieval English Borough*, 1936, 172–9.

[120] Beresford and St Joseph, 200–6; W. G. Hoskins, *The Making of the English Landscape*, 1955, 88–91; Carus-Wilson, 'Stratford-upon-Avon', 46–63; H. E. Salter (ed.), *Cartulary of Eynsham Abbey*, vol. II, Oxford Historical Society, LI (1908), xli; M. W. Beresford, 'The Six New Towns of the Bishops of Winchester', *Medieval Archaeology*, III (1959), 187–215; *V.C.H.*, Wiltshire, VI, 69, 138.

markets developed, but the great fairs such as St Ives became increasingly prominent and towns were themselves granted the right to hold fairs, attracting specialist sellers, providing for the less frequent needs of the surrounding area. Though some fairs and some of the less successful towns were to fade away, the developments of the twelfth and thirteenth centuries were the basis for the greater growth of internal trade in the post-medieval period.[121]

Our picture of the development of English production and wealth in the thirteenth century shows an unbalanced growth. Agricultural production was restricted by static techniques and a land-hunger which both held back capital investment and ensured an uneven distribution of wealth. Yet the development of food-trading built up exchanges, towns and markets could in theory have supplied larger urban or industrial populations. But employment opportunities in such a sector were restricted by the lack of a mass market, and towns grew up as mercantile rather than manufacturing centres, developing their trading at a greater rate than their craft capital.

This pattern has emerged from our survey of wealth both in national terms, in the sense of resources and facilities, and in terms of the prosperity of groups within the population. Our impression must be that in the agricultural part of the economy, in which the great majority of people were involved, the rift between demand and supply could only continue to grow at the risk of serious consequences. It is to these, and to the occurrences which restored the balance, that we must now turn.

[121] Beresford and St Joseph, 160–4.

Chapter two

The Wealth of England in an Era of Underpopulation, 1315–1500

The turning-point of 1315–17 and its aftermath

The problems of the second and third decades of the fourteenth century forcibly illustrate the effects both on estate and peasant wealth of the failure of agricultural production to keep pace with population. In the years 1315–16 two particularly bad harvests followed a series whose yields had been below average; heavy rainfall occurred over much of Europe in both years, and low resistance to disease may have led to abnormal mortality. The second disaster occurred in the mid-1320s, when to poor harvests were added a series of livestock epidemics, which were particularly serious amongst sheep in the south of England.[1] The effects of the poor harvests are clear; the price of food rose as a result of wheat crops which were 57 per cent and 62 per cent of normal in 1315 and 1316 respectively. In Southern England, the price of wheat reached two or three times its usual level in 1316 and 1317, and a clear relation emerged between grain prices and high death-rates, which continued into the 1320s. Contemporary chroniclers such as John de Trokelowe of St Albans support this impression with their lurid descriptions of high mortality.[2] Communities short of land found that two severe harvests stretched their resources severely. However, it was not new for poor crops to bring some increase in death-rates on early-cleared lands of Southern England, for on Winchester estates the number of money heriots paid by those too poor to have livestock had risen in line with wheat prices on five occasions since

[1] H. S. Lucas, 'The Great European Famine of 1315, 1316 and 1317', *Speculum*, V (1930), 343–77; C. E. Britton, *A Meteorological Chronology to A.D. 1450*, Met. Office Geophysical Memoirs, LXX (1937), 132–3; H. van Werveke, 'La Famine de l'An 1316 en Flandre et dans les Régions Voisines', *Revue du Nord*, XLI (1959), 5–14; J. Z. Titow, 'Evidence of Weather in the Account Rolls of the Bishopric of Winchester', *Ec.H.R.*, 2nd ser., XII (1960), 385–7; R. A. L. Smith, *Canterbury Cathedral Priory*, 1943, 156.

[2] Barley crops were between 59 per cent and 77 per cent of normal. B. H. Slicher van Bath, *The Agrarian History of Western Europe, 500–1850*, 1963, 120; D. L. Farmer, 'Some Grain-Price Movements in 13th-Century England', *Ec.H.R.*, 2nd ser., X (1957), 212–8; M. M. Postan and J. Z. Titow, 'Heriots and Prices on Winchester Manors', *Ec.H.R.*, 2nd ser., XI (1959), 407; H. T. Riley (ed.), *John de Trokelowe, Annals* (Chronica Monasterii S. Albani), Rolls Ser., 1886, 92–6.

1251, and there the point had been reached where cottagers and small-holders had difficulty in maintaining a subsistence diet one year in three, a problem made no easier by the tendency to lease the poorer parts of demesnes to the growing peasant community.

The Winchester manor of Taunton is an example of the worst effects of overpopulation, though applied nationally such figures would probably exaggerate the problem. It has indeed recently been suggested that the crisis of 1315–17 only brought a levelling of the population trend, probably not a fall, and more recently still that the proportion of the mortality of 1315–17 caused by epidemics rather than by starvation has been underrated, that the late thirteenth-century fall in peasant living standards has been exaggerated and that this period of bad harvests has been invested with undue significance.[3]

But prices of grain did decline from the 1320s onwards, and despite attempts to attribute this to shortage of coin, it seems clear that real wages in terms of wheat did rise enough to suggest that there was some population change which brought about a significant easing of food supply and even a shortage of labour.[4] What is important about the period 1315–17 is that it illustrates what could happen in certain early fourteenth-century communities, it draws attention to what had already begun to happen in the thirteenth century on the Winchester lands, and it foreshadows the comments of the *Nonarum Inquisitiones* on the poverty of the uplands of Cambridgeshire, Bedfordshire and Buckinghamshire in 1342. It is unreasonable to suggest that all estates had reached the same stage of pressure on land and living standards; the variations in the levels of entry fines, in the sizes of holdings, or their levels of fertility, are clear, and, although most places show similar trends, over lowland England there may have been a 50-year gap between the worst and the best. This is suggested, despite the small sample available, by a recent examination of population replacement-rates in the century after 1250 on a number of manors in Eastern England; though the evidence is necessarily incomplete, the lowering of replacement-rates, particularly between 1280 and 1340, does deserve attention.[5]

[3] B. F. Harvey, 'The Population Trend in England, 1300–1348', *Trans. Roy. Hist. Soc.*, 5th ser., XVI (1966), 23–42; J. C. Russell, 'The Pre-Plague Population of England', *Jnl Brit. Studies*, V (1966), 1–21. Whether such a distinction between starvation and disease is valid is in doubt: chronic malnutrition could well cause low disease-resistance.

[4] W. C. Robinson, 'Money, Population, and Economic Change in Late Medieval Europe', *Ec.H.R.*, 2nd ser., XII (1959), 63–76; M. M. Postan, 'Note', *ibid.*, 77–82. See particularly M. M. Postan, 'Some Economic Evidence of Declining Population in the Later Middle Ages', *Ec.H.R.*, 2nd ser., II (1950), 221–46.

[5] A. R. H. Baker, 'Evidence in the *Nonarum Inquisitiones* of Contracting Arable Land in England in the Early 14th Century', *Ec.H.R.*, 2nd ser., XIX

Changes in agrarian life in the first half of the fourteenth century are consistent with a halt in the growth of population, and perhaps with a slight decline. In 1300 any incentive to lease lands was still because high rents were available from a growing peasantry whose preferences were for more land. In communities where population was still rising it was even worthwhile for an estate to buy land, as was done by Ely in the 1290s, for leasing rather than for direct farming. But after the 1320s the reasoning was apt to change to a more defensive line; demesne income was threatened by falls in food prices, but a backlog of demand for land allowed leasing to safeguard total revenue. At the Ely Manor of Shelford the decline in agricultural prices is clearly seen: income from sales fell by more than half between 1325 and 1333, years during which only one seventh of the demesne was let. On Cistercian lands the trend to leasing seen sporadically from 1280 onwards quickened between 1300 and 1350, particularly after 1315, when the General Chapter recognised what was happening by setting out the safeguards to be adopted.[6]

Some estates maintained direct farming for as long as they could. At Canterbury, Henry of Eastry continued investment in bought-in seed well into the 1320s, and reduced the size of demesnes only after high mortality among the priory sheep flocks in 1324–6; proceeds from wool sales had been vital to maintain income when grain yields were poor, despite attention to seed, and this loss of a third of the sheep enforced the change to the leasing of grazing lands. Some manors belonging to Durham Cathedral Priory maintained grain production to the end of the 1320s and in certain cases into the 1340s. But the pressures against direct farming affected most estates to some degree before the Black Death. The tendency for wages to rise became clear in the 1320s; on Winchester and Westminster manors this was significant by the end of the decade, and at Canterbury and Ramsey there were attempts to keep wage-bills in check by continuing the operation of labour services. This, however, was apparently unsuccessful, for with more land available there were marked objections to performing works which diverted men from their expanding holdings, and in the 1330s the best Ramsey manors, Shillington and Pegsdon, were leased out as the Abbey's income from sales declined.[7]

(1966), 518–32; S. L. Thrupp, 'The Problem of Replacement Rates in Late Medieval English Population', *Ec.H.R.*, 2nd ser., XVIII (1965), 101–19.

[6] E. Miller, *The Abbey and Bishopric of Ely*, 1951, 105; J. S. Donnelly, 'Changes in the Grange Economy of English and Welsh Cistercian Abbeys, 1300–1540', *Traditio*, X (1954), 399–458. By 1336 substantial parts of the Vale Royal estates were leased, and Fountains had applied for permission to let lands on five of its granges.

[7] R. A. L. Smith, *Canterbury Cathedral Priory*, 1943, 134; E. M. Halcrow, 'The Decline of Demesne Farming on the Estates of Durham Cathedral

There does seem to have been sufficient general growth in leasing at this period to meet some of the pent-up demand for land, and some discrimination by tenants is apparent as their holdings reached the largest size they could work or afford to buy. There are instances of marginal lands that were not always easy to rent out. Even in 1320 the Merton College manor of Kibworth Harcourt, Leicestershire, had begun to record increasing arrears of rent, and clay grass-lands on the Chertsey Abbey Manors of Great and Little Bookham seem to have been reluctantly taken up in the 1330s. The *Nonarum Inquisitiones* show this trend in 1342; over a quarter of the parishes of Cambridgeshire land totalling 4,870 acres had gone out of cultivation since 1291, and in Bedfordshire and Buckinghamshire uncultivated ground was becoming noticeable, the uplands being particularly affected. However, such cases were fewer than after 1348, and the position on Durham estates in the 1330s and 1340s, where tenants were still anxious to take single acres on short leases, was not exceptional.[8]

Assarting continued on the fringes of late settlements in both lowland and highland areas. Woodlands were still being cleared in Warwickshire; in the south-east peasant efforts continued in East Kent, where the tenants asked the Prior of Canterbury to share the cost of reclaiming 700 acres of marsh at Seasalter. In the north expansion continued in Rossendale and on the Duchy of Lancaster lands in Derbyshire, although in the Vale of Pickering and at Wakefield assarting and abandonment went on concurrently, suggesting a transfer from exhausted ground to workable waste.[9] There appears generally to have been less need to retain the poorest lands, resulting perhaps in some decrease in the area under cultivation, but, one would assume, without a proportional drop in production. Even so, whilst some peasants continued to assart, bringing in these new grounds which would help to maintain the overall average of yields per acre, those who took on leased-out demesne could find their resources stretched, particularly on those poorer lands requiring heavy dressing which lords were apt to lease out first. Thus, though the very worst grounds of which we know in Yorkshire or the South-East Midlands may have gone out of production, underinvestment on old demesne may still have held yields

Priory', *Ec.H.R.*, 2nd ser., VII (1954), 345–6; W. H. Beveridge, 'Wages on the Winchester Manors', *Ec.H.R.*, VII (1936), 22–43; 'Westminster Wages in the Manorial Era', *ibid.*, 2nd ser., VIII (1955), 18–35; J. A. Raftis, *The Estates of Ramsey Abbey*, Toronto, 1957, 239–41; see also M. Morgan, *The English Lands of the Abbey of Bec*, 1946, 104–16.

[8] R. H. Hilton, 'Kibworth Harcourt, a Merton College Manor in the 13th and 14th Centuries', *Studies in Leicestershire Agrarian History* (ed. W. G. Hoskins), Leics. Arch. Soc., 1949, 33; Harvey, 35; Baker, 525–8; Halcrow, 350.

[9] Harvey, 'The Population Trend . . .', 40–1; R. H. Hilton, *The Stoneleigh Ledger Book*, Dugdale Soc. Pubs No. xxiv, 1960, xxxix–xl; Smith, *Canterbury*, 187.

below the average we might expect. Indeed, many of the Cambridge-shire and Bedfordshire abandonments were put down to the scantiness of peasant resources.[10] Investment on many large estates declined: Glastonbury Abbey reduced its reclamation on Sedgmoor; on Ely lands expenditure on mills and sheepfolds virtually ceased after 1333; the comparatively high rate of spending on land reclamation, marling and seed purchase at Canterbury fell about 1330; and at Ramsey there was little improvement of drainage or buildings after the prosperous decade ending in 1310—here resources were sufficiently stretched for central funds to be unable to replace cattle lost in the 1319 epidemic, leaving reeves to make gradual purchases over the subsequent 15–20 years.[11]

But whatever the level of investment or the standards of tenant farming, living conditions among those peasant communities where land had become available can hardly have worsened. Rents were static or falling, allowing tenants to retain a greater proportion of their output, and real wages were rising; the desire to take on as much land as possible might lead to voluntarily low standards of nutrition and comfort, but there was a greater element of choice in consumption for a larger proportion of the population than since the middle of the twelfth century. The losers were the landowners: demesne incomes declined and rents did not provide complete compensation; the increasing incidence of taxation on property under Edward I and Edward II brought an added burden; and whilst some, such as Canterbury, could retain a proportion of their demesne for wool, the only product with a buoyant market, others, such as Owston Abbey or Durham Cathedral Priory underwent complete changes in their relationships with their tenants. From relying for their food supplies on demesnes cultivated by customary labour, by the time of the Black Death they were purchasing their grain from those to whom their lands had been leased.[12]

The period of epidemics

Although the Black Death of 1348–9 has been shorn of much of its former reputation as the major turning-point in medieval economic history, by awareness of changes earlier in the century and of the effects of the plagues of the 1360s and 1370s, it clearly accelerated earlier trends and put an end until the sixteenth century to serious

[10] Baker, 525–8.
[11] *C.E.H.E.*, I, 565; Miller, *Ely*, 106; Raftis, *Ramsey*, 240–1.
[12] J. F. Willard, *Parliamentary Taxes on Personal Property 1290–1334*, Camb., Mass., 1934, 9–13; Smith, *Canterbury*, 156; R. H. Hilton, *The Economic Development of Some Leicestershire Estates in the 14th and 15th Centuries*, 1947, 135–6; Halcrow, 351.

peasant land-shortage. Figures for death-rates are not hard to find and show that communities suffered the loss of from one-third to three-quarters of their adult populations. On the lands of Crowland Abbey 35 out of 50 tenants died at Oakington, 20 out of 42 at Dry Drayton, and 33 out of 58 at Cottenham. On two manors at Blackmore, Essex, it is estimated that half the inhabitants died. Where proportions are not available comparisons between deaths in normal and plague years often are. At Petworth four heriots were received in 1347-8 while the total was 58 in 1348-9 and at West Thorney, Sussex, where there were no recorded deaths in 1347-8, seven died in 1348-9 and three in 1349-50.[13]

The evidence from the years immediately after the plague shows significant local contrasts in its effects. In some manors there was comparatively little difficulty in filling vacant holdings. At Abbots Langley 71 tenants of St Albans Abbey died by May 1349, and of the successors 44 were men or women of full age, 21 were minors, six were other tenants and only two holdings were left in the lord's hands. On the lands of Durham Cathedral Priory, the majority of holdings went straight to new tenants without long vacancy, and on the thickly settled and more fertile manors of the Bishop of Winchester in Southern Hampshire tenements were largely filled in the early 1350s. That the replacement was often rapid indicates the size of the reservoir of potential tenants. At Petworth it is clear that absent sons were willing enough to risk returning to the manor during the epidemic, to take over their dead parents' holdings, some dying of plague themselves.[14] The number of willing takers may be gauged from six manors in the Isle of Avalon belonging to Glastonbury Abbey, for here in the early fourteenth century there had been 260 full customary tenants, and 350 with a quarter-virgate or less, 150 of these having only cottage holdings. Thus a 50 per cent death-rate in 1349 would still have left more than enough tenants to occupy the holdings of viable size.[15] Where heirs or landless neighbours were not available the disruption was greater. There were reports of harvest losses through crops remaining in the fields at Crowland, and of sudden rises in prices and wages in the plague years.

The mid-1350s give an idea of the range of problems landowners had to face in maintaining their incomes, particularly where tenancies

---

[13] F. M. Page, *The Estates of Crowland Abbey*, 1934, 120-1; J. L. Fisher, 'The Black Death in Essex', *Essex Review*, 52 (1943), 13-20; L. F. Salzman, *Ministers' Accounts of the Manor of Petworth*, Sussex Record Society, LV (1955), xxxiii.

[14] Slicher van Bath, 84; A. E. Levett, 'The Black Death on the St Albans Manors', in *Studies in Manorial History*, 1938, 253; Halcrow, 345-56; Salzman, 'Petworth', xxxiii.

[15] Postan, 'Declining Population', 242-3.

were less easy to fill. After the death of the Bishop of Worcester royal escheators could collect so little revenue from the estates that a commission was sent to test the validity of their returns; in such circumstances estates had to offer inducements to fill vacancies, encouraging peasant mobility. This may be seen in reverse at Ramsey, where in 1356 manorial officials were finding it hard to keep tenants within the manor. At Cuxham in Oxfordshire all nine half-virgate holdings vacant were filled by 1355 by men from outside the village, some taking over from tenants for whom heriots were not rendered in 1349 and who may themselves have moved away to still better ground.[16]

Marginal land was a major problem. Tilgarsley, Oxfordshire, was one of the poorest hamlets of Eynsham Abbey, and like many upland settlements was never resettled after all its occupants died in 1349. Further, better land was becoming 'marginal'. Seacourt in Berkshire was gradually deserted by the early fifteenth century, although at the end of the thirteenth it had enjoyed considerable prosperity, probably from stock-raising on the Isis watermeadows and the sale of wool or carcases in Oxford. Other villages must have been more attractive to Seacourt's inhabitants, for the village gradually declined until in the 1420s only one house was left occupied, in contrast to the rebuilding of the timber houses in stone which had taken place a century before.[17]

Later plagues prolonged the shortage of tenants and the effect of the 1361 outbreak was particularly damaging, due to its relation to the Black Death. In 1348 adults were prone to infection, but in 1361 child mortality was high. Coming after 12 years the second outbreak attacked the offspring of the survivors of the first, and the gap in the able-bodied population, which might otherwise have been filled by the 1370s after early marriage and occupation of holdings by the survivors of 1349, was prolonged for another generation. The gap was made still larger by the 1368–9 plague, which again affected adults, killing 13·4 per cent of incumbents in the diocese of York compared with the normal annual death-rate of three or four per cent, and endemic plague prevalent until the 1420s prolonged low replacement rates.[18]

After the outbreak in the 1360s, which largely removed the backlog of demand for tenancies, estates' major problem was to ensure that existing tenant-land produced some return, and that demesne lands, the market for their produce in decline, were either effectively managed

[16] R. M. Haines (ed.), *A Calendar of the Register of Wolstan de Branford*, Historical Manuscripts Commission, 1966, liii; J. A. Raftis, *Tenure and Mobility*, 1964, 143; Harvey, *Cuxham*, 135–40.
[17] H. E. Salter (ed.), *Eynsham Cartulary*, Oxford Hist. Soc., XLIX (1906–7), xxvi, and LI (1908), xxvi; M. Biddle, 'The Deserted Medieval Village of Seacourt, Berkshire', *Oxoniensia*, XXVI–XXVII (1961–2), 74–84.
[18] *C.E.H.E.*, I, 675; Thrupp, 118–9.

direct or let out without risk of dilapidation in the saturated market. An obvious answer, and one which could hardly fail to benefit crop yields, was the consolidation of holdings into sizes attractive to the wealthier peasantry. At the Winchcombe manor of Sherborne a majority of tenements in the 1340s had been virgates, but by 1355 several were much larger; at Bledington virgates were taken back by the estate when tenants were hard to obtain and relet in different combinations of lands; and at Crowland numerous villeins accumulated holdings over the second half of the century paying entry fines with their growing resources of cash. Terms of tenancy were eased, and labour services, rents and fines were reduced. Where leasehold had been rare it was introduced and where it had appeared at or before the Black Death the terms were lengthened.[19] It became unrealistic to insist on labour services on any but the remaining thickly populated manors. At Ramsey works were cut early in the 1350s to encourage villeins to cultivate their own lands effectively and to take up vacant lands *ad censum*. However, the process could be a slow one. At Crowland works, though decreasing in number, were still in operation in the 1380s and were only sold off in large numbers between 1387 and 1395. An enquiry held before the Justices of Kings' Bench at Brentwood in 1389 showed the reluctance of some Essex estates to liberalise their attitudes on status.[20] But almost all rents and entry fines declined late in the fourteenth century; some reeves had tried to cash in on the rush for better holdings in the 1350s, but by the 1380s such attempts were rare and Ramsey was typical in asking negligible fines. Rent reduction sometimes lagged, for conventional figures survived, but mounting arrears showed tenants' strength when charges were unrealistic.[21]

If rent and conditions were right, an estate could still maintain lands in good order, for there was still a demand at the turn of the century for fertile holdings which could be profitably run or sub-let. But where conventional rents and services died hard, long-term values of lands had by this time suffered from tenant neglect, and Ramsey, Crowland and Durham all recorded dilapidations, with holdings uncultivated, repairs neglected, and byelaws ignored. An excellent example of the effects of dilapidation occurs at the upland Osney Abbey hamlet

---

[19] R. H. Hilton, 'Winchcombe Abbey and the Manor of Sherborne', *Gloucestershire Studies* (ed. H. P. R. Finberg), 1957, 103; Page, 152–3.

[20] Raftis, *Ramsey*, 251; Page, 126; N. Kenyon, 'Labour Conditions in Essex in the Reign of Richard II', *Ec.H.R.*, IV (1933), 429–51.

[21] A striking account of the strength of the tenants' position is given by Page (pp. 141–55) for Crowland. It is also illustrated by the decline in rents seen in some Leicestershire cases (Hoskins, *Midland Peasant*, 84) to be down to one-third of their mid-thirteenth-century level by the 1440s. While this may be an extreme example 60-per-cent reductions in the century after the Black Death are not hard to find.

of Brookend, Oxfordshire, where the drift of population was by 1400 failing to be made up by migrants from still poorer lands. Rent reductions became necessary and tenants took on extra holdings, but redundant buildings decayed and the Abbey faced the dilemma of frightening tenants away by insisting on repairs or of allowing the collapse of its property, leading to an irreversible change to pastoral farming.[22]

The solution of leasing demesnes as units was not new: even in the 1330s some Midland manors had leased their demesnes *en bloc* if tenants had resources enough to keep land in a condition adequate to pay a high rent: this was certainly so on widely spread ecclesiastical estates where the home-farm function did not apply, but between 1350 and 1450 complete leasing became general, comparatively early examples being Cuxham in 1359 and Tamworth on the Duke of Clarence's Warwickshire estates in 1381. By the early fifteenth century peasants frequently took on these demesne leases, whereas a century earlier leases of large blocks had generally been taken only by bailiffs or reeves. Thus good land could maintain its value: at Cuxham, although the 1361 farm of £20 sank to £18.10.0 in 1395 it was back to £20 in 1401.[23] From the turn of the century the lands which could most profitably be leased over much of England were those suitable for sheep; the Duke of Norfolk and Sir John Fastolf, Winchcombe, Gloucester and Dorchester Abbeys are examples of the many landowners who could ease themselves out of the problems of the labour-market. Indeed, with the growing profitability of pasture-farming in the fifteenth century, Canterbury Cathedral Priory undertook improvement to Appledore Marsh expressly directed at attracting high rents from farmers selling wool to the textile industry of South Kent.

Except for sheep-farming, direct management was rarely a satisfactory solution, for apart from a sudden peak during the food shortage of 1349–40 product prices continued and intensified the downward trend dating from the 1320s. Rising labour costs were a serious problem, shown by an index of agricultural real wages for the Winchester estate:

1300–19	*1320–39*	*1340–59*	*1360–79*	*1380–99*	*1400–19*	*1420–39*
100	140	148	154	235	210	200

This pattern was caused both by rising money wage-rates and by falling food prices. On the lands of the Abbey of St Mary des Prés rates

[22] Raftis, 1964, 34; Page, 147; Halcrow, 352–3; T. H. Lloyd, 'Some Documentary Sidelights on the Deserted Oxfordshire Village of Brookend', *Oxoniensia*, XXIX–XXX (1964–5), 116–28.
[23] *A Medieval Oxfordshire Village*, 13, 94–6; R. H. Hilton, 'Ministers' Accounts of the Warwickshire Estates of the Duke of Clarence, 1474–80', *Dugdale Soc.*, XXI (1952), xviii–xx.

for harvesting wheat, rising from 6d. to 8d. per acre in 1349–50, never fell back, and at Ramsey money wages of *famuli* doubled during the 1350s.[24]

Unskilled labour, important in agriculture, rose particularly in cost as workers took on holdings, and on the estates of Winchester and Westminster Abbey the skill-differentials between carpenters and labourers had shrunk to less than half those of 1300 by the end of the century. The friction which developed over increases was a measure of the changed relationship in the employment market, and although the Statutes of Labourers and local regulations hindering mobility were only sporadically implemented they did much to encourage the wage-labourer to make himself independent by acquiring land.[25]

However, some determined attempts were made to revive demesne farming on the best lands. In the 1380s Ramsey maintained liveries from the manors of Upwood and Holywell at their early fourteenth-century levels, and made improvements to land and buildings in doing so. Likewise, Leicester Abbey increased its grain production over the 20 years before 1408, perhaps in response to the development of the Lynn grain trade. Where was an industrial market for foodstuffs or wool, demesne farming could be worthwhile. The Catesbys in South Warwickshire worked two demesnes; one, Ladbroke, was arable, employing wage-labour and the other, Radborne, was made up of sheep pasture. At Tavistock the part of the demesnes which was of particularly high quality was intensively farmed and improved to supply the Stannary market. In these cases direct farming was profitable, but in others it was practised half-heartedly, largely, perhaps, as with the Duke of Clarence's manor at Sutton Coldfield, because nobody else would take the demesne on.[26]

We have dealt with the difficulties of leasing or direct arable farming; if estates found that neither policy could maintain their incomes, one alternative might be to convert to sheep pasture. This could give some insulation from rising labour costs, and wool prices fell less than those of other products. But there were problems in the development of flocks which are illustrated at Ramsey, where shortage of capital

[24] Postan, 'Declining Population', 226; A. E. Levett, 'The Accounts of St Mary des Prés', in *Studies in Manorial History*, 1938, 287; Raftis, 257; A. E. Levett, 'Notes on the Statute of Labourers', *Ec.H.R.*, IV (1932), 77–80; J. Schreiner, 'Wages and Prices in England in the Later Middle Ages', *Scandinavian Ec.H.R.*, II (1954), 61–73.

[25] Beveridge, 'Wages in the Winchester Manors', 26, and 'Westminster Wages', 18–35.

[26] Raftis, *Ramsey*, 261; Hilton, 63, 83–4; N. S. B. Gras, *The Evolution of the English Corn Market*, 1915, 172–6; R. H. Hilton, 'A Study in the Prehistory of English Enclosure', *Studi in Onore di Sapore*, I, Milan, 1957, 673–85; H. P. R. Finberg, *Tavistock Abbey*, 107–15; Hilton, 'Ministers' Account of the Duke of Clarence', xx–xxi.

meant a slow increase in stock numbers, made worse by bad weather and sheep epidemics in the 1360s. On the Cotswolds the change occurred between 1350 and 1450. Conversion of poorer ground for sheep was common, and when Cotswold villages such as Upton were deserted late in the century their land was put to pasture. An early example was Osney Abbey, which had wintered small numbers of hogasters on its outlying lands at Chastleton before the Black Death, but in 1355 pastured a large mixed flock there for most of the year. These early conversions were apt to be defensive, but by the second quarter of the fifteenth century landowners as well as tenants were seeing the positive value of grazing lands as English textile output grew. One example was Winchcombe Abbey, which increased its specialisation, controlling its flocks centrally and allocating particular functions to its manors. Here numbers grew during the fifteenth century, 1,900 sheep being shorn at Sherborne in 1468 and 2,900 in 1485.[27]

This account of agrarian change prompts two main questions: how much did agricultural output as a whole run down and what were the effects on standards of living? The overall position, it might be argued, mattered little provided *per capita* output was maintained, but the total of land kept under cultivation has some relevance to the problems of food-supply encountered when population recovered in the sixteenth century.

There is a strong case for arguing that a significant amount of land was more suitably used after the mid-fourteenth century. Arable was less overcrowded and overcropped and yields show slight, even if hardly spectacular, increases.[28] The most significant rationalisation lay in the conversion of poor arable to pasture. Studies of deserted villages have shown that many of the fifteenth-century sheep conversions were carried out on lands which had not been prosperous before 1349. Some villages disappeared before 1450, when their inhabitants moved to better ground. Villages such as Standelf, Oxfordshire, or Wyville, Lincolnshire, were cases of poor settlements which could not hold those tenants who survived the plagues. 'The three carucates are worth little, for the land is poor and stoney, and lies uncultivated for want of tenants after the pestilence'; such was Wyville. The number of complete abandonments between 1350 and about 1440 was smaller than is sometimes assumed. Of the recorded deserted sites in Northamptonshire of all periods, 17 per cent fall between these years, a figure slightly smaller than for Oxfordshire, somewhat larger than for Leicestershire.

---

[27] Raftis, 1957, 258; Lloyd, 121; Hilton, 'Winchcombe', 110; R. H. Hilton and P. A. Rahtz, 'Upton, Gloucestershire, 1954–1964', *Trans. Bristol and Glos. Arch. Soc.*, 85 (1966), 73.
[28] B. H. Slicher van Bath, *Yield Ratios, 810–1820*, A. A. G. Bijdragen 10, 1963.

And of the villages depopulated in the next century, up to 1550, many had also been small. In Northamptonshire the average given by the 1334 Subsidy Assessment of villages eventually deserted was only 40 per cent of the county average; in Oxfordshire the average village in 1377 had 77 taxpayers, but the figure for those to be deserted was only 33. These were the places which were liable to disintegrate before 1450, or would be simplest for enclosing landowners to deal with in the following century.[29]

How much the total of pasture increased cannot be measured with any accuracy. Some impression of overall growth can be gained from our knowledge of the textile industry and of wool exports,[30] but this involves uncertainties over the extent of the increases in grazing for meat production, which in the West Midlands was clearly important. Against the growth of lowland pasture must of course be set any lessening in the use of poorer upland grazing in Wales and the south-west. The abandonment of villages in Devon and Cornwall in this period is clearly significant in this context.[31]

The conversion trend may have gone rather too far, with sheep being run on grounds which could have grown good crops if labour had been available to till them. This did not matter when demand for food was low, but it was to have more serious consequences in the second half of the sixteenth century where buildings and drainage had been neglected, even though converted land was at least kept manured.

But conversion went too far in another sense; whereas early in the fifteenth century it had largely been prompted by trends in population, from 1450, when the decline had certainly ended and had probably been reversed, enclosure continued, and gave rise to evictions. John Rous' account of depopulation in Warwickshire, though written in the 1480s, refers to this period, and illustrates a movement which was to attract attention for almost a century.

In addition to more suitable use there is evidence that capital-formation in agriculture, after a slack period in the mid-fourteenth century was little below the thirteenth-century level. Its form perhaps was different; enclosure produced benefit for a small outlay: at least it was a means of attracting tenants to poor land, as Eynsham Abbey attempted to do at Tilgarsley late in the fourteenth century. The enclosure at Quarrendon, Buckinghamshire, which Richard Beauchamp,

[29] M. W. Beresford, *The Lost Villages of England*, 2nd ed., 1965, 159–62; K. J. Allison, M. W. Beresford and J. G. Hurst, *The Deserted Villages of Northamptonshire*, Univ. of Leicester, Dept of Eng. Local Hist., Occ. Paper 18, 1966, 10; *The Deserted Villages of Oxfordshire*, Occ. Paper 17, 1965, 6–7, 26.

[30] See p. 76 below.

[31] D. Dudley and E. M. Minter, 'The Medieval Village at Garrow Tor, Bodmin Moor, Cornwall', *Medieval Archaeology*, vi–vii (1962–3), 272–94.

Earl of Warwick, supervised in 1421 may not have been much more, for the village was later depopulated for sheep.[32] But fifteenth-century enclosures of good land raised values from 10 to 16 years' purchase, and a Warwickshire example, the manor of Kingston, shows that a Coventry grazier would pay in 1437 a rent double the 1394 value of the unenclosed ground.[33] Where land was of high quality and worth improving, men such as the Abbots of Ramsey and Tavistock were prepared to invest in soil-dressing or building or, in the case of Furness Abbey, in marsh reclamation. At Hampton Lucy the Bishop of Worcester invested 10 per cent of the total manorial income on building, enclosures, and equipment between 1387 and 1393, and in 1480 capital investment on the rural estates of the earldom of Warwick came to nine per cent of receipts. Further, the difficulty of obtaining tenants led to some houses and farm buildings being repaired as an attraction, and fifteenth-century leases commonly contained undertakings by the owner to maintain farm buildings. Peasants' investment is less easy to identify. Their capital was largely committed in rents, in the purchase of new lands and, in particular, in the buying of livestock.[34] But peasant enclosures certainly took place. In the 1380s Titchfield Abbey let out lands to be run in severalty, and in the fifteenth century licences to enclose were issued on the Duke of Clarence's estates. The amount spent by tenants on livestock matched demand for wool; in Worcestershire the thriving local cloth industry and the needs of town butchers led to peasant flocks of up to 200 sheep, and references to overstocking of commons and trespassing on arable ground suggest that in this area land surplus and the decline of rents must have ended by the middle of the fifteenth century.[35]

Our second major signpost as to how far the changes of this century affected agricultural production is the extent of alterations in the standards of living of the agrarian community, and the redistribution of income within it. We have already found a good deal of evidence that rents and demesne profits fell between 1350, or earlier, and 1450. How far do individual cases back this up, and, in particular, were losses a spur to greater efficiency? In the early decades after the Black Death large estates maintained their revenues to a considerable degree.

[32] Salter, xlviii; C. D. Ross, *The Estates and Finances of Richard Beauchamp, Earl of Warwick*, Dugdale Soc. Occ. Paper 12, 1956–9.
[33] *V.C.H.*, Leics., 1954, 189–90; Hilton, 'Prehistory of Enclosure', 682.
[34] C. M. L. Bouch and G. P. Jones, *The Lake Counties*, 1951, 49–50; R. H. Hilton, 'Rent and Capital Formation in Feudal Society', *Internat. Econ. Hist. Conf., Aix 1962*, 1965, 47–53.
[35] *V.C.H.*, Hampshire, V, 1912, 421; Hilton, 'Ministers' Accounts of the Duke of Clarence', xxii; R. K. Field, 'Worcestershire Peasant Buildings, Household Goods and Farming Equipment in the later Middle Ages', *Medieval Archaeology*, IX (1965), 105–45.

The lordship of Usk, for instance, had an income in the 1370s which was generally less than 10 per cent below that of the 1340s, and the lands of the bailiwick of Clare in East Anglia almost regained their old income in the 1370s. Much of the wealth of Usk came from pastoral farming, less affected by rising labour costs than arable, but it would seem that on the lowland Clare estates the drop in population was not reflected by any severe fall in income from rents. The major difficulties seem to have arisen between about 1370 and 1450–70. All the Clare demesnes were leased out by 1400, rents on the lordship of Denbigh became increasingly hard to collect after 1370, a feature seen at Usk in the 1390s. The chronology of the fall in baronial incomes is understandable in the light of the effects of the later plagues. Tenants became really hard to obtain in the final quarter of the century, and it is thence right through to the third quarter of the fifteenth that we see pressure on large estates. The rents of the Duchy of Lancaster were falling in 1400 and decreased by a further 20 per cent by 1475: on the estates of the Percies income from lands in Cumberland dropped by between a quarter and a third, in Northumberland by up to a half, and in Yorkshire by rather less than a quarter. The agricultural profits of the Earls of Stafford from their Gloucestershire estates fell by a half. The recovery came late in the fifteenth century, although in particular cases it may have been earlier; the Archbishop of Canterbury's estate income, for instance, was steady in the mid-fifteenth century with a distinct upturn after 1480. Here the demand of London for foodstuffs was already being felt, and tenants were comparatively easy to find for the farms of North Kent.[36]

The problem is whether decreases led the largest landowners to make any radical revision of their management. Contemporaries held the view that they were able to maintain a high, in Fortescue's opinion an excessively high, standard of living, a 'prodigious' opulence in Thorold Rogers' view. Household expenditure seems hardly to have diminished; the Black Book of Edward IV puts a normal baron's household costs at £500 per year, considerably greater than those typical of the thirteenth century, after a century or more of declining prices. The level of living standards to which royal and baronial groups were accustomed can be gauged from the purchases made by Henry, Earl of Derby, for his expeditions to the Baltic and the Mediterranean in 1390 and 1393. Expenditure on servants and personal retinues was inflated by the needs of the Hundred Years War and the Wars of the Roses. In

[36] G. A. Holmes, *The Estates of the Higher Nobility in 14th-Century England*, 1957, 90–115; Postan, 'Declining Population', 237; J. M. W. Bean, *The Estates of the Percy Family*, 1958, 41 *seq.*; C.E.H.E., I, 597; F. R. H. Du Boulay, 'A Rentier Economy in the Later Middle Ages: the Archbishopric of Canterbury', *Ec.H.R.*, 2nd ser., XVI (1964), 427–38.

1420–1 Richard Beauchamp Earl of Warwick spent £250 on wages of officials, and £123 on annuities to retainers in a war year when most retainers could rely on Crown pay; in other years the total rose to £490. Even some relatively small landowners employed large forces on campaigns, for while the Duke of Lancaster took 1,500 men on the 1373 campaign, Sir Thomas Dagworth had taken 200 to Brittany in 1346–7. In the fifteenth century the pattern was the same, and from a fairly modest social level there was involvement and expenditure in the Wars of the Roses. MacFarlane writes: 'Not to be of the Duke of Suffolk's affinity in East Anglia in the 1440s was to ask for trouble.' Expenditure on building, servants, and annuities continued at a high level, and if the decline in landed incomes reached and exceeded the 25 per cent that the few available runs of accounts suggest, some further explanation seems necessary.[37]

In the first place, some caution is needed over any estimate of incomes. The assessment for tax in 1436, an apparently convenient fixed point, is suspect due to incomes net of expenses being taxable; the definition of legitimate expenses was a clear field for dispute and pressure on assessors, which some families seem to have exploited to the full. The problem with tax assessments of this type, together with *Inquisitions Post Mortem* and escheators' accounts is that they represent the position only in a single year, and few continuous accounts are available or really useful; the case of those of Richard Beauchamp, in which overlap has been seen between the records of different estate officials, may be cited as a clear warning.[38]

Secondly, some landowners who appear to have been able in the short term to support high expenditure on war and consumption were aided by the concentration of estates that seems to have taken place partly by accident and partly as a result of the disputes of the middle of the century. The Earl of Warwick held not only the family inheritance but, through his wife, the lordship of Lisle and a contested title to the Berkeley lands. With his second wife, Isabel Dispenser, came 50 manors, and in 1435 he inherited the lands of Abergavenny. Such

[37] J. Fortescue, *The Governance of England*, ed. C. Plummer, 1885, 17–18, 130; J. E. Thorold Rogers, *Six Centuries of Work and Wages*, 1884, 307; J. B. Pugh and C. D. Ross, 'The English Baronage and the Income Tax of 1436', *Bull. Inst. of Hist. Research*, XXVI (1953), 2; N. Denholme-Young, *Seigneurial Administration in England*, 1937, 22; L. T. Smith (ed.), *Expeditions to Prussia and the Holy Land Made by Henry, Earl of Derby, 1390–1, 1392–3*, Camden Soc., N.S., LII (1894), 5–34, 220–4; Ross, *Estates of Richard Beauchamp*, 15; K. B. McFarlane, 'Bastard Feudalism', *Bull. Inst. Hist. Res.*, XX (1945), 161–80.
[38] H. L. Gray, 'Incomes from Land in England in 1436', *Eng.H.R.*, XLIX (1934), 607–39; C. D. Ross and T. B. Pugh, 'Materials for the Study of Baronial Income in 15th-Century England', *Ec.H.R.*, 2nd ser., VI (1953), 185–94.

accumulation perhaps on a rather smaller scale was not uncommon. Richard Earl of Arundel for instance, bought 20 manors in Sussex in the mid-fourteenth century. Although the incomes of individual properties may have been declining, the survivors or purchasers had more of them. Whether the profits of war made any net addition to baronial incomes is dubious in the extreme: the costs of retinues and ransoms were considerable, and the good fortune of Sir John Fastolf really seems to have been exceptional. It would perhaps be fair to say that by means of demographic accident and lower prices certain known members of the baronial group got by without any great pressure on their pattern of consumption; they got by sufficiently safely not to examine the possibilities for increasing their incomes with any sense of urgency, and a man such as Richard Duke of York took no apparent action to reduce the leakage of income of 15–30 per cent due to dishonesty and inefficiency. But the surplus remaining was probably not large and where it was adequate for capital investment the rewards were hardly great enough for it to be worth diverting funds from building and personal consumption. Those who did invest did so only to a small extent in land for leasing, deterred by depressed rents, and rather more, in the manner of the Hungerfords of Sir John Fastolf, in sheep, and towards the end of the century in good-quality enclosed pasture.[39]

The evidence for smaller landowners is less abundant but it suggests that their wealth increased. Many were in a position to extend their estates, taking advantage of the active fifteenth-century land market. The Stonors' South Oxfordshire lands grew over the century, and, despite the particular tendency to faction in East Anglia those of the Pastons also increased, particularly under William Paston in the first half of the century.[40] Sir John Fastolf is perhaps a remarkable case, a man who made full use of his exceptional war profits, but the growth of his estate from the basis of his inheritance, £46 per annum, to the £1,061 which they were worth in 1445 shows how much was available for the alert who were prepared to tackle the contemporary problems of uncertain land titles. These families certainly seem to have been aware of the profitability of pasture lands, but their purchases were not at the expense of living standards. The property of Fastolf was no doubt exceptional, the inventory of Caister Castle listing 40 tapestries on hangings, two of which had cost together £220. His jewellery con-

[39] L. F. Salzman, 'The Property of the Earl of Arundel, 1397', *Sussex Arch. Colls*, XCI (1953), 32–52; J. T. Rosenthal, 'The Estates and Finances of Richard, Duke of York, 1411–60', *Studies in Medieval and Renaissance History*, II (1965), 115–204.

[40] C. L. Kingsford, *Prejudice and Promise in 15th-Century England*, 1925, 62–3; N. Davis (ed.), *The Paston Letters*, 1958 edn., viii.

tained stones amongst the most precious outside royal hands, and his plate was worth over £2,400. But less notable families maintained comfortable standards of food and housing. Dame Alice de Bryene of Acton Hall, Suffolk, recorded in her household book purchases of spices, wines, and fruit from London, and the Stonors bought a similar range from barge-owners trading up the Thames.[41] The income of the endowments of a Bridport chantry allowed its priest to maintain a comfortable standard perhaps equivalent to the circumstances of those smallest gentry with income around £20 per year.[42] This group was also able to improve its living conditions. The Stonors rebuilt their house, and despite the rising costs of timber for building the fourteenth and fifteenth centuries saw considerable enlargement of house-plans for which men in this income-range were responsible.[43] The aisled hall of the thirteenth century developed servants quarters and solars, and frequently wings at either end. There are many examples in the south and east of well-finished buildings, erected by the gentry and yeomanry, of which the Wealden House type is typical.[44]

We are perhaps better served with information on the living standards of the peasantry, ranging from the emerging yeomanry to wage workers. There is plentiful evidence of the increasing size of peasant holdings late in the fourteenth century. At Cuxham from about 1380 onwards, half-virgate tenants were taking on second holdings; at Chippenham in the late fourteenth century about one fifth of holdings mentioned in Court Rolls were over 30 acres, but by 1471–83 the proportion was one third; there are examples at Ramsey of peasants taking long leases on sizeable pieces of demesne; John Poulton and John Bennett, for instance, farmed over 180 acres of demesne in about 1430. Some of these larger tenants could certainly be regarded as yeomen, if not small gentry, and there was apparently a gap emerging between the substantial peasant who would have a surplus with which he could buy more land, and those who found the initial stages of expansion hard. The rate of investment among the larger men had to be fairly high, and it is here that doubts arise about how well the leased lands were farmed, whether men taking on complete demesnes could really afford to stock them adequately unless they had stock-and-land

---

[41] K. B. McFarlane, 'The Investment of Sir John Fastolf's Profits in War', *Trans. Roy. Hist. Soc.*, 5th ser., vii (1957), 91–116; V. B. Redstone (ed.), *The Household Book of Dame Alice de Bryene*, Suffolk Inst. of Arch. and Nat. Hist., 1931, 116–39; C. L. Kingsford (ed.), *Stonor Letters and Papers, 1290–1483*, Camden Soc., 3rd ser., xxx (1919), 45–6.

[42] K. L. Wood-Leigh, *A Small Household of the 15th Century*, xviii–xxiii.

[43] L. F. Salzman, *Building in England down to 1540*, 1952, 206–9.

[44] J. T. Smith, 'Medieval Aisled Halls and their Derivatives', *Archeological Jnl.*, 112 (1955), 76–94; R. T. Mason, 'Three Medieval Houses in East Sussex', *Sussex Arch. Colls*, XCI (1951), 20–31.

leases; also, with the high cost of labour, whether good arable land could be properly farmed by the tenant without a large family. At the lower end of the scale it was not always as easy to increase the size of a holding as may appear at first sight. Assuming the peasant and his family survived the late-fourteenth century epidemics as anything like an intact group there were estates which took long to wake up to the realities of the land market and continued to insist on high customary rents; in the 1390s, even, the impression emerges that smaller peasants were not having their share of the general improvement of the market, and land acquisition over the fourteenth century could be a very laborious business. The Grene family at Cuxham had held three acres and three roods besides their messuage in 1279; by the 1450s they built up possessions in seven parishes, made up of 11 plots totalling perhaps rather over 24 acres, with 20 shillings worth of rents. Such a cumbersome holding could hardly have been effectively farmed, and if we return to Ramsey we find that some very dilapidated peasant holdings were reverting to the estate after 1400.[45]

Even so, it is quite clear that there were opportunities for many small men, and wage-earners too could find themselves with the chance to become small cultivators, while wages were strikingly higher over the period 1400-1500 than in the 1330s, a time when they were themselves a considerable improvement over the late thirteenth century. Even though the enforcement of the wage and mobility provisions of the Statute of Labourers was capricious, the step into land tenure or ownership was simpler, as landowners' anxiety over the condition of empty holdings increased. At Elton, on Ramsey lands, 'men from the town', landless artisans, appeared in lists of new smallholdings about 1400.[46] However, the problems of the small man with insufficient capital applied to new tenants; in Worcestershire notable deficiencies have been seen in the agricultural equipment of smallholders, and the fifteenth-century improvement in housing standards only applied to the more substantial peasantry. It is worth noting that in Leicestershire in 1381, 28 per cent of men in a sample of villages were classed as wage-earners, and in 1524 the proportion in the county was 30 per cent. How far rising population since late in the fifteenth century had contributed to the latter figures we cannot say, but this impression that the transfer away from wage labour in the century

[45] Harvey, *Cuxham*, 115-8, 139; Raftis, *Ramsey*, 264-5, 288-9; Spufford, 37.
[46] E. H. Phelps Brown and S. V. Hopkins, 'Seven Centuries of Building Wages', *Economica*, N.S. 22 (1955), 197-9; 'Seven Centuries of Consumables Compared with Builders' Wage Rates', *ibid.*, N.S. 23 (1956), 300-5; Raftis. *Ramsey*, 281-2.

after 1381 had not been great should at least be mentioned in connection with the problems of smallholders.[47]

Although a comparison of the experiences of different sections of the population shows some apparent downward redistribution of wealth, the gains of the lower income-groups seem unlikely to have come greatly at the expense of large estates, for the latters' fall in income appears to have been small, certainly insufficient to bring about any real attempt at reform of their affairs. It seems clear that much the greatest proportion of the peasant gain came from the supply of land, which had dwindled less rapidly than population, and had provided wider opportunities for the peasantry to obtain not only more, but, and this is of major importance, better ground. Despite the dilapidations and abandonments of the century there seems no doubt that *per capita* income rose, which possibly explains the emergence of a rising population trend late in the fifteenth century. While there may not, in 1500, have been an acreage comparable with 1300 to feed these growing numbers, such land as was in use was of higher quality and capable of greater yields.

Industry: its development under conditions of labour-scarcity

Industrial output in the fourteenth and fifteenth centuries must inevitably have been affected by population change. But the relation was a complex one, and it would be unwise to assume that a numerically smaller market, on the one hand, and on the other the rising cost of labour led to any proportional reduction in production. We will see that in two industries, textiles and iron, external factors had an overriding effect, leading to notable developments in scale and techniques.

Throughout the later Middle Ages the textile industry was England's largest industrial employer, and despite the reduction in the labour-pool in the fourteenth century its output rose over the period to a remarkable extent. In the late thirteenth century English cloth had largely belonged to the medium and lower ranges of quality, the demand for the best being met by imports from Flanders, whose industry had been largely using English wool. But between 1300 and 1350 English production of all grades grew, largely because of the protection conferred by the export duties levied on raw wool from the 1280s, the uncertainties of the wool export trade in the hostilities of the 1330s, and the political disturbance of the period in the Flemish cloth towns. It is not possible to estimate total cloth production. Export figures, however, are available from 1349 onwards, and their trend is significant; within an average annual figure of 19,249 cloths between 1350 and 1400, we find that in the 1350s the highest total for a year

[47] Field, 123–4; *V.C.H.*, Leics., II (1954), 187.

was 10,324, whilst after 1382-3 there was no figure below 20,000, and the recorded totals for the decade after 1392 are all over 30,000. Even in the worst years of the post-1410 decades the total remained above 20,000, and the average over the fifteenth century was over 42,000.[48] What we are unable to establish is the course of production for the home market.

One possible guide-line is the decline in imports of Flemish cloths in the first half of the fourteenth century. In the years 1303-11 these averaged 12,000, declining by the 1330s to 9,000-10,000 each year, and falling sharply to a mere 2,000 in 1340.[49] It is not certain how far this gap in the upper quality-ranges was made up by English clothiers, nor is it possible to measure the output of poorer grades. At first sight the Ulnage returns, purporting to show how many cloths were sealed in each of the manufacturing areas, should provide this information, but it has been shown that their reliability is suspect in the fourteenth century and negligible in the fifteenth.[50]

We can, perhaps, suggest some of the variables affecting the industry and its output. It was aided in foreign sales by export duties, lower on cloths than on raw wool, which gave it a cost-advantage over the Flemings of about 15 per cent in European markets. Its concentration on heavily-fulled yet undyed products enabled advantage to be taken of the labour-saving, water-powered fulling mill, yet to avoid the labour-costs of dyeing. Further, the tendency was for production to be concentrated in those hilly rural areas where power was available and where arable farming was limited enough for labour to be anxious for industrial employment, in particular before the Black Death and in the latter half of the fifteenth century. On the market side the position is less certain; the Hundred Years War's demand for military clothing may have aided growth, although the intermittent nature of hostilities and the disruption the war caused to cross-channel routes puts the overall balance of advantage in doubt. The effect of the decline in population is even less clear. The purchasing-power of the early fourteenth-century peasantry, bent on using surpluses to acquire more land, was inadequate to provide a really large-scale market even for cheap cloth. The epidemics, releasing land, probably brought to many surviving families a prosperity their forebears had not known for a century, but their priority in spending would still be for land. When they had acquired holdings of a profitable size their tastes might turn

[48] Bridbury, *Economic Growth*, 36; E. M. Carus-Wilson and O. Coleman, *England's Export Trade, 1275-1547*, 1963, 138.
[49] E. M. Carus-Wilson, 'Trends in the Exports of English Woollens in the 14th Century', *Ec.H.R.*, 2nd ser., III (1950), 184. n. 2.
[50] H. L. Gray, 'The Production and Consumption of English Woollens in the 14th Century', *Eng.H.R.*, 39 (1924), 20-9; E. M. Carus-Wilson, 'The Ulnage Accounts: a Criticism', *Ec.H.R.*, II (1929), 114-23.

elsewhere, but to quantify such demand, where it turned towards cloth, is virtually impossible.

But despite these uncertainties there is every reason to think that in most regions textile manufacture expanded and prospered, and this development is probably as good a guide as export figures to the growth of production and the contribution the industry made to national wealth.

All the rural clothing areas shared this growth. The Wiltshire-Gloucestershire industry grew on the basis of good wool-supplies and available water-power: landlords such as Sir John Fastolf or the Abbeys of Syon and Caen realised the profitability of leasing fulling-mill sites and tenements unbound by manorial restrictions.[51] The West Riding, too, grew on a basis of power, wool and labour in settlements short of arable, and, producing a lower grade of cloth than the West Country, developed an important home market, in contrast to the overseas sale of Wiltshire broad-cloth. Whereas these areas saw a decline in urban production, particularly in Yorkshire where the West Riding villages virtually replaced York and Beverley, in East Anglia rural and urban centres alike prospered.[52] The worsted industry in Norwich was integrated with its suppliers of yarn in surrounding villages[53]; in Suffolk and Essex the traditional cloth industry of Colchester was maintained as the growing villages, Lavenham, Long Melford, or Halstead, developed their own specialities in the fifteenth century.[54] Some towns were less successful; in the West Midlands Worcester and Coventry kept their prominence into the sixteenth century, but the crafts of Oxford, Lincoln and finally York, amongst those well known for cloth in the thirteenth century, suffered declining fortunes.[55]

This expansion, taking place when labour was short, emphasises the profitability of the industry, and the wealth of the fifteenth-century clothier families, the Springs of Lavenham and their Wiltshire contemporaries, gives it due emphasis.[56] In addition it was easily the largest industrial employer; a total is unobtainable, due to the number of part-time workers involved, but it has been suggested that after the fourteenth century the number, full and part-time, may have increased

---

[51] E. M. Carus-Wilson, 'Evidence of Industrial Growth in Some 15th-Century Manors', *Ec.H.R.*, 2nd ser., XII (1959), 190–205; *V.C.H.*, Wiltshire, iv, 121–38.
[52] H. Heaton, *The Yorkshire Woollen and Worsted Industries*, 1965 edn., 74–86; J. Le Patourel (ed.), *Documents Relating to the Manor and Borough of Leeds*, Thoresby Soc., XLV (1957), 31.
[53] K. J. Allison, 'The Norfolk Worsted Industry in the 16th and 17th Centuries; I: The Traditional Industry', *Yorks. Bull. Ec. and Soc. Res.*, 12 (1960), 73–83.
[54] G. Unwin, *Studies in Economic History*, 1927, 262–301.
[55] J. N. Bartlett, 'The Expansion and Decline of York in the Later Middle Ages', *Ec.H.R.*, 2nd ser., xii (1955), 22–3.
[56] B. McClenaghan, *The Springs of Lavenham*, Ipswich, 1924, 62 *seq.*

by 25,000.[57] In national terms expansion was important in two ways. In the shorter run it increased the return in foreign exchange for each sack of wool produced by English farmers, due to the value added by making up into cloth rather than exporting raw; in the long run it laid the foundations of an industry which was to be able to expand in the rapidly growing European cloth-markets of the first half of the sixteenth century.

In the extractive industries also there seems to have been little absolute decline in production in the later Middle Ages, and in the most important iron, tin and coal, production per head of the population would appear to have risen. In the late fourteenth century tin output rarely sank below the high levels reached in the early thirteenth century, and output in the peak year, 1400, had only been equalled on three previous occasions, all in the 1330s.[58] Coal output gradually grew, being increasingly used as a domestic fuel where outcrops occurred in areas with a shortage of timber. The traffic along the east coast grew, and developed into an export trade, with about 10,000 tons per year being shipped from Northumberland to Zeeland and Brabant.[59]

Perhaps the iron industry shows most clearly how the pressure of labour costs could encourage technical innovations which in turn increased output not only per worker, but perhaps also in absolute terms. The early fourteenth-century bloomery forge, smelting ore by a process dating back to the prehistoric iron age, used hand and foot power for bellows and the hammer. Such have been the types excavated in recent years, corresponding well with the series of accounts surviving for the works at Tudeley, Kent. These accounts show the marked increase in labour-costs which took place about 1350, and it is in the following century that the iron industry saw a major increase in the use of water-power.[60] At the powered bloomery at Byrkeknott, Co. Durham, built in 1408, costs were cut to one sixth of those at hand-operated works, and the annual output was 10 times greater.[61] What, however, is not known is how many of the power-blown hearths were built, and how many manually operated examples were aban-

---

[57] Carus-Wilson, 'Trends . . .', 177, n.3.

[58] Bridbury, *Economic Growth*, 24–6.

[59] *C.E.H.E.*, II (1952), 127, 133; J. B. Black, 'The Medieval Coal Trades of North-East England: Some 14th-Century Evidence', *Northern History*, II (1967), 1–26.

[60] M. S. Giuseppi, 'Some 14th-Century Accounts of Ironworks at Tudeley, Kent', *Archaeologia*, LXIV (1912–13), 145–64.

[61] G. T. Lapsley, 'The Account Roll of a 15th-Century Ironmaster', *Eng. H.R.*, 14 (1899), 509–29; H. R. Schubert, *History of the British Iron and Steel Industry to 1775*, 1957, 134–8; R. A. Mott, 'English Bloomeries (1329–1589)', *Jnl Iron and Steel Inst.*, 1961, 149–61.

doned. But the indications, in the form of such significantly lowered costs and prices, are that total output might well have increased around 1400, at a time when the agricultural demand for iron would be rising with the increase in wealthier peasants' surplus for improvements.

England's growing wealth from foreign trade

A remarkable feature of England's trading position in the fifteenth century was the apparent size of her favourable trade balance. It has been suggested that this was as high as £37,700 for the years 1446–8, and averaged £15,300 over the years 1478–82.[62] These are figures for visible trade, to which adjustments may be necessary for smuggled imports, any invisible earnings deficit, and, during the Hundred Years' War, any net costs or benefits from ransoms, booty or disruption of trade.

One obviously advantageous development was the change from raw wool to cloth exports. In the mid-fourteenth century only four per cent of exported English wool went out in the form of cloth. By the middle of the fifteenth century the figure had reached 50 per cent and, by the 1540s, 86 per cent. Even though the amount of wool exported in all forms was similar to the total in 1300, its early sixteenth-century value was roughly double, with the increase in the processing it had received.[63] This change, important in itself in providing employment and foreign earnings, had further beneficial effects. The wool trade of the early fourteenth century was vulnerable to disruption in its markets, which were limited to the textile industries of Flanders and Italy. Over the fourteenth and fifteenth centuries the area covered by English exporters gradually widened, and although war might upset trading, as it clearly did in the early 1370s, local fluctuations in demand became less significant. The north-west seaboard of Europe was the most consistently successful market, although from it must be excluded Flanders, where there was understandable reluctance to purchase cloth from the rival English industry. But the Netherlands trade grew through the period to be the major outlet, taking in the fifteenth century the position Gascony had held on a far smaller scale in the fourteenth, and, with the permanent facilities established by the Merchant Adventurers in the 1490s at Antwerp, the market took shape for the major expansion of the first half of the sixteenth century, selling into Germany and Central Europe. Despite the growing importance of the Netherlands route, English traders took opportunities further afield; in the 1390s they reestablished themselves

[62] E. Power and M. M. Postan, *Studies in English Trade in the Fifteenth Century*, 1933, 20, 37.
[63] E. M. Carus-Wilson, *Medieval Merchant Venturers*, 1954, xix–xx.

in Danzig, taking advantage of the internal weaknesses of the Hanseatic League to gain an outlet for cloth and a centre for the purchase of grain. This was not a settled trade over the subsequent century, for intermittent pressure upon English residential privileges in Danzig never allowed the Eastland trades the predictability enjoyed at Antwerp. Nor were English efforts in Scandinavia entirely successful. The Northern Baltic trade was subject to many of the uncertainties seen at Danzig, and at Bergen also the Hanse did much to exclude English wares from a market in which they had been sold since the twelfth century.[64]

If the northern fringe of English trading was subject to uncertainty, efforts in Southern Europe, particularly in the fifteenth century, met with rather more success. The Mediterranean was never a large market, being in the hands of Italian merchants, but after the 1430s, when *The Libelle of Englyshe Policye* was pointing out the missed opportunities in the south-west, interest in the Spanish trade grew, and Bristol merchants saw the peninsula as an outlet for the cloths of Gloucestershire and Wiltshire. From the middle of the century this became a steady trade, with returns of iron, salt, wine and fruit in quantities which suggest rising standards of consumption in and around Bristol.[65]

The balance of trade was helped by the lack of manufactured products amongst England's imports. There were, it is true, the heavy cloths of Italy and the Near East and the decorated earthenware of Spain and Italy, and, amongst the semi-finished products, the iron of Northern Spain, but more significant was the growing quantity of foodstuffs, dominated by the wines of Gascony and Spain, and salt, fruit, and olive oil. Similarly, in the northern trades England imported primary products, cod from Norway and Iceland, and timber and naval stores from the Baltic.

There would seem every reason, then, to take estimates of a favourable visible trade balance seriously, but if the figures reached in the fifteenth century were really so large, it is surprising that there is little sign of bullion inflow, indicated by any significant rise in prices. We need, therefore to look at the invisible items, and here too there is little sign that England's position worsened; indeed, the overall picture is of an increasing proportion of England's trade coming under the control of English merchants, of improving institutional facilities and of an expanding merchant fleet. The changes in the control of trade can be seen from the reign of Edward I onwards; at the end of the thirteenth century Flemish and Italian merchants had controlled about

[64] G. D. Ramsay, *English Overseas Trade in the Centuries of Emergence*, 1957, 96 *seq.*
[65] G. F. Warner (ed.), *The Libelle of Englyshe Policye*, 1926 edn., 4–8; Carus-Wilson, *Medieval Merchant Venturers*, 49 *seq.*

two-thirds of the exports of English wool; Gascons imported two-thirds of the wine; Flemings sold cloth in England, merchants from Picardy managed the dyestuffs trade, Italian merchants were settled in Southampton, there were thriving Hanseatic trading settlements, not only in London but also in the east coast ports, and, of major importance, the business of Italian merchants in London was greatly aided by the presence of the agents of their banking houses who, indeed, provided loans for the English Crown. During the fourteenth century increasing xenophobia weakened the position of the Italians, their prestige harmed by the financial failures of the Frescobaldi and the Bardi in the 1340s, and London goldsmiths were thus given the opportunity to develop a banking function on the basis of their charter of 1327.[66]

The establishment of the staple brought the wool trade into English hands, apart from those Italians shipping direct who were exempt from the Staplers' monopoly operating through Calais. By the end of the fourteenth century other commodities had come under English control; the wine trade was almost entirely in native hands, and Picard and Flemish merchants had largely disappeared; in the second half of the fourteenth century Englishmen controlled more of the cloth export trade than Hanse and other alien merchants added together, and they held their position in a majority of seasons in the fifteenth century. Even in Norway, Denmark and the Baltic, vulnerable to Hanse pressure, English merchants made headway during the fifteenth century. They had less success in the Hanseatic ports themselves; after the favourable climate of the 1390s referred to above, only in the late 1430s, with the treaty of 1437, were English residential privileges again asserted on a comparable scale. Indeed it was the Hanse, and to some extent the Italians, who in the fifteenth century interrupted this pattern of increasing English control of trade. Despite the overall English predominance in cloth exporting, the Hanse were able to retain their facilities at the London Steelyard to good enough purpose to more than double the number of English cloths they handled in the period 1400–80; the Italians too, kept a good foothold in England, for working on the basis of their privilege to ship wool direct to Italy, and their community in Southampton, they maintained their traffic in Near Eastern luxuries and developed the import of woad and alum into England as an offshoot of their established trade in finishing materials to the Netherlands.[67]

[66] Bridbury, *Economic Growth*, 36–8; Power, *Wool Trade*, 57–60, 86 *seq.*; C.E.H.E., III, 451 *seq.*

[67] G. A. Holmes, 'Florentine Merchants in England, 1346–1436', *Ec.H.R.*, 2nd ser., XIII (1960), 193–208.

In the fifteenth century England probably achieved some savings by the expansion of her shipping. The ownership of vessels was regarded as a sound investment and absorbed an appreciable proportion of available capital, as a wide range of landowners, goldsmiths, traders and even clergy invested in them. Specialist shipowners were men of consequence; William Canynges the younger of Bristol, with 10 ships in 1474, employed 800 men as crew and several hundred more on ship-maintenance ashore. Amongst members of Parliament were ship-owning merchants; John Bourton, a Bristol importer of Gascon wines, sat in the Commons in 1422, as did John Tamworth of Winchelsea, involved in cross-channel freighting for the campaigns of Henry V. Ship design improved, particularly for deep-water trades such as the Icelandic route, and the many ships bought or captured abroad lent their design features to new vessels built in home yards.[68]

Thus a survey of the invisible elements in trade does little to suggest any clear compensation for the favourable visible balance. Other possibilities are even less susceptible to analysis. Some outflow obviously resulted from Papal taxation, but whilst this may be calculable the results of visits of ecclesiastics to Rome, the costs of diplomatic activity and of war lend themselves far less readily to assessment. The balance of costs and advantages during the Hundred Years War has been debated at length.[69] A major problem is that hostilities were sufficiently lengthy yet sufficiently sporadic for the grossing-up of gains and losses over the whole period to be of questionable value. The campaigns varied widely in character, and we have seen that the emergence of the fifteenth century's favourable trade balance took place only over the later periods of hositility. However, several points are worth considering. It is clear that much of the money collected in taxation went out of the country; it is true that much of the equipment for a campaign was bought in England and contributed to internal economic activity, but once on campaign maintenance of troops meant payments abroad. How much was brought back to compensate in the forms of booty and ransoms? Of the spoils much was immediately spent, particularly the captures of the lower ranks, and the case of Sir John Fastolf shows that it needed financial contacts and business expertise to return large sums of money without a great deal rubbing off. The bill businesses of English and Italian financiers in London were used

[68] Carus-Wilson, *Medieval Merchant Venturers*, 84 *seq.*; G. V. Scammell, 'Shipowning in England, c.1450–1550', *Trans. Roy. Hist. Soc.*, 5th ser., XII (1962), 105–22; J. S. Roskell, *The Commons in the Parliament of 1422*, 1954, 53.

[69] M. M. Postan, 'Some Social Consequences of the Hundred Years' War', *Ec.H.R.*, XII (1942), 1–12; K. B. McFarlane, 'England and the Hundred Years' War', *Past and Present*, 22 (1962), 3–13; M. M. Postan, 'The Costs of the Hundred Years' War', *ibid.*, 27 (1964), 24–53.

by the astute and purposeful Fastolf; many lesser men would have any preference for immediate spending in France strengthened by the complications of remittance.[70] And apart from such problems there is no real evidence that, overall, English gains on ransoms exceeded those of the French; only in particular compaigns might the advantage definitely go one way or the other. But what is clear is that large sums were spent on the maintenance of garrisons; Calais cost £9,000 each year in the early fifteenth century, and this level of expenditure, more regular than the sporadic costs of campaigns, must have eaten into the favourable trade balance.[71] It would be wrong to leave the subject of war without referring to the ways in which hostilities retarded English growth. The income from England's French territories was reduced by French attack and conquest and the established wine-import trade from Gascony was indeed weakened enough to send the merchants of Bristol to Spain for their supplies. Foreign trade was held back by embargoes, particularly in the first half of the fourteenth century, by the diversion of shipping to the servicing of campaigns, and by the high incidence of piracy on the fringes of the wars which raised the costs of trading in the English Channel.

Urban wealth in late medieval England

The pattern of trade does something to explain trends in urban prosperity in the fourteenth and fifteenth centuries. There was an increasing tendency towards concentration on London, due to the comparative ease of transport to and along the North Sea coast. Thus London grew from having three times the population of Bristol in 1334 to be 15 times its size in the 1520s. But concentration was not complete. Italian merchants used Southampton as an outport for London and maintained a thriving trade, importing wine for London and Salisbury, woad for the Coventry 'blues' and certain types of Cotswold and Mendip cloth, and exporting wool to Italy and cloth to Southern Europe. Bristol's prosperity was more striking; its trade relied on a productive hinterland and an advantage of distance over London in trading with Gascony, Iberia and the Mediterranean. Cloth exports from Coventry and the Cotswolds, iron and timber from the Forest of Dean, and the imports of wine, salt, dyes and fish saleable in the West Midlands and the Cotswolds were the basis of its trade, the growth in its shipping and the wealth of its merchants. The improvement of the town's streets and the rebuilding of many of its houses in the fifteenth century show an activity which, though periodically

[70] K. B. McFarlane, 'The Investment of Sir John Fastolf's Profits of War', *Trans. Roy. Hist. Soc.*, 5th ser., vii (1957), 91–116.
[71] Power and Postan, 20.

threatened by disturbances to its traders in Gascony, Iceland and Ireland, was to lead the author of the *Italian Relation* to say that there were 'scarcely any town of importance except ... two, Bristol ... York ... besides London'.[72]

There were other, smaller, towns which maintained their prosperity for particular reasons. Coventry was the centre of a dyed cloth area; Colchester maintained its cloth industry, and acted as a centre for a developing textile-producing hinterland; Ashburton and Tavistock were Stannary towns and their comparatively low reductions in taxation in the 1445 assessment indicate the prosperity of the tin industry. But the condition of towns relying solely on their functions as markets for agricultural produce does suggest that lowered population resulted in less internal trade being done in England in the century after 1350. At Oxford there was a definite physical contraction of that area outside the north wall which had been built up in the late thirteenth century. Plots occupied then were left abandoned in the fifteenth century and were only built on again late in the sixteenth. While complaints about poverty were notoriously aimed at the ears of tax assessors there appears to have been some justification in those of Lincoln. York's survival was perhaps exceptional: in the middle of the fourteenth century its textile industry flourished as immigrants arrived from the Low Countries, and the number of textile workers becoming freemen increased sixteenfold. When the competition of the West Riding and later the bypassing of York by cloth exported direct through Hull threatened its position, it still had its marketing and supply function, unique in that the area it supplied was exceptionally large, with a prosperity attested by the late fifteenth-century rise in wine imports and the success of the York crafts.[73]

There is some analogy between the fortunes of towns and those of merchants and traders. The men who prospered were the financiers and those in export trades where least regulation occurred. Merchants working under rules, the Staplers or, at the end of the fifteenth century, the Merchant Adventurers, may have been stifled to a degree, but their opportunities for high incomes and living standards were far greater than those working in trades under gild control and with inelastic home markets. In London housing conditions point out the contrast between those at the shopkeeper and craft level and the merchants.

[72] O. Coleman (ed.), *The Brokage Book of Southampton, 1443–4*, I, Southampton Rec. Soc., IV (1960), xxvi-xxxv; Ramsay, *Overseas Trade*, 6, 132–5; Carus-Wilson, *Medieval Merchant Venturers*, 1–97.
[73] W. G. Hoskins, 'The Wealth of Medieval Devon', *Devonshire Studies* (ed. W. G. Hoskins and H. P. R. Finberg), 1952, 228; R. L. S. Bruce-Mitford, 'The Archaeology of the Site of the Bodleian Extension in Broad Street, Oxford', *Oxoniensia*, IV (1939), 89–146; Bartlett, 17–33.

Merchants' houses might have similar ground-plans to shops, although most of the latter would be very much smaller, but merchants could build higher and their house layouts frequently followed the rural hall-houses of the period, and some occupied several plots on a quadrangular plan. Furnishings often followed the tastes of the nobility, and the privacy of separate rooms was common. Similarly, in Bristol the house of William Canynges was built in less-congested Redcliffe, and had not only a hall but a stone tower. The smaller merchant houses in the centre of the town, such as that of Alice Chester, who traded with Spain and Flanders, had several storeys, hers having four floors, two with oriel windows, and a high standard of furnishing. It was this class that provided the major demand for imported quality goods such as linen and tapestries, Mediterranean foods, and wines.[74]

Over the fourteenth century the wealth of the merchant class became more widely spread, and the wool trade provides a good example. About 1300 the export trades were concentrated into the hands of men approaching the wealth of William de la Pole, Lawrence of Ludlow, or Thomas Daurant of Dunstable. From the mid-fourteenth century the composition of the Company of the Staple was very different, consisting of men of whom none controlled more than a fiftieth and few more than a hundredth of the total of wool exported. The system was to 'level up or down to the scale of a substantial but not over-powerful merchant class', a comment not inappropriate to many other trades where opportunities for profit were never immense and where both export and internal trading required considerable effort in static markets.[75] This climate fostered mobility; many of the most enterprising had rural origins among the yeomanry and small gentry, from the Randulls of Wigston Magna, who became Leicester grocers in the mid-fifteenth century, to men such as the Springs of Lavenham, the Marlers of Coventry, and, at the height of achievement, the Canynges in Bristol. The traffic was a two-way one; those who came from the land often returned, as did the Springs after three generations. The purchase of land by merchants was common throughout the period; in 1350 Simon Hauberk, a London mercer, bought lands at Scalford, Leicestershire; in the 1450s a City merchant would often have one third to one half of his wealth in land, bought for its intrinsic value, as a security for loans and as provision for survivors, apart from its prestige attraction. Bristol merchants did likewise: their purchases were frequently in Somerset and Gloucestershire, but many went as far as the Midlands.[76]

[74] S. L. Thrupp, *The Merchant Class of Medieval London*, 1948, 130–5; Carus-Wilson, *Medieval Merchant Venturers*, 73–4.
[75] *C.E.H.E.*, II (1952), 219–20; Power, *Wool Trade*, ch. VI.
[76] W. G. Hoskins, 'English Provincial Towns in the Early 16th Century',

Recent comment on the later Middle Ages has questioned the extent to which England's economy was depressed by the drastic reduction in population between 1349 and the 1370s. Dr Bridbury has, in Professor Miller's words, 'turned the established view on its head' by stressing that examples of deserted farm-lands and depressed towns can be outweighed by the prosperity of a peasantry with viable holdings, the forerunners of the yeomen of Tudor England, the expansion of the cloth industry and the prosperity of merchants and ports.[77] The argument, if there still is an argument, involves measurements firstly of the total of national wealth, which may well have declined, at least between 1350 and 1400, and wealth *per capita*, which certainly rose, and, in rising, acquired a more even spread. The key to this period lies less in the details of readjustment than in the circumstances from which they began, the thirteenth-century overpopulation of the country and the poverty of so many of its inhabitants, with their low standards of production and of consumption. When holdings grew larger and surpluses increased, not only could greater care be taken of the land and the worst ground be relinquished but also a home market appeared for the products of the cloth industry, which needed a reliable base of demand to back its expansion in what were often unreliable overseas markets. Both in agriculture and in industry this period, and the fifteenth century in particular, provided a breathing space which allowed national resources to develop to meet the needs of a new century of rising population and expanding foreign markets.

Trans. Roy. Hist. Soc., 5th ser., VI (1956), 1–9; *V.C.H.*, Leics., II, 1954, 188; Thrupp, 118–27.

[77] E. Miller, 'The English Economy in the Thirteenth Century', *Past and Present*, 28 (1964).

Chapter three

Readjustment to a Rising Population, 1500–1600

Throughout the sixteenth century there are clear signs that the English economy was going through a process of adjustment in the exploitation of its resources in order to accommodate a growing population. Market forces slowly produced changes in agriculture, where rising food prices broke the trend towards conversion to wool pasture, in the exploitation of minerals, in the manufacture of consumer goods, and in foreign trade, where raw wool gave way to semi-finished and then finished textiles. But the rising national income produced by these changes failed to benefit all ranges of society, as is shown by the growing problem of the relief of the poor. While those who could take advantage of demand for their products prospered, many others suffered a decline in their real incomes.

Agriculture: the problems of inadequate techniques and under-utilised resources

Overall estimates of population in the sixteenth century are subject to great uncertainty, but information derived from the 1524–5 subsidy, the 1547 Chantry Certificates and the Diocesan returns of 1563 and 1603 suggests that a total at the beginning of the sixteenth century of 2½ million or slightly more may have grown to 4 million by 1603, perhaps passing 3½ million in the 1540s.[1] The differing nature of the sources makes this an approximate picture, but local studies have shown its general validity. A study of the 1563 and 1603 returns for Leicestershire has suggested a 58 per cent rise; in one village a doubling appears between 1525 and 1625. There were local peculiarities; a recent study of a Cambridgeshire village shows little growth in the early sixteenth century, but a 34 per cent rise in the century after 1563.[2] The picture in Wales seems much the same as in North-West England, with about 50 per cent more people in 1670 than 1545–63.

[1] J. Thirsk, 'Sources of Information on Population', *Amateur Historian*, IV (1959), 129–33; G. S. L. Tucker, 'English Pre-Industrial Population Trends', *Ec.H.R.*, 2nd ser., XII (1963), 205–18.
[2] *V.C.H.*, Leics., III, 140; W. G. Hoskins, *The Midland Peasant*, 85; M. Spufford, *A Cambridgeshire Community*, University of Leicester, Dept of English Local Hist., Occ. Paper 20, 1965, 44; J. Thirsk (ed.) *The Agrarian History of England and Wales*, vol. IV., 1500–1640, 1967, 204.

Clearly many of these local figures are upset by migration: the north of Wales may have benefited by immigration from England, and some of the lower figures in Midland England may reflect enclosure depopulations, but the examples of new holdings pressing on common rights and the building of new cottages over much of England reinforce the general view.[3] The causes of this rise seem fairly clear. The early sixteenth century was largely free of epidemics by comparison with the early fifteenth. The population density of the mid-fourteenth century was not regained by 1500, and even allowing for the disruptions of the late fifteenth century sheep-conversion it may be assumed that around 1500 most areas had sufficient holdings to allow an earlier age of marriage and larger families than two centuries before, bringing a steeper rise in population. However, as the sixteenth century progressed the rise was more precariously based, and it has been suggested that it took only the comparatively minor influenza epidemic of the 1550s to reduce the rate of increase.[4] But there is clear evidence that in the 1570s and 1580s good harvests predominated and provided conditions for the further rises suggested by local studies. Numerous specific points may also apply. Among them, improvements in housing standards among middle-income groups may have reduced infant mortality.[5] The undoubted attractions of London did something to maintain the availability of holdings, and where enclosure improved arable farming some reduction in the acreage needed for subsistence might allow holdings to be split.

What is clear is that the food resources of the country were not developing at a similar rate. The causes of the sixteenth-century price rise have been discussed at length elsewhere, and it is proposed to do no more than stress the part played by the growing demand for food. Debasement and uncertainty over the currency contributed to the peaks above the rising mean in the 1540s and early 1550s, but the general rise can be seen in terms of population pressure; wage-rates did not keep in step with prices due to the growing supply of labour, and food prices rose more quickly than those of manufactured goods, whose production could be expanded to meet demand.[6] The position was made worse by the disproportionate growth of London, with its dis-

[3] L. Owen, 'The Population of Wales in the 16th and 17th Centuries', *Trans. Hon. Soc. Cymmrodorion*, 1959, 99–113.
[4] F. J. Fisher, 'Influenza and Inflation in Tudor England', *Ec.H.R.*, 2nd ser., XVIII (1965), 120–9.
[5] W. G. Hoskins, 'The Rebuilding of Rural England', *Past and Present*, 4 (1953), 44–59.
[6] Y. S. Brenner, 'The Inflation of Prices in Early Sixteenth-Century England', *Ec.H.R.*, 2nd ser., XIV (1961–2), 'The Inflation of Prices in England, 1551–1660', *ibid.*, 2nd ser., XV (1962–3), 256–84; E. H. Phelps Brown and S. V. Hopkins, 'Wage Rates and Prices: Evidence for Population Pressure in the 16th Century', *Economica*, N.S. 24 (1957), 289–306.

torting effect on prices, which had to rise markedly in order to attract supplies from outside the normal area, the Home Counties and the hinterland of the Thames Valley.[7] Towards the end of the sixteenth century this exaggerated the effect of the quality of harvests on prices, and considerable distress was caused during runs of two or more consecutive poor crops.[8] It can certainly be suggested that the growth of food production shows no sign at all of having exceeded the probable 60 per cent increase in population over the century.

There were, however, two major pressures for the expansion of food production. From within the rural community came a growing need for more holdings and better methods to support rising numbers, to which was added a demand for food from urban and industrial communities which encouraged specialisation for the market. Some room remained for clearance of wastes and commons: for while thirteenth-century expansion had taken many settlements to their boundaries, sixteenth-century observers such as Alderman Box still saw room for improvement.[9] Pressure on common land increased: on the Lincolnshire Wolds it reduced the grazing grounds relied upon by many smallholders, and in the Fens the worsening overstocking of commons led to frequent disputes. Upland communities expanded their cultivated lands towards the hillsides as rising returns on crops pushed the margin of cultivation outwards. A Commission of 1571–2 enquired into enclosures in Westward Forest in the Lake District and found that 127 enclosures had encroached on 545 acres; 32 were completely new farms, while the rest had been made to enlarge existing ones.[10] Typical was Grindleton, on Duchy of Lancaster lands in North Yorkshire, where villagers agreed with the estate over an enclosure of fell that would ease the problems of fragmenting holdings. In the Fens the Highmarsh at Fosdyke and Sutterton was enclosed and sold off, while at Harlaxton no waste remained by 1600. The picture is repeated over the whole country, highland and lowland, and by the end of the century the

[7] N. S. B. Gras, *The Evolution of the English Corn Market*, 1915, 75, 119; F. J. Fisher, 'The Development of the London Food Market, 1540–1640', *Ec.H.R.*, V (1934–4), 46–64; J. Thirsk, *Tudor Enclosures*, Hist. Assoc. Pamphlet, Gen. Ser., 41 (1959), 3.

[8] W. G. Hoskins, 'Harvest Fluctuations and English Economic History, 1480–1619', *Ag.H.R.*, 12 (1964), 28–46; M. Campbell, *The English Yeoman*, New Haven, 1942, 185–6. For the diversion of commercial capital to the financing of grain imports in the years 1596–7, see L. Stone, 'Elizabethan Overseas Trade', *Ec.H.R.*, 2nd ser., II (1949–50), 30–58.

[9] R. H. Tawney and E. Power, *T(udor) E(conomic) D(ocuments)*, I (1924), 72–6. For cases of reductions in stints, see W. O. Ault, 'Open Field Husbandry and the Village Community', *Trans. Am. Phil. Soc.*, N.S., 55 (1965), 26–7.

[10] C. M. L. Bouch and G. P. Jones, *The Lake Counties*, 1961, 77–8; G. Elliott, 'The System of Cultivation and Evidences of Enclosure in the Cumberland Open Fields in the 16th Century', *Trans. Cumberland and Westmorland Archaeological Society*, N.S. LIX (1959), 85–104.

majority of Midland villages had very little waste left. The position is clearly shown in Leicestershire, where by 1600 less than one-half per cent of the south of the county was made up of woodland.[11]

Where there were few possibilities for the extension of husbandry some effort seems to have been made to increase output by intensive improvement, although there is little evidence of enquiry into farming methods on the scale of the period after 1650. Pressure on land gave rise to more rigorous attitudes on the part of landowners, who looked for tenants able to pay higher rents. Thus, with the tendency to lease out holdings hitherto held by customary tenure for shorter and shorter terms, tenants had to improve their methods to pay more. The major improvement possible was usually the consolidation and enclosure of strip-holdings. Traditional open-field farming gave conservatism in a community full opportunity to frustrate experiment: planting and harvesting schedules had to be generally agreed if situations were to be avoided such as at Fulbeck, Lincolnshire, where in 1630 300 cattle had to be tethered to graze the stubble between unharvested strips.[12] There had been gradual progress towards consolidation in open-field England through the Middle Ages, but much remained to be done: in a Cambridgeshire village in 1544 only seven per cent of parcels were over one acre in size, and even on a holding where consolidation had progressed relatively far $27\frac{1}{2}$ acres were divided into 16 parts.[13] Contemporaries were clear about the benefits of enclosure: Fitzherbert considered that even on a 20-year lease it was worth a tenant's while to enclose, particularly as the cost of temporary fencing represented a major item for the open-field farmer. John Hales agreed:

> 'Experience showeth that tenaunts in common be not so good hus-bandes as when every man hath his part in severall.'

The survey of Mudford and Hinton, Somerset, put the case likewise in 1554:

> 'For when the fields are inclosed every man will use a further trayvale and dylygence with his Londe to converte yt to the best use and purpose, whiche before they coulde not, for no man was master of his owne, but to use the same as plesed his neighbour.'

John Norden, the surveyor, indeed reckoned that enclosed land was worth at least 50 per cent more than unenclosed. Only occasionally did enclosure fail to benefit: it has been suggested that outside the regulations of the open field some tenants attempted to overcrop,

[11] *T.E.D.*, I, 81–4; Thirsk, *English Peasant Farming*, 1957, 21, 97; *V.C.H.*, Leics. II, 211.
[12] Thirsk, *Enclosures*, 16–17.
[13] Spufford, 41–2.

leading to exhaustion of the ground.[14] The amount of Midland England enclosed for arable in the sixteenth century is at first sight small, seen in terms of large-scale estate enclosures for pasture. But piecemeal peasant and yeoman enclosure was common; the 1549 Enclosure Commission found that yeomen and small gentry in Warwickshire had commonly enclosed areas of 20–30 acres at a time. Between 1550 and 1607 19 per cent of known Leicestershire enclosures were carried out by small tenants, and the pace quickened in the late sixteenth century with increasing enclosure by yeomen.[15]

Open-field farming cannot be totally condemned, in spite of contemporaries' enthusiasm for enclosure, for there was room for some flexibility; Leicestershire examples, Lutterworth and Wigston Magna, show how folding with temporary fencing, though costly, could overcome some problems of cattle on neighbours' stubble, and experiments were practised with catch crops, longer rotations and the inclusion of fodder crops.[16] Even so, enclosure by agreement was clearly increasing, and the advantages of consolidation gradually overcame that peasant conservatism which was so clearly a legacy of the century of depopulating enclosure before 1550.

How far were sixteenth-century farmers aware of possibilities— besides enclosures—for improving output? Certain manuals of husbandry did appear during the century: Fitzherbert wrote *The Boke of Husbandry* and *The Boke of Surveying* in the 1520s. The former went through eight editions in the sixteenth century, while the *Hundreth Good Pointes of Husbandrie* of Thomas Tusser, published in 1557, were enlarged to *Five Hundreth . . . in* 1573. These are the two best known: Fitzherbert presented a summary of contemporary practice, perhaps rather better than the average and stressing the benefits of enclosure; Tusser, however, wrote in verse, and never achieved any great precision in his directions. Apart from these two authors Leonard Mascall wrote treatises on livestock-care late in the century and Scot on hop-growing in 1534, while in 1577 Barnaby Googe revised and translated a continental treatise which, although inappropriate in many respects, contained a measure of useful material. None of these added a great deal to Walter of Henley's advice; the most significant suggestions

[14] Lord Ernle (R. E. Prothero), *English Farming Past and Present*, 1961 edn., 65; J. Hales, *A Discourse of the Common Weal of this Realm of England*, ed. E. Lamond, 1893, 49; *T.E.D.*, I, 60–2; J. Norden, *The Surveyor's Dialogue*, 1618, Book III, 16, 18; *V.C.H.*, Wilts., IV, 54; Campbell, 85–6.
[15] *V.C.H.*, Leics., II, 202; R. H. Tawney, *The Agrarian Problem in the 16th Century*, 1912, 152; R. H. Hilton, *The Social Structure of Rural Warwickshire in the Middle Ages*, Dugdale Soc. Occ. Paper 9, 1950, 25.
[16] Hoskins, *Midland Peasant*, 152, 161–4; *V.C.H.*, Leics., II, 212; Campbell, 178–9; J. Cornwall, 'Farming in Sussex, 1540–1640', *Sussex Arch. Colls*, XVIII, 49–50.

came perhaps from Barnaby Googe, that worn-out pastures benefit from ploughing-up, though not going as far as suggesting replanting with grasses, and that the Netherlands practice of using turnips as winter feed was beneficial. However, what is not clear is the extent of the circulation or influence of these manuals.[17]

No book could tell farmers exactly the best combination of crops for their land, for with cultivation and fertilisation far below modern standards local conditions varied widely. This can be seen by comparing various areas of the Midlands; Leicestershire had a tendency to pasture, with grain near the markets, the Thames Valley areas of Oxfordshire produced barley and pulses, East Anglia grew predominantly grain. The best crop was dependent on local experience reflecting conditions of soil and the needs of the market in particular. Thus, in Leicestershire, inventories show variations in the proportions of peas, barley, wheat, oats and rye grown at different times in the sixteenth century, as town requirements grew.[18] Rotations could be lengthened, giving a higher effective yield over a period, or the actual quality of the crop could be improved by better soil-care or seed quality. The mixing of seeds had been advocated by Walter of Henley, and Harrison implied in the 1570s that it was common practice.[19] Different varieties were known, Fitzherbert recognising three of barley, three of oats, and six of wheat, but how far they were seen by farmers as fitting particular grounds is not clear.

New specialised crops were a significant addition in the late sixteenth century: the influence of the Netherlands was strong and hops were introduced from Flanders into the Home Counties and the West Midlands. Late in the century oil seed was grown in the East Midlands. Vegetable-growing on a commercial scale within reach of London dates from the end of the century, developing a taste which had grown from imports and from private vegetable gardening in larger households. Vegetables were grown in Fulham and other villages west of London; Sandwich became noted for carrots and Suffolk developed a thriving vegetable trade with London through the port of Aldeburgh.[20]

Stress continued to be laid on treatment of the soil; this was vital

[17] G. E. Fussell, *The Old English Farming Books from Fitzherbert to Tull*, 1947, 4–20; Campbell, 412–3.

[18] M. A. Havinden (ed.), *Household and Farm Inventories in Oxfordshire, 1550–90*, Hist. MSS. Comm., 1965, 35; W. G. Hoskins, *Essays in Leicestershire History*, Liverpool, 1950, 160 *seq.*

[19] *T.E.D.*, III, 74.

[20] W. Harrison, *A Description of England*, ed. F. J. Furnivall, New Shakespeare Soc., Ser. VI, I, 1877, Bk. 2, 324–5; G. E. Fussell, 'Low Countries' Influence on English Farming', *Ec.H.R.*, 74 (1959), 611–22; W. H. Brace, *History of Seed-Crushing in Great Britain*, 1960.

in lengthening rotations and increasing yields, and reflects the major shortcoming of pre-eighteenth-century agriculture, the lack of manure. To some degree the manuring of ground was restricted by open-field husbandry: as fields were enclosed they could be allowed to grass for more than a season, not only to let them recuperate but also to use them as high-quality pasture to raise the numbers of stock and gain from manuring; as a result longer rotations became possible by the end of the century. But there was still in general a severe lack of manure and there were many local expedients: Norden reports the spreading of river dredge by Thames Valley farmers, street refuse and city ash in Middlesex and seaweed in Cornwall. Scraping and burning stubble and heathland was common throughout the West Country on land described by Camden as 'lean and barren but bearing fruit'. The great increase recorded by Carew in Cornish yields, which led to a grain surplus late in the sixteenth century, was a result of dressing and the improving of marginal land.[21] Liming and marling had been known for centuries as beneficial to acid soils. Marling involved heavy expenditure: Adam Martindale, a Lancashire yeoman, remembered his father running into debt in reclaiming land this way, but its benefits were noted by Norden and Leland.[22] Lime was extensively used in Wiltshire, Devon, Berkshire, Shropshire, Yorkshire and Pembrokeshire, to judge from contemporary comments on spreading and on lime-burning kilns. In Cornwall an effective substitute was a mixture of sand and shells.[23]

Many of the practices outlined above had been carried on in the medieval period, but the crucial point, the provision of more manure and better pasture, does seem to have received increasing attention in the late sixteenth century. This was partly ensured by the demand for meat and dairy produce, which tended to raise stock numbers; but some farmers kept their stock more for manure than for wool or meat, and the hiring of flocks to manure ground was not uncommon. The most significant sign of progress towards a solution of the problem was the increasing attention paid to ley grasses, which are seen even in the open fields. Temporary enclosures are known in Midland villages where strips were left to grass for a few seasons: their purpose in Leicestershire was to allow land to recover under manure and stock tread, providing in the second season a valuable pasture supplement.

[21] William Camden, *Britannia*, 1610, 199; R. Carew, *The Survey of Cornwall, 1602*, ed. F. E. Halliday, 1955, 86, 102, 111; G. E. Russell, 'Crop Nutrition in Tudor and Early Stuart England', *Ag.H.R.*, III (1955), 95–106.

[22] R. Parkinson (ed.), *The Life of Adam Martindale*, Chetham Soc., 1st ser., IV (1845), 2–3.

[23] *V.C.H.*, Wilts., IV, 55; Trow-Smith, *English Husbandry*, 100; Campbell, *op. cit.*, 173–4; G. E. Fussell, 'Four Centuries of Farming Systems in Shropshire, 1500–1900', *Trans. Shropshire Arch. Soc.*, LIV (1951–3), 1–29.

In Lincolnshire villages pasture-rents were in places so high that these temporary conversions may have been designed particularly to provide extra grazing.[24] Difficulty could occur when temporary enclosures fell foul of anti-enclosure legislation, and the 1597 Act expressly permitted them. There are a few recorded cases of planting of grass seed; in 1591 John Andrew of Stainton-le-Hole in Lincolnshire had nine acres sown with 'leyseed', one of several cases in the county. In Leicestershire inventories show a sudden increase in the qualities of hay in certain farmers' stocks, and while only a very few cases have been identified (involving the planting of grass seed on boggy ground), the beginnings of true ley farming appear to lie in this period.[25]

However, it is not clear how far the more intensive use of enclosed land was accompanied by better yields from seed. Figures are very scarce, although it has been estimated that averages for wheat, $8\frac{1}{2}$ bushels to the acre late in the fifteenth century, may have improved to 11 by 1650. Actual yield ratios, to seed planted, are too scarce to allow firm conclusions. In none of the developments outlined was improvement spectacular, but there was a general rise in standards from medieval open-field practice to a point where the innovations of the century after 1650 would be appreciated by most farmers.[26]

Besides the importance of livestock for manure, there was a strong market demand for wool, meat, and dairy products. For a century after about 1450 the demand for wool was sufficient to lead Midland land-owners with dual-purpose ground to change to sheep-raising even where tenants were displaced and settlements depopulated. The rate of conversion appears to have slackened in the first quarter of the six-teenth century, and its incidence thereafter may have been exaggerated by the pathological nature of many of the recorded disputes.[27] In the early sixteenth century the author of *The Italian Relation* wrote:

> 'But still more do they derive from their extraordinary abundance of wool which bears such a high price and reputation throughout Europe.'[28]

The dominance of cloth among English exports and the resulting demand for wool was clear until the early 1550s, and, although diminished by less favourable trading conditions in the second half of the century, cloth still remained by far the largest exported commodity.

[24] Thirsk, *Agrarian History*, 178, 180.
[25] Thirsk, *Enclosures*, 17; *Peasant Farming*, 89.
[26] Fussell, 'Nutrition', 95–106; B. H. Slicher van Bath, *Yield Ratios 810–1820*, A. A. G. Bijdragen, 10, 1963, 41–2, 75. 119, 159.
[27] M. W. Beresford, *The Lost Villages of England*, 102–33.
[28] C. A. Sneyd (ed.), *A Relation or Rather a True Account of the Island of England*, Camden Soc., XXXVII (1847), 420–3.

One of the interesting problems in the history of sixteenth-century agriculture is how such outside forces affected the balance between arable and pastoral farming. Trends in cloth exports hint that pressures might change in favour of arable after 1550, and it has been suggested that the rate of increase in wool prices slackened in the later sixteenth century.[29] Up to mid-century men at all levels found sheep profitable, and the strength of the wool-growing interest hindered the implementation of legislation against enclosure and, in particular, the 1549 poll tax on sheep. Later the balance did change slightly: clearly the land-use appropriate to most of England was dictated by conditions of the ground; slight market shifts had little effect in much of the highland zone, but in the Midlands they did.[30] Families like the Bacons of East Anglia ceased direct sheep-farming in the 1560s. The Fitzwilliams in Northamptonshire leased out their sheep-closes in the 1570s[31] and the availability of grain in the 1580s suggests reconversion, a peaceful change which does not enter legal records.[32]

However, many found that, given the economies of earlier enclosure, they could still make profits on sheep-farming; yeomen on narrow margins might get into trouble, and Oxfordshire inventories show a lower rate of increase in the value of sheep than of cattle, but families such as the Spencers continued to prosper, maintaining large flocks of 13,000–14,000 sheep.[33] But the position is partly obscured by increasing reliance on mutton for profits, and by the use of pasture, as in Oxfordshire, for cattle-raising. References to mutton become more frequent; in Norfolk the Townshends sent sheep to Norwich market in increasing quantities from the 1540s onwards, and sold direct to drovers working in the London trade. In Lincolnshire the salt marshes were used for fattening, the sheep in turn helping to convert the land into good grazing.[34] Stock-raising increased in Kent, the West Midlands, Cheshire, Dorset and the borders; young stock from Wales, Scotland and Ireland, sold through the Shrewsbury, Falkirk, and Liverpool markets, could be driven towards London for final fattening in the South-East Midlands. The possibilities of dairying were also increasingly seen, and, while

[29] P. J. Bowden, 'Movements in Wool Prices, 1490–1610', *Yorkshire Bull. of Soc. and Econ. Research*, IV (1952), 109–24.
[30] M. W. Beresford, 'The Poll Tax and the Census of Sheep', *Ag.H.R.*, I (1953), 9–15, II (1954), 15–29; J. Thirsk, 'The Content and Sources of English Agrarian History after 1500', *Ag.H.R.*, III (1955), 66–79.
[31] A. Simpson, *The Wealth of the Gentry*, 1963, 65; M. E. Finch, 'The Wealth of Five Northamptonshire Families, 1540–1640', *Northants Rec. Soc.*, XIX (1956).
[32] Thirsk, *Agrarian History*, 639.
[33] Finch, 63.
[34] P. J. Bowden, *The Wool Trade in Tudor and Stuart England*, 1962, 8–10; K. J. Allison, 'Flock Management in the Sixteenth and Seventeenth Centuries', *Ec.H.R.*, 2nd ser., XI (1958–9), 98–112; Thirsk, *Peasant Farming*, 69–70.

London demand had a considerable influence on the Home Counties, North-west Wiltshire and, further afield, Cheshire and Staffordshire also developed as dairying areas, Camden making particular reference to Uttoxeter as a cheese market and to the trade from the Dee to London.[35]

With this interest in pastoral farming, some improvement in livestock standards might be expected, particularly if the indiscriminate breeding of the open fields could be eliminated. But evidence of changing standards is scarce. Some large sheep farmers did acquire a reputation for high-quality stock: John Spencer of Althorp is a clear example, and Richard Carew claimed that Cornish sheep had improved over the sixteenth century to approach those of the lowland counties for size and, significantly, for rapid fattening.[36] Fleece-weights showed some general increase, an average for the middle of the century being 1·9 lbs compared with 1·4 lbs in the fourteenth century and 3·5 lbs in the eighteenth. Some areas did much better: Norfolk sheep might only produce 1–2 lbs, but the fleeces of Northamptonshire (3–3½ lbs), Hampshire (2–3 lbs), and Oxfordshire, Buckinghamshire, and Worcestershire (commonly 4–7 lbs) approach or exceed the eighteenth-century national average, which of course includes upland stock.[37] But a good deal of caution must remain, for it has been argued and in turn challenged that improved grazing will rapidly produce a heavier though coarser fleece without selective breeding. There is no question about the change in wool quality; the broadcloth producers found increasing difficulty in finding their traditional supplies of fine short-staple wool and resorted to upland suppliers, and the makers of new draperies in East Anglia welcomed the increasing staple-length of Midland fleeces.[38] Better pastures may have had as much effect as breeding in increasing fleece-weights, for advice on selection is remarkably sparse in contemporary manuals of husbandry. Lambing rates remained low enough to suggest that standards of health were poor, and any great improvement in a flock would have taken many generations. Carcase weights improved, but this was not only, if at all, due to breeding. As farming for mutton became more common, purpose-fattened sheep increasingly reached the market, rather than beasts culled from flocks, as useless

---

[35] C. Skeel, 'The Cattle Trade between Wales and England from the Fifteenth to the Nineteenth Centuries', *Trans. Roy. Hist. Soc.*, 4th ser., IX (1926), 35–58; R. Trow-Smith, *A History of British Livestock Husbandry to 1700*, 1957, 178–9, 209, 224–9.

[36] Finch, 41; Carew, 106–7.

[37] Allison, 'Flock Management', 104–8.

[38] P. J. Bowden, 'Wool Supply and the Woollen Industry', *Ec.H.R.*, ser. IX (1956), 44–58; M. L. Ryder, 'Sheep Breeds in Britain, II', *Ag.H.R.*, XII (1964), 65–82, esp. 70–1; Bowden and Ryder, 'Rejoinders', *Ag.H.R.*, XIII (1965), 125–6.

for anything else.[39] It is probable, therefore, that gradual improvement took place on the basis of the traditional regional breeds, held back where common grazing survived, as on the Norfolk fold courses—a good instance of an area where fleece-weights lagged—but advancing enough on enclosed grounds to prompt the reference in the scheme for the 1547 subsidy to:

> 'Pasture men ther catell is bothe greater and carrieth more woole ...'[40]

Had any cure for diseases such as liver fluke, to which marsh flocks were so vulnerable, or scab become available, the position might have improved further, but in fact all the careful breeder could do was to use the traditional remedies, avoid contact with village stock, and have as little as possible to do with markets, which were recognised as dangerous sources of infection.[41]

Improvement by tenants was to some extent a result of pressures on rent by landowners, and it is important to decide how far attempts by landowners to maintain their real incomes contributed overall to the national rise in agricultural production. A good deal of effort went not so much into increasing estate production as to ensuring a redistribution in favour of the owner. If this was the intention, it clearly had the indirect effect of forcing tenants to consider means of increasing their own income in order to meet the new demands. However, there was probably a distinct lag in this effect. Rents might increase between 1540 and 1640 at a rate similar in the case of the Wiltshire estates of the Herberts to wheat price increases,[42] but the pressure on the better-off tenant to improve his crops over the sixteenth century itself was less severe, because many estates took time to raise rents and tenants could benefit from an unearned increment brought by rising product prices. Up to 1550 many did not fully realise the extent of the price rise, a failure partly due to the small scale of increases before the 1540s, but in the third quarter of the century the difference between the alert and the lethargic landowner becomes clear. There could be numerous restrictions on estate income; in the Midlands there were many entrenched customary tenants who both claimed copyhold by inheritance and paid rents more appropriate to the fourteenth than the sixteenth century; rents of 6d per acre, standard after the epidemics of the fourteenth and fifteenth centuries, were still paid in Leicestershire in the sixteenth.[43] In particular, management on

[39] Campbell, 199; Thirsk, *Agrarian History*, 644–5.
[40] *T.E.D.*, I, 182.
[41] Campbell, 201; Bowden, *Wool Trade*, 15–16.
[42] E. Kerridge, 'The Movement of Rent, 1540–1640', *Ec.H.R.*, 2nd ser., VI (1953–4), 16–34.
[43] Hoskins, *Midland Peasant*, 106–7.

ecclesiastical estates had frequently been slack early in the sixteenth century: leases had been granted for as long as 41 years on Leicester Abbey lands; there had been many complaints of slack or abusive officials; and inspections of Missenden Abbey in 1518 and 1530 had found no rent-roll or estate book—no surveys had been conducted, buildings were in disrepair and woods had been felled by the bailiff for his own purposes. More general evidence comes in the years following the Dissolution, when the selling prices fixed by the Court of Augmentations on the basis of the *Valor Ecclesiasticus* of 1535 show that its estimates were based on slack management.[44] The opportunities are well illustrated by the cases of the Suffolk lands of Mettingham College granted to Sir Anthony Denny after the Dissolution. Here rents were renewed but hardly increased by the Dennys as late as 1562, and when Sir Nicholas Bacon purchased the estate in that year a survey disclosed that many were fixed at no more than half the market rate, a state of affairs which the purchaser had obviously suspected, to judge by the price he was willing to pay.[45]

The controlled release of monastic lands into the market over the decades after 1540 supplied and stimulated a demand governed by profit and prestige. Purchases by a wide range of society, from the peerage to the yeomanry, took lands into the management of the more enterprising, who, successful in managing these, were on the look-out for more.[46] Apart from rent increases the careful landowner could do much to improve his income by surveying his property, with the intention of fixing rents from exact knowledge of what he was letting, and the activities of Norden and other surveyors are proof of its value.[47] The results are seen in the trend to short tenures and to leasing rather than agreements of an archaic nature. In Chippenham, Cambridgeshire, this is clear in the century after 1560. In that year, 126 out of 1,225 holdings were leasehold and 1,099 copyhold and freehold, while in 1636 the figures were 702 and 523 respectively, out of 1,275.[48] Opinion varied as to how far the new tenancies and rising rents caused hardship. A great deal of ill-feeling could be generated, but whether this was always a result of genuine hardship or of the loss of the benefits

[44] *V.C.H.*, Leics., II, 195–6; J. G. Jenkins (ed.), *The Cartulary of Missenden Abbey*, III, Hist. MSS. Comm., 1962, xviii–xix; H. J. Habakkuk, 'The Market for Monastic Property', *Ec.H.R.*, 2nd ser., X (1957–8), 362–80.

[45] Simpson, 204.

[46] Campbell, 71; J. Youings, 'Devon Monastic Lands: Calendar of Particular for Grants 1536–1558', *Devon and Cornwall Rec. Soc.*, I (1955), xxii–iv.

[47] E. G. R. Taylor, 'The Surveyor', *Ec.H.R.*, XVIII (1947), 121–33; D. Chilton, 'Land Measurement in the Sixteenth Century', *Trans. Newcomen Soc.*, XXXI (1957–9), 111–29; M. C. Hill, 'The Wealdmoors, 1560–1660', *Trans. Shropshire Arch. Soc.*, LIV (1951–3), 276–87.

[48] Spufford, 44.

of archaic rents is less clear.[49] Propagandists like Lever might condemn rack-renting, yet it remains that these rising rents could always find a taker.

'For if a Gentelman have land to let; he'll have it, at what price so 'ere 'tis set.'[50]

Thus even under these conditions alert tenants could farm to some profit,[51] so the suggestion that resources had been underdeveloped early in the sixteenth century must be taken seriously. But some contemporary opinions should be mentioned at this stage. Robert Furse, a Devonshire yeoman, noted the dangers of irresponsible rent-increases. Sir John Gostwick, a Bedfordshire landowner, came to the same view.[52] It was better to keep a contented tenant who would maintain buildings and land in good order than to let to a man who, to pay a high rent, took more from the land than he put in and reduced its long-term value.

Despite this evidence of improvement of management and methods in agriculture, the final judgment on their effectiveness must lie with the course of food prices. During the 150 years from 1500 some rose no less than fivefold, and, even allowing for the part played by monetary factors, it is hard to escape the conclusion that increases were due in large measure to the failure of production to keep pace with a rising demand largely brought about by growth in population. What seems to have been lacking was any radical improvement in soil fertility comparable with the improvements of 1650–1800, with the result that yields in 1600, though better, were not strikingly different from those of 1200. All that sixteenth-century agriculture seems to have achieved was the avoidance of a spiral of soil exhaustion and falling yields which could have led to a catastrophic decline in lower-class living standards comparable with the late thirteenth century.

The wealth of rural England

There was a considerable redistribution of agricultural wealth, not simply upwards, but also towards those best able to sell at rising prices to expanding markets. In determining the extent of such a shift there is less need in the sixteenth century to rely on evidence of the broad pressures of population, land or status on which the medieval picture rests. For in the sixteenth century a significant middle range of the

[49] L. A. Parker, 'The Agrarian Revolution at Cotesbach', *Studies in Leicestershire Agrarian History* (ed. W. G. Hoskins), 41–76.
[50] *T.E.D.*, III, 47–50; Campbell, 80.
[51] *V.C.H.*, Leics., II, 199.
[52] H. J. Carpenter, 'Furse of Moreshead', *Trans. Devonshire Assoc.*, XXVI 1894), 167–83; A. G. Dickens, 'Estate and Household Management in Bedfordshire, c. 1540', *Beds. Hist. Rec. Soc.*, 1956, 40.

population was covered by probate inventories, whose details suggest trends in personal wealth. Inventories were generally made of the movable possessions of persons ranging from such labourers, craftsmen and husbandmen as had goods worth listing to the yeomen and, at the top of the scale, those smaller gentry whose wills were not proved in the Prerogative Court of Canterbury.[53]

The differences between wage-labourer and peasant smallholder, and between the smallholder, the husbandman with an adequate holding and the yeoman farmer, are indistinct. Low in the range of inventories there appears a group relying partly on wages and partly on land, and whose position altered little over the century. A man such as Robert Jarvice of Wigston Magna, who in 1581 had goods worth £4.2.8., mostly household property, with a pig, hens, straw and hay, appears to have had no land, and probably relied on wages. Yet William Bradshaw, though described in 1586 as a labourer and owning property worth under £2, had an acre divided between barley and peas. Better off, though still described as a labourer, was John Winter, with property worth over £17 in 1603 including a cow and 15 sheep, and occupying a two-roomed cottage with outbuildings; he presumably grazed his stock on common land or on his employer's ground. Those with holdings of up to 10–15 acres thus relied on the exchange of labour for grazing ground and the loan of implements.[54] In this group an increasing division took place during the century between those with enough land and common grazing to keep a family, and men at and below the bottom margin of those making inventories. At Chippenham, in Cambridgeshire, while one yeoman lessee farmed one fifth of the open fields and one third of the tenants had 30 acres or more, half held no more than a house and two acres each. Similar patterns appear over most of the Midlands, and the gap became wider as the upper group added to their lands and frequently became indistinguishable from the yeomanry. Growth of income still rested to some degree on status: the freeholder had a secure basis from which to expand, while the copyholder and customary tenant were more vulnerable to landlord pressure, though even they were often able to lease lands and to strengthen their position by reducing the proportion of land on insecure tenure.[55]

There was some improvement in living conditions among the better-off smallholders; their houses were frequently single-roomed early in the century, but from about the 1560s references to second and upstairs rooms became common, and glazed windows appeared even at this

[53] See in particular W. G. Hoskins, 'The Leicestershire Farmer in the 16th Century', *Essays in Leicestershire History* (ed. Hoskins), Liverpool, 1950, 123–183; Havinden, *op. cit.*, introduction.
[54] Hoskins, *Midland Peasant*, 171–4.
[55] *T.E.D.*, I, 29–39; Tawney, 27–40.

level. Building materials would also depend upon wealth; the Midland cottage of one or two bays and timber crucks on rubble sills with wattle, mud and plaster walls remained typical of the smallholder, but transported brick or stone came within reach of the small farmer.[56] The standard of contents improved among those approaching yeoman wealth; they had more linen and pewter, and the number of furnishings increased, often reaching 15 per cent of the value of an inventory. The best guide to wealth in an inventory is the quantity of crops; if other evidence is absent the crops growing or in store indicate the amount of land held, and land was the best buffer against bad years. This stratum of rural inventories also covered tradesmen, craftsmen and sometimes the clergy; and village smiths, wheelwrights, butchers, or bakers were frequently part-time farmers. For the Redley family in Wigston Magna, agriculture was certainly as important as smithing, judging from the value of their equipment. Similarly, clergy in livings with small endowments relied heavily on land, and suffered a decline in real incomes if dependent solely on the money income of the living.[57]

The wealth of these groups overlapped at their top end with that of the yeomanry, the range of whose incomes lay between about £30 and £500 per year. Thomas Wilson noted that:

> 'Many yeomen . . . are able yearly to despend betwixt 3 or 5 hundred pounds by their lands and leases and some twise and some thrise as much.'

Wilson was the younger son of a gentry family jealous of yeoman success, and his jealousy leads to exaggeration, but there were clearly many wealthy yeomen whose prosperity is not always easily detectable from the land that they actually owned, due to the amount held on lease.[58] But their possessions show very clearly a general improvement in wealth and living standards, particularly in the latter half of the century, among those who had saleable surpluses and no urgent pressures to ostentatious extravagance. The more successful were able to rehouse themselves in a style little different from many gentry; the substantial farmhouses still surviving in many parts of England are the result. This house-building followed the wave of yeoman land-purchases in the middle of the century, and was paid for out of the proceeds of the crops they yielded. While the range of yeoman wealth

[56] M. W. Barley, *The English Farmhouse and Cottage*, 1961, 38–125; V. R. Webster, 'The Cruck-framed Buildings of Leicestershire', *Trans. Leics. Arch. Soc.*, XXX (1954), 26–58.

[57] W. G. Hoskins, 'The Leicestershire Country Parson in the 16th Century', *Essays in Leicestershire History*, 1950, 1–43.

[58] Thomas Wilson, *The State of England (1600)* (ed. F. J. Fisher), *Camden Miscellany* XVI, Camden 3rd ser., LII (1936), 19.

increased, so did its mean, and in Leicestershire samples the median values of farmers' inventories in 1500–31, 1570–1 and 1603 were respectively £14.7.11., £46.16.8. and £67.2.4., a rate of increase faster than that of the prices of durable goods.[59] The size of houses grew, with lofting over halls to provide upper floors and development of staircases from ladders. Glazed windows became common, and many more chimneys were built, some with flues suitable for coal fires. The amount and standard of linen, furniture, wall-hangings and vessels grew. There is a clear trend in a sample of Oxfordshire inventories towards a greater proportion of wealth being made up of such household effects. In the 1550s a quarter would be other than farm stock, by the 1580s the amount had grown to a half: this was for a group of medium farmers, and those at the top of the range show similar tendencies. Contemporaries noted the change: Richard Carew, after describing the worst of Cornish housing comments on the adoption of the standards normal in Eastern England, while Robert Furse and Robert Loder noted the improvements they had made to their own houses. This improvement occurs consistently: in Essex, in Yorkshire, in Monmouthshire, in the Midlands, a movement aptly called the Great Rebuilding.[60]

Thomas Wilson, dealing with the gentry, estimated a total of about 500 knights, with incomes ranging between £1,000 and £2,000, mostly from rents. He reckoned that there were about 16,000 esquires, whose incomes lay between £500 and £1,000.[61] He then dealt with the peerage, but there is much to be said for treating the whole range from esquire to peer together: much has been written in recent years attempting to contrast the fortunes of gentry and peerage,[62] but as more individual studies have emerged, separation of these groups has been called in question, and many of the pressures leading to success or failure have been seen to apply over the entire range of landed families.[63]

To calculate the wealth of the gentry is frequently difficult: subsidy assessment could undervalue landowners' income; where accounts do

[59] Hoskins, *Essays*, 132 seq.; J. Cornwall, 'The People of Rutland in 1522', *Trans. Leics. Arch. and Hist. Soc.*, XXXVII (1961–2), 7–28.

[60] C. Fox and Lord Raglan (F. R. Somerset), *Monmouthshire Houses*, 3 vols, Cardiff 1951–4, vol. 3, *passim*; Campbell, 222 *seq.*; Barley, 62 *seq.*; Hoskins, 'Rebuilding', 44–59; S. Jones and J. T. Smith, 'Medieval Timber-Framed Houses in Cricklade', *Wilts. Arch. and Nat. Hist. Mag.*, 55 (1954), 344–52; Havinden, 2–33.

[61] Wilson, 23–4.

[62] Summarised: J. H. Hexter, *Reappraisals in History*, 1961, 117–62; D. C. Coleman, 'The "Gentry" Controversy and the Aristocracy in Crisis, 1558–1641', *History*, 51 (1966), 165–78.

[63] Notably, M. E. Finch, 'The Wealth of Five Northamptonshire Families, 1540–1640', *Northants. Rec. Soc.*, XIX, 47 (1956); A. Simpson, *The Wealth of the Gentry, 1540–1660*, 1963.

survive they may be misleading, for Valors' statements for one particular year could be distorted by the incidence of fines; surveys may give a mistaken impression if beneficial leasing rather than rack-renting were practised; or a rental may make no mention of the value of land in hand.[64] Wills are a guide, and some probate inventories were made for lesser gentry, where property was insufficient for the will to be proved in the Prerogative Court of Canterbury. On the income side there were certain clear dangers to which larger land-owners were exposed. There was, in particular, a tendency to concentrate upon leasing, rather than direct demesne farming. The astute could maintain their receipts in real terms, by strict scrutiny of rent and fines, by surveys, and by the encouragement of tenant-enclosure into more viable holdings, but, in view of the experience of many of their yeoman tenants of the profitability of direct farming for the market, the reluctance of some estates to resume land at the expiry of agreements needs explaining. The problem was one of control, and the unsatisfactory nature of contemporary accounting systems was largely to blame. There was a horror of dishonest servants, and the charge and discharge system of accounting so concentrated on checking their frauds that it paid less than due attention to profitability. But some did farm directly. The Midland sheep-farmers were conspicuously successful on large rationalised estates; the Spencers were regarded as the richest family in England in mid-century, and when sheep-farming for wool lost its attraction, some, the Bacons and the Spencers among them, ran stock for mutton. But many did no more than the Fitz-williams at Dogsthorpe in using an estate for household needs. Where possible an astute landowner would make direct use of other resources. Woods could be kept in hand; the Pelhams of Laughton in Sussex enclosed common land to increase their timber supply[65]; Sir John Newdigate of Griffin, Warwickshire, took a return of eight per cent on his coal mine, and the Earl of Shrewsbury's mine brought as high a figure as £50 from an outlay of £62.[66] Though industrial profits were not always spectacular, coal might at least save expenditure on high-cost timber, and an ironworks could provide a use for unsaleable wood.[67]

Other sources of income were significant; if a landowner with Court connections could keep his social expenditure within bounds, he might profit by attendance; this was perhaps not from office (William

[64] Havinden, 8–10; L. Stone, *The Crisis of the Aristocracy, 1558–1641*, 1965, 130–6.

[65] J. S. Moore, *Laughton*, Univ. of Leicester, Dept of Local History, Occasional Papers, 19 (1965), 44.

[66] *V.C.H.*, Warwickshire, ii, 221; L. Stone, 'An Elizabethan Coalmine', *Ec.H.R.*, 2nd ser., III (1950–1), 97–106.

[67] Stone, *Crisis*, 295.

Fitzwilliam claimed he made little from his position), but from information available in London about the land market. And, conversely, it is noticeable how many Catholic families, cut off from Court or local office or contacts, failed to maintain their real incomes late in the century.[68]

Larger landlords were, however, subject to great pressures towards extravagant living. Certain standards of consumption were socially accepted, and involved heavy irregular items, in particular hospitality, dowries and building. For comparison, a three-bay yeoman farmhouse would cost about £40 in the 1560s: as early as 1525–9 Thomas Kytson spent £3,000 on Hengrave Hall, and Bacon probably spent £6,000–£7,000 on building at Stiffkey, Gorhambury, and Redgrave, in spite of using estate bricks and timber. House-types differed from those of the yeomanry: a temptation to display led to the gentry building on courtyard plans emulating the aristocracy, rather than the rectangular plans of the yeoman farmhouses.[69] Contents of houses showed similar trends. Glazing was standard and open-roofed halls rare; privacy, better heating and tapestry wall-hangings became more common and more linen and vessels were used.[70] Once a house was built how often could it be used to display the ostentation intended? Hospitality could to some extent be met from home farms, but strain came from the growing availability of imported overseas luxuries at inflated continental prices. Insofar as entertainment had a high labour-content, the problem might be kept under control with the lagging wages of servants, but some costs, court living and marriage portions, rose faster than income. Many were aware of the dangers: among documented Midland landowners Thomas Isham was one who clearly geared his expenditure to his income, but others, the Treshams, did not, following an extravagant course of hospitality and costly litigation.[71] The case of Henry Percy, Ninth Earl of Northumberland, illustrates both sides of the problem; up to 1595 lavish spending forced him to sell estate timber on a vast scale, yet later careful land management during a time of diminished spending, admittedly partly spent in prison, brought by 1616 an income nearly four times that of 1595.[72] Failure meant borrowing either on bond, or, in more extreme circumstances, on mortgage, and at worst it led to the sale of lands. The Treshams

---

[68] J. E. Mousley, 'The Fortunes of Some Gentry Families in Elizabethan Sussex', *Ec.H.R.*, 2nd ser., XI (1958–9), 467–83; Finch, 76.

[69] Simpson, 53–61; E. Mercer, 'The Houses of the Gentry', *Past and Present*, V (1954), 11–32.

[70] O. Ashmore, 'Household Inventories of the Lancashire Gentry, 1550–1700', *Trans. Hist. Soc. of Lancs. and Cheshire*, 110 (1958), 59–105.

[71] Finch, 25, 82.

[72] G. R. Batho (ed.), 'The Household Papers of Henry Percy, Ninth Earl of Northumberland', *Camden*, 3rd ser., XCIII (1962), xlviii, 59.

of Rushton, spendthrift, were driven to all three. Thomas Wilson wrote of the Earl of Oxford,

> 'who in the yeare 1575 was rated at 12,000 a yeare sterlinge, within 2 following was vanished and no name of him found having in that time prodigally spent and consumed all even to the selling of the stores timber and lead of his castles and howses'.[73]

Who were the most successful? Certain groups can be recognised among landowners who maintained their wealth more effectively than the average. Many with mercantile or lawyer origins did so, and one may argue that competence in one field was likely to reappear in another, citing cases such as William Fitzwilliam, Merchant Adventurer and Warden of Calais, then Essex and Northamptonshire landowner, William Rede, Norwich Mercer, who bought land in the 1540s, or Robert Brudenell of Deane, Justice of the King's Bench in 1507, who invested his profits in estates in the Midlands. But a major advantage lay in their varied sources of income, allowing lean years in agriculture to be weathered from professional or trading sources. Not that this was always the pattern, for John Isham retired from his Mercer's business in London in the 1570s to run his Lamport estates after a discouraging period in European trade.[74]

But because families were open to consumption pressures and in a number of cases suffered accordingly this does not mean that they did not benefit from redistribution of wealth towards landowning groups: their increased income was merely spent the sooner. Despite all the variations in fortune there is no question that landowners were able to consume at a higher level in 1600 than in the late fifteenth century. The pressure on land and the demand for its products made this inevitable and brought them a larger share in the slowly rising total of agricultural production, at the expense in particular of wage-earners and the smallest and least secure of tenants.

The response of industry to growing markets

The sixteenth century saw an unprecedented development in technology and its industrial applications. However, while the new heavy industries are of great interest both for their methods and their organisation, their scale remained small by comparison with the textile industry.

Cloth made a significant contribution to the national income, in providing a market for the wool grower, employment over much of the West Country, East Anglia and Yorkshire, and 90 per cent of

---

[73] Wilson, 22.
[74] Finch, 100; Simpson, 35; G. D. Ramsay, *John Isham's Accounts*, Northants Rec. Soc., XXI (1962), lxxxi.

England's exports. But it was a vulnerable industry upon which fluctuating trade had strong repercussions. Textile-makers were faced by
a major problem of unsteady demand.[75] The mean of London cloth
exports shows a rising trend over the first half of the century, but
rapid fluctuations took place, many of which are obscured by even
triennial averages. There were short-term variations in purchasing
power in the traditional Northern and Central European markets, and
the position was worsened by the debasement of the English coinage
of the 1540s, which had the effect of making English goods cheap in
continental markets, taking the peaks of the booms of the 1540s to
increasing heights and causing, in turn, increasing dislocation in the
intervening slumps. The chronic weakness was the narrowness of the
market. The facilities of the port of Antwerp and the power and
influence of London merchants led to the concentration of trade on
one route and on the Antwerp hinterland; thus the security of the
Rhineland both as a route and a market was of the utmost importance.
Few attempts were made in the early part of the century to widen
trading contacts: development of the Baltic routes was slow, little
interest was taken in the sea route to the Mediterranean or in the new
discoveries, and the warnings of Barlow and Thorne in the 1520s went
largely unheeded.[76] Thus there were no means of cushioning the effects
of German recession on the English cloth industry; these effects were
felt intermittently from the late 1520s until the great setback of 1551,
when a long period of depression set in after the attempt at restoration
of the English coinage. Only then and in the 1560s with the closure
of Antwerp was much attempt made to remedy the position.

The structure of the industry maximised the effects of these market
fluctuations. The basic problem lay in its capital structure; most
capital was employed in the circulating stocks of raw and semi-finished
materials. Men like Matthew Kyng in Wiltshire, Tucker of Burford,
or the Springs in Suffolk could control the output of whole villages
but had little equipment themselves.[77] A solitary exception was the
renowned William Stumpe of Malmesbury, who set up a factory in
the buildings of the dissolved Abbey. Stumpe must have found some
advantage in centralisation, in supervision of quality or the reduction
in capital by the elimination of transit time, for he planned though
never operated a further integrated unit, at Osney Abbey; however, no
other clothier followed suit, leading to the conclusion that only the

[75] F. J. Fisher, 'Commercial Trends and Policy in 16th Century England',
Ec.H.R., X (1940), 95–117.
[76] *T.E.D.*, II, 19–23; J. A. Williamson, *The Ocean in English History*, 1941,
56–85.
[77] R. H. Gretton, *The Burford Records*, 1920, 219, 656; B. McClenaghan,
The Springs of Lavenham, Ipswich, 1924, 48–52.

cheap monastic buildings available to Stumpe could make the arrangement pay.[78] Thus there was no incentive during recessions to maintain production to keep fixed capital at work or to stock-pile cloth; any direct labour could be laid off or, where dependent craftsmen took in work from clothiers, putting-out could be stopped, to be resumed when trade improved. The position was made worse for workers by their poor bargaining position in the labour market: an increasing number of the rural population found their holdings inadequate for subsistence, particularly if subject to subdivision by partible inheritance, and welcomed the fresh source of income which domestic cloth-working could provide.[79] The traditional correctives no longer applied. When cloth-making had been largely an urban occupation the gilds had done something to steady output by using apprenticeship regulations to restrict entry into trades. Rural industry was free of these restraints, and although urban pressure-groups succeeded as late as the 1530s and 1550s in securing legislation hindering rural clothiers, there was little effective urban competition.[80]

The problem of restricted markets was made worse by the beginnings of a change in tastes in Central and Southern Europe towards lighter cloths, the New Draperies, encouraged by increasing familiarity with silks and lightweight materials coming from the east through the Levant and the Mediterranean. The beginnings of adaptation to this change come somewhat fortuitously in the 1550s and 1560s when immigrants from the Low Countries settled first at Sandwich,[81] then in Norfolk, Suffolk, and Essex. The effects of their arrival were complex. Little is heard of the Walloons at Sandwich, apart from the migration of some of their number to Norwich, but the East Anglian groups clearly prospered. They were particularly fortunate in Norfolk, for they encountered only limited opposition from native craftsmen. The traditional local worsted industry had been in decline since the previous century; its quality could not compete in export markets with cloths made of long-staple wool in the Low Countries, and at home it was priced above many of the varieties produced by the small textile industries of the south of England. Thus skilled labour was available in Norfolk and it was thought that retraining should present little difficulty. In fact assimilation proceeded slowly, but the secondary effects on the prosperity of Norwich were considerable. Further,

[78] G. D. Ramsay, *The Wiltshire Woollen Industry in the 16th and 17th Centuries*, 1965, 31–49.
[79] Ramsay, *Wiltshire*, 15–16; J. Thirsk, 'Industries in the Countryside', *Essays in the Economic and Social History of Tudor and Stuart England* (ed. F. J. Fisher), 1961, 70–88.
[80] *T.E.D.*, I 119–21, 173–5.
[81] W. K. Jordan, 'Social Institutions in Kent', *Archaeologia Cantiana*, LXXV (1961), 2.

supplies of the long-staple wool necessary for the New Draperies and previously used for worsteds were increasingly available from Midland pasture-farmers.[82] The Suffolk-Essex industry had different problems, being established in a traditional broadcloth-manufacturing area which had retained much of its prosperity; here local opposition was greater, and Dutch craftsmen had to compete for supplies of wool. However, their meticulous attention to standards of workmanship brought prosperity, and a gradual integration took place in Colchester and inland, despite friction as serious as the exodus of settlers from Halstead in protest against English counterfeiting of their seals. The sixteenth century ended with a strong Suffolk industry: New Draperies were increasing their sales both at home and abroad, and while the output of the less saleable white broadcloths had declined, the local dyed broadcloths maintained their markets through the efforts of the Levant Company in the Eastern Mediterranean.[83]

Wiltshire clothiers, however, showed themselves less alert to changes in demand. Apart from the revival of the making of coloured medley cloths the main product remained undyed broadcloth, despite the signs that it was less easy to sell; indeed, disputes were frequent between the Merchant Adventurers, who claimed that its quality was deteriorating, and clothiers who suggested that slack selling was at fault. That Wiltshire manufacturers only seriously began to change their products in the 1620s suggests that the growing interest of Suffolk clothiers in New Draperies and dyed broadcloths delayed the point when the dwindling market for whites would force the west to change.[84]

We are no nearer to attaining figures for total cloth production for the sixteenth century than in earlier periods. It is not clear how many home sales have to be added to known export totals. Numerous small centres of production existed which had little or no export reputation; weavers in Worcestershire or the Welsh border, South-West Surrey or East Kent appear in lists of exported cloths only as makers of lower grades, and produced mostly for the home market.[85] More is known of the West Riding industry, the major home supplier, which, competing increasingly and successfully against the regulation-ridden towns

[82] K. J. Allison, 'The Norfolk Worsted Industry in the 16th and 17th Centuries', *Yorkshire Bulletin of Economic and Social Research*, 12 (1960), 73–8, 13 (1961), 61–77; Bowden, *Wool Trade*, 64.

[83] J. E. Pilgrim, 'The Rise of the New Draperies in Essex', *Univ. Birmingham Hist. Jnl*, vii (1961), 36–59; *V.C.H.*, Suffolk, II, 256–67; Bowden, *Wool Trade*, 44, 52 *seq.*

[84] *V.C.H.*, Wiltshire, IV, 148–53; Ramsay, *Wiltshire*, 50–8.

[85] Bowden, *Wool Trade*, 50–1; T. C. Mendenhall, *The Shrewsbury Drapers and the Welsh Wool Trade*, 1953, 48–79; G. D. Ramsay, 'The Distribution of the Cloth Industry in 1561–2', *Eng.H.R.*, 57 (1942), 361–9; B. C. Jones, Westmorland Packhorse Men in Southampton', *Trans. Cumberland and Westmorland Ant. & Arch. Soc.*, N.S. LIX (1960), 65–84.

of Beverley and York, managed to expand its export trade in kerseys through London. The industry in Yorkshire was based on very small units and its weavers had to have exemption from legislation against middlemen, as their available capital was insufficient to buy in bulk at infrequent markets. This industry, many of its weavers working to provide a supplement to hill-farm income, had been based on local sales, and, though we cannot measure totals, its home market appears to have grown in volume and area throughout the sixteenth century.[86] Yeoman inventories show increasing ownership of textiles and draperies, sufficient to provide a market for a thriving medium-quality industry, such as the West Riding, but whether their purchases could offset the stagnation of total foreign demand is uncertain on present evidence. The surest guide is the levelling of the rise in wool prices apparent in the second half of the century; this, with the change of graziers to mutton, though partly caused by the demand for food, does suggest that cloth manufacture increased little if at all after the early 1550s.

In heavy industry, the scale of operations increased out of all recognition during the sixteenth and seventeenth centuries. This was particularly the case in coalmining, for the problem of fuel supplies became pressing by the middle of the sixteenth century; wood prices rose throughout the period and by the 1540s were attracting particular attention in London and the south-east. Numerous contemporary comments attest to the shortage:

> 'The commodity of Newcastle and such like coals is of late years known to be of more value than in times past, for wood being grown to dearth and the severity of it felt more every day, causes many of the said coals to be used for fuel in London and other places.'[87]

The use of coal was not without its problems. Domestic flues frequently induced inadequate draught, and air pollution in towns brought frequent complaints and projects for charking coal or making of briquettes in order to lessen the smoke. In industry coal spread from traditional uses such as lime-burning and smithing to the boiling of salt, sugar and soap, alum, copperas and saltpetre making, dyeing and brewing, processes where great technical problems arose; further, it was adopted for pottery and malt-making, where considerable obstacles were overcome under pressure of high wood prices. Only iron-smelting continued

[86] H. Heaton, *The Yorkshire Woollen and Worsted Industries*, 2nd edn., 1965, 47–88; Ramsay, *John Isham's Accounts*, xxvi-vii.

[87] *T.E.D.*, I, 231–8; *State Papers Domestic, Elizabeth*, vol. 105, 30, Aug. 24, 1575.

to resist the substitution of mineral fuels. The available resources of coal were plentiful:

> 'Of coalmines we have ... plentie in the north and westerne parts of our Island as may suffice for all the realme ... and so must they doo hereafter ... if wood be not better cherished than it is at this present.'

However, the difficulties of extraction grew during the century requiring a capital investment which was only possible with the prices brought about by the scarcity of wood.[88]

In the major field supplying London, the Tyne Valley, the need for capital increased as the accessible deposits close to the river were worked out. Transport, drainage and ventilation were major problems; the pumping techniques of the period limited deep working to the seams where adit-draining was possible, thus increasing the problem of transport from pithead to river and requiring wooden-railed wagonways and the building of new staithes. There were numerous complaints from London in the 1580s and 1590s about the high coal prices charged by the Newcastle Hostmen's monopoly. Little is known about their actual capital expenditure, but the evidence of new sinkings to replace worked-out mines, taken with accounts such as those of the Willoughbys, Nottingham coal-owners, who faced very high capital expenditure under conditions of great risk, suggests that high prices may have been to some degree justified for the provision of working capital.[89]

While the Newcastle to London trade was of major national importance, the smaller coal producers' significance should not be underrated. Nef's classification of 'sea-sale' and 'land-sale' separates mine-owners whose mass markets required and allowed a high level of investment from those whose trading area was limited by land transport. The latter kept fuel costs down over their localities. In the north and the Midlands coal was in common use for domestic purposes, supplied from collieries that were generally small, employing, in the case of a Sheffield pit, no more than five to eight men, with no mechanical pumping, and hand haulage. Considerable efforts were made by landowners to extend the scale of marketing and mining, but the Willoughbys' mines at Wollaton and Huntingdon Beaumont's costly failures in Leicestershire illustrate the problems of transporting

---

[88] Harrison, *Description of England*, book 3, ch. 16; J. U. Nef, *The Rise of the British Coal Industry*, I (1932), 158–64, 192–6.
[89] C. Singer *et al.* (ed.), *A History of Technology*, III, 1957, 16–83; P. M. Sweezy, *Monopoly and Competition in the English Coal Trade, 1550–1750*, 1938, 4–10; R. S. Smith, *The Willoughbys of Wollaton*, unpublished Ph.D. thesis, 1964, 110.

output. Some were more successful: the Earl of Derby's pits at Prescot provided coal for export through Liverpool by the 1560s; Sir George Bruce was expanding production at Culrose both for the Forth salt-pans and for export; and by the end of the century coal was the principal item exported from Pembrokeshire. In fact such developments raised fears for local suppliers. As Owen put it:

> 'The lower partes as the hundreds of Narberth and Rowse make some gains by sellinge of seacoale by sea to Irelande and Frannce, but generally the countrie people dislike with the selling of this commoditie, lease in tyme yt growe soe scarce that the countrie shall want it, being the greatest fuell, as it hath already enhaunsed the price thereof.'[90]

The development of coal-mining provided a significant addition to national wealth: whereas 35,000 tons were being mined annually in the 1560s, by the first decade of the seventeenth century the average was 200,000 tons, and the provision of coal on this scale removed a potential check on the expansion of fuel-using industries.

Sixteenth-century heavy industry saw a new scale of capital investment, which involved problems of management never before encountered in such severe form. These were particularly marked in industries such as iron when complex manufacturing processes were involved. While total investment in the iron industry probably lay well below that in coal-mining, it significantly reduced reliance on iron imported for military needs and for secondary working.

Late in the fifteenth century iron was made in bloomeries which in their most advanced form produced no more than 30 tons of bar annually. In 1496 the first blast furnace was built in Sussex, and in the following 50 years the Weald industry developed to serve the needs of the London building and ironmongery trades, the Thames and Portsmouth dockyards and the coastal defences of Kent and Sussex. Blast furnaces, developed from the continental 'high bloomery', represented a complete break from English tradition; even in the first half of the sixteenth century a furnace could supply enough pig to make four to five times the wrought iron made by a bloomery, was capable of producing castings of high quality, and extracted a greater proportion of iron from the ore.

The rapidity of the change in techniques depended largely on the

[90] *V.C.H.*, Warwickshire, II, 220–1; Stone, 'An Elizabethan Coalmine', 97–106; M. J. Ellis, 'A study in the Manorial History of Halifax in the 16th and 17th Centuries', *Yorkshire Arch. Jnl*, 40 (1959–62); F. A. Bailey, 'Early Coalmining in Prescot, Lancashire', *Trans. Hist. Soc. of Lancashire and Cheshire*, 99 (1947), 1–20; Nef, I, 42; G. Owen, *Description of Pembrokeshire*, I, 1892 edn., 57; Stone, *Crisis*, 340.

availability of local markets. The cost advantage per ton of bar was not greatly in the furnace's favour before the late sixteenth century, and the major incentive was the quantity of iron which could be made wth available ore and water-power and the ability to produce cast-iron goods.[91] For the Weald the market clearly existed: specialised gun-casting furnaces were set up at Buxted, Worth, and Cowden, but others were linked with finery forges to which they sent their pig for conversion; by 1550 there were 20 furnaces in operation and by 1580 about 50.[92] In the West Midlands, the Forest of Dean, and South Yorkshire change came later, and there were periods of overlap between the new and the old processes. In Staffordshire and North Warwickshire the first furnace, at Cannock, was in operation by 1568, but bloomeries still worked in 1600. In South Yorkshire, Wadsley and Kimberworth furnaces dated from the mid-1580s, but Barnby bloom-ery was in use until about 1650.[93]

A landowner's decision to change was based on the local demand and on the available raw materials. While the secondary metal trades of Birmingham and Sheffield were active in the mid-sixteenth century neither expanded their markets at the pace with which London and its demand for nails and constructional iron grew. Also, raw materials represented a major problem; ironworks were frequently intended to use unsaleable timber, and, in his accounts, Sir Richard Shireburn, owner of a bloomery at Esholt, Yorkshire, calculated how his profits would have been reduced had he needed to buy wood. A limited timber supply would discourage a change to the new process, and the prob-lems of a furnace owner with inadequate woodlands are clear in the case of Sir Henry Sidney's works at Robertsbridge, where periods of declining profit corresponded with the need to buy outside the estate or to cart highly friable charcoal from outlying woods. Skilled iron-founders were few in the early years, and they were of great impor-tance in maintaining the efficiency of the more complex method of smelting, particularly as sixteenth-century accounting made difficult

[91] H. R. Schubert, *A History of the British Iron and Steel Industry to 1775*, 1957, 157–208; E. Straker, *Wealden Iron*, 1931, 38 *seq.*; R. F. Tylecote, *Metal-lurgy in Archaeology*, 1962, 217–307.

[92] M. S. Giuseppi, 'The Accounts of the Ironworks at Sheffield and Worth in Sussex', *Archaeological Jnl*, 69 (1912), 296–307; H. R. Schubert, 'The Northern Extension of the Wealden Iron Industry', *Jnl Iron and Steel Inst.*, 160 (1948), 245–6; 'The First Cast-Iron Cannon Made in England', *ibid.*, 148 (1942), 131–40.

[93] R. A. Pelham, 'The Migration of the Iron Industry towards Birmingham during the 16th Century', *Trans. Birmingham Arch. Soc.*, 66 (1950), 192–9; Smith, 281–337; G. G. Hopkinson, 'The Charcoal Iron Industry in the Sheffield Region, 1588–1775', *Trans. Hunter Arch. Soc.*, VIII (1961), 122–51; A. Rais-trick and E. Allen, 'The South Yorkshire Ironmasters', *Ec.H.R.*, IX (1939–40), 170.

the location of poor performance whether in the furnace, the finery or the chafery. However, a successful works could be profitable. The capital required, between £200 and £300 for a complete works in the 1540s could be recouped in three years, and Sir William Sidney could keep crudely calculated costs below 75 per cent of selling prices. To maintain this level of success after estate resources had been exhausted, with coppicing a rarity, meant either leasing works to tenant iron-masters or joining one of their combinations. A number of loose group-ings appeared in Sussex late in the sixteenth century, commanding numerous furnaces, forges, ore and woodlands: the high rents which men such as Michael Weston were able to pay suggest that these specialists had developed skills and resources to a considerable de-gree.[94]

The total national output cannot be calculated before the late seven-teenth century due to the continued existence of small bloomeries, few of which have left accounts and whose total is in doubt. However, assuming an annual output of 140 tons of bar-iron-equivalent, blast furnace production may be estimated thus[95]:

1500	*1540*	*1570*	*1600*
140	1,400	7,000	10,000

The secondary metal trades were increasing their output at this time. Coventry and the villages in the Birmingham area contained numerous scythesmiths and nailmakers, and families who had pursued these trades as a side-line increasingly operated on a full-time basis; more building meant greater demand for nails, and the market for edge-tools expanded with agricultural prosperity. Sheffield smiths and cutlers were similarly active, and provided a growing custom for local coal-owners.[96] One bottleneck in these trades was in the making of high-quality iron and steel, and imports remained important. In theory the use of blast furnaces in iron production brought a new possibility for increasing steel supplies, for instead of increasing the carbon content of wrought iron, as had traditionally been done, it was possible to decarburise pig-iron into a steel. The first attempt to do

[94] B. G. Awty, 'Sir Richard Shireburn's Esholt Ironworks', *Bradford Antiquary*, N.S. 40 (1960), 243–54; D. W. Crossley, 'The Management of a 16th Century Ironworks', *Ec.H.R.*, 2nd ser., XIX (1966), 273–88.

[95] Clearly, more has to be added to the early figures to take account of bloomery production, so the total growth will in fact be less steep, although the later furnaces, in use by 1600, probably had rather greater capacity.

[96] W. G. Hoskins, 'English Provincial Towns in the Early 16th Century', *Trans. Roy. Hist. Soc.*, 5th ser., VI (1956), 1–19; W. H. B. Court, *The Rise of the Midland Industries, 1600–1838*, 1938, 33–44; G. P. Jones, 'Early Industrial Development', *Sheffield and its Region* (ed. D. L. Linton), 1956, 149. For a Kentish smith with water-powered grinding-wheels see F. R. H. Du Boulay (ed.), *Documents Illustrative of Kentish Society*, Kent Records, XVIII (1964), 276.

this in England took place at Sir Henry Sidney's works in Sussex in the 1560s, using cast 'plates' brought from his Glamorgan furnaces. Although initially successful, Baltic imports' prices were reduced to undercut the Sussex steelworks, which made increasing losses until its virtual closure at the end of the decade. Until Eliot and Meysey's patent in 1614 England had to rely very largely on imports to provide steel for blade edges and other high-quality applications.[97]

After wool and cloth, lead and tin had been the largest exports in the medieval period, and their production was aided during the sixteenth century by advances in mining, ore-preparation, and smelting. The practice of streaming tin was declining due to the exhaustion of surface deposits, and in Cornwall German miners were called in by landowners, the Godolphins and Carnsews, to advise on methods of deep mining.[98] However, in the undertakings financed by London merchants there was a reluctance to provide capital in the large amounts required for deeper mining; also, the organisation of labour on the tribute system hindered expansion, for miners had to pay such high fees and duties on output that their income was restricted and uncertain.[99]

In the lead-mining industry, the mechanical crushing of ores and the development of improved smelting furnaces and sieves—both under the Mineral and Battery Company's patent and by established Derbyshire workers—enabled output to respond to the demands of building, and the three major producing areas, Derbyshire, Alston Moor and the Mendips, all developed during the century.[100] Copper was in a rather different position; it had never been mined on a commercial scale in medieval England, nor had attempts in Scotland in the 1520s been developed, but in the 1560s the possibility of the introduction of brass-making provided a fresh incentive, and the likelihood of finding silver with copper was thought to be strong. Negotiations began for copper-mining in the Lake District in 1561, Letters Patent were granted in 1564, and the Company of the Mines Royal, incorporated in 1568, began operations with German workers and over a third German capital. The problem was to find a market, for the Crown

---

[97] H. R. Schubert, 'The Economic Aspects of Sir Henry Sidney's Steelworks at Boxhurst and Robertsbridge', *Jnl Iron and Steel Inst.*, 164 (1950), 278–80; T. Bevan, 'Sussex Ironmasters in Glamorgan', *Trans. Cardiff Naturalists' Soc.*, 86 (1956–7), 5–12; R. Jenkins, 'Notes on the Early History of Steelmaking in England', *Newcomen Society Transactions*, III (1922–3), 16–32; Singer *et al.*, III, 79.

[98] A. L. Rowse, *Tudor Cornwall*, 1941, 54–9; Halliday, *Carew*, 88–100; G. Agricola, *De Re Metallica*, 1556 (ed. H. and L. Hoover), 1950 edn., 338–90.

[99] G. R. Lewis, *The Stannaries*, 1907, 176–208.

[100] A. Raistrick and B. Jennings, *A History of Lead Mining in the Pennines*, 1965, 49–65; M. B. Donald, *Elizabethan Monopolies*, 1961, 142 seq.; J. W. Gough, *The Mines of Mendip*, 1930, 112–53.

required less for the Mint after the recoinage of 1561, and copper export was banned until the Crown was pressed in 1570 to end its prohibition. The Mineral and Battery Company, which had been expected to make brass wire and plate from the copper, concentrated on iron wire.[101] However, the Lake District copper mines had a considerable effect on the prosperity of the towns on the Cumberland coast and, in spite of many of the workers being German, new employment was created for the local population. The national effect, however, was small; returns were poor and the mines lost money.[102] Some of the English shareholders of the Mines Royal also held shares in the Mineral and Battery Company, founded in 1565, which was intended to provide an outlet for copper by making sheet brass, and wire for wool cards, reducing the amount imported. But although the Mineral and Battery Company took up its monopoly of prospecting for zinc ore, finding deposits in the Mendips, and undertook experiments in brass-making, it produced little brass. Not until Martyn, a Londoner, bought the brass rights from the Company in 1582 and set up a works at Isleworth was brass made on any scale, and even then without any great success until Van Herrick's Rotherhithe brass works took over the patent in 1594.

The Mineral and Battery Company illustrates the difficulties of management in early multi-process heavy industry. When capital requirements were high joint-stock organisations suffered from the system of proportional shares whose holders were subject to further calls. Works management was unsatisfactory: by 1569 it was clear that the patentees and shareholders included none suitable to act as a direct manager, and rather than have a company servant in charge the works at Tintern were leased. However, the fixing of the rent, on the basis of the lessees' profits, was hindered by the difficulty of establishing what these profits really were, for even the investigation of the tenants' books seems to have served little purpose. This failure of an industrial concern to use up-to-date accounting methods was typical; in the Sussex Iron industry the double-entry system was apparently not used, and there is no sign that its introduction into London merchant houses had spread significantly into industry.[103]

The anxiety in the 1560s about England's trade balance which led to the enquiry of Thomas Coleshill into London trade explains the Government's encouragement of new industries by the grant of Letters

[101] M. B. Donald, *Elizabethan Copper*, 1955, 17–25, 242.
[102] W. R. Scott, *The Constitution and Finance of English, Scottish and Irish Joint-Stock Companies to 1700*, II, 1910, 383–99; H. Hamilton, *The English Brass and Copper Industries to 1800*, 1926, 1–31.
[103] Scott, II, 413–24; Hamilton, 31–41; Donald, *Monopolies, passim*; B. S. Yamey, 'Scientific Book-Keeping and the Rise of Capitalism', *Ec.H.R.*, 2nd ser., I (1949), 99–103.

Patent.[104] However, the debates of 1603 and 1624 exhibited strong feeling against the private interests which had infiltrated this system, and it is hard to evaluate the benefit to the country beneath the welter of criticism. It does seem that in the 1560s and 1570s the Government genuinely intended to harness private interest to national advantage by patents to make goods hitherto imported. In the case of the Mines Royal and the Mineral and Battery Works, although the initiative may have come from private interests, there was none of the abusive disregard for an established trade so common later in the century. The justification of the early patents was that a skill should be genuinely new and that there should be sufficient uncertainty about techniques and markets to allow the first entrepreneurs an initial freedom from competition. The definition of innovation raised problems; Wilkes' salt-boiling process, even though using coal fuel and iron vats, differed little in essentials from the methods used by established East Coast salt-makers, and failed to produce low-cost salt.[105] In the case of glass-making, while the craft had certainly existed on a small scale early in the sixteenth century,[106] contemporary comment suggests that it was moribund[107]; the encouragement the patents of the 1560s and 1570s gave to Becku and Carré for window glass, and Jacob Verselini for the manufacture of glass drinking vessels, did come at a time when expanding demand might otherwise have attracted imports on an undesirable scale.[108] From the 1570s it became clear that too many patents were either being granted for the wrong reasons or falling into the wrong hands. Many of those debated in the Commons in 1601 had never satisfied the criteria of innovation or risk, and established manufacturers had been hurt by their award, in that the major benefit to the patent-holders was too frequently the collection of fees paid by existing workers. Many grants were being used as Court currency, rewards which cost the Crown nothing, but whose wider effects were harmful.[109]

Despite the hesitancy of the search for improved methods in agriculture, the vicissitudes of the textile industry, and the varying rates

[104] L. Stone, 'State Control in 16th-Century England', *Ec.H.R.*, XVII (1947), 112.

[105] *T.E.D.*, II, 254-62.

[106] D. W. Crossley, 'Glass-making in Bagot's Park, Staffordshire, in the Early 16th Century', *Post-Medieval Archaeology*, I (1967), 44-83.

[107] T. Charnock, *Breviary of Natural Philosophy*, 1557.

[108] E. S. Godfrey, *The Development of English Glassmaking, 1560-1640*, unpublished Ph.D. thesis, Chicago, 1957, 13-62; G. H. Kenyon, *The Glass Industry of the Weald*, 1967, 120-4.

[109] *T.E.D.*, II, 269-92; W. H. Price, *The English Patents of Monopoly*, Harvard, 1906, 82-101. A non-industrial monopoly bringing net benefits involved marine insurance, which was much in need of central registration—W. J. Jones, 'Elizabethan Marine Insurance—the Judicial Undergrowth', *Business History*, II (1959), 53-66; *T.E.D.*, II, 246-51.

of development in heavy industries, it is clear that growing population was leading to a measure of rising production and an expansion in trade. It is as well at this stage to see where the institutional checks to progress lay, and how far the infrastructure of economic life developed during the period.

There is plentiful evidence for the lack of internal transport. By 1600 little attempt had been made to improve river navigation, leaving much of Midland England, the central south and most of the north more than 15 miles from navigable water[110]; little attempt had been made to improve roads and their impassability in winter was taken for granted. It was only in coastal traffic that costs were low enough for bulk cargoes to be transported any distance, and this determined the areas where subsistence farming could give way to specialisation and where accessible markets could justify large-scale production in industry. Particular development took place on the east coast, with the Newcastle coal trade acting as a spur to ship design, leading to an increase in size and a decrease in manning requirements.[111] The grain trade illustrates the importance of coasting; prices in areas which could easily supply London were generally higher throughout the sixteenth century. The Thames Valley and the south-east coastal areas could supply London in years of good harvests, but in average or poor years the supply radius crept outwards as far as Yorkshire or Exeter: by the end of the century longer hauls were normal, and the hinterlands of Lynn and Boston were regular suppliers.[112] Barley for beer went to London in increasing quantities; Cambridgeshire farmers sold peas to dealers shipping on the east coast as far as Berwick, and beans went from the Lincolnshire marshlands to Newcastle and Hartlepool. In fact there were complaints about shortages in these areas; the villagers of Yaxley, Huntingdonshire, petitioned about heavy advance-buying of local peas, and there were protests by Cambridge to the Privy Council in 1565 about the effect of London's demand upon local wheat supplies.[113] Other areas had outgrown their own local food resources; the West Midlands drew increasingly from the border counties, Wiltshire and Gloucestershire textile areas drew through Bristol, while the West Riding was supplied not only from the Vale of York but via Selby from the Lincolnshire claylands. These links

[110] T. S. Willan, *River Navigation in England, 1600–1750*, 1936, 1–2 and map (frontispiece).

[111] T. S. Willan, *The English Coasting Trade, 1600–1750*, 1938, 11; Nef, I, 390; G. V. Scammell, 'English Merchant Shipping at the End of the Middle Ages; Some East Coast Evidence', *Ec.H.R.*, 2nd ser., XIII (1960–1), 327–41.

[112] Thirsk, *English Peasant Farming*, 12.

[113] *T.E.D.*, I, 144–6; Thirsk, *ibid.*, 77; Gras, 124.

developed despite poor transport, and Leland commented favourably on the cheapness and availability of food at Wakefield market.[114]

There was an increase in the specialisation of town markets. In the Middle Ages most markets covered a wide range of wares, but there was a tendency not only to act as retail units, but to forward local specialities to distant centres. In the East Midlands and East Anglia an increasing number of markets specialised in grain, while in the west specialisation was in stock. This tendency was marked in the Home Counties, where towns such as Hertford established themselves as forwarding centres and the Lea Valley villages built up their milling as a service industry to London. But town markets were not the only means of supply. During the sixteenth century an increasingly wide belt around London was visited by buyers of foodstuffs; some were wholesalers, the middlemen anathematised for alleged profiteering and stock-piling by sixteenth-century writers and legislation. Others were retailers whose London custom had grown beyond the unpredictable quality, price and supplies of the markets within the city itself. They traded outside, some in the specialised markets within the counties up to 100 miles around, others direct with the producers. Their effect was in bringing the farming community from a reliance on subsistence-cropping of small quantities of a comprehensive range of products to a measure of specialisation. They were regarded with suspicion not only in London but also in the country, for the less sophisticated and literate farmers seem often to have misunderstood the complications of forward buying. Despite suspicion from all sides, typified by legislation for regulation of grain badgers and middlemen in the various food trades, there is no question that such men performed an economic function.[115] Communications were such that few farmers or retailers had time to undertake their own long-distance transport; the growth of London in particular was such that distances involved were continually increasing. Hence the importance of the intermediary; his activities serving to increase the wealth and purchasing power of yeomen farmers and landowners whom he presented with access to new markets.[116]

Contrasts in wealth, in trade and industry

The fortunes of towns and the living standards of their occupants reflect the changes seen in agricultural marketing and in the location of industry. The traditional industrial towns of Eastern England, in decline in the fifteenth century, sank further after 1500. Lincoln, its textile

[114] Heaton, 78.
[115] Campbell, 191; Thirsk, *Agrarian History*, 466 *seq.*; Fisher, 'London Food-Market', *Ec.H.R.*, V (1934–5), 46–64.
[116] *T.E.D.*, I, 144–6.

industry gone, could only continue as a marketing centre; but the markets and fairs which it maintained could hardly support the population which had grown up in the thirteenth century and references to derelict property extend into the sixteenth.[117] Stamford, similarly, was unable to rebuild its former textile-based wealth. Even though it stood on the Great North Road and could link differing agricultural regions, it was never able to regain its former prosperity; purchasing power in the Fenland was insufficient, and the landowners of the adjacent heathlands used other markets in addition.[118] York was hit less hard; its textile industry was in decline in the first half of the sixteenth century, but it retained its place as a marketing centre for durable goods for much of the north and north-east.[119] The towns which could grow in wealth, marked by rebuilding and expansion, specialised in either food-marketing or craft industry, or combined the two. London's suppliers, Kingston, Ware and Hertford among them, benefited from the wealth of grain merchants. The specialised industrial towns of the Midlands maintained their position. Coventry, while its textile industry may have declined, kept its secondary metal trades, and Northampton and Leicester evidently specialised in leather; their goods found a ready market among rising farmers, and other towns attempted to introduce industries to restore employment. Stamford's scheme to introduce foreign workers to make canvas was unsuccessful, but the Flemings and Walloons making New Draperies in Norwich clearly prospered.[120]

The concentration of wealth on London is perhaps best illustrated by the wealth of its merchants. London was a magnet for the most able:

'It is well knowne that att this time (1600) there are in London some merchants worth 100,000 l. and he is not accounted rich that cannot reach to 50,000 l. or neer it.'[121]

Wilson may have exaggerated, but the attraction of London can be seen in its physical expansion, both within in new building for merchants and outside the walls to house the service occupations which accompanied new wealth and filled the areas to the north-east, upon whose squalor Stow commented in 1603.[122] The wealth of London

[117] J. W. F. Hill, *Medieval Lincoln*, 1948, 288; *Tudor and Stuart Lincoln*, 1956, 2, 30, 85.
[118] J. Thirsk, 'Stamford in the 16th and 17th Centuries', *The Making of Stamford* (ed. A. Rogers), 1965, 58–76.
[119] J. N. Bartlett, 'The Expansion and Decline of York in the Later Middle Ages', *Ec.H.R.*, 2nd ser., XII (1959–60), 17–33.
[120] W. G. Hoskins, 'English Provincial Towns in the Early 16th Century', *Trans. Roy. Hist. Soc.*, 5th ser., VI (1956), 1–19.
[121] Wilson, 20–1.
[122] C. L. Kingsford (ed.), *John Stow: A Survey of London (1603)*, II (1908),

merchants appears in their purchases of lands. Henry Becher, a Muscovy merchant, had property in eight counties and Sir Rowland Heyward owned 18 manors. Urban property was frequently owned on some scale; Robert Downe had 23 cottages and 30 shops, Sir Thomas White a comparable amount. High standards of living are apparent in the numbers of servants kept by merchants, the quality of the houses built, the amount of personal property they bequeathed, and their legacies, not only to families but for charitable purposes.[123]

Provincial merchants' fortunes were markedly smaller. Among the wealthiest Exeter merchants, the Hursts had seven manors, while Christopher Spicer left £4,200 in 1600 and John Periam £3,000 in 1573, but a normal Exeter merchant's estate was worth under £500.[124] In the smaller ports the level of wealth was still lower. Henry Tooley of Ipswich rose from being eleventh in order of wealth among the inner group of 41 burgesses in 1522 to preeminence in the assessment of 20 years later and to wealth which invited comparison with London merchants. But his total wealth at his death, at least £2,400, was exceptional and his income from rents, £46, hardly compared with the £152 of such Londoners as Henry Becher, the £240 of Henry Brunker, or the £2,400 of Sir Thomas Gresham.[125]

There was a striking tendency for sixteenth-century urban wealth to be uneven in distribution. This was not solely due to an over-abundance of labour, but also to the capital required in the more prosperous trades. The larger merchants and traders of wool or leather in Leicester, Northampton or Coventry, the clothiers of the Suffolk or Wiltshire towns, the hostmen of Newcastle, or grocers such as the Marlers of Coventry and the Jannys of Norwich maintained their prosperity, accumulating large stocks of goods. In Exeter seven per cent of the population owned two-thirds of the wealth in 1525, in Leicester 13·5 owned 65 per cent and in Nottingham 12·5 per cent owned 67 per cent,[126] and there was a noticeable pattern of the more able merchant families living in towns for perhaps three generations and then using their accumulated wealth to purchase rural estates. Only in towns where there were thriving crafts—Sheffield, York or Norwich—was there perhaps a wider distribution. A significant group town and industrial workers, were hard-hit by falls in real wages. Hal

42–4, 69–91; E. J. Davis, 'The Transformation of London', *Tudor Studies* (ed. R. W. Seton-Watson), 1924, 287–314.

[123] T. S. Willan, *The Muscovy Merchants of 1555*, 1953, 47–68.

[124] W. G. Hoskins, 'The Elizabethan Merchants of Exeter', *Elizabethan Government and Society* (ed. S. T. Bindoff), 1961, 163–87.

[125] J. Webb, 'Great Tooley of Ipswich', *Suffolk Rec. Soc.*, 1963, 141–5.

[126] D. Charman, 'Wealth and Trade in Leicester in the Early 16th Century' *Trans. Leic. Arch. Soc.*, XXV (1949), 69–93; W. G. Hoskins, 'Leicester, an Elizabethan Town', *Studies in Social History* (ed. J. H. Plumb), 1955, 33–67.

the population of sixteenth-century Coventry were close to subsistence even in good years, as were one third of the inhabitants of Leicester or Exeter.[127] This is consistent with the increasing concern over poor relief and the tendency for towns to develop schemes for its administration.[128]

In the rural textile areas the problem was comparable; in the West Riding even J.P.s were concerned by 1600 about the results of their laxity in fixing wage-rates under the terms of the Statute of Artificers; in Wiltshire there was little increase in rates in the 50 years after 1560, and the Justices had to be pressed into upward revision by a draft bill of 1593 and by legislation in 1597. Even if rates were fixed they were often ignored, and in 1605 40 Wiltshire clothiers were fined for non-payment. There were frequent local complaints about a rising crime-rate involving textile workers, and the embezzlement of stocks by spinners was explicable partly in terms of low pay.[129] The problem was at its worst for those who had no opportunity for supplementing their wages from other part-time work, from land, or from common rights, and who were exposed to a situation where prices rose more rapidly than their rates of pay; their real incomes were falling.

But wages do not necessarily provide a yardstick for living standards; Thomas Wilson commented of labourers that they

'lyve chiefly upon contry labor workeing by the day for meat and drinke and some small wages'.[130]

In the case of servants, as the accounts of the Cornwallis' household show, wages were a small proportion of income, less important than bed and board or the constant tips and perquisites of a large establishment.[131] Rural wage-workers received rewards in kind: housing, meals and the right to graze stock; grazing on common land was the major rural escape from low wages, and in industrial areas, dwindling rights were jealously guarded; in some towns commons survived; at Launceston burgesses were allowed four beasts on the town fields and other inhabitants could still each keep two.[132] A recent sample of inventories in Oxfordshire shows labourers with very small numbers of stock; Thomas Hakins of Stonesfield did at least have two hives of bees; more typical was a servant, Richard Baker of Duns Tew, with his six

[127] W. T. MacCaffery, *Exeter, 1540–1640*, 1956, 247–50.
[128] *T.E.D.*, II, 313–26; E. M. Leonard, *The Early History of English Poor Relief*, 1900, 95–137.
[129] Heaton, 110–17; *V.C.H.*, Wilts., IV, 149–50; Ramsay, *Wiltshire*, 14.
[130] E. H. Phelps Brown and S. V. Hopkins, 'Seven Centuries of the Prices of Consumables Compared with Builders' Wage Rates', *Economica*, N.S. 23 (1956), 296–314; Wilson, 20.
[131] Simpson, 169.
[132] R. H. Tawney, *The Agrarian Problem in the 16th Century*, 1912, 53; Rowse, 38.

sheep and three lambs in 1594.[133] Extra part-time work was also taken among the regularly employed; at a Sheffield coal-mine one pickman regularly had one or two days off each week, and saints' days were observed by Pembrokeshire miners, perhaps not only for celebration, but to maintain plots and stock, creating a vicious circle of low wages and absenteeism in order to work their land. Clearly the annual earnings of barrowers at the Sheffield mine, £6.1.0., would require some form of supplement.[134]

Thus the incomes of those able to supplement their wages were not as low as suggested by published indices; but wages of urban workers, who were least able to do this, approached subsistence minimum. The Phelps Brown and Hopkins index might thus be taken, in dealing with mainly urban building workers, as indicating the position of the worst-off.[135] However, this is only partially true, for there is every sign of prosperity and a demand for labour in the building trades, which the index covers; they grew in London; and in Oxford, whence some of the wage information comes, the town was expanding beyond its walls after a lull in the fifteenth century; rural building of all types, from yeoman farms to large houses, was increasing. The Statute of Artificers provides striking supporting evidence; in Clause 23 the restriction on apprentices by parental property qualification was relaxed for a group of trades largely in the building industry.[136] This suggests that building tradesmen were short enough for any check on entry to affect costs, of which M.P.s would be well aware from their own building operations. Thus there must be reservations as to whether this index represents the worst-off, and whether the decline in real incomes may have been more severe in other urban trades.

The enlarging pattern of foreign trade in the later sixteenth century

So close was the connection between England's foreign trade in the early sixteenth century and the manufacture of textiles that the significance of the pattern of commerce has been discussed in relation to the industry.[137] The connection remained after 1550, but the direction and form of mercantile activity began to alter. Turning points came in the early 1550s and in 1565. The last of the great cloth booms collapsed in 1551, and thereafter English cloths never again achieved such large sales through Antwerp; in 1563 the port was temporarily closed to English shipping, only reopening briefly before final closure in 1565.

---

[133] Havinden, 5, 13.

[134] Stone, 'Elizabethan Coalmine', 101–2.

[135] E. H. Phelps Brown and S. V. Hopkins, 'Wage-rates and Prices, Evidence for Population Pressure in the 16th Century', *Economica*, N.S. 24 (1957), 289–306.

[136] *T.E.D.*, I, 346–7.

[137] See p. 101 *seq.*

The loss of the carefully developed financial links, trading contacts, warehousing and privileges brought a problem of readjustment which led many London merchants to consider investment in trading ventures outside the traditional centres of the Low Countries and North-West Germany, for none of the ports used to replace Antwerp, Emden, Hamburg or Stade proved entirely satisfactory.

By the 1570s the trading pattern had changed noticeably since the time, 50 years before, when Robert Thorne had regretted the concentration on the Low Countries. In 1555 the Russia Company was formed, following Chancellor's voyage to Archangel of 1553, and although this, the earliest of the trading joint-stock companies, only found the Persian part of its activities really profitable, it was a model for others in the development of an organisation closer-knit than that of the Merchant Adventurers, the greatest of the Regulated companies.[138] The Levant and Barbary merchants increased their activities in the 1560s and 1570s. Both at first traded without formal company organisation, as groups of merchants spreading risks among their members. The Levant Company was formed in 1581, the value of its charter lying in privileges in the Middle East brought by the backing of the Crown. However, merchants working in partnerships and joint stocks could operate on routes of high risk without charters; the Barbary merchants operated thus until 1584, when Leicester's scheme for a company, unwelcome to many of those involved, brought to foreign trade the questionable motives seen in the field of industrial monopolies.[139] The longer-distance routes' main importance lay not so much in the value of the goods they carried (by the 1590s the Barbary and Levant Companies were together responsible for no more than eight per cent of English exports),[140] rather in the greater quantity of capital required and the wider circle whence it came. Costs were greater, particularly on the Russian run, with its need for seaworthy vessels, and on the Levant and Barbary coasts where piracy necessitated larger crews and armed vessels. Further, goods were longer in transit and returns on investments were slower, particularly when running joint-stocks were employed with redistribution after several voyages rather than at the end of each. But in spite of diversification the bulk of English commerce still lay within Europe. Most of the merchants who changed trades went no further than the Baltic or France. From the mid-1560s the Eastland trade, moribund since the late fifteenth century, began to revive, and the Eastland Company, formed on a

[138] G. D. Ramsay, *English Overseas Trade in the Centuries of Emergence,* 1957, 105; T. S. Willan, *The Early History of the Russia Company, 1553–1603,* 1956, 107.
[139] T. S. Willan, *Studies in Elizabethan Foreign Trade,* 1959, 93–137, 163–87.
[140] L. Stone, 'Elizabethan Overseas Trade', *Ec.H.R.,* 2nd ser., II (1949), 51.

Regulated basis in 1586, accounted for 11 per cent of English exports by 1590. Trade with France grew on a less formalised pattern; many of the more independently minded Merchant Adventurers traded with the northern and western ports, and the wine trade of the south-west became increasingly active.

This widening pattern laid the foundations for seventeenth-century expansion in long-range trades. Merchant Adventurers, independent interlopers and foreign merchants still carried over 75 per cent of English exports in 1590, but the experience of the long-range companies and the great increase in distant navigation during the Spanish War laid the foundations for a trading pattern which by 1700 was to have reversed the importance of European and Oceanic operations. But the changing picture of trade does more than suggest the widening opportunities for capital investment, the more extensive overseas facilities and the development of a future asset. It also illustrates, by the wares traded, some of England's strengths and weaknesses. In the export field the pattern changed little over the century; the dominant commodity was cloth which, though not regaining the scale of the late 1540s until the first decade of the seventeenth century, increased rather than reduced its proportion of the total. Wool's share continued to decline, and the quantity of tin and lead recorded as exported fell, whether due to home demand or, in the case of tin, because of increases in smuggling. There was little else. The coal-export trade, though attracting strident criticism from London consumers, only amounted to 0·5 per cent of the value of exports in 1590, and the export of arms, though volubly criticised and subject to Crown investigation in 1574, made little significant contribution.

The character of the goods imported was very different, and posed a dilemma for Tudor Government, which feared that undesirably large quantities of luxury imports were contributing to an adverse balance of trade and a consequent drain of bullion. Yet the Government had to face the risk that discouragement of imports, or their substitution by home-produced goods, could well lessen overseas sales of textiles and thus harm employment in the industry. There would have been less concern had foreign exchange contacts been sufficiently developed to allow multilateral transactions embracing all routes, but there remained those, particularly in the Middle East where 'want of returns' for luxury goods necessitated the use of bullion. A proportion of imports were necessities: linen and canvas, valued at 17 per cent of imports in 1565, materials for cloth-finishing and dyeing (13 per cent) and metal goods (6 per cent) could only be replaced slowly by state encouragement of industry. Many Baltic shipping stores could not, nor could wine, at 10 per cent of the total. Grain imports, it is true, accounted for considerable sums in bad years, but the £15,500 worth of corn imported in 1559–60 may be compared with £14,600 worth exported in 1565. Although the fine cloths (6 per cent) and exotic foodstuffs (10 per cent), the 'deceitful wares', between them barely equalled the value of linen and canvas, it was an unavoidable fact that imports of goods demanded by higher living-standards among middle- and upper-income groups would continue; after 1551 and in particular 1565 trading conditions for cloth were difficult enough without restrictions on returns, quite apart from any damage import control might do to Customs revenues.[141]

England's invisible trade position was weak in the mid-sixteenth century. The proportion of trade in the hands of aliens in 1565 (valued at 38 per cent of imports and 25 per cent of exports) was a matter for concern and is reflected in pressure on the Hanse, who, it was claimed, handled trade for merchants of other nationalities within the privileges of the Steelyard.[142] Shipping also was to a great extent foreign-owned in the 1550s: contemporaries commented on the number of derelict English vessels; in about 20 years after 1544 92 ships of over 100 tons had decayed, a basis for comparison being the 76 of 100 tons or more belonging in 1560 to all ports except Bristol and its neighbours. Late in the century Government subsidy did much to correct this situation, being available for the construction of vessels of over 100 tons. Fifty-one were built between 1571 and 1576, and in the decade before 1582 the English long-range merchant fleet approximately doubled in size. The interest of the 1590s in long-range trade and privateering seems to have caused a further wave of building, 48 ships receiving subsidy between 1592 and 1595—although, because of the subsidy on tonnage, the building of smaller ships may have declined.[143]

There was a significant tendency for trade and wealth to concentrate on London after 1500. In 1548 90 per cent of cloth exported was shipped from London, and in 1559–60 the proportion had reached 93 per cent[144]; even early in the century the obvious wealth of the city had excited the Venetian ambassador's comment.

> 'In one single street, named the Strand, leading to St Paul's there are fifty-two goldsmiths shops, so rich and full of silver vessels great and small, that in all the shops in Milan, Rome, Venice and Florence put together, I do not think that there would be found so many of the magnificences that are to be seen in London.'[145]

[141] *Ibid.*, 43–50.
[142] *T.E.D.*, II, 34–7.
[143] *T.E.D.*, II, 122.
[144] Stone, 'State Control', 105, 119; 'Elizabethan Overseas Trade', 39.
[145] C. A. Sneyd (ed.), *A Relation or Rather a True Account of the Island of England*, Camden Soc., XXXVII (1847); Sneyd, *An Italian Relation*, 42–3.

The attractions of the short route to Antwerp had been the basis of this trend, and even after the 1560s any revival of outport activity was due to exceptional and identifiable circumstances. Ports without a specialist trade declined. Southampton had expanded due to Italian trading, the establishment of a tin staple in 1492, the Gascon wine trade, and, as late as the 1520s, a thriving Breton trade; but, while early in the sixteenth century London merchants had made increasing use of the port, they returned to the capital in the 1530s. This left Southampton with little enough trade to be classed as 'decayed' in 1587; Italian wine ships went increasingly to London and the Spanish trade from the port declined after the formation of the Spanish Company in 1577.[146] A similar pattern appears at most eastern ports; merchants moved to London, ports silted, and unless a specialist trade could be maintained town wealth declined. Ipswich and Lynn were saved by the increasing grain trade to London, Great Yarmouth by its fish trade and, above all, Newcastle prospered by the export of coal, but Hull's trade was bypassed by ships sailing further up the Humber and by the decline of its Merchant Adventurers.[147] In the west, Exeter and Bristol had better fortunes. Citizens of Exeter attempted to improve their port; the Haven scheme which was begun in 1560, though beset by constant difficulties of construction, was in satisfactory operation by 1597; the Exeter Company of Merchant Adventurers was chartered in 1558 in an attempt to strengthen the trade with France and Spain, and despite friction over the monopoly to retail imported goods claimed by its members it achieved considerable influence in representations to the Government over piracy and relations with foreign governments.[148] Bristol—like Exeter, outside the London orbit and able to compete in western trade—improved its wealth late in the century. It took a prominent part in oceanic ventures and largely regained its former position.[149]

It is in the financial infrastructure for trade that the contrast between London and the provinces is most striking. Between London and the major trading ports of North-Western Europe reciprocal facilities had been built up, largely due to the activities of Italian and Flemish banking houses. Some traders, particularly Mercer members of the Merchant Adventurers, had taken to bill-broking as a sideline to their main cloth-export business. Even so, it is evident that these facilities were inadequate in times of crisis and on some of the less frequented routes, particularly to the Baltic. The foreign exchange business was

[146] A. A. Ruddock, 'London Capitalists and the Decline of Southampton in the Early Tudor Period', *Ec.H.R.*, 2nd ser., II (1949), 137–51.
[147] *T.E.D.*, II, 49–50.
[148] MacCaffrey, *Exeter*, 126–59.
[149] Ramsay, *Overseas Trade*, 235–41.

still beset by uncertainties over exchange rates; even the mint par was sometimes hard to gauge when a currency might be made up of coins differing in fineness from one denomination to another, and communications were slow enough to allow specie-point to be reached through sudden demand at one port, without this being known at the other end of a trade-route.[150] The suspicion with which foreign-exchange business was regarded in England even by the tolerably well-informed arose partly from fears for the balance of trade, partly from xenophobia directed at foreign speculators, and also from suspicions over interest payments inseparable from the business, held by the remaining opponents of usury. There was indeed sufficient public unfamiliarity with this aspect of trade to suggest that internal bills of exchange were not greatly used in England.[151] We have some glimpses of internal traders' use of bills; when the Earl of Shrewsbury wished to transmit funds from his northern estates to his London household he paid West Riding clothiers for a bill of exchange drawn on their Blackwell Hall factors, avoiding the transmission of cash. Insecurity of transport made such developments an urgent matter. However, the legal uncertainties surrounding bills were apt to slow the development of the mechanism of credit.

There was as yet a shortage of banking facilities, because few scriveners or goldsmiths had begun to specialise in attracting deposits and making loans, as they were to do during the seventeenth century. Thus the amount of hoarded cash must have held business activity back and there are numerous instances of landowning families who kept large quantities of coin idle.[152] The Crown's difficulties in replacing foreign sources of loans in the 1570s also suggest a general shortage of available funds, and when individuals needed capital they frequently borrowed from relations or from business contacts.[153] There was some tendency for the circle of men investing in trade ventures to widen; there was certainly a notable coincidence between the arrival of newly elected M.P.s in London and their first investments in overseas trading companies, which emphasises the existence of under-employed landed wealth. Of course, the circle of regular attenders at Court contained men who were keen to invest, even to speculate, as the composition of the backers of the privateering ventures of the 1590s shows; but the circle of shareholders in joint-stock companies

[150] R. de Roover, *Gresham on Foreign Exchange*, 1949, 102–40.
[151] *T.E.D.*, II, 168.
[152] Stone, *Crisis*, 508–13; R. D. Richards, 'The Pioneers of Banking in England', *Ec.Hist.*, I (1929), 485–502.
[153] R. B. Outhwaite, 'The Trials of Foreign Borrowing: the English Crown and the Antwerp Money-market in the Mid-sixteenth Century', *Ec.H.R.*, 2nd ser., XIX (1966), 289–305; F. C. Dietz, *English Public Finance 1558–1641*, 1932, 16–19, 26–27; Ramsay, *John Ishman*, lxxxi.

was in general a tight one.[154] Whether the usury laws had any great effect in hindering the growth of financial institutions has never been satisfactorily established; certainly they cannot have helped. The legal prohibition on charging interest was relaxed to allow a maximum of 10 per cent in 1545, reimposed in 1552, and again relaxed in 1571 to allow 10 per cent. Prohibition did not stop the making of loans; as stated in the Commons debate of 1571, it merely tended to drive rates up, hinder trade due to the element of uncertainty introduced by the activities of Common Informers, and do nothing to change the high pawnbroking rates accepted as reprehensible by both sides of the argument over mercantile interest charges.[155]

Conclusion

We have seen that as the total of England's wealth grew in the sixteenth century, so its social and geographical distribution changed. Thus to pay too much attention to the growth-points would give a false impression; to stress the wealth of the Elizabethan farmers and of the more astute among the larger landowners, with their high standards of consumption, would obscure the position of smallholders under pressure from worsening forms of tenure or labourers hit by contracting common lands for their beasts. In the towns the differences were comparable, between a rising merchant class, particularly prosperous in London, and labouring groups entirely lacking the means to supplement falling real wage rates. The geographical contrasts are striking; London's growth was one of the outstanding features of the century, and its effects diffused over a large area; food and fuel were drawn in for its population, talent and capital for its trade. At the centre of these changes came a rising population, growing beyond the capacity of England's resources, forcing a redistribution of wealth towards those with food to sell, thus creating the purchasing power which developed much of London's import trade. Many more of the changes in the economy may be traced back, directly or indirectly, to the population factor, which was of just such an extent to encourage enterprise but not to create those conditions of miserable poverty seen three centuries before.

[154] T. K. Rabb, 'Investment in English Overseas Enterprise, 1575–1630', *Ec.H.R.*, 2nd ser., XIX (1966), 70–81; K. R. Andrews, *Elizabethan Privateering*, 1964, 61–80.
[155] R. H. Tawney (ed.), *Thomas Wilson's Discourse on Usury (1572)*, 1925, 86–104.

Chapter four

Agriculture and Commerce:
The Beginnings of Expansion, 1600–1689

Late in the seventeenth century we come to the first sets of estimates of national income and wealth. The figures of William Petty (1665) and Gregory King (1688) are the first with any degree of accuracy, but the changes which they suggest may be amplified and put into context by examining some of the long-term trends in the economy over the whole century. We find that in this period the pressure on food supplies was noticeably relieved, both by increased agricultural output and by an easing of population-increase, but that the most striking field of growth was in trading activity and facilities, a sector which increasingly attracted the attention of the investing public and by 1690 was recognisably developing the structure which was to sell the products of the Industrial Revolution.

The relaxation of pressure on agriculture

From Gregory King's figures, gathered in 1688, it appears that at the end of the seventeenth century agriculture contributed a total of about £25 million to a national income of £48 million. The first figure is made up of rents, profits and wages, and is an overestimate due to the inclusion of the part-time industrial earnings of many freeholders and cottagers.[1] Unfortunately, it is not possible to gauge the position of agriculture earlier in the century: the figures of Wilson (1600) and Petty (1665) do not lend themselves to numerical comparison of agriculture with other sources of income, and any attempt to use them thus involves uncertainties greater than the likely differences between them. However, intervening changes in agriculture may provide a guide. While there is a suggestion over the century that it lost ground as a source of national wealth, particularly to overseas trading, it did succeed in providing foodstuffs in increasing variety and at lower prices to a population which rose from $4\frac{1}{2}$ to $5\frac{1}{2}$ million[2] and a grain

[1] P. Deane and W. A. Cole, *British Economic Growth, 1688–1959*, 1964, 156.
[2] G. S. L. Tucker, 'English Pre-Industrial Population Trends', *Ec.H.R.*, 2nd ser., XVI (1963), 205–18. Local studies bear out the suggestion of an easing of the rate of growth during the century—see E. A. Wrigley, 'Family Limitation in Pre-Industrial England', *Ec.H.R.*, 2nd ser., XIX (1966), 82–109; W. G.

surplus which turned England into a net exporter after 1670. Indeed, agriculture succeeded to the extent of reducing product-prices enough to lessen the incentive to purchase land, leading to some diversion of funds to mercantile and industrial investment. But its importance as a source of employment remained; three million out of a population of $5\frac{1}{2}$ million were directly occupied in agriculture, and its products were the basis of the work of many others in trade and industry.

This increase in the productive capacity of agriculture was achieved by a diversity of means. Sixteenth-century improvement in methods has been seen to concentrate on enclosure, which brought higher returns without any great changes in technique. This movement continued after 1600 and, acre for acre, it came to contribute more to the increase in national food supply than in the previous century. This was because the slackening demand for wool meant that more care was given to using pasture for its best purpose; lands clearly suited for grazing were, when enclosed, still used for stock-rearing, but often for meat rather than wool, while others were reconverted to arable. This trend had begun after the peak of cloth exports of the early 1550s, and was hastened by the dwindling sales of the second and third decades of the seventeenth century. Further, when pasture-land fit for arable farming came to be ploughed up there were often social benefits in terms of rural employment, and enclosure tended to lose the overtones of moral condemnation it had justifiably earned early in the sixteenth century, and which had survived as late as 1607 when harvest-crises called forth a scapegoat for rural distress. Thus enclosure took place freely at all levels. In Lincolnshire landowners enclosed for sheep on the thinly populated uplands and on the clays in order to improve the arable. Bentham might still regard Northamptonshire as an open-field county in 1649, but here and in Leicestershire enclosure by agreement proceeded on an appreciable scale.[3] In Wiltshire, though much of the chalk was still unfenced in the middle of the seventeenth century, the dairying areas, enclosed from the late sixteenth century onwards, were by 1650 enjoying increased production from better soil-dressing and the planting of leguminous crops.[4] Much

Hoskins, 'The Population of an English Village', *Trans. Leics. Archaeol. Soc.*, XXXIII (1957), 15–35.

[3] J. Thirsk, *English Peasant Farming*, 1957, 159 *seq.*; M. W. Beresford, 'Habitation Versus Improvement; the Debate on Enclosure by Agreement', *Essays in the Economic and Social History of Tudor and Stuart England* (ed. F. J. Fisher), 1961, 40–69; R. Lennard, *Rural Northamptonshire under the Commonwealth*, 1916, 128–9; W. E. Tate, 'Inclosure Movements in Northamptonshire', *Northamptonshire Past and Present*, I, 2 (1949), 19–33; W. G. Hoskins, 'The Leicestershire Farmer in the 17th Century', *Agric. Hist.*, XXV (1951), 9–20.

[4] *V.C.H.*, Wiltshire, IV, 55.

enclosure was carried out by landowners with large capital resources, who drained, hedged, and consolidated farms as leases ran out, but small farmers and tenants had much to gain by at least consolidating widespread strips in the open field. Some of the latter do seem to have suffered from lack of capital for adequate fencing and drainage, but the general effect was beneficial, as buoyant yeoman incomes suggest.

This trend towards consolidation in open-field areas should be stressed; it allowed more farmers to grow the old crops to their ulti-mate, and yeoman farmers taking the first steps towards greater returns realised the possibilities for yet further experiment. This must have been so for Robert Loder, the Berkshire farmer whose accounts sur-vive for the second decade of the seventeenth century. His farm was largely made up of partially consolidated strips in the open fields of Harwell; he suffered the usual shortage of manure, which he had to supplement with bought-in dressings such as malt-dust, and he ap-pears, from the care with which he recorded his manuring, to have been experimenting to find the most effective. In his careful account-ing he may not have been typical of the smaller farmer in South-East England, but there must have been many within the pull of the London market who had every reason to think like him.[5]

As evidence for experiment, Loder's accounts are more satisfactory than the manuals of husbandry of the period, of whose effects on the practices of their readers little can be said. Manuals' advice, in the first half of the seventeenth century at least, contained little that was radical, but even they frequently complained of rural conservatism, suggesting a great range of efficiency between Loder at one extreme, and those mentioned by John Norden, the surveyor, who 'only shape their courses as their fathers did, never putting into practice any new device', or who, as Walter Blith claimed in 1652, 'no issues nor events shall change'.[6] However, one group of writers did discuss detailed innovations. Sir Hugh Plat (*A Newe and Admirable Art of setting of corne*, 1600) and Edward Maxey (*New Instructions of plowing and setting of corn*, 1601) were concerned with the effects of haphazard seed-sowing and their enquiries foreshadowed experiments with mechanical seed-drills[7]; early in the seventeenth century Francis Bacon conducted experiments in the germination of wheat, comparing the effects of different manures and soil-dressing under controlled con-ditions.[8] But the best writers of the mid-century such as Blith and

[5] G. E. Fussell (ed.), *Robert Loder's Farm Accounts, 1610–20*, Camden 3rd ser., LIII (1936), vii–xxxi.

[6] J. Norden, *The Surveyor's Dialogue*, 1618, 210; Walter Blith, *The English Improver Improv'd*, 1652, preface.

[7] C. H. Wilson, *England's Apprenticeship, 1603–1763*, 1965, 27.

[8] E. J. Russell, *A History of Agricultural Science in Great Britain*, 1966, 16 *seq*.

Worlidge provided general manuals covering many aspects of farming practice; while they show less care and calculation than Loder, they compare in standard with the diary of Henry Best, the Yorkshire farmer who, writing in the 1640s, presents a picture of perhaps rather above-average competence.[9]

As one writer has put it: 'An ingenious husbandman could break away from the traditional pattern when he was so inclined.'[10] Early in the century, before the major changes in rotations and crops, there were numerous possibilities for producing new crops if local markets were available. In the Home Counties more hops were being grown, particularly in Essex, Hertfordshire, Kent and Surrey, catering for London brewers and using methods developed in Flanders; hemp was cultivated in the East Midlands, and market garden produce became the specialised crop of villages such as Fulham and Chelsea on London's western fringes during the first half of the century. Fruit in increasing variety was grown in the Home Counties; in 1637 John Shermenden, a Surrey yeoman, had crops of apples, strawberries, raspberries, gooseberries, cherries, plums, peaches and quinces.[11] But among more traditional crops the influence of the market was also strong. London's effect on grain specialisation in East Anglia had been clear in the sixteenth century and it was apparent in the seventeenth not only in Kent and Norfolk but in Lincolnshire and East Yorkshire; there is indeed evidence of an increasing southward trade from as far away as Scotland by the middle of the century.[12] The development of river and coastal navigation came both as response and further stimulus to this trend. Foodstuffs from the Upper Thames Valley benefited from low transport costs, and the increase in the average size of coasting vessels using the port of Lynn paralleled the development of the grain trade from the Wash ports.[13]

Thus at all levels of the farming community awareness of the needs of the market could have its effect on income without the need for large capital investment. But, with more capital, greater improvements could be made. Large-scale enclosure is the prime example, but there

[9] J. Worlidge, *Systemæ Agriculturae*, 1669; *The Farming and Account Books of Henry Best*, Surtees Soc., 33 (1857).
[10] G. E. Fussell, 'Farming Methods in the Early Stuart Period', *Jnl Mod. Hist.*, VII (1935), 1–26, 129–40.
[11] F. J. Fisher, 'The Development of the London Food Market', *Ec.H.R.*, V (1934–5), 46–64; 'The Growth of London as a Centre of Conspicuous Consumption', *Trans. Roy. Hist. Soc.*, 4th ser., XXX (1948), 37–50; J. Thirsk, 'Stamford in the 16th and 17th Centuries', *The Making of Stamford* (ed. A. Rogers), 1965, 64; M. Campbell, *The English Yeoman*, 1952, 182.
[12] N. S. B. Gras, *The Evolution of the English Corn Market*, 1915, 106–7.
[13] T. S. Willan, *River Navigation in England, 1600–1750*, 1936, 119; 'The Navigation of the Great Ouse between St Ives and Bedford in the 17th Century', *Bedfordshire Hist. Rec. Soc.*, XXIV (1946), 2–29; *The English Coasting Trades, 1600–1750*, 1938, 11–13.

were other more specialised opportunities. In Wiltshire and Hereford-shire the practice of floating the water-meadows increased from late in the sixteenth century. Rowland Vaughan told in 1604 of his use of the method in Herefordshire, and in Wiltshire it became normal prac-tice in the seventeenth century to construct banks and sluices to allow the winter flooding which would provide both grazing in April and a four-fold increase in the supply of hay.[14] Requiring vastly more capi-tal were the major drainage schemes of Eastern England. The reclama-tion of Canvey Island in the 1620s was carried out by Dutch engineers to meet the needs of London butchers for good pasture.[15] The demand here was sufficient to ensure success, but the more grandiose projects for Fenland drainage had mixed results. Around the Nene and Wel-land silting had reduced the amount of flood-free land during the sixteenth century, and after 1618, when the Privy Council directed the Commissioners of Sewers to clear the channels, interest grew in converting marshland to arable use. In 1634, Vermuyden began work on drainage for Undertakers headed by the Earl of Bedford to provide 90,000 acres of land free from summer flooding. In 1638 a new plan, with the Crown as Undertaker, set the old project aside for a more complex scheme to free the area from winter flooding. This was probably the most ambitious yet carried out in England, but the techniques of the time were unequal to the magnitude of the problem: peat shrank as it dried, lowering ground-levels; the fall of the river channels was insufficient to prevent silting; and lands hitherto immune from flooding became more vulnerable. The effect on the economy of the district was as varied. New crops such as coleseed, first grown on the restored lands, were found to be suitable elsewhere in the area, and the proportion of local farmers who grew oats rose from one in 11 in the 1630s to one in two in the 1690s. But there remained the problem of any drainage scheme, the effect on those who had relied on marsh products to supplement their income, made clear by the reoccupation of land by its former holders during the Civil War. In 1710 3,400 acres near Spalding allocated to Crown drainers before 1640 were still held by Commoners, and late in the seventeenth cen-tury the overall pattern of land-use in the Fens differed a good deal less from that of 1620 than the Undertakers had envisaged.[16]

These improvements cannot be clearly separated from those of the sixteenth century; an increase in available capital and reduced objection

---

[14] E. Kerridge, 'The Sheepfold in Wiltshire and the Floating of the Water Meadows', *Ec.H.R.*, 2nd ser., VI (1954), 282–9; 'The Floating of the Wiltshire Water Meadows', *Wilts. Arch. and Nat. Hist. Mag.*, 55 (1963), 105–10.
[15] B. E. Cracknell, *Canvey Island: The History of a Marshland Community*, Univ. of Leicester, Dept of English Local Hist., Occ. Paper 12, 1959.
[16] Thirsk, 112–35; H. C. Darby, *The Draining of the Fens*, 1940, 23–116.

to enclosure probably allowed more rapid progress, but before 1640 we see few of the beginnings of the improved husbandry associated with the eighteenth century. Some writers have been sceptical over how far improved farming—lengthened rotations and the use of new fodder crops—contributed to production before 1700. Lord Ernle's view was that the pace of improvement slackened between 1640 and 1670, with little adoption of roots and clover, and that the reputation of writings on agriculture was jeopardised by the more eccentric authors.[17] More recent views suggest that Ernle was over-cautious, and that while the number of farmers using improved methods before 1690 was not large in total, their example was of the greatest importance to later development and was indeed making a contribution to output in the last quarter and certainly the last decade of the century.[18] If we are to indicate the effects of innovation on total output, the problem is to decide not only when changes were first introduced, but when their scale became appreciable. Some evidence is apt to be misleading; the questionnaires of the Royal Society's Georgical Committee, beginning in 1665, did elicit some information, and this survives for six English counties. This is enough to establish rotations, but those who gave details were at the literate extreme of the farming community, unrepresentative enough to make this evidence of limited value.[19]

A major early influence was Sir Richard Weston, who, writing in 1645, advocated the methods of stock feeding on turnips and clover used in the Low Countries. The light sandy soils of East Anglia were well fitted to root-growing, and rotations incorporating the oats, turnips and clover which suited the poor soils of Flanders and Brabant were used on an increasing scale in Suffolk and Norfolk, and formed the origin of the later standard four-course rotation. The new crops also appeared further west. In the sandy soils of the Vale of Pewsey turnips were regularly grown in the late seventeenth century, while clovers and ryegrass were in use about 1650 and were normal practice after 1675.[20] The total national acreage of new crops was probably small; it is estimated that besides home supplies, which must have been increasing, only enough cloverseed was being imported annually in the 1690s

[17] Lord Ernle (R. E. Prothero), *English Farming Past and Present*, 1932, 103 *seq.*, 135 *seq.*
[18] E. Kerridge, 'Turnip Husbandry in High Suffolk', *Ec.H.R.*, 2nd ser., VIII (1956), 390-2; G. E. Fussell, 'Low Countries Influence on English Farming', *Eng.H.R.*, 74 (1959), 611-22; A. H. John, 'The Course of Agricultural Change, 1660-1760', *Studies in the Industrial Revolution* (ed. L. S. Pressnell), 1960, 125-55.
[19] R. Lennard, 'Agriculture under Charles II', *Ec.H.R.*, IV (1932), 23-45.
[20] *V.C.H.*, Wilts., IV, 53-5; G. E. Fussell, 'Agriculture from the Restoration to Anne', *Ec.H.R.*, IX (1938-9), 68-74.

to plant 15,500 acres, but, considering the importance of the parts of East Anglia and Wiltshire where the turnips and new grasses are best attested, the effect on agricultural thinking cannot be disregarded. The significance of these innovations was to relax some of the 'inexorable pressures of diminishing returns' in the older agricultural areas.[21] Before 1650 the problem had been that, unless permanent pastures were available, intensification of arable husbandry was limited by lack of manure. Turnips and grasses, allowing greater numbers of stock, accelerated the progress towards better crop nutrition which had begun with early ley farming in the sixteenth century, while the properties of clover further improved grazing.

Some measure of the effect of these changes may be seen in livestock numbers. In Lincolnshire totals per holding declined from about 1590 to 1630, changed little until the 1670s, but then rose, particularly in the 1690s. The increasing prosperity of grazing arose from the ability of the new fodder crops to reduce costs in a way as yet impossible in arable farming,[22] and from an increasing demand for meat which encouraged large-scale grazing. Further, more fertile pastures and higher yields of year-round fodder lessened seasonal fluctuations in meat prices. Late in the century lands which were marginal between arable and pasture were frequently put to the latter and enclosed, and in this way the Midland claylands were strikingly changed: while 10 per cent of Leicester had been enclosed in 1607, the figure for 1730 was 52 per cent, much of this for grazing.[23] But one side-effect of the ability to raise the numbers of stock appears to have been a lack of interest in breed improvement. All authorities agree that little progress had been made towards better-quality stock by 1710. On unimproved pastures there were the same nutritional problems that kept sixteenth-century stock quality poor, and where greater numbers could be kept meat output was in any case raised, without much attention to selective breeding. In the manuals of husbandry detailed discussion of breeding principles is rare, and while Loder and Best show that their practice was ahead of Markham or Mascall, known figures of, for example, lambing ratios show only slight improvements.[24]

How did agricultural changes affect the standards of living of sections of the rural community? In general smaller farmers' conditions improved less rapidly in the seventeenth than in the sixteenth century; incomes were restricted, for production for the market on an adequate

[21] John, 130.
[22] Thirsk, 137, 173.
[23] Hoskins, 15–19.
[24] Trow-Smith, 234–45; L. Mascall, *The Countryman's Journal: or the Government of Cattle*, 1680, 134; K. J. Allison, 'Flock Management in the 16th and 17th Centuries', *Ec.H.R.*, 2nd ser., XI (1958–9), 98–12.

scale was apt to require more capital for improvement. This tendency for the ability to invest to determine the fortune of peasant families in the seventeenth century explains examples of polarisation of income among the husbandmen-yeoman group. Those who were unable to increase the sizes of their holdings enough to reduce their vulnerability to fluctuations in product-prices were apt to sell their land to larger farmers, and in Midland England a gulf emerged over the century between smallholders and those yeomen and small gentry whose ancestors had begun the enlargement of holdings in the sixteenth century. The 1670 Hearth Tax returns for Wigston Magna show how far this could go in a typical Midland village; here those either exempt from the tax or paying on two or less hearths outnumbered those with three hearths or more by nine to one.[25]

In this context the period can be divided between the first 40 years of the century, when rising population still made for land shortage and rising product-prices, and the second 50 years, when the problem was rather different. About 1650 population levelled off and the general rise in prices eased; thus it was no longer so easy for the small farmer to accumulate capital from selling to the market. Prices fluctuated around a stagnant mean, for poor harvests no longer brought great increases, and particularly in the 1670s and 1680s high yields frequently meant glut-level prices. So a good living could only be made if prices remained within close limits. The pastoral village had more resilience; in the Lincolnshire marshlands and fenlands common rights made holdings of two to five acres of arable adequate, and the average size of fenland peasant flocks rose from 50 to 62 between 1660 and 1690.[26] By and large, however, the position of the smallholder and agricultural worker was a precarious one by mid-century and is reflected in the pattern of building: the rate of peasant house-construction decreased after about 1620, and in the succeeding 90 years building was far more common among the upper yeomanry and gentry.[27] When, after about 1640, agriculture began to feel the effects of the end of rising product-prices, problems of poverty became acute. The increasing interest in poor-relief and schemes for employment provide adequate commentary on a situation where the poor were becoming increasingly conspicuous; while in the sixteenth century they had been largely the aged and infirm, by 1670 it was not uncommon for half the 'exempt' category in Hearth Tax returns to be able-bodied.

Within the agricultural sector this trend in peasant living-standards was not altogether balanced by improvements in the incomes of land-

---

[25] Hoskins, 185–215.
[26] Thirsk, 118 *seq.*, 195
[27] M. W. Barley, *The English Farmhouse and Cottage*, 1961, 129 *seq.*

owners. While rents in general kept pace with rising prices up to 1640,[28] due to the continuing need of a rising population for land, in the following years the demand declined to the point where, late in the century, good tenant-farmers were hard to find. Corresponding to the levelling population trend, market demand for foodstuffs was less keen, and was replaced by a home and, increasingly, an export market for grain in which prices were low enough to be profitable only to the large-scale farmer. This explains property-distribution within the land-owning class; the amount of land owned by those with gross annual rentals below £800 declined in the 60 years after 1680, while those with greater rent rolls managed to hang on. It seems, then, that estates were not the attractive investments they had proved in the sixteenth century; there was less expectation of rising rents and land values, and Land Tax imposed an additional burden.[29]

A reduced demand for land is probably the main reason why development of improved methods in farming proceeded no faster than it did. There was no longer the same desire to buy land as a capital investment, and fewer merchant purchasers appeared. Those who bought estates did so largely for prestige reasons,[30] and both among this group and existing landowners less capital was made available for improvement, while a developing money market and growing foreign trade provided more effective opportunities. Only in stock-rearing did this pattern not entirely hold good. Graziers found young stock and feeding grains cheap in the 15 years after 1675 and the meat market continued to expand; dairy products, similarly, were more favourably placed than grains, and only wool represented a hazard, its declining profitability spanning the century.

Thus we may confirm the impression gained from commentators of the 1690s that agriculture, while still the direct or indirect source of income of a majority of the population, no longer remained the buoyant sector of the economy that it had been in the sixteenth century. It would seem that a smaller proportion of national income reached the farming and landowning community, for, while the living standards of the rural lower classes probably declined, this was not entirely due to an upward redistribution. It might perhaps be argued that English agriculture had been geared to a steady rise in population for a century and a half before 1640. Even though much scope remained for improvement, slackening of demand led to a measure of over-production,

[28] E. Kerridge, 'The Movement of Rent, 1540–1640', *Ec.H.R.*, 2nd ser., VI (1953–4), 16–34.

[29] H. J. Habakkuk, 'English Landownership, 1680–1740', *Ec.H.R.*, X (1939–40), 2–17; 'The Long-term Rate of Interest and the Price of Land', *Ec.H.R.*, 2nd ser., V (1952), 26–45.

[30] L. Stone, 'Social Mobility in England, 1500–1700', *Past and Present*, 33 (1966), 16–55, esp. 18–19.

illustrated by the capacity to export grain without any severe dearth at home. The offer of the Export Bounty may perhaps have attracted some capital to improvement that might otherwise have gone else-where, but over-production brought prices down to a point where many thought twice about much further investment, a reluctance leav-ing much to be done in the following century, when population again began to put pressure on the food supply.

Industry: the consolidation of earlier developments

Seventeenth-century industry is more noteworthy for consolidation than for major innovations, but by 1700 minor improvements produced a wider range and a higher quality of goods. The scale of growth is not easy to determine, due to the difficulty of estimating home con-sumption. It is possible to make a reasonable estimate of the trend in exports of cloth, the major exported industrial product, but with industries whose export markets were small we have less evidence. In the sixteenth century it is possible that home sales of goods had risen at about the rate of population increase, assuming that some lessening in the purchasing power of the landless sections would be made up higher in the social scale. In the seventeenth century this probably still applied, but, while population continued to rise until the 1640s, there seems adequate evidence for a levelling in the second half of the century. Both early and late in the century there would be reason to expect a decline in lower income groups' surplus for the purchase of manufactures; before 1640 the pressure of rents was maintained, while we have seen that after 1680 declining agricultural profits bore hard on tenants and smaller landowners. Gregory King's figures are perhaps significant in this context, for he placed a majority, 2,825,000 people, in families whose income averaged £10 per year, compared with the 2,675,000 where family income averaged £67, a group which included the 870,000 in the categories of small free-holders, farmers, artisans and tradesmen with under £50. Further, in the latter part of the century, for which we do have some estimates, upper-class saving appears to have been significant. Thus, over the whole century there is little reason to think that the home market in goods such as cloth, leather or metal products, would grow much faster than the 20–25 per cent by which population increased, par-ticularly as the growth in the variety of foodstuffs, both imported and home-grown, may have diverted some spending into the provision of a more varied diet.

The major growth in productive capacity occurred in industries where there was change in market tastes or technology. The obvious examples are cloth and coal. In the textile industry demand for the lighter New Draperies grew rapidly in the seventeenth century, largely at the expense of the producers of the older types of heavy cloths. This affected the traditional English industry in two ways. The old draperies, heavy broadcloths, frequently undyed, which had still formed 90 per cent of English cloth exports in the 1590s, continued their decline, and only the dyed varieties still kept a market of any size. The first 15 years of the seventeenth century were exceptional, with a revival in foreign trade after the end of the war with Spain, when even undyed broadcloths sold sufficiently to prevent unemployment in Wiltshire; but this phase was ended in 1614 by Alderman Cockayne's unsuccessful scheme to restrict textile exports to dyed cloth,[31] and by currency depreciation in Central and Eastern Europe in the 1620s which priced exports out of these markets.[32] By the 1630s, therefore, traditional exports had declined sufficiently to make all but the most conservative manufacturers look for new possibilities.

In Wiltshire the trend away from broadcloth, slow in the sixteenth century, grew as the proportion of coloureds increased, made initially from Spanish dyed wool and as techniques improved, dyed as cloth. Makers of coloureds such as Jeremy Pottecary were able to maintain their sales in the most depressed years of the 1620s, keeping men in employment as white broad-clothiers laid weavers off, and a reputation for high-quality medley cloths arose among men such as Benedict Webb of Kingswood, on the Gloucestershire edge of the main producing area. In the 1630s experiment became more frequent and mixtures appeared made from Spanish and English wools. Quality improved after the Civil War with the introduction of Dutch workers and techniques, and in the middle of the century the area's industry was in a far healthier state than had earlier seemed likely.[33]

The change had taken place earlier in Norfolk; the settlement of Dutch and Walloon weavers had revived the old industry of the area, and after 1600, apart from dornix cloths, its products were entirely based on immigrant styles. The 'Norwich stuffs' brought unprecedented activity, and in spite of problems of wool-supply the industry only came under any serious threat late in the century with the expansion of Devon serge and Lancashire fustian and cotton producers.[34] Suffolk was less fortunate. The production of New Draperies in Colchester

---

[31] A. Friis, *Alderman Cockayne's Project and the Cloth Trade*, 1927, 224 seq.
[32] B. E. Supple, *Commercial Crisis and Change in England, 1600–42*, 1959, 73 seq.
[33] G. D. Ramsay, *The Wiltshire Woollen Industry in the 16th and 17th Centuries*, 1943, *passim*; *V.C.H.*, Wilts., IV, 155–8.
[34] K. J. Allison, 'The Norfolk Worsted Industry in the 16th and 17th Centuries; II, The New Draperies', *Yorks. Bull. of Soc. and Econ. Research*, 13 (1961), 61–77.

and on the Essex border had developed after the arrival of the Dutch community, but in the mid-seventeenth century competition from Norwich reduced its prosperity and the major activity became the preparation of yarn for the Norfolk bay makers. The dyed broadcloths of Suffolk had, predictably, become less saleable, though they were still profitably made when Wiltshire undyed products were hard to sell: the Eastland Company kept a thriving trade to the Baltic until the second quarter of the seventeenth century.

Yorkshire presents a rather different problem. The area was traditionally one of second-grade products, and it suffered particularly in the second and third decades of the seventeenth century from the poor market in undyed cloths. Some weavers attempted to cut prices by reducing quality, but this brought the standard down to those of the native products of Central Europe where Yorkshire cloth had traditionally been sold. In the 1630s some improvement in quality seems to have taken place, but the problem of wool supply, in competition with the industries of Southern England, restricted an expansion which was temporarily halted by the severity of Civil War damage to Bradford and Halifax and by the effects of epidemics in 1644–5. The major growth of the West Riding industry hardly appears within the seventeenth century. Much of the market for lower and medium grades of cloth was acquired by the Lancashire industry, whose production of fustians and linen mixtures was increased late in the century by the arrival of Huguenot refugees, and, although production of bays modelled on Norwich stuffs began in the North Riding in the 1650s as a Poor Relief measure, development on a commercial scale only took place after the 1680s.[35]

An exceptional area was Devon. The traditional industry had made kerseys in relatively small quantities, but in the mid-seventeenth century it rapidly developed the manufacture of serges. These cloths used both long and short-staple wool, the long being shipped from Ireland, the short coming from Spain or from local suppliers. The industry grew up around Tiverton and Exeter, the more highly capitalised finishing being concentrated around the latter while the spinning and weaving stages took place in and around Tiverton on the traditional putting-out basis.[36]

The English textile industry as a whole is thought to have maintained its total output during the seventeenth century, although between 1660 and 1700 cloth's share of the value of all exports fell

---

[35] H. Heaton, *The Yorkshire Woollen and Worsted Industries*, 1965, 185 *seq.*, 266 *seq.*; A. P. Wadsworth and J. de L. Mann, *The Cotton Trade and Industrial Lancashire 1600–1780*, 1931, 4–25, 98–106.
[36] C. Wilson, 'Cloth Production and International Competition in the 17th Century', *Ec.H.R.*, 2nd ser., XIII (1960), 209–21.

from 75 per cent to under 50 per cent. As the total of England's exports was increasing over this period, the absolute volume of cloths may have been maintained, and, if there was a reduction, home sales of some finer varieties may have compensated. If the contribution made by textiles to national income changed little, some addition to the national capital may have come from internal changes. Firstly, textiles had perhaps the least fixed plant of any industry of the period. Circulating capital was infinitely more important, for a clothier's re-sources were made up of raw and semi-finished materials in the hands of out-workers, many of whom owned their own looms. The capital equipment of the industry was found in the finishing stages, which changed markedly in character during the century. Broadcloth had been heavily fulled, and water-operated fulling mills had represented the main capital investment. In the case of lighter cloths, the New Draperies, and their derivatives, far less fulling took place, and in many varieties there was no need for the raising and felting of the nap at all. On the other hand the proportion of dyed cloth increased, whether dyed as cloth or wool. Thus there was a reduction in capital employed in fulling, but a growing expenditure on dye vats. Perhaps more im-portant is the extent to which the textile industry provided employ-ment; it had been the claim of those favouring schemes for dyeing before export that much potential employment and profit was left to the Dutch finishing trades when broadcloth was shipped in the white. The dyed says and worsteds of the seventeenth century provided a clear gain both in employment and in terms of value added, for while, with broadcloth, fulling had accounted for five per cent of the selling price, dyeing could make up as much as 45 per cent of the value of New Drapery cloth.

There was one threat to this picture of modest gains in wealth and employment. In the seventeenth century increasing quantities of cotton cloths and calicoes entered the country from the east. These made some inroads into the home sales of the cheaper light materials, and in their printed forms acquired a considerable market, particularly after 1678, when imports of French silks and linens were prohibited. How-ever, efforts to perfect a printing method in England, although at first unsuccessful in producing acceptable colour-fastness, did give good results after 1690, when Gillet's patent process and Indian methods were increasingly used in the calico-printing works of Essex and Surrey.[37]

Significant change occurred in one other industry, coal-mining. This is apt to be obscured because no great developments took place in techniques of drainage or ventilation, which remained as restrictions

[37] P. J. Thomas, 'Calico Printing in England', *Eng.H.R.*, 39 (1924), 206–16.

on growth even with Savery's pumping experiments in the 1690s, and until the development of Newcomen's engines. But the industry clearly expanded rapidly during the seventeenth century, both in output and in capital employed. Between the 1550s and the 1690s total production increased fourteenfold and that of the Northumberland and Durham coalfield by more than twentyfold. Much of this occurred during the seventeenth century and made it necessary for mine-owners to operate on less accessible seams. Mainly responsible was the growth in the industrial use of coal; domestic consumption continued to rise steadily, particularly with the expansion of London, but the rate of increase in industrial coal consumption was many times greater; processes hitherto unsuited to coal, brewing, glass-making, brick-making and many others were modified under pressure of increasing wood-fuel costs. As diminishing returns set in, with the need to mine deeper and employ more capital, costs of fuel at the pit-head tended to rise. But the consumer was partly protected from these as mines were enabled to sell their product over greater distances by improved river navigation. The West Riding mines benefited from improvements to the Aire and Calder, and Tyne coal no longer enjoyed large sales into their hinterlands. The pits of the West Midlands gained from the improvement of the Stour, and thus the fuel costs of the metal trades of Birmingham and Wolverhampton tended to fall.[38]

In consequence, the industrial processes using coal were enabled to expand their output as falling fuel costs allowed lower prices. Notable was the glass industry, which, under Mansell's patent of 1615, became exclusively a user of coal. This development depended on closed crucibles to prevent gases from the coal affecting the colour of the molten glass. New glassworks, such as those of the Willoughbys near Nottingham, were set up to use coal, and the output of the industry, which had been increasing from the 1560s with the widening demand for window glass, continued to grow as glass bottles and containers became cheaper. Despite his non-industrial background, Mansell appears to have taken his patent rather more seriously than most monopolists of the time, and though the users of wood-fuel resented his position and persistently attacked his patent the development of glass as a common product in the seventeenth century owed something to his management.[39]

Improved coal supplies were of great significance to the metal trades.

[38] J. U. Nef, *The Rise of the British Coal Industry*, I, 191; Willan, *River Navigation . . .*, 135–6.

[39] E. S. Godfrey, *The Development of English Glassmaking, 1560–1640*, unpublished Ph.D. thesis, Chicago, 1957, 131–262; R. S. Smith, *The Willoughbys of Wollaton*, unpublished Ph.D. thesis, Nottingham, 1964, 338–46; W. H. Price, *The English Patents of Monopoly*, 1906, 73–9.

The secondary industries of Birmingham and Sheffield widened the range of processes where coal rather than wood could safely be used, and only specialities such as gun-making remained users of timber. In Birmingham and the Black Country these industries developed during the seventeenth century as the traditional metal-working villages increased their specialisation still further. In addition to making iron articles, the Birmingham trades expanded their use of brass and copper, particularly in the years between 1660 and 1700. For these the degree of skill was high and the weight of raw materials and finished products low, mitigating the problems of poor transport; after the Act of 1662 preventing the import of buttons, brass manufacturers developed under protection and diversified into numerous other ranges of small items, besides continuing their manufacture of cast brass and copper utensils.[40]

These products of the Midland crafts were widely sold; ironmongers such as Ambrose Crowley I and II had connections and outlets in London, and themselves took part in manufacture. Ambrose II had two forges near Stourbridge in the 1680s, he appears to have been making steel, and he entered a partnership for building an iron furnace in Glamorgan.[41] Their capital requirements were comparatively large; the ironmongers put work out to nailers and controlled circulating stocks which in the case of copper or steel were of considerable value. While the nailers were hand workers, the makers of cutlery and scythes needed water-powered grinding equipment, the suppliers of bar used slitting mills, and steel-makers operated cementation furnaces of the type patented by Elliott and Meysey in 1615. This pattern of capital equipment was repeated in Sheffield. Here the cutlery trades, previously regulated by the manorial court, founded the Cutlers' Company in 1624, and by the end of the seventeenth century the town had achieved a degree of specialisation with few parallels in the period, up to half the working population being employed in metal trades. The degree of mechanisation was high, for the town was well supplied with water-power to operate grinding wheels and tilt hammers, and its products ousted the competition not only of other northern knife-makers, particularly in York, but of London also. Here again, coal and transport provided advantages which cut costs and allowed penetration of wider markets; the local coal pits increased in number, and the improvement of the River Idle to Bawtry reduced the transport cost of Baltic steel imported through Hull.[42]

[40] W. H. B. Court, *The Rise of the Midland Industries*, 1938, 71; H. Hamilton, *The English Brass and Copper Industries*, 1926, 122–30.
[41] M. W. Flinn, *Men of Iron: The Crowleys in the Early Iron Industry*, 1962, 8–14.
[42] G. P. Jones, 'Early Industrial Development', *Sheffield and Its Region* (ed. D. L. Linton), 1956, 149–51.

A major industry where few alterations in technique occurred was ironmaking itself. The greatest change was in location, and the erection of new plant incorporating accumulated innovations increased the capital stock. In the sixteenth century the great majority of works had been situated in Sussex, and here the change from the bloomery to the blast furnace was virtually complete by 1600.[43] But in Glamorgan, the Forest of Dean, the West Midlands, South Yorkshire and the north-west, the iron market had not developed sufficiently to justify a complete change to the new processes. Indeed, in the north-west the old methods were still in use at the beginning of the Civil War and a new bloomery was put up in Eskdale, Cumberland, in 1623.[44] During the seventeenth century this pattern changed. The small Sussex works relied on streams inadequate for the lengthening periods for which seventeenth-century techniques allowed furnaces to keep in blast. There was a decline until the Civil War, when certain works were reopened, but the total fell again until, in the eighteenth century, only a handful were used. The Thames dockyards were the major customer for castings and without their demand the Weald industry would hardly have lasted as long as it did.[45] The Midland ironmakers found the markets for their products increasing throughout the seventeenth century and their capital investment in furnaces, forges and slitting mills, though not involving as many units as had sprouted in Sussex in the 1570s, created a greater capacity due to the larger size of plant. This brought problems of raw-material supply similar to those encountered in Sussex in the previous century, and in the 1650s there grew up large-scale partnerships covering wide resources of charcoal and complementary ranges or ores. In 1669 the capital of the Foley Partnership in the Stour Valley was £68,830, an amount comparable with the largest undertakings in coal-mining, and by 1692 the 'Ironworks in Partnership' in which the Foleys were involved controlled 14 works both there and in the Forest of Dean and had links with the 'Staffordshire ironworks' north of the Trent, which were in turn linked to a Derbyshire and Nottinghamshire group. The same approach appeared in Yorkshire, where the Spencer interest was a common feature, enabling furnaces to have guaranteed outlets to forges and thence to the slitting mills which provided rods for nailers.

[43] E. Straker, *Wealden Iron*, 1931, 60–68; H. R. Schubert, *A History of the British Iron and Steel Industry to 1775*, 1957, 175 *seq.*
[44] Excavated by Dr R. F. Tylecote, 1967; report forthcoming. A. Raistrick and E. Allen, 'The South Yorkshire Ironmasters, 1690–1750', *Ec.H.R.*, IX (1938–9), 170; C. M. L. Bouch and G. P. Jones, *The Lake Counties*, 1961, 129–30.
[45] W. K. Jordan, 'Social Institutions in Kent, 1480–1660', *Archaeologia Cantiana*, LXXV (1961), 2–3; D. C. Coleman, 'Naval Dockyards under the Later Stuarts', *Ec.H.R.*, 2nd ser., VI (1953), 134–55, esp. 147.

The important point was that the linked interests of partners enabled the works to have a more predictable supply of charcoal; for only widespread supplies and careful coppicing could guarantee the quantities which late seventeenth-century furnaces required.[46] The problems of management are explained by the growth in furnace capacity; detailed development of design raised average annual pig outputs from 200 to 750 tons per furnace over the century, and hearth-life from 20 to 60 weeks. Mineral fuel, strong enough to bear the weight of a large charge, could further have increased the size of furnaces, but the first large-scale use of coke in the furnace was not to come until 1709, when Abraham Darby successfully used it at Coalbrookdale.[47] But in the light of the general increase in scientific and technological enquiry in the seventeenth century it is worth noting that the experiments of Dudley beginning in the 1620s may have been more practical than some critics have suggested. Even if he did not use coke for smelting on a commercial scale, his correct identification of some of the problems crucial to the adoption of mineral fuel urge that his attempts be taken as seriously as those of Savery with steam power in the 1690s.[48] Even without coke during the seventeenth century the industry appears to have achieved a growth in production of 30–60 per cent, an increase probably reached with a 60 per cent reduction in the number of furnaces.[49]

In the non-ferrous metal industries, coal was used in improved reverberatory furnaces and was particularly important in reducing costs in tin-smelting. Celia Fiennes saw the Cornish coal-fired furnaces at the end of the century, reducing costs which had been rising as mining in Cornwall concentrated on the deep deposits of the west.[50] Lead production also increased, with the ability to smelt greater quantities at lower costs with new furnaces. Late in the seventeenth century deeper mines were sunk in Derbyshire and long soughs were dug for drainage; in 1688 Cromford sough cost £30,000, while Durham and Cumberland lead deposits attracted renewed attention for their silver content.[51] Despite the demand for brass wares and the develop-

[46] B. L. C. Johnson, 'The Foley Partnership', *Ec.H.R.*, 2nd ser., IV (1952), 322–4; A. Raistrick, 'The South Yorkshire Iron Industry, 1690–1756', *Trans. Newcomen Soc.*, 19 (1938), 51–86; B. G. Awty, 'Charcoal Ironmasters of Cheshire and Lancashire', *Trans. Hist. Soc. of Lancashire and Cheshire*, 109 (1957), 71–124.
[47] A. Raistrick, *Dynasty of Ironfounders: The Darbys of Coalbrookdale*, 1953, 37–8.
[48] G. R. Morton, 'The Early Coke Era', *Bull. Hist. Metallurgy Group*, VI (1966), 49–59.
[49] M. W. Flinn, 'The Growth of the English Iron Industry, 1660–1760', *Ec.H.R.*, 2nd ser., XI (1958–9), 144–53.
[50] E. Griffiths (ed.), *The Diary of Celia Fiennes*, 1888 edn, 218; cf. G. R. Lewis, *The Stannaries*, 1907, 24–5.
[51] A. Raistrick and B. Jennings, *A History of Lead Mining in the Pennines*,

ment of brass working in the Midlands, copper-mining was largely neglected before 1690. Little had been done between 1600 and 1640 by the Mines Royal and the Mineral and Battery Company to increase the supply of home-produced copper and brass, and at the time of the Civil War only Welsh copper was being mined. Swedish copper and German brass sheet and wire were imported in large quantities before the passing in 1689 of the Mines Royal Act, which was intended to encourage home production unfettered by Crown claims on copper as a precious metal. The result was the foundation of six copper mining companies within the next decade—although the development of new smelting furnaces at this time was probably as influential as legislation, particularly as the Crown still had a right of preemption of copper. Even so, the suspicion that imported copper and brass were of higher quality and the comparatively small requirements of the brass-workers restricted the annual output of mines to about 160 tons in 1697.[52]

The experience of these industries suggests that in the seventeenth century significant technical developments took place only in the last decades, apart perhaps from the change in textiles to New Draperies. The old industries, many of whose innovations dated from the sixteenth century, increased in scale; coal to the limits of pumping technology, iron to the greatest size of furnaces charcoal would allow, and textiles with more out-workers using traditional equipment. In each case there were factors limiting further growth, and it is only late in the century that enquiry into innovation really appears.[53] Up to this point our calculation of industrial wealth means counting cloths, mines, furnaces and, most of all, heads. But after the Restoration we begin to see a fresh factor. The development of experimental science, particularly under the auspices of the Royal Society, brought experiments in physics; typical of these were schemes for pumping, using the effect of atmospheric pressure on a vacuum and leading to the inventions of Savery and Newcomen. But even with increasing interest in astronomy which encouraged the developing skills of the clock- and instrument-makers, precision in early engineering practice was limited, and it took much of the eighteenth century before engineers approached clock-makers' standards of accuracy.[54] But we do find late in the seven-

1965, 71–2, 116–18; J. D. Chambers, *The Vale of Trent, 1679–1800*, Ec.H.R. Supplement no. 3 (n.d.), 6–8; W. R. Scott, *The Constitution and Finance of English, Scottish and Irish Joint Stock Companies to 1720*, II (1910), 440–2.
[52] Scott, II, 430–6; Hamilton, 56–64, 101–8; C. Singer et al., *A History of Technology*, 1957, III, 80.
[53] D. C. Coleman, 'Technology and Economic History, 1500–1750', *Ec.H.R.*, 2nd ser., XI (1958–9), 506–14.
[54] W. H. Dickenson, *A Short History of the Steam Engine*, 1938, 1–53; Singer et al., II, 629–74; IV, 168–75.

teenth century a greater willingness to seek to reduce costs, not only by keeping wages low but also by introducing new equipment—the reverberatory furnaces for non-ferrous metals, Dutch ribbon looms for Manchester small-wares—improved methods for the making of white paper, and, perhaps of greatest importance, a more serious study of dyeing. Immigrants had considerable effect; the finer types of linens, paper, instruments and glass all owed much to foreigners (in particular to Huguenots) for improved standards of quality which had an important influence on the industrial wealth of the period.[55]

New skills in labour-intensive crafts and the increasing proportion of industry devoted to secondary manufacture meant increased employment for what contemporaries regarded as the least utilised of England's resources, her labour-force. But real wages are a limited guide to this; the Phelps Brown and Hopkins index of real wages of building workers, calculated in terms of provisions, indeed shows a modest rise between 1600 and 1700, steepening slightly later in the century. This could support a rise in industrial demand for labour, but it is complicated both by the levelling in population after 1650 and by the end of the rise in prices. In fact money wages rose only slightly over the century, reflecting the well-publicised view that wage-costs had to be held down to maintain the competitiveness of industrial products.[56] The standard of living of industrial workers was still largely dependent on their means for supplementation of wages: as in the sixteenth century, those in rural industry with access to smallholdings or commons were in a stronger position than those in towns, who were often forced to spend long periods as journeymen in master craftsmen's households before opportunities appeared for independence. For the city labourer the position was still worse, and the degree of squalor in the suburbs east and north-east of London commented upon by Stow at the beginning of the century was if anything worse by 1700.

The new pattern of trading

At the end of the seventeenth century observers thought of foreign trade as the buoyant feature of England's economy, contributing more to the increase in national income in the interval between the observations of Petty and Gregory King than any other sector. Davenant and King saw capital being ploughed back into trade rather than leaving the City for land-purchase in that circuit of wealth so typical of the sixteenth century. What they also saw was a trade pattern which was

[55] D. C. Coleman, *The British Paper Industry, 1495–1860*, 1959, 54–80.
[56] E. H. Phelps Brown and S. V. Hopkins, 'Seven Centuries of Building Wages', *Economica*, N.S. 22 (1955), 195–206; 'Seven Centuries of the Prices of Consumables Compared with Builders' Wage-Rates', *ibid.*, N.S. 23 (1956), 296–314.

far less vulnerable, relying less on concentrated markets for narrow ranges of goods, and capable of weathering depressions in particular outlets. The optimism with which English trade was viewed in the 1690s contrasts strikingly with a century earlier. For the later mercantilists trade was the key to the 'improvement' of the whole economy, providing employment for underutilised labour and natural resources, increasing capital and giving the incentive for the development of the infrastructure of credit, shipping and inventiveness. The early seventeenth century took a far more defensive attitude, and Mun's predecessors thought less in terms of progress through trade than the risks of degeneration without it. The fears were of a weak navy, should the merchant marine and fishing fleets not provide training for seamen, or of problems in war finance if unfavourable trade-balances depleted the stock of bullion.

Development in English trade in the seventeenth century involved changes in commodities, markets and methods. Dependence changed from a limited range of textiles to a wide range of manufactures and reexported colonial primary products; trade developed from the narrow hinterland of the Northern European seaboard first to the Mediterranean, later to Africa, Asia and the Atlantic; from undercapitalised individual ventures under the aegis of restrictive regulated companies to the activities of such bodies as the East India Company, which in 1700 had a capital of £4 million, compared with the £68,373 of its first voyage in 1601.[57] The change is seen most clearly in figures for the total value of trade. Whereas in the 1660s the value of exports amounted to £4·1 million and imports £4·4 million, by 1696 exports had risen to £6·36 million and imports, less rapidly, to £4·75 million.[58]

The trade pattern in the first 30 years of the seventeenth century goes far to explain any pessimism in the outlook of men such as Misselden or Malynes. The Indian Summer of the decade after the end of the Spanish war in 1604 was little less precariously based than the textile booms of the 1540s, for, although the Mediterranean trades had expanded, over three-quarters of the broadcloths on which the prosperous trade of James I's reign was based went to the traditional Central European markets, and any stoppage comparable with that of the mid-1580s would have had scarcely less serious an effect. As we have seen, the contraction came not only from problems abroad but from the damage done by Cockayne's scheme, which by threatening

[57] R. W. K. Hinton, 'The Mercantile System in the Time of Mun', Ec.H.R., 2nd ser., VII (1954–5), 277–90; F. J. Fisher, 'The Dark Ages in English Economic History?', Economica, 24 (1957), 2–18; K. N. Chaudhuri, The English East India Company, 1965, 209.
[58] C. H. Wilson, 'Treasure and Trade Balances', Ec.H.R., 2nd ser., II (1949), 152–61.

the Netherlands' finishing industry brought an embargo on English cloth exports to the Low Countries. In the depression of the 1620s a new factor appeared; currency-manipulation in Germany and Poland priced English cloth out of the market, and the reduction of purchasing power and the uncertainty of communications in the early years of the Thirty Years' War threatened trade still further. The only expanding area at this period was the Mediterranean, where in particular the Levant Company maintained its sales and cut into the markets of the Venetian traders. Tin and lead, dyed broadcloths, and kerseys found ready sales; these textiles, together with the English-produced New Draperies which tended to replace them from the 1630s, increased the traffic both of the Levant Company in the Eastern Mediterranean and of the traders with Spain and Italy, who brought in return the traditional ranges of Eastern goods among which silk was particularly prominent, trebling in quantity between 1621 and 1669.[59] It was into this longer-range trading that mercantile capital was attracted during the reign of Charles I. The second and third decades of the century showed that little improvement could be expected in sales to Europe and that attempts to reduce prices by sacrificing quality were self-defeating. Hence investors looked more to Levantine and Spanish routes, although the main interest in the Indian trade was yet to come. The early ventures to the East Indies in the first quarter of the century had been of limited success, for the Dutch, first on the scene, were better equipped and backed by greater resources, and forced English merchants to concentrate on the Arabian Sea trade. The East India Company did not attract sufficient capital in this period; terminable stocks failed to give Company policy the continuity it needed to match competitors' forts and shipping, and the trade only developed on a really large scale after the reaffirmation of the Charter in 1657.[60]

The character of the trades was also changing. Capital was attracted not only into conventional exporting, but to the business of importing new primary products and reexporting, largely to Europe. This had grown out of the early seventeenth-century interest in American colonial projects, and initial disappointment at the lack of conventionally valuable raw materials disappeared as demand for tobacco and sugar increased. By 1640 reexports equalled in value all English exports of non-textile manufactures, and growth continued over the century. In 1615 50,000 lbs of sugar were imported; in 1663-9 the figure averaged 14·8 million lbs and in 1699-1701 37·1 million lbs, while in the latter years home consumption was only one-third of this

[59] R. Davis, 'England and the Mediterranean', *Essays on the Economic History of Tudor and Stuart England* (ed. F. J. Fisher), 1961, 117-37.
[60] G. D. Ramsay, *English Overseas Trade in the Centuries of Emergence*, 1957, 63-95.

total. In the 1650s four-fifths of the pepper brought to Europe by English merchants was sold on the Continent, and in 1700 two-thirds of English calico imports were reexported.[61]

It was seen in the middle of the century that this entrepôt trade did little to stimulate English industrial skills; except for a proportion of sugar, goods were reexported without processing, and other maritime nations were as capable as England of doing this. Thus preoccupation with Dutch naval power had a real basis, and the Navigation Acts were their obvious result. The Dutch, indeed, demonstrated the inadequacies of English naval resources on repeated occasions. The failure of the fishery project in the 1630s to present any challenge to Dutch supremacy in the North Sea herring grounds meant that a large source of overseas earnings was lost. The problems of the East India Company illustrated the willingness of the Dutch to invest to a higher extent in oceanic trading. The ability of the Dutch to undercut rivals in the Baltic trade suggested that English shipping costs were high, and the ability to negotiate the lump-sum toll agreement with Denmark in 1648 showed how English shipping could be hindered by lack of diplomatic assistance to trade. The Navigation Acts were the result of the frustrations which these problems aroused, and the balance of their long-term effects is particularly hard to measure. The war of 1664–7 was a particular set-back to England; its cost both to the Exchequer and in terms of disruption to trade was high. The restrictions on direct colonial trading with Europe benefited English trade in the medium term, but probably held back colonial development of resources. English shipping did in fact challenge Dutch power in the latter part of the century; this may have been partly because of the number of vessels captured in the First Dutch War, but English owners purchasing Dutch vessels in the 1660s still demonstrated the Netherlands yards' skill in building ships suitable for the nearer trades. The next change came later in the century, as the balance of activity shifted further towards oceanic trading and the products of English shipyards became more suitable than those of the Dutch for the carriage of tobacco and timber from America. It is a measure of the eventual decline in the Dutch merchant marine that while fewer English merchant ships were built after 1689 English traders could maintain their superiority in the Atlantic during the reign of Anne.[62]

The most striking feature of English trading in the second half of the century was the greatly increased interest shown by the business community, expressed by reinvestment of profits in further ventures

[61] R. Davis, 'English Overseas Trade, 1660–1760', *Ec.H.R.*, 2nd ser., VII (1954), 150–60.
[62] C. H. Wilson, *Profit and Power*, 1957, 143 *seq.*

rather than in land. This did much to solve the chronic undercapitalisation which had hindered trade earlier in the century. Examples of the resilience of the trading community may be seen in the decades after 1660; the damage caused by the Great Fire of London in 1666, reckoned at £10 million, was rapidly made good; in 1671 the issue of the Royal Africa Company, though one third of it was earmarked to buy out its unsuccessful predecessor, was 11 per cent oversubscribed after one month; and, in 1677, the same company had no difficulty in reducing rates on its bonds from six per cent to five per cent. These examples suggest an ability to weather periods of trading depression, and the start of war in 1689, the poor harvests of the 1690s and a depreciating currency had few of the consequences of earlier crises. The trade pattern as a whole was more broadly based, and its capital was drawn from a wider field, even though the insecurity of stocks led the smaller investor to confine himself to bonds.[63]

This interest in trade was no longer confined to London. The differential growth in favour of the capital's trade seen since the end of the Middle Ages slackened in the mid-seventeenth century, and while London still grew in absolute terms, by 1700 others were enjoying a prosperity unheard of in the sixteenth century. Exeter grew to be the third largest English port, and other west coast towns, Bristol, Liverpool and Whitehaven, benefited from activity in the Atlantic. Bristol had declined in the sixteenth century as its traditional carrying trades were captured by Dutch and Scottish shipping, the textile industries of its hinterland had turned to the market facilities of London, and the Icelandic trade was barred. From the 1620s onwards, Bristol shipowners found the American tobacco trade and Newfoundland codfishing increasingly profitable and triangular operations developed between North America, Europe and Bristol. The port's potential was shown by its rapid recovery from Civil War damage, aided in particular by the revival of trade with Portugal, the growth of sugar-refining in the 1650s, and the quantity of Midlands manufactures exported to the American colonies. The development of Liverpool was similarly based on the Atlantic trade, together with the addition of Chester's coasting trade after the silting of the Dee and the increasing exports of Cheshire rock-salt shipped down the improved River Weaver. The result was an improvement in port facilities which came at the time of the early growth of Lancashire cotton cloth production, much of which came to be shipped to the West Indies in return for tobacco and sugar.[64]

[63] Davis, 'English Overseas Trade...', 161.
[64] Ramsay, *English Overseas Trade*, 141–62.

The new pattern of investment

The investigations of the Inspectors General of Imports and Exports, beginning in 1696, confirm the impression of Davenant and Gregory King that foreign trade had come to be the fastest-expanding source of wealth. This buoyancy of trade throws a good deal of light on the impression we have gained of a reduction of investment in agriculture late in the seventeenth century, a process of declining profitability of land which diverted capital to trade and, in a vicious circle, starved the improvement of agriculture. Where industry stands is less simple to judge. It is clear that writers such as Child, Fortrey and Dudley North, while encouraging investment in overseas trade, saw that there remained potential in the development of national resources. But the speed of innovation in industry was insufficiently great to attract capital on a comparable scale. The major means of holding down costs was still to keep wages low—hence the preoccupation with avoiding wasteful underemployment or wages high enough to raise production costs.[65] However, this weighting of investment towards overseas trade achieved a valuable basic infrastructure of institutions and experience. Routes and depots were established, the reputation of products was built up abroad, and many of the foundations of the great eighteenth century expansion of trade were laid down. The addition to the national wealth lay in this invisible but vital network.

Even so, as late as the 1690s it was abundantly clear that foreign and domestic trade were still being hindered not only by shortage of capital but also by imperfections in its application. The need for capital clearly grew: in the distant trades goods were in transit for longer periods and expenditure on ships and fixed installations abroad increased; the East India Company, for instance, required forts in India, and the Levant Company's shipping had to withstand the Barbary Corsairs and their successors.[66] The total tonnage of English shipping increased over the century, from 115,000 tons in 1629 to 200,000 tons in 1660, and to 340,000 tons by 1686, and the capital invested in shipbuilding grew also with the need for more complex vessels.[67] The growth in companies' capital is clear; in 1660 the East India Company had a paid-up total of under £400,000, while in 1703 the East India trade, now divided into Old and New Companies, had a total of £4 million. Overall, the estimates of national capital of the time give a similar impression, with a growth of £70 million between

---

[65] D. C. Coleman, 'Labour in the English Economy of the 17th Century', *Ec.H.R.*, 2nd ser., VIII (1956); C. H. Wilson, 'The Other Face of Mercantilism', *Trans. Roy. Hist. Soc.*, 5th ser., IX (1959), 81–101.

[66] Ramsay, *English Overseas Trade* . . . , 54–59.

[67] R. Davis, *The Rise of the English Shipping Industry*, 1962, 27.

the 1660s and 1688, much of which was involved in trade.[68] Industry also needed funds. The financing of lead-mine drainage in Derbyshire, of coal-mining, of increasing circulating stocks in the new textile areas, Devon and Lancashire, and new industrial investment in paper and copper-smelting, brought new provincial needs for capital, a problem altogether more difficult than its provision in London.[69]

There is no doubt that by the third quarter of the seventeenth century the willingness to invest was growing. Earlier it had been less clear; interest rates had been high[70] and much available capital had either gone into land in the uncertain trading conditions before the Civil War or had been drawn off in the form of loans to the Crown. Later, however, the sources of funds widened, not only through ownership of shares but also through fixed-interest bonds, which had a comparatively wide following.[71] This expansion was particularly apparent in the 1690s, when the collapse following the recoinage of 1696 showed how many stock-jobbers and brokers had entered the market. Investment in foreign ventures had reached boom proportions in the early 1690s, and many of the more gullible had been hurt by promoters of bogus companies.[72] No organised stock-exchange in any way comparable to the Amsterdam Bourse had developed, and it required the Act of 1697 restricting the number of brokers to 100 to impart an air of respectability to their dealings. Thus it is hard to speak of a formal money market in London until late in the century, but experience in the provision of loans had developed much earlier with the needs of the Crown. London loans had been nothing new in 1600, although the Crown's reputation as a borrower had not been high during the reign of Elizabeth and the City's concern during the reigns of James I and Charles I lay in establishing some assurance that Crown debts would cease to be bad ones. Increasingly, loans were secured by future revenues, and in the 1630s farmers of customs and other revenues relied on future years' income to repay loans from the City which they took up to meet Crown needs.[73] As the inducements offered by the Crown grew with the severity of its financial problems, there seems to have been some attraction of funds which might otherwise have

[68] Scott, I, 315–16.
[69] G. D. Ramsay, 'Industrial Laissez-Faire and the Policy of Cromwell', *Ec.H.R.*, XVI (1946), 93–110; J. K. Horsefield, *British Monetary Experiments, 1650–1710*, 1960, 237–40.
[70] F. J. Fisher, 'Tawney's Century', *Essays* . . . (ed. F. J. Fisher), 1–14.
[71] K. G. Davies, 'Joint Stock Investment in the Late 17th Century', *Ec.H.R.*, 2nd ser., IV (1952), 283–301.
[72] Scott, I, 357–60.
[73] R. Ashton, 'Deficit Finance in the Reign of James I', *Ec.H.R.*, 2nd ser., X (1957), 15–29; 'Revenue Farming under the Early Stuarts', *Ec.H.R.*, 2nd ser., VIII (1956), 310–22.

been used for mercantile and industrial purposes.[74] After the Restoration, however, in the climate of confidence inspired by the new trade-routes mercantile investment became more attractive, although funds deposited with bankers were still advanced to the Crown in anticipation both of hereditary revenues and extraordinary grants. This was the pattern of the early 1660s, and was adequate for Crown needs as long as home expenditure was kept under control. But the Second Dutch War and the Fire of London raised Crown expenditure and temporarily reduced the supply of loans, a position from which the Exchequer could not extricate himself before 1672, when repayments of loans to lenders had to be stopped. The result was both a further swing of preference towards mercantile investment and a setback to the growth of banking houses, with the bankruptcies following the Stop of 1672.

The vicissitudes of dealing with the Crown necessarily affected the emergence of a private banking system, for London finance houses were frequently involved in both kinds of business. Here perhaps lay one of the most serious restrictions on economic expansion in the seventeenth century, and the failure of liquid credit facilities to grow at the rate of foreign trade was a problem of which contemporaries were well aware.[75] Banking had grown up in the hands of three groups: the billbrokers were largely concerned with bills of exchange and, although their activities led to an increasing transferability of bills, they contributed least to the development of general private deposit banking; the scriveners, who specialised in land transfers and mortgages, spread in numerous cases into the taking of deposits and the making of loans on the security of land; the goldsmiths (perhaps most important of all), though particularly concerned with Crown loans, were in an obvious position to accept private deposits of temporarily unwanted cash. Both the latter groups were recognised by seventeenth-century opinion as having a banking function, making loans at interest, and were still the object of attacks over the practice of usury.[76] Their skills and facilities developed with their increasing use of the accounting systems encouraged by the circulation of the textbooks of the sixteenth and seventeenth centuries,[77] and their provision of credit instruments of high liquidity, though not expanding as rapidly as trade

---

[74] R. Ashton, 'Charles I and the City', *Essays in the Economic and Social History of Tudor and Stuart England* (ed. F. J. Fisher), 1961, 138–63; Scott, I, 213 *seq.*

[75] D. C. Coleman, 'Sir John Banks, Financier; An Essay on Government Borrowing under the Later Stuarts', *Essays . . .* (ed. F. J. Fisher), 1961, 204–30.

[76] R. D. Richards, 'Early English Banking Systems', *Jnl Econ. and Bus. Hist.,* I (1928), 36–7.

[77] B. S. Yamey, H. C. Edey and H. W. Thomson, *Accounting in England and Scotland, 1543–1800,* 1963, 167.

required, was an important contribution to the economy. But there remained major problems in transferring funds. Bills of Exchange were fairly common in inland business by 1650, but their transferability was not fully recognised by Common Law, as a buyer could not claim a better title than the seller, and until 1710 the legal fiction survived that the holder of a bill was the 'agent' of the payee. Other instruments were 'informal' promissory notes, whose legal validity was also in doubt, and cheques, whose status was equivalent to that of Bills of Exchange. However, by the 1680s cheques were in common use, drawing on 'running cashes', accounts held with goldsmiths.[78]

Provincial banking was more slow to develop, and its absence perhaps left the Londoner in ignorance of the field for industrial investment. With the expansion of the western ports industrial areas became less dependent upon London as their outlet and found themselves lacking facilities. Apart from the exceptional Thomas Smith of Nottingham, provincial specialists were largely absent before 1700 and their place was taken by merchants in the longer-distance trades, particularly in wool and grain, some of whom were to become the country bankers of the eighteenth century.

Conclusion

These impressions of change in agriculture and industry and in particular in the direction and infrastructure of trade compare well with the estimates and opinions of Petty (1664–5), and Davenant and King (1688). The figures of Petty and King for national income and wealth, while not strictly comparable, do indicate the major trends:

Income	1664–5 (Petty)	1688 (King)	Wealth	1664–5	1688
Real property £m	8	13		210	234
Labour	32	30·5			
Personal property				40	86
	40	43·5		250	320[79]

It is difficult to break these figures down to show changes in particular sectors, but from all we have seen it is hard to escape the conclusion that foreign trade was to a large extent responsible for the 28 per cent increase in national capital. It also brought a considerable part of the increase in national income, and Davenant considered that

[78] Coleman, 'Sir John Banks . . .', 208–9.
[79] Scott, I, 315–16.

savings from this were as high as £2·4 million per annum, auguring well for investment in future expansion.

As for the income figures, whether there was a slight increase in the earnings of labour must depend on their reliability, but there was clearly no increase comparable with that from property. The index of builders' money wages does in fact suggest a slight decrease, disguising a rather greater one in real terms. But income from real property rose significantly, and, despite the suggested high level of savings, spending on personal goods and property also showed a remarkable growth. It is clear that there was rising upper-class purchasing-power for the increasing range of imported wares, and it is likely that it was mercantile rather than landed groups in whose hands this increasingly lay.

It is, however, advisable to make one proviso when discussing this apparent increase in wealth over the third quarter of the century; there must be some caution over how far figures for wealth in the early 1660s were affected not only by the Civil War, but by the war with Spain and the trade depression of the later 1650s. It has been shown that the economy was capable of a very high level of activity by 1666, the year of the Great Fire, but 1660–4 should perhaps be regarded as a period of reconstruction after a decade of considerable disquiet in both Government and City circles over the cost of war and the prospects for trade. Thus the contrast between 1664 and 1688 may slightly exaggerate the longer-term rate of growth.

But there can be no doubt that by the final quarter of the seventeenth century the economy was in an excellent position to continue the development of a structure of agriculture and trade equal to the demands and opportunities to be presented by the rising population of the mid-eighteenth century.

Chapter five

The Years of Commercial Supremacy, 1689–1760

The England of Gregory King

At the time of the Glorious Revolution, England was not yet certain of having overcome the Dutch dominance of European trade, and appeared to be economically much weaker than France; 70 years later, Great Britain was secure in her commercial supremacy in Europe. The outward signs of this rise were the expansion of the colonial empire, the size of the trading fleet, and the wealth of the mercantile classes. Indeed, perhaps the outstanding characteristic of this era is the rising importance of commercial fortunes. But behind this growth of commerce stood the expansion of agriculture, and the beginning of a transformation of industry.

We are fortunate in possessing a most useful set of estimates of the wealth of England at the outset of this period, compiled by Gregory King.[1] Although in minor matters King's views have to be treated with caution—e.g. his assumption of a decline in incomes between 1688 and 1695 hardly seems credible[2]—it is nevertheless recognised today that on the whole his figures were firmly based on much reliable evidence used intelligently.[3] According to King, the total population of England and Wales in 1695 amounted to 5·5 million, and total personal incomes in 1688, to £43·5 million, or £7.18.0 per head; when

---

[1] King's tabulations were not fully published in his lifetime, and first received wide currency when they were included as an appendix in George Chalmers' *Estimate of the Comparative Strength of Great Britain* in 1802. A recent version was edited by George E. Barnett as *Gregory King, Two Tracts*, Baltimore, 1936, and the basic tables have been reprinted many times since, e.g. in G. N. Clark, *The Wealth of England from 1496 to 1760*, Oxford, 1946, 192–3, and G. M. Trevelyan, *English Social History*, 3rd edn, 1946, 277.

[2] Chalmers, *Estimate*, 1794 ed., 76.

[3] P. E. Jones and A. V. Judges, 'London Population in the Late Seventeenth Century', *Ec.H.R.*, VI (1935), 56. Also, Phyllis Deane, 'The Implications of Early National Income Estimates for the Measurement of Long Term Economic Growth in the United Kingdom', *Economic Development and Cultural Change*, V (1955), 5 *seq.*; D. V. Glass, 'Gregory King's Estimate of the Population of England and Wales, 1695', *Population Studies*, III (1950), and 'Two Papers on Gregory King' and 'Population and Population Movements in England and Wales, 1700–1850' in D. V. Glass and D. E. C. Eversley, *Population in History*, 1965, 221 *seq.*

recalculated to meet modern conventions, incomes should be set at £48·6 million, or about £8.14.0. per head. By themselves, such figures may not convey a great deal, but the detailed breakdown into classes, families and income groups, which is carried through with a remarkable degree of internal consistency, allows us to draw certain other conclusions about social structure in England around 1690. King's tables present an income pyramid of an extremely wide base, and a very narrow apex.

Number of families, by occupation, in 1688

Landowners	16,560	1·2%
Professions, including Clergy	46,026	3·4
Merchants, shopkeepers	50,000	3·7
Artisans and handicrafts	60,000	4·4
Farmers, freeholders	330,000	24·3
Labouring people and out-servants	364,000	26·8
Cottagers, paupers	500,000	29·4
Armed services	94,000	6·9
	1,360,586	100·1

The disparity is even greater than might appear at first sight, for while in the top two categories only one person, at most, was gainfully 'employed', it must be assumed that among all the lower orders much more than one person per family, on average, was actually at work. Even if we also include among the comfortably-off and educated class the overseas merchants and army and navy officers, they still formed a thin veneer of only six per cent of families, and considerably less in terms of occupied population. The 'landowners', comprising 1·2 per cent of the families, had an income exceeding that of the 'labouring people', forming over one quarter of the population; and the top two classes, with an income of nearly £10·3 million, or nearly 24 per cent of the total, greatly exceeded the lowest two orders, who formed over 51 per cent of the population, but received only 17 per cent of the total. Every single family of a 'temporal lord' had *on average* an income equivalent to that of 70 artisans' families, 187 labourers' families, or 431 'cottagers'' and 'pauper' families. Secondly, the bulk of the population still obtained its income from the land. Unfortunately, no exact figure can be derived from King's tables, but a reasonable estimate for the proportion of income arising in agriculture would appear to be about £24·2 million or 56 per cent.[4] The importance of landed wealth is also shown by the fact that, while peers averaged an income of £2,800 and mere 'esquires' still averaged £450, even the 'eminent merchants and traders by sea' averaged only £400, and lesser merchants and traders by sea £200, a good deal less than the undifferentiated 'gentlemen' at £280.[5]

Finally, it is evident that much of English wealth is still spent on personal service. With the average family put at just over four souls, the two lowest classes appear to have one person per family away on service, to allow peers to amass total average households of 40, bishops 20, and even 'gentlemen', 'persons in greater offices and places', and 'eminent merchants', an average of eight. The total servant population is given as 13 per cent in London, 11 per cent in other towns and 10 per cent in the countryside.

The effects of the new husbandry

Agriculture still being the main occupation and source of income of the people, the outstanding fact of the next 70 years or so was the ability of the food-producing section of the economy to keep its volume of output ahead of the population increase, while employing a decreasing share of the population and of national resources in general. The importance of this favourable development, which had begun around 1640 and had become increasingly evident before 1689, on an economy of the type of the English in the eighteenth century, need hardly be stressed.[6] It was made possible by the fact that, while population continued to increase only slowly, husbandry improved

[4] Derived as follows (in £000)

Landowners	5,622
Freeholders, Farmers	16,960
Cottagers and Paupers	2,000
37% of 'Labouring People, etc'	2,020
50% of Clergy	257
	£26,859

Less incomes from urban and mining rents and urban paupers. Compensated in part by the agricultural produce of industrialists	2,500
	£24,359

Dean and Cole, *British Economic Growth, 1688–1959*, Cambridge, 1962, 156, table 35 and note 1, giving only £19·3 million, or 40 per cent, are quite unrealistic, as they have omitted 'hemp, flax, woad' etc. (valued at £1 million), fruit, green vegetables, etc. See also Deane, 'Implications', 9.

[5] According to Mathias, there are errors in the printed versions, and esquires' average incomes should be £400 only, and gentlemen's £240: 'The Social Structure in Eighteenth-Century Society', *Ec.H.R.*, X (1957), 32, note.

[6] E. G. John, C. H. Fei, and Gustav Rahis, *Development of the Labour Surplus Economy*, Homewood, III, 1964.

more rapidly, gradually increasing both output per acre (partly by cultivating previously waste land) and output per man.

The population of England and Wales, put at 5·5 million by Gregory King, is estimated by modern statisticians to have been around 5·8–5·9 million at the turn of the century. After a further slow rise, it fluctuated about the six million mark for 20 years, c.1720–40, and then continued its upward trend for another 10 to 15 years, reaching perhaps 6·6 million by 1760. The average annual growth of 5–8,000 in the first half of the century (compared with 60,000 a year after 1760),[7] though sustained for a long period, was no faster than has been recorded in earlier centuries and among other traditional societies. There was little sign yet, before 1760, of the population explosion generally associated with industrialisation, and it seems likely that the irregular upward curve was the result of the traditional interplay of birth- and death-rates[8] in a primitive society rather than a spectacular rise in nutrition, comfort, or medical skill. There were, indeed, good schools of medicine arising, as in Edinburgh, and hospitals were built for the first time in large numbers in this period; but medical practice was still partly based on superstition and was as likely to harm as to benefit the patient, while hospitals certainly increased the risks of death severalfold.[9] It was only the end of bubonic plague and the curtailment of smallpox by inoculation, as well as of scurvy, that made any substantial difference to death-rates.[10] London, in its gin-drinking phase c. 1720–50, killed off not only its own citizens, but many of those born in the provinces and sucked into the vortex of the capital; its high death-rate contributed to the slowing-down of growth before 1750, as its sharp improvement helped the faster growth later.[11] Scotland, with perhaps 1·3 million in 1760, had grown as fast as England; Ireland, with about 3·3 million, grew significantly and dangerously faster.[12]

In Great Britain, at least, the production of the staple foodstuffs more than kept pace with this slow population growth. Wheat prices were low and were falling; all classes fed better, and grain exports

[7] A. H. John, 'Aspects of English Economic Growth in the First Half of the Eighteenth Century', reprinted in Carus-Wilson (ed.), *Essays in Economic History*, II (1962), 362.

[8] See the arguments of H. J. Habakkuk, 'English Population in the Eighteenth Century', *Ec.H.R.*, VI (1953) and G. S. L. Tucker, 'English Pre-Industrial Population Trends', *Ec.H.R.*, XVI (1963).

[9] T. McKeown and R. G. Brown, 'Medical Evidence Relating to English Population Changes in the Eighteenth Century', *Population Studies*, IX (1955).

[10] P. E. Razzell, 'Population Change in Eighteenth-Century England. A Reinterpretation', *Ec.H.R.*, XVIII (1965); C. Lloyd and J. L. S. Coulter, *Medicine and the Navy, 1714–1815*, III, 1961.

[11] Dorothy George, *London Life in the XVIIIth Century*, London, 1925, 26.

[12] K. H. Connell, *The Population of Ireland, 1750–1845*, 1950.

were growing, reaching their maximum in 1749–51.[13] Exact output figures are not known, but the fact that prices fell steadily (subject to sharp, temporary fluctuations owing to variation in harvests), at a period of growing (bounty-fed) exports and growing prosperity, to reach their lowest point about 1755, is an eloquent sign of rising output. Falling prices would encourage higher consumption; but, even assuming stationary consumption per head and rising exports, average harvests must have risen by at least 15 per cent between 1700 and 1760.

By comparison with other countries and earlier ages, England ate well in the first half of the eighteenth century. The mid-century estimate of an average wheat consumption of one quarter of wheat per person per annum[14] was not a bad standard. Perhaps the most striking proof of this was the spread of wheat as the basic form of grain food: whether superior or not, it was considered so, and more and more Britons felt that they could afford it.[15] It spread from the south, and one informed guess stated that 89 per cent of Londoners were on a wheat diet by 1764. The northern counties, poorer than the south early in the century, continued longer on barley and rye, and took to potatoes sooner. But as they were gradually overtaking the purely rural districts in prosperity they took to wheat also, though some areas held out against it, with the help of local meat and milk supply, until the end of the century.[16] Scotland kept to its old diet until the last. 'The country people of North Britain live chiefly on oat-meal, and milk, cheese, butter and some garden-stuff, with now and then a pickled herring, by way of delicacy; but flesh-meat they seldom or never taste', according to Smollett in 1771.[17]

But, as Adam Smith observed in the 1770s, not only grain

> 'but many other things from which the industrious poor derive an agreeable and wholesome variety of food, have become a great deal cheaper. Potatoes ... turnips, carrots, cabbages; things which were formerly never raised but by the spade, but which are now commonly raised by the plough. All sorts of garden stuff, too, has become cheaper.'[18]

---

[13] D. G. Barnes, *A History of the English Corn Laws, 1660–1846*, 1930, 297–299.

[14] Elizabeth W. Gilboy, *Wages in Eighteenth-Century England*, Cambridge, Mass., 1934, 22, n. 3.

[15] Sir William Ashley, *The Bread of Our Forefathers*, Oxford, 1928, lecture I; D. G. Barnes, 108 *seq.*; T. S. Ashton, 'Changes in the Standards of Comfort in Eighteenth-Century England', *Proc. British Academy*, XLI (1955).

[16] e.g. William Marshall, *A Review of the Reports to the Board of Agriculture from the Western Department of England*, York, 1810, 11–12, 110–11.

[17] Tobias Smollett, *Humphry Clinker*, Everyman edn, 1943, 256.

[18] *Wealth of Nations*, McCulloch ed., 1863, 35; also, Gustav F. Steffen,

Though the evidence is less certain, all the indications are that the consumption of other foods, such as meat and beer,[19] also increased, malt and other feeding stuffs also having fallen in price to the 1750s at least.

In part, these results were achieved by increasing the acreage under cultivation: by the 1790s, if contemporary reports are to be believed, some two million acres had been added in England to King's 11 million acres under the plough, either by reducing the fallow or by taking in the waste. The bulk of the conversion of the waste land was completed only during the French wars, but even by the 1780s Sir Hubert Mackworth was not the only landlord of whom it could be said that 'the country around him was barren—now they are mowing 3 loads of hay from each acre! His mountains are planted with trees, and his vallies are cover'd by beeves.'[20] Others were draining fens and marshes, cutting down and paring shrubs, or ploughing the uplands.

This was not yet the time for massive enclosures by Acts of Parliament, but much change in organisation went on piecemeal. Slow adaptations led to vital regional specialisation, even though the changes are hard to discern in the national statistics. In the south, farms became larger to furnish the exports to the cities and abroad; in the industrial north, encroachment on the grasslands or hillside wastes for sheep, cattle or potato patches created a new class of smallholders, whose part-agrarian, part-industrial life formed, by the 1760s, the apparently stable, almost idyllic society that many men looked back to in the later days of the factories.[21] In some areas improvements began in the home farm, in others among the small farms or herdsmen. Often it involved new crops such as turnips or clover, and improvement might mean conversion to pasture or ploughing up the grassland; it might employ fewer workers than before as on the Midland clay soils turned to grass, or more, as in the lighter soils of the south.

Yet despite the new lands and the new methods much of the additional output was produced under decreasing returns and by an ever-declining share of the occupied population. The critical factor, whose input was increased more than proportionately, was capital. Agricul-

Studien zur Geschichte der Englischen Lohnarbeiter, Stuttgart, 1901, 3 vols, I, 470 *seq.*, 486–7.

[19] T. S. Ashton, *Economic Fluctuations in England, 1700–1800*, Oxford, 1959, Appendix Tables 1, 2, 3; B. R. Mitchell and Phyllis Deane, *Abstract of British Historical Statistics*, Cambridge, 1962, 354; Deane and Cole, 72; A. H. John, 'The Course of Agricultural Change, 1660–1760', *Studies in the Industrial Revolution* (ed. Pressnell), 144–5.

[20] *Torrington Diaries*, 4 vols, 1934, I, 299.

[21] e.g. William Radcliffe, *Origin of the New System of Manufacture*, 1820, 59–60.

tural capital in this period took many forms: farm houses and barns, even perhaps some new cottages; drains and wells; more stock or new ploughs and implements; and, possibly most significant of all, new roads. The turnpike era began in earnest in the 1740s, and in most areas the economic backbone of road-building was the agrarian economy. Just as the later enclosure commissioners were to insist on new roads among their first commands,

> 'Arthur Young ... rejoiced to note that when a good turnpike road was made, opening out new markets and enabling new ideas to circulate by the come-and-go of more frequent travel, rents in the district soon rose with the improvement in agriculture.'[22]

Where a road was built to the nearest market town or navigable river, the agriculturist not only found a market for his produce, but also for the products of other regions, and thus regional specialisation, one of the most potent factors making for a total increase in output in this period, was further encouraged.

Thus it was the general wealth of the country, and particularly the availability of capital, which helped to break in the eighteenth century the vicious Malthusian cycle of rising population, paralleled by less than proportionately rising food supplies, followed by famine and declining population, so well known in other eras and in contemporary Ireland. Capital kept down real costs in agriculture and created links with markets and helped, for most of a century, to feed well the bulk of a growing population in all but a handful of bad harvest years.

It needs no stressing that the urban population benefited by low food prices: the terms of trade turned in their favour, and the growing share of income left over after buying food was largely spent on manufactures and imports—in the first seven decades of the century the share of a typical town labourer's wage spent on flour or bread fell from perhaps 60 per cent to 50 per cent and that of a craftsman's wage fell from 40 per cent to 30 per cent.[23] The building wages series shows an index of purchasing price of a carpenter's wage of 51 in 1683–7, 53 in 1710–14 and 61 in 1758–62. William Playfair calculated an even more rapid increase in the purchasing power of a 'mechanic' by concentrating on the falling corn prices, putting the days of work necessary to buy a quarter of wheat as:

1675–99	35
1700–24	23½
1725–49	17
1750–74	14

[22] Trevelyan, 381.
[23] E. W. Gilboy, *passim*; A. H. John, 364.

'Take . . . a carpenter, a smith, a weaver, or any such workman . . .
that is industrious', Defoe wrote as early as 1709. 'If the gentle-
man eats more puddings, this man eats more bread, if the rich
man drinks more wine, this man drinks more ale and strong beer . . .
if the rich man eats more veal and lamb, fowl and fish, this man
eats more beef and bacon. . . .'[24]

The urban middle classes benefited equally, and although some of the
margin gained was used merely to increase the consumption of foreign
wines, which, if they were smuggled, did not even contribute to the
revenue, on the whole the additional purchasing power of all classes
gave home industry and the import trade a valuable stimulus.[25]

It is not nearly so certain that the low and falling food prices
would benefit the agricultural interest, still representing half the
nation: 'Corn was cheap in the first half of the century', asserts Mrs
Dorothy George,[26] 'and if this was bad for landlords and farmers it
was good for labourers and cottagers and artisans'. The issue has
often been debated, and clearly depends on circumstances.[27] Here, however, the pessimistic view is misplaced, for the debate usually turns on
the effects of the low price of agricultural produce in occasional good
harvest years. In the first half of the eighteenth century prices were
low because of a rise in real productivity, or a fall in real costs, on
the land, in the face of an expanding market and a long period of
internal peace, which had itself encouraged these improvements.
Hence the agricultural interest was by no means depressed, and it had
in any case the political power to look after itself, by export bounties
and other means, though there were bad periods, especially around
1740–1.[28] In any case, that 'interest' was composed of several distinct
sections, such as landlords, freehold and tenant farmers, smallholders,
labourers and cottagers.

Comprehensive statistics are lacking, but all the evidence points to
the fact that rents were high and, with periodic setbacks, were rising,
not only on urban or coal-bearing land but also on agricultural estates.
Clerical incomes, drawn largely from similar sources, showed startling
aggregate increases. This was the age of the country house, and while

[24] *A Review of the State of the British Nation*, VI/36 (1709), 142. Defoe went
on to calculate that the feeding of every average adult required the produce of
three good, or four average acres.
[25] D. E. C. Eversley, 'The Home Market and Economic Growth in England,
1750–80', in *Land, Labour and Population in the Industrial Revolution*, 1967,
206–59.
[26] M. Dorothy George, *England in Transition*, 1931, 14.
[27] E.g. Charles Wilson, *England's Apprenticeship, 1603–1763*, 1965, 249–55;
A. H. John, 'Agricultural Change', 128–32.
[28] G. E. Mingay, 'The Agricultural Depression 1730–1750', *Ec.H.R.*, VIII
(1956).

the wealth of some estates had been accumulated outside, in trade or politics, most of it was based on rents. In the building of great houses, 'it is a common and reasonable impression that the end of the seventeenth century and the first half of the eighteenth were times of exceptional activity'.[29] This was the time when the squires' manor houses began to equal Jacobean houses of the nobility in size and splendour, and the houses of the nobility became like palaces of former ages, overshadowing even the Court. As Europe, made familiar in the fashionable Grand Tour, was being ransacked for its marble, its statues and its pictures, the landed society of England used the services of the new professions of architects and landscape gardeners to build itself lavish monuments to its growing wealth, which remains impressive even today. It was out of this kind of surplus that many great schemes, from drainage and improved husbandry to road works, harbours and coal mines, were financed.

But if rent income was rising, was it not being squeezed out of tenants and farmers by bleeding them dry, as in contemporary Ireland or France? All the indications are otherwise. Life improved for the larger farms as much as for their landlords, and some of the evidence for this is also still with us. 'The farmers in the main were becoming more prosperous, though possibly fewer in number, and they demanded accommodation in keeping with their increasing wealth, when new farm houses were built.'[30] Many fine, solid farmhouses still standing show the standards required. They are built of solid materials, stone, brick, or half timbered, with tall sashed windows; while the kitchen is still the main room on the ground floor, it has become larger and better equipped, and is flanked by substantial dairies and butteries; and there may now also be a parlour and even a gun room or embryonic office.

But there were many among the 140,000 smaller freeholders and 150,000 farmers enumerated by Gregory King who could not stand the pace, and who sank down to the level of cottager, labourer or pauper: the more agriculture became specialised and market-oriented, the more difficult it became for the man of small means to keep up with the new techniques and pay the higher rents.[31] The day of mass

[29] H. J. Habakkuk, 'Daniel Finch, 2nd Earl of Nottingham: His House and Estate', *Studies in Social History, A Tribute to G. M. Trevelyan* (ed. J. H. Plumb), 1955, 141; also his 'English Landownership 1680–1740', *Ec.H.R.*, X (1940); Trevelyan, *Social History*, 400 *seq.*

[30] G. E. Fussell and C. Goodman, 'The Housing of the Rural Population in the Eighteenth Century', *Economic History*, II (1930), 65; also Rosamond Bayne-Powell, *Housekeeping in the Eighteenth Century*, 1956, 19 *seq.*; G. E. Mingay, *English Landed Society in the Eighteenth Century*, 1963, chapter X.

[31] A. H. Johnson, *The Disappearance of the Small Landowner*, 1909, and Joan Thirsk's introduction to the 2nd edn, 1963; also J. D. Chambers, *The Vale of Trent 1670–1800*, Ec.H.R. Supplement, 41.

redistribution by enclosure was not yet, but the position of those living on the fringes of the village became less and less secure as the century wore on. In the industrial areas of the north and the Midlands, demand from industry enhanced the ability of part-time farmers to survive, and kept up rural labourers' wages: indeed, it is likely that rural wages in the vicinity of industrial centres rose faster than any others in this century, and cottage building there improved after about 1750.[32] But elsewhere, especially in the south away from London,[33] the cottager and labourer saw his condition worsen, hardly benefiting from the price fall to 1755, and suffering from the rise thereafter. Unable to escape his rural drudgery, he was suffering the loss of rural timber supplies and easy poaching or grazing, without the compensation of cheap coal to heat his hovel and cook his meals, or a wage surplus to buy his meat. This was the class whose miserable cottage, built of mud or unmortared stone, covered with turf, its single room housing men and animals, its earthen floor, often below ground level, and its unglazed windows, shocked innumerable travellers in the second half of the century when they ventured into the fastnesses of rural England and Wales. Because of the local limitations on cottage building, surviving until 1775, 'cottages ... swarm with children, and may have double, treble, and even quadruple families', according to Arthur Young.[34]

This was the only substantial section of the agricultural community to shows signs of deterioration, and it was the low wages of southern labour which helped to lower the costs of grain production for the home market and for export. For the rest, the wealth of the agrarian population increased in this period, as a revolution in husbandry permitted it to lower its prices yet increase its incomes with its output, and partake of the greater wealth created by the other two main sections, the commercial and industrial population. No estimate comparable with King's can be found for the end of this period, but Arthur Young, when his scattered figures are reassembled[35] gives a total net output of £58 million for agriculture about 1770. Even if this estimate is too high, it is certain that the incomes generated in agriculture had more than doubled (from £24 million) between 1690 and 1760, while prices had certainly not risen and the agricultural population could not have increased by more than 15–20 per cent, at most. On the other hand, the share of incomes due to the agricultural sector

[32] Gilboy, 220, 241; *Torrington Diaries*, II, 209.
[33] Arthur Young claimed a direct mathematical relationship between the distance from London and the reduction in typical wages—cf. Gilboy, 39, 189.
[34] Fussell and Goodman, *op. cit.*; Young, *Northern Tour*, IV, 416.
[35] Deane, 'Implications', 21.

had fallen substantially, from 56 per cent in 1688 to 46 per cent in the nearest equivalent estimate, that of Massie, 1760.[36]

The expansion of trade

The growth of commerce was certainly faster than that of agriculture. As merchandise imports rose from 16s. *per head* of population in the 1690s to £1. 12. 0. in the 1760s, and exports from 18s. to £2.2.0., growing at the rate of $1\frac{1}{2}$ per cent per annum throughout, it was not only the quantity traded which changed substantially, but also its composition and direction. Even in the 1690s, the trade bore the aspect of that of an advanced country, imports consisting mostly of food and raw materials, and exports of manufactures, and it had become even more clearly polarised by the 1760s.[37] At the same time, the trade with Europe almost stagnated, imports from Europe falling from 53 per cent at the beginning of the century to 44 per cent in the middle and 31 per cent at the end; exports, from 78 per cent to 63 per cent and 45 per cent.[38] By contrast, trade increased by leaps and bounds with such areas as the North American colonies, the West Indies, Africa and India and the Far East. Of reexports, over 80 per cent went to Europe throughout.

The North American colonies supplied Britain with some necessities, such as naval stores and iron, in the normal way of trade: much of it was carried in Yankee-built ships. But most of the rest of the trade was quite exceptionally lucrative, and, as this developed under

---

[36] **(in £000)**

Landowners	8,720	
Freeholders, farmers	16,950	
Husbandmen	3,000	
Country labourers	2,500	(including labourers in provincial towns)
Clergy ($\frac{1}{2}$)	325	
	31,495	
Less deductions, as above	3,500	
	£27,995,	or *c.* 46% of £60,962

Mathias, *loc. cit.*, Tables I and III.

[37] English foreign trade, averages:

		1699–1701	1772–4
% **Exports:**	Manufactures	55·9	54·1
	Food and raw materials	13·2	8·8
	Reexports	30·9	37·1
% **Imports:**	Manufactures	31·7	16·9
	Food and raw materials	68·3	83·1

R. Davis, 'English Foreign Trade, 1700–1774', *Ec.H.R.*, XV (1962).

[38] The figures are for England and Wales for 1701–6, 1751–6 and 1796–1800 respectively—T. S. Ashton, *An Economic History of England: The Eighteenth Century*, 1955, 154; E. B. Schumpeter, *English Overseas Trade Statistics 1697–1808*, 1960.

the Navigation Acts, the gain went to the British mercantile community. Thus a large part of the colonial imports was reexported again to Europe, reexports running at just under one third of total export values throughout, and in the process yielded profits of perhaps 15 per cent of the trade to British shippers and merchants, as well as encouraging new industries such as tobacco-curing and sugar-refining. Nor did it end there, for British manufacturers were employed in making goods to exchange for slaves and British merchants engaged in the slave trade itself, which yielded steady profits when it stopped being exceptionally risky.[39] The plantation economy in the West Indies and in parts of the North American continent itself was ultimately financed from England, and yielded its profits to England.[40] 'As ... slaves are the Produce of the British Commerce in their *African* Factories', Defoe recognised in 1728, 'they are so far a Branch of the *British* Exportation, just as if they were first brought to *England, landed here, and then sent Abroad again'*.[41] Similar conditions applied in other triangular trade patterns: for example, much of the wealth created in the East India trade reappeared in England in the pockets of returned 'nabobs', and was invested in land, titles or further commercial ventures. In turn, this thriving commerce, including the valuable entrepôt trade, created banks and other financial institutions, particularly insurance companies,[42] which not only furthered British trade, but were responsible for yet more 'invisible' earnings from foreigners. The terms of trade fluctuated in long waves, being unfavourable to 1704, favourable from then until 1720-2, turning against Britain again until 1735, and then swinging heavily in her favour until the early 1760s. However, since in this period, as in most others, exceptional export surpluses were associated with unfavourable terms and *vice versa*, the total foreign trade 'gains' to this country may not have been greatly affected.[43]

To these has to be added the vast growth of internal trade, creating

---

[39] C. N. Parkinson, *The Rise of the Port of Liverpool*, Liverpool, 1952; F. E. Hyde, B. B. Parkinson and S. Marriner, 'The Nature and Profitability of the Liverpool Slave Trade', *Ec.H.R.*, V (1953); Eric Williams, *Capitalism and Slavery*, 2nd edn, 1964.

[40] R. B. Sheridan, 'The Wealth of Jamaica in the Eighteenth Century', *Ec.H.R.*, XVIII (1965); K. G. Davies, 'Empire and Capital', *Ec.H.R.*, XIII (1960); D. A. Farnie, 'The Commercial Empire of the Atlantic, 1607-1785', *ibid.*, XV (1962).

[41] Defoe, *A Plan of the English Commerce*, Oxford, 1927 ed. of *Works*, X, 183.

[42] D. M. Joslin, 'London Private Bankers, 1720-1785', *Ec.H.R.*, VII (1954), and 'London Bankers in Wartime, 1739-84', in *Studies in the Industrial Revolution* (ed. Pressnell), 1960; A. H. John, 'The London Assurance Company and the Marine Insurance Market of the Eighteenth Century', *Economica*, N.S. XXV (1958).

[43] Deane and Cole, 48-9 and Table 85, also 319-21; 'Aspects', 363-4.

the beginnings of modern means of transport and bringing the 'putting-out industries' to their highest stage of development.[44] Not only mercers and drapers, but other shopkeepers also could become opulent. 'A pastrycook's shop, which twenty pounds would effectively furnish at a time ... (could now) cost upwards of three hundred pounds', wailed Defoe in 1725,[45] and cutlers' shops were furnished equally lavishly.

The 'Glorious Revolution' had marked a certain turning-point here also. The 1690s, despite (or perhaps because of) the high cost of the war, had seen a promotion mania of joint-stock companies,[46] many of which were for trading purposes. This phase ended with the collapse of the South Sea Bubble in 1720, after which the typical commercial firm was composed of individual merchants, grouped in shifting personal partnerships of different kinds. Even the great overseas trading companies changed their character, the African Company losing its exclusiveness in 1698 and the Levant Company in 1754, and only the East India Company—increasingly a political unit[47]—and the Hudson's Bay Company preserved the old monopoly form. Directors of these companies were among the élite of the merchant class, but in the course of the century, independent traders and planters could overshadow them in wealth.[48]

Evidence of the new commercial wealth was there for all to see. Defoe had already marvelled at the bustle and activity in ports and trading centres, and at the large numbers of ships to be found around the British coast. Total British Tonnage rose from 323,000 in 1702 to 496,000 in 1763, and the tonnage engaged in foreign trade alone has been estimated at 123,000 in 1702 and 304,000 in 1773. Entries and clearances from English ports were 827,000 tons in 1686, 358,000 tons in 1692–3 and 1,451,000 tons in 1765. London built its Greenland Dock, and other maritime cities like Bristol and Liverpool followed.[49] These were the towns in which much of the new commercial

[44] R. B. Westerfield, *Middlemen in English Business, 1660–1760*, Yale U.P., 1915; T. S. Willan, *River Navigation in England, 1660–1750*, Manchester, 1936, and *The English Coasting Trade 1660–1750*, Manchester, 1938.

[45] *Complete English Tradesman*, Oxford, 1841 ed. of *Works*, XVII, 206.

[46] W. R. Scott, *The Constitution and Finance of ... Joint Stock Companies to 1720*, 3 vols, Cambridge, 1911–12, I, 327; K. G. Davies, 'Joint-Stock Investment in the Later Seventeenth Century', *Ec.H.R.*, IV (1952), 292.

[47] L. S. Sutherland, *The East India Company in Eighteenth Century Politics*, Oxford, 1952.

[48] W. E. Minchinton, 'The Merchants in England in the Eighteenth Century', 27, in *The Entrepreneur* (Papers read at the Economic History Society Conference, 1957).

[49] Chalmers, *An Estimate of the Comparative Strength of Great Britain*, 1794, 235 *seq.*; Ralph Davis, *The Rise of the English Shipping Industry*, 1962, 26–7; D. Defoe, *A Tour Thro' the Whole Island of Great Britain (1724–6)*, Oxford, 1928, 2 vols; T. C. Barker, 'The Beginnings of the Canal Age in the British

wealth was concentrated in fine streets and houses: Bristol, the second city in England in 1700, had grown from 20,000 to 64,000 inhabitants in 1801, and other towns engaged in overseas trade, like Liverpool, Glasgow and Whitehaven were growing fast, if not faster.[50] Above all, it was London that revealed the new wealth, and the share of it that was commercial.

The continuous built-up area around the cities of London and Westminster contained perhaps one eighth of the population of England and Wales in 1690, and one seventh, or about a million, in 1760. In many respects, life in London had become different from life in the rest of the country. Dwellings were much more overcrowded—'It was common for a family to live in a single room'[51]—and even tradesmen's families had no more than one floor each in the three- or four-storied houses[52]; food prices were higher. 'London, tho' the dearest place in the Kingdom to live at, is by far the cheapest for purchasing Household Goods',[53] sanitary conditions were far worse, and in the gin-drinking era which ended only with the Act of 1751 the death-rate was appallingly in excess of the birth-rate. On the other hand, for the common people, wages were higher and opportunities to rise were greater, and this is mostly what attracted a constant stream of migrants from the country. The common people here, too, benefited by falling food prices until the 1750s, and by rising wages thereafter.

Rising standards, however, were most evident among the trading and upper classes. It was in this period that the nobleman who maintained his town house, and the rich merchant, left the confined streets of the city and went to live in the new open squares and wide streets of Mayfair and the northern suburbs, advancing towards what is now the Euston Road and its extensions. By the middle of the century, improvement was extended to public property also. 'London and Westminster are much better paved and lighted than they were formerly', it was said in 1771. 'The new streets are spacious, regular and airy; and the houses generally convenient.'[54] The Westminster Paving Act was passed in 1762. The Fleet River was covered over, the city gates pulled down, culverts and bridges built. Other cities were soon to follow this lead. 'It is not easy', wrote T. S. Ashton, 'to set an initial

Isles', in *Studies in the Industrial Revolution*; W. M. Stern, 'The First London Dock Boom', *Economica*, XIX (1952).

[50] N. E. Minchinton (ed.), *The Trade of Bristol in the Eighteenth Century*, Bristol Record Society, 1957.

[51] George, *London Life in the XVIII Century*, 85.

[52] *Wealth of Nations*, 54; Rosamond Bayne-Powell, *Eighteenth-Century London Life*, 1937, 82.

[53] Josiah Tucker, *Four Tracts on Political and Commercial Subjects*, 3rd edn, Glasgow, 1776, 39–40.

[54] *Humphry Clinker*, 83.

date to any social or economic improvement. But what was known as "improvement" seems to have arisen in the early fifties and to have got under way in the middle of the Seven Years War.' Old Corporations or new Commissions began the paving, lighting and improving of large towns.[55]

London had some industries, including the consumption industries, and others, like silk, brought in by immigrants. But it also included some of the richest, and some of the poorest, families in the kingdom, and among the former was an increasing number of commercial occupations. Some of the most obvious signs of the new affluence, the coffee house, the drinking of tea and chocolate, the consumption of sugar, the use of china, Chinese lacquer and wallpaper, and the transformation of furniture-making into a delicate art, which depended so much on the introduction of mahogany, were derived directly from the new ranges of imports now available. Trade figures are notoriously unreliable because of the incidence of smuggling,[56] which may have accounted, for example, for two-thirds of the actual tea importation, and they are affected by war conditions, but for what they are worth, they show the following changes[57]:

Retained imports

	Coffee cwts	Tea 1,000 lb	Rum 1,000 gal.	Sugar 1,000 cwts	Tobacco mill. lb
Annual average					
1700–04	4,763[a]	26[a]	2·3[a]	255[b]	14·0[b]
1720–24	5,029	685	80·1	553	8·8
1758–62	2,455	3,198	998·2	1,075	10·5

[a] Average of 3 years.   [b] Average of 4 years.

The upward movement of commerce was beset by serious fluctuations, sometimes of great destructiveness, but none of these, not even those caused by war, could hold up the expansion. Armed conflicts, indeed, were of major significance, since England was at war for about half the period under review, and it is natural to assume that the destructive effect of war, especially on shipping, and in the diversion of resources (including capital), the decline in building, and the manpower employed in the field abroad rather than productivity at home,

[55] *Economic Fluctuations*, 97; Ashton goes on to quote Dr Plumb: 'This growth of local authorities is the most important social development of the second half of the eighteenth century and the least stressed.'
[56] G. D. Ramsay, *English Overseas Trade During the Centuries of Emergence*, 1957, chapter 6; W. A. Cole, 'Trends in Eighteenth Century Smuggling', *Ec.H.R.*, X (1958).
[57] E. B. Schumpeter, Table XVIII.

would have slowed up economic growth and left England worse provided than peaceful evolution would have done.[58] Yet in this period, if perhaps in no other, such conclusions would be hard to sustain.

The diversion of resources was minimal. The total forces mobilised amounted, at the peak, to no more than 2·4 per cent of the population at the beginning of the century, and three per cent in 1760.[59] Even naval impressment could not prevent the number of merchant mariners increasing rather than declining in the war years. Loans were raised partly from abroad and mainly from London, where they had little effect on productive investment in the provinces, and taxes (if spent at home) tended to direct resources from the idle to the active population. Shipping losses[60] were generally made up by prizes and more building, and trade tended to be greater at the end of each war than at the beginning, having grown at the expense of enemy trade, normally the French, though it was carried by a larger proportion of foreign ships.[61] War borrowings, it is true, created and enlarged the National Debt, which contemporaries considered to be a great economic burden; but today we are more inclined to stress the beneficial effects these operations had on the early development of the London Money Market.

A wide range of industries was greatly furthered by the wars, above all iron and non-ferrous metal-smelting, coal-mining, animal-breeding and leather-working, canvas and woollens, shipbuilding and chemicals, and even luxuries like silk, as foreign imports were taxed, prohibited or hampered. It is not merely that these industries were enlarged; many of them were driven to develop cost-reducing processes, and to accept a positive attitude towards innovation, both of which were of permanent and critical importance.[62] Indeed, the momentum of the commercial expansion of this period as a whole depended on war and conquest. The creation and absorption of overseas settlements, markets and sources of supply, the dynamics of active trade penetration, the replacement of passive economies (such as the Spanish or Portuguese) by active ones in contact with overseas countries, depended on the wars and the victories of this era. Perhaps without wars there would have been no American and no French Revolution, and the

---

[58] E.g., Ashton, *Fluctuations*, 49–83, 91 *seq.*

[59] W. W. Rostow, *The Process of Economic Growth*, 2nd edn, Oxford, 1960, 150.

[60] Mercantile shipping losses were estimated at 2,000 vessels in 1702–12, over 3,000 in 1739–48, and rather less than that in 1756–63—Ralph Davis, *The Rise of the English Shipping Industry*, 1962, 317.

[61] George Chalmers, *Comparative Strength, passim*; R. Davis, 334; G. N. Clark, 'War Trade and Trade War 1701–1713', *Ec.H.R.*, I (1927).

[62] A. H. John, 'War and the English Economy, 1700–1763', *Ec.H.R.*, VII (1955).

Bourbons might have continued to govern France.[63] Wars were as indispensable to the development of commercial capitalism in the eighteenth century as slavery was to the development of the sugar plantation.

Thus history herself seemed to follow the merchant and the trade, as all conditions conspired to enlarge his power and his wealth.

> 'An ordinary tradesman now ...', Defoe wrote in 1725, with but little exaggeration,[64] 'shall spend more money by the year than a gentleman of four or five hundred pounds a year can do, and shall increase and lay up every year too ... and as for the lower gentry, from a hundred pounds a year to three hundred ... a shoemaker in London shall keep a better house, spend more money, clothe his family better, yet grow rich too. It is evident where the difference lies: an estate's a pond, but trade's a spring.'

In his calculation of material incomes in 1760, Massie added a whole new category of rich merchants over and above those listed by King, averaging incomes of £600 a year. These were the

> 'substantial merchant magnates, princes of wealth, drawing their riches from all parts of the world ... easily distinguishable from the "middling sort" of folk, local factors and agents, engaged in domestic trade, men who "though highly useful in their stations, are by no means entitled to the honours of higher rank" '.[65]

The growth in total incomes of this class, according to Massie's judgment, was equally striking[66]:

	King, 1688	Massie, 1760
Proportion of families engaged in trade and distribution	7·3%	18·9%
Proportion of total incomes gained by them	11·6%	23·3%

The manufacturing industries

Both the development of agriculture, which left more money in people's pockets for non-food goods, and the expansion of overseas markets and domestic commercial wealth were bound to provide much stimulus to industry, and the manufacturers of the period proved able and willing to use their opportunities. Monopolies had either been abolished by 1690 or proved impossible to enforce in an increasingly hostile environment. Apprenticeship restrictions were broken where

[63] Charles Wilson, *England's Apprenticeship, 1603–1763*, 1965, 281 *seq.*
[64] *Complete English Tradesman*, I, 245.
[65] Asa Briggs, *The Age of Improvement 1783- 1867*, 1959, 11, quoting the *Political Register* of Jan. 1763.
[66] Mathias, *loc. cit.*, Tables I and III.

they hindered industrial progress, but were newly established or strengthened for several emergent or important crafts, e.g. in building and engineering. Mercantilism was still strong enough to maintain a selective body of protection against foreign-manufactured imports, while Great Britain herself formed the largest Free Trade area in Europe. Conditions could hardly be more favourable.

Total industrial output grew substantially faster than population or agricultural production, even if somewhat erratically. Statistics for this period are notoriously unreliable and narrowly based, but for what they are worth the best available series show the following increases[67]:

	Dean and Cole (Real Output)			Hoffmann
	Export industries	*Home industries*	*Total industry and commerce*	*Industrial production, including building*
1700	100	100	100	100
1730	142	105	127	128
1760	222	114	148	157

These growth-rates were still slow compared with those after 1760, but beyond them, there now also began a basic transformation in structure.

First, there was the growth in the division of labour. By the 1760s it had reached such complexity in Adam Smith's pin factory, Boulton's 'toy' factory at Soho and Wedgwood's pottery at Etruria, as to permit reductions in cost of staggering proportions, by improved organisation and a limited amount of better equipment. In a different direction, an efficient and highly developed 'putting-out' system gave central mercantile control over raw material supply, orders, quality and usually some finishing processes and dispatch, and allowed a range of industries to improve their performance greatly by division of labour and specialisation. These included wool, cotton, and linen-spinning and weaving, silk-weaving, framework-knitting, mail-, file- and tool-making and watch- and clock-making.

Secondly, not only were important technical inventions introduced and adopted, but, what was perhaps of greater consequence, they were accompanied by innumerable minor improvements and developments, the symbols of a progressive economy. Some of these, again, were labour-saving; others, almost equally important, saved horse-power;

[67] Deane and Cole, 78; W. G. Hoffmann, *British Industry, 1700–1950*, Oxford, 1955.

others still permitted operations or created products unknown or impossible before. Nearly all of them tended to substitute capital for other factors of production. Among the best-known were silk-throwing, Kay's flying shuttle and Strutt's process for producing ribbed hose, in the textiles; the reverberatory furnace for non-ferrous metals, Darby's coke-smelting process for iron, and Huntsman's crucible process for steelmaking, in metals; new chemical processes, including an improved method for producing sulphuric acid; the development of such relatively new industries as glass, paper and tinplate, and substantial improvements in hydraulic engineering for the use of water power, and for pumping, including the Newcomen atmospheric engine, by such engineers of genius as Serocold, Smeaton, and Brindley. In addition, instrument-making and instrumentation were much improved, and the costs of transport were reduced by much turnpike roadmaking, by river improvements and by the laying of rails in the coal and iron districts and elsewhere. The very fact that, spreading outwards from London, activities such as brewing, baking, and spinning were increasingly transferred from the home to professional workers was bound to make for greater efficiency, though it may have temporarily inflated some production statistics. The movement out of the high-wage area of London of industry such as silk-weaving, framework-knitting or high-grade pottery lowered prices, even if it did not lower real costs.

It was significant that many of these innovations were introduced, or widely adopted, only towards the end of this period. By that time, British manufactures had been cheapened sufficiently to achieve larger and sometimes mass sales at home, while undercutting foreign producers abroad, despite higher wages paid in Great Britain. For British products, according to Dean Tucker,[68] benefited by

> 'established trade and Credit, large correspondences, experienced Agents and Factors, commodious shops, work-houses, magazines, etc. also a great Variety of the best Tools and Implements in the various Kinds of Manufactures, and Engines for abridging labour; —add to these good Roads, Canals and other artificial Communications; Quays, Docks, Wharfs and Piers; Numbers of Ships, good Pilots and trained Sailors....'

and they explain not only how output was enlarged, but costs reduced.

Conclusion

The period 1689–1760 saw several serious crises, some setbacks and some years of stagnation, but on the whole it was an age of rising wealth and rising incomes per head. To this improvement, all the main sectors of the economy contributed.

[68] *Four Tracts*, 30.

Agriculture, helped by innumerable local improvements in transport, succeeded in expanding the output of corn faster than the total consuming population, without reducing the production of meat. At the same time, supplies became more regular as localised famines became rare, at least in England and Wales, and there are no longer any noticeable increases in the death-rate that can be attributed to famine as such.[69] The consumption of home-grown fruit and vegetables spread to the poorer classes, and the supply of dairy products was larger than in previous centuries. As the bulk of the population spent 60–80 per cent of their incomes on food, this improvement was of major significance.

Though forming a much smaller share of total expenditure of all but the very rich, the increased availability of imports and of manufactured products was of greater significance still in raising the general level of comfort. The larger expanses of glass in the newly-built houses, the brass goods, the pottery ware to be found in the homes of all but the very poorest; the rising sales of newspapers, prints, and even books; the new Sheffield plate, allowing the middle classes to copy the solid silver of their betters, the enamelled and ormolu goods, lace and clocks; the growing quantities of soap and candles consumed, according to the taxation returns, and of coal and salt, were all proof of improvement. As for the poor, 'the great improvements in the coarser manufactures of both linen and woollen cloth', wrote Adam Smith,[70] 'furnish the labourer with cheaper and better clothing; and those in the manufactures of the coarser metals with cheaper and better instruments of trade, as well as with many agreeable and convenient pieces of household furniture'.

Most significant is the rising chorus of complaint about the alleged extravagance of the poor. About textiles Dean Tucker wrote, with some exaggeration:

'Females of all Ages and Conditions hardly use any Woollens at present, except those of the finest Texture, and made of the finest Wools. Silks, Cottons, and Linens, combined in a thousand forms ... are now almost the universal wear, from her Grace in the drawing-room down to the lowest Scullion in the Kitchen. ... And as to Males, even they wear ten times the Quantities of Cottons and Silks ... more than was usual for them to do.—Respecting Ruggs, and other Coarse Articles, they are in a manner banished from all the Houses in Towns and Cities;—and are scarcely to be found anywhere but in country cottages.'[71]

[69] Chambers, *Vale of Trent*.
[70] *Loc. cit.*, 35.
[71] Josiah Tucker, *Reflections on the Present Low Price of Coarse Wools*, 1782, 9

Regarding food and drink, Deering was equally emphatic in the Nottingham of 1751:

'People here are not without their Tea, Coffee and Chocolate, especially the first, the Use of which is spread to that Degree, that not only Gentry and Wealthy Travellers drink it constantly, but almost every Seamer, Sizer and Winder will have her Tea in a Morning ... and even a common Washerwoman thinks she has not had a proper Breakfast without Tea and hot Buttered White Bread.'[72]

The consensus of opinion on this point is too great to be accounted for merely by class prejudice, and there is no doubt that many types of workmen in many areas could afford some types of consumption goods in the 1750s that were beyond their reach in the 1690s, either because of higher incomes or because of lower prices. Yet, measured by modern standards, the mass of the population was still appallingly poor. The bulk of the population still lived a family to one room or perhaps two, ill-furnished, and barely heated outside the coal-bearing regions. They rarely had more than one change of clothing, and a good coat lasted a lifetime. The artefacts of modern life were still absent, or held as single, treasured possessions. Disease was often fatal, even without the aid of a doctor, and the law was very harsh on the poor.

In some respects, indeed, conditions may have deteriorated in those years. Urban living for most citizens, with its growing sanitary problem, was worse than rural living. The uncertainties of life, such as unemployment, sudden death at work, robbery, or violence, struck more often in the towns than in the country, and more people now lived in the towns. With the rising incomes of merchants and squires, economic inequalities became, or appeared to become, greater and thus less bearable.

Aggregates and averages are misleading, even if they were in themselves reliable. The three main independent estimates showing a *per capita* income for England and Wales of about £8 a year in 1688, £9. 10. 0. in 1760 (Massie) and £18 in 1770 (Young), measured against fairly stable prices, are too varied to have much reliance placed on them. However, they do at least not conflict with the assumption of rising standards, and make it clear that this was precisely the assumption which the two later authors intended to convey.

[72] Quoted in Chambers, *Vale of Trent*, 24.

Chapter six

The Onset of Industrialisation, 1760–1815

The Industrial Revolution

The years from 1760 to 1815 include the early decades of the Industrial Revolution which transformed the British economy in every major respect. In more recent parlance, they include the decades of the 'take-off' into that sustained growth which has, since then, expanded and enriched the material life of the population in two centuries of 'unbroken progress'. It was a period in which many of the old landmarks disappeared, and many new ones were erected. The task of describing the changes in the wealth of Britain therefore becomes particularly difficult for these years.

The overriding impression which this period has left on historians is one of progress, and this impression was undoubtedly shared by most contemporaries, beginning with David Hume, who confidently described its political, and Adam Smith, who traced its economic preconditions. Yet despite the obvious signs of new wealth, the factory chimneys in the north, the new suburbs of London in the south, the canal and dock works and the piles of new commodities, there were critics like Charles Hall and Robert Owen who were not convinced that progress had been universal. Recent, more detailed research supports the contention that the period, despite its profound qualitative changes in the economy, did not see any marked improvement in the standards of wealth and material comfort of the mass of the population, and may even have witnessed a decline.

This chapter sets out to describe the developments behind this apparent paradox, which became the background to a generation experiencing some of the greatest social stresses in British history. They were largely the consequences of the interplay of five parallel developments: the growth of population, the transformation of agriculture and of industry, the course of commercial expansion, and the wars, particularly the long years of strife between 1793 and 1815.

Food and population growth

It cannot be stressed too often that the reequipping of the British economy in its early stages of industrialisation, as indeed in its later phases, had to be carried out at a time of unprecedented growth in total population. On the one hand, innovations of all kinds were stimulated by this population explosion; at the same time, it put great strain on the resources available for consumption and for investment.[1]

Estimates of the change in numbers of population are still too much based on guesswork to identify its detailed course with certainty, but it is most likely that, after the relatively moderate rise described in the last chapter, population growth accelerated from about 1780 onwards, to reach well over nine million people by the time of the first Census in 1801. Growth in Scotland was similar, and in Ireland it may have been even faster.[2]

A growth of this order of magnitude of well over 50 per cent in six decades, in a country in which there were no wide and fertile open spaces left for settlement, and at a time when foreign trade in foodstuffs was no more than marginal, was bound to lead to a race between the additional mouths to be fed, and the ability of home agriculture to feed them. The 'new' husbandry, and other changes in the structure of British agriculture, ensured that the race was not cut short by widespread famine, as had happened in other countries and other centuries, and was to happen in Ireland in the 1840s; but the adjustment was by no means smooth or straightforward.

In the first two-thirds of the eighteenth century, when population growth was still slow, agriculture had gone into the lead and as a result the people as a whole were better fed. Whatever the view of contemporaries, the experience of the following era tended to make men look back on these years as a golden age:

'During the first half of the eighteenth century the food of the people was mixed, nutritious and in general adequate. . . . For at least fifty years prior to 1770 the workers in this country were free from anxiety as to their immediate needs in respect to food and shelter, to an extent unknown to later generations.'[3]

The timing of the turning point is not clear, but a good indication of it is provided by the foreign trade in corn. Up to the 1760s there were large and growing export surpluses, and as late as 1766 a French merchant could call the United Kingdom the 'granary of Europe'.[4]

[1] S. Pollard, 'Investment, Consumption and the Industrial Revolution', Ec.H.R., XI (1958).
[2] The classic description and explanation of this growth will be found in T. H. Marshall, 'The Population Problem during the Industrial Revolution', Economic History, I (1929) and 'The Population of England and Wales from the Industrial Revolution to the World War', Ec.H.R., V (1935), both reprinted in E. M. Carus-Wilson (ed.), Essays in Economic History, 1954. For a new view see J. T. Krause, 'Changes in English Fertility and Mortality 1781–1850', Ec.H.R., XI (1958).
[3] R. N. Salaman, The History and Social Influence of the Potato, Cambridge, 1949, 465, 470; cf. also Lord Ernle, English Farming Past and Present, 6th edn, 1961, 262.
[4] C. R. Fay, The Corn Laws and Social England, Cambridge, 1932, 28.

There was a rough balance in the 1770s, and from about 1780 onwards England required substantial, and mounting, imports to feed her population.[5] Corn prices began to rise faster than other prices and faster than wages, and there is some evidence that the price of bread rose faster still, indicating that even the additional imports failed to keep pace with demand. Years of shortage, amounting at times to 'famine', became more frequent, marked local shortages reappeared,[6] and bad harvest years increasingly imperilled home consumption, and with it the social peace of the towns and industrial districts. Shortages were felt most severely during the war years, when the price of bread rocketed and kept far ahead of wages and other incomes: according to Salaman, the wheat available for the population of the *United Kingdom* fell from 1·5 lbs *per capita* daily in the 1760s to about 1 lb at the end of the war, though this was partly offset by an increase in the supply of potatoes.

Whereas the fat years before 1770 had seen a spread of the consumption of the wheaten loaf, now in the lean years, when prices moved against the consumer, he refused to revert to the old diet. As the typical labourer's family (if surviving budgets are any guide) had to increase its expenditure on bread from 40–50 per cent of its income in the 1760s to 50–60 per cent,[7] it began to drop its former consumption of meat, cheese, beer or milk, and survived substantially on a bread (and butter) diet, augmented by tea and occasional bacon, which also became the standard diet of the new factory proletariat. Thus contemporary critics were unjust in railing at the labouring classes for indulging in needless luxury bread. With the loss of the power to buy other kinds of food, the labourer's white bread and tea provided a cheap, if unvarying diet of minimum nutrition and physical warmth and comfort.[8]

Regional differences were significant, and the northern labourer on his rye, potato, and milk diet, supplemented by some meat, tended to do better than the farm hand in the south; the developing industrial centres in the north ensured that his wages kept up better with prices. In England, as in all industrialising countries since, the early industrialists had to attract their labour in part by paying higher money wages

---

[5] Ernle thought bad harvests as well as rising population to have been responsible for this reversal—*op. cit.*, 268.

[6] Janet Blackman, 'Changing Marketing Methods and Food Consumption', *Our Changing Fare* (ed. T. C. Barker, J. C. McKenzie and John Yudkin), 1966, 35–6.

[7] E. H. Phelps Brown and Sheila V. Hopkins, 'Seven Centuries of Consumables, Compared with Builders' Wage Rates', *Economica*, XXIII (1956), 297.

[8] John Burnett, *Plenty and Want. A Social History of Diet in England from 1815 to the Present Day*, 1966, 3, 7.

than was customary in existing occupations in handicraft industry and in agriculture; but in England, unlike many present-day economies, this differential was created by depressing the latter at least as much as by raising the former. This process was aided by social change in the village, particularly the enclosures; it was made possible by the fact that at the outset, in the 1760s, labourers and wages were well above the subsistence level and there was therefore room for some reduction. It was an interesting comment on this development that the diets of workhouses and similar institutions, which had been comparable with labourers' diets earlier on, appeared to be superior to those enjoyed by free labour by the end of the century,[9] and contributed to the middle-class revolt against the existing Poor Law.

This growing imbalance, the temporary failure of the English food supply, which lasted from about 1770 to 1800, was basically due to the marked increase in population, together with the increase in the numbers of horses, which represented a substantial investment in that phase of the industrial and agrarian revolution in field, road and towpath.[10] The increase was large enough not only to gobble up the former marginal export surplus and turn England into a net importer of grain, but also to outpace the increases in home food production stimulated by this growing demand itself.

Although it failed to meet the total requirements in the short term, English agriculture nevertheless increased its output substantially in absolute terms,[11] and did so while releasing labour for other sectors of the economy; the agricultural share of employment fell from perhaps 45 per cent to perhaps 35 per cent, as measured as a share of incomes or employment.[12] This was achieved largely by diverting an important share of the nation's investment effort to agriculture in this period.[13] The success of this effort is all the more remarkable if it is borne in mind that agriculture, over a wide range, worked under decreasing returns, that some of the concrete investments had a long period of gestation, like drainage, or spread their benefits to other sections, as in the case of roads built on the instruction of the enclosure awards. Further, there were institutional factors which delayed until

[9] J. C. Drummond and Anne Wilbraham, *The Englishman's Food*, 1957 ed., 222 *seq.*; Sir F. M. Eden, *The State of the Poor*, 1797.

[10] One horse consumed enough oats to feed two persons *on an oats diet.* Arthur Young, *The Question of Scarcity Plainly Stated*, 1800, 68. Also David Grigg, *The Agricultural Revolution in South Lincolnshire*, Cambridge, 1966, 74.

[11] W. E. Minchinton, 'Agricultural Returns and the Government during the Napoleonic Wars', *Ag.H.R.*, I (1953).

[12] François Crouzet, *L'Economie Britannique et le Blocus Continental 1806–1813*, Paris, 2 vols, 1958, 53–6.

[13] Lord Ernle, *English Farming Past and Present*, 6th edn., 1961, 210–13, also 265–7; W. Rostow, *The Process of Economic Growth*, Oxford, 2nd edn, 1960, 157; David Grigg, 22 *seq.*, 39 *seq.*, 65.

the early nineteenth century some of the most immediate and spectacular gains to be achieved by ploughing up the wastes.[14] The net effect of all these influences, according to Arthur Young's careful calculations, was to keep the average yield *per acre* constant between c. 1770 and c. 1800,[15] or even 1815, according to modern researches, the increase being achieved by increases in acreage under the plough in some areas, by new rotation or taking in the waste, and by an increase in output *per head* in other areas.[16]

As the shortage was due not to an increase in demand, rather a shortfall in supply, one might have expected it to have affected all kinds of foodstuffs; the reasons why the pressure was concentrated on corn included the changing habits of consumption and the income effect of high corn prices on the poorer classes, as described above; a possible similar shift in the habits of many well-to-do families, from the gluttony of the eighteenth century gentry to the frugality of many of the new industrialists; and growing imports from Ireland. It is likely that total production of meat rose no faster than that of corn, though mutton replaced beef within this total,[17] and *per capita* consumption of meat must have fallen likewise towards the end of the century from its mid-century peak, despite the conversion from arable to pasture in early enclosures. Meat prices rose more steadily than grain prices, but ultimately reached a similar level of $2\frac{1}{2}$ times the pre-war figure.[18]

The nadir was reached in the last years of the century, 1795–1800, when the position was aggravated by a series of poor harvests. A succession of deficient harvests was to recur in the latter years of the war, when there were four particularly bad years between 1809 and 1812, and the quartern loaf, retailing at $4\frac{1}{2}$d.–6d. in the 1760s, 8d. in the early 1790s and 13d. in 1799, rose to a maximum of 17d. in 1812, yet in some degree the corner had been turned. Imports were fluctuating according to the state of the harvest, but provided around one tenth to one twentieth of total consumption. An appreciable proportion of exports was used to finance food imports: the Commons Committee on the Corn Laws reported that £58·6 million was spent by Great Britain on foreign grain in 1792–1811 and £2·8 million on import bounties in 1796–1803. Some corn and flour was also saved by sumptuary laws restricting its uses in starch, hair powder and distilling; and between

[14] G. Slater, *The English Peasant and the Enclosure of Common Fields*, 1907, App. A and B; Barnes, 110.
[15] *The Question of Scarcity*, 8–16.
[16] According to Drescher, the total acreage under cultivation in England and Wales rose from 21 million acres to 27·9 million acres between 1700 and 1812, and the acreage under wheat from 2,795,000 acres in 1771 to 3,160,000 in 1812 —*Manchester School*, XXIII (1955), 167; also David Grigg, 58, 192.
[17] Deane and Cole, 68–75.
[18] W. S. Jeans, 'On the Variation of Prices', *J. R. Statistical Soc.* XXVIII (1865).

c. 1800 and c. 1814 the average harvest yield went up by perhaps two million quarters of wheat, or by over one-fourth.[19] Besides, potatoes were used in many districts to eke out the diet of the poor.[20] At the end of the period, a good harvest such as that of 1813 could produce a sizeable surplus. Thus food consumption per head probably fell no further, despite the rapid growth of the population,[21] though the level at which it settled was low by the standards of an earlier generation.

Since this increased output was obtained at great cost, largely under decreasing returns, the incomes of the agricultural sector, i.e., those of farmers and receivers of rent, increased at the expense of those of other sectors of the community.[22] This was the period of the Malthusian doctrine on population and the Ricardian theory of rent. It is likely that the heavy expenditure necessary on food production also diverted funds from other sectors, including industry. The benefits, however, did not extend to farm labourers. While rent rolls soared and farmers experienced unprecedented opulence, the farm hands were turned out from their quarters, 'living-in' gave way to payment in cash in order to throw the burden of higher food prices on them, and the villages were being demoralised by the Speenhamland system in its many variants.

Effects of the rise of modern industry

In spite of the important changes in agriculture, it would be generally agreed that the outstanding innovations of this period occurred not in the agrarian sector, but as part of the rise of modern industry and the new means of communication, including the great canal schemes of the late 1760s and the early 1790s, and the growing output of manufacture and mining receiving a new spurt from about 1780. What effect did they have on the income and wealth of the population?

There is no dispute about the transformation of industry and transport: an indication of the orders of magnitude involved is given by the following tentative estimates of eighteenth-century growth[23]:

[19] Crouzet, 97; also, W. F. Galpin, *The Grain Supply of England during the Napoleonic Period*, New York, 1925, 196–7.
[20] Salaman, 509; W. Marshall, *A Review of the Reports by the Board of Agriculture from the Western Departments of England*, York, 1810, 110.
[21] Mancur Olson Jr, *The Economics of the Wartime Shortage*, Durham, North Carolina, 1963, 55, 65, 69.
[22] According to the farmers themselves, agricultural costs per acre less than doubled between 1790 and 1813, including wage costs and rents; selling prices more than doubled. Moreover, landlords benefited by having more acres under cultivation—Select Committee on the Corn Laws, 1814–15, quoted in L. P. Adams, *Agricultural Depression and Farm Relief in England, 1813–1852*, 1965 ed., 35. McCulloch estimated the rent roll at £22·5 million in 1800, and at over £34 million in 1815—*The British Empire*, 2 vols, 1837, I, 531 *seq.*; Deane and Cole, 166.
[23] Deane and Cole, Table 19 and footnote, p. 78.

Real Output Index (1700 = 100)

Approx. date	Export industries	Home industries	Total real output p. head (inc. Agric., etc.)	
			Inc. Government and Defence	Excl. Government and Defence
1700	100	100	100	100
1760	222	114	130	121
1780	246	123	129	117
1800	544	152	160	147

If these figures are even approximately correct, there seems to have been a substantial jump in output per head in the last years of the century, just when food production began to lag. This fast rate of growth continued in the nineteenth century. It is our problem to explain why it was not reflected in any obvious rise in popular consumption.

The reasons for the discrepancy are complex. Some hints are provided by the table above. The striking increase is confined to the 'export industries': home industries lagged behind population growth. To be sure, the former supplied the home market also, but they were limited to a narrow range of goods, and of these only three groups were of major significance in the consumption of the majority of the population: textiles and clothing made from them; metals, which allowed a reduction in the costs of such goods as tools, table knives and nails; and pottery, where concentration and mass-production reduced prices in the cheaper ranges. The evidence about other products, such as soap, glass or paper, is either doubtful,[24] or may have affected only better-off households.[25] Such estimates as tend to rely on the margin between the necessary food and total income as a measure of prosperity[26] will understate the benefits accruing to ordinary households in this period, for manufactured articles bought out of this margin did become substantially cheaper in real terms and more easily available. At the same time, quality may have deteriorated

[24] An approximate index of quantities paying duty, *per head*, may be summarised as follows (England and Wales):

	White glass	Bottles, etc.	Soap	Paper	Candles
1759–1761	100	100	100	100	100
1779–1781	122	75	110	120	109
1799–1801	134	87	124	177	114
1814–1816	101	89	150	208	118

Based on Mitchell and Deane, 262–7.

[25] A. J. Taylor, 'Progress and Poverty in Britain, 1780–1850: A Reappraisal', *History*, N.S. 45 (1960), 22–3.

[26] E.g., those of E. W. Gilboy.

in the early days of machine manufacture, though this may have been hidden from contemporaries, who might still think of calicoes, for example, no matter how badly produced in the mills, as a newly desirable luxury since they were brought up to consider hand-spun calico as such; just as food bought in town markets may have been inferior to apparently similar food produced in cottage gardens. But in all these comparisons certainty is hard to find.

Many 'home industries', i.e. industry producing for the home market, did not even keep up with population. Whatever value this fact may have for the explanation of the origin of the drive to industrialise, it is clear that it will have helped to keep incomes low in this period. Perhaps building is the best example: Shannon's brick index rose by 1·192 per cent per annum in 1786–1816, against a population increase of 1·191 per cent.[27] This striking coincidence is of no particular significance, since it is clear that with growing work on canals, factories and public works, house building did not keep pace with the population which was less well housed at the end of the period, even disregarding the fact that urban housing of equal quality was then far less desirable, on other grounds, than the rural housing it replaced.

Moreover, the conversion of a rising output limited to one sector, manufacturing, into rising real incomes, labours under a grave handicap in the early stages of industrialisation. The growing productivity depends on growing investment and more roundabout methods of production, and this investment (together with the needs of a rising population) may well at that stage swallow up all the modest increase. Thus a canal which ultimately reduces freights between Birmingham and Liverpool or the costs of imported raw materials in Birmingham may take 10 or 15 years to complete, meanwhile swallowing up a large part of the growing resources; and, when it is completed, it may not even then immediately lead to cost reductions, for there is no merit in consumption away from the scene of production or imports, unless in turn it can lead to cost reductions (by mass production, for example) in the long run. Thus the first generation of industrialisers may be sacrificed to the second, and even the second, if its investment is significantly larger than that of its predecessor, may not enjoy the increase in consumption, but use it all up for even better future performances.[28] This is particularly evident if, as in Britain at the time, the rising productivity is limited at first to a small sector of

[27] H. A. Shannon, 'Bricks, a Trade Index, 1785–1849', *Economica*, N.S. I (1934).
[28] The marginal capital-output ratio may thus be very high for considerable periods, though in the long run, experience shows, it tends to unity or less— cf. the literature reviewed in R. M. Hartwell, 'The Rising Standard of Living in England, 1800–1850', *Ec.H.R.*, XIII/3 (1961), 402, note.

industry, and is only gradually spreading to others, while the benefits of the first are lost by diffusion among the whole economy. It is virtually impossible to be certain about the burdens of investment carried by the British economy in those years; but trial calculations show[29] that they may have increased from about 6½ per cent in the 1760s to eight or nine per cent during the French wars, to rise further to 11 per cent by the early 1830s. War expenditure, in this respect, had the same effect as investment. The striking increase in building, to revert to our earlier example, from the early 1760s onwards after a long period of near stagnation must have absorbed a large part of the newly available productive resources, yet was largely used up in providing accommodation no better than that already in existence for the rising population, particularly in the provincial towns.[30]

Lastly, a proportion of the increase was exported. How large this was may be seen by the proportion of *total* output (a very different matter) exported, according to an estimate for 1805.[31]

		Estimated output 1805–6		*Real values of exports 1805*
Cotton goods	£m.	15–20	£000	11,457
Woollens		18		9,000
Linens		4		966
Silk		3		699
Metal goods		10–17		4,859
Pottery and glass		4		842

Total industrial production was then estimated at £100–£110 million (produced by 1,130,000 workers) and exports (not all of which consisted of manufactures) at £40 million. It is clear that most of the increase in the output of these critical commodities was sent abroad. How were these exports used? One part merely went to investments abroad, having the same effect of 'arresting' immediate production in order to contribute to later rises in productivity, as investment at home. A further proportion paid for the war and subsidies to the Allies. Yet a third paid for the imports of food which the lag in

[29] Read by Professor Pollard to the Third International Economic History Conference, held in Munich in 1965, and to be published in the Conference Report. The percentages are those of gross capital formation over Gross National Product.

[30] J. Parry Lewis, *Building Cycles and Britain's Growth*, 1965, figure 2.1 (p. 12), esp. series a, c and d, and pp. 189–91; A. K. Cairncross and B. Weber, 'Fluctuations in Building in Britain, 1785–1849', *Ec. H.R.*, IX (1956); also p. 175 above.

[31] François Crouzet, *L'Economie Britannique et le Blocus Continental (1806–1813)*, 2 vols, Paris, 1958, I, 64.

agricultural output behind population increase had made necessary. A fourth went to pay for the rising imports of raw materials contained in the exports themselves, such as raw cotton or raw silk. And a fifth was lost in worsening terms of trade, which were the other side of the coin of rising productivity at home. Only the remainder brought imports which could be viewed as the converted product of home industry used for home consumption, and this remainder, in the early decades of industrialisation, might often be negligible or even negative. Where it was positive, it did contribute, in the form of colonial products, to rising standards of consumption, helped also by Pitt's Customs and Excise reforms; but the effects on the whole were minimal. Figures of *per capita* consumption of some imported items moved as follows (in lbs)[32]:

	Coffee (G.B.)	Tea (U.K.)	Sugar (U.K.)	Tobacco (U.K.)
1789–1791	0·10	1·16	14·7[a]	0·85[c]
1799–1801	0·07	1·48	20·0	1·17
1814–1816	0·51	1·27	15·5[b]	0·92

[a] 1793.   [b] 1814.   [c] 1790–1.

Changes in the standard of consumption

Thus much of the growing output was required to furnish investments at home and abroad, to provide for a rising population, to pay for wars, allies, and food imports as well as for raw material imports. What was left over for consumption still had to be divided among the different classes. It was not at all certain that any of it would necessarily be available to benefit the average income of labour. What wage figures we have are deficient and particularly difficult to interpret in a period of structural change in the economy.

In the view of many historians, there was a turning point in the movement of wages about the middle of the 1790s,[33] though they are not wholly agreed in which direction the 'turn' occurred. In the period 1760–95 the rise registered up to 1760 had given way to stagnation in real wages or perhaps a slight downturn: a recent study, summarising several earlier findings, estimated average wages to have risen by about 25 per cent, and the cost of living by 30 per cent,[34] though this average hides a definite rise in the industrial north,[35] and a distinct

[32] Mitchell and Deane, 355.
[33] E. J. Hobsbawm, 'The British Standard of Living, 1790–1850', *Ec.H.R.*, X (1957), 61.
[34] Deane and Cole, 20 *seq.*
[35] Lancashire real wages averaged 127 in 1759–61 (1700=100) and 138 in 1799–1801, having been as high as 164 in 1779–81. E. W. Gilboy, 'The Cost of

fall in London and the agricultural counties, representing rather more than half of the country.

For 1795–1815, prices and wages rose so fast that even a slight error in the indices would make a large difference to any conclusions we might wish to draw, and the indices, in fact, are not too reliable.[36] Some recent figures present the following picture:

	Index of average weekly wages[37] (1840 = 100)	Real wages, using the Gayer–Rostow–Schwartz price index[38] (1800 = 100)
1790	70	125
1795	82	113
1800	95	100
1805	109	127
1810	124	129
(1812–14)	(123)	(121)

They show stagnation with some years of serious falls during the war. In this total, however, it is likely that the agricultural labourer did rather better than his urban contemporary, except for certain scarce trades in provincial towns[39]—a consequence of the prosperity of

Living and Real Wages in Eighteenth-Century England', *Rev. of Economic Statistics*, XVIII (1936), 137, 140.

[36] Thus Joseph Lowe, the only contemporary who attempted comparative statements of national income (*The Present State of England, 1822*), concluded that there was an appreciable rise in *per capita* incomes to 1792–1806, and then a levelling-off at a high plateau in 1806–14. Had he used any of the modern price indices, he would have reached the more plausible conclusion of stagnation during the war, and a rise afterwards. P. Deane, 'Contemporary Estimates of National Income in the First Half of the Nineteenth Century', *Ec.H.R.*, VIII (1956), 345–6. Also, compare the following two series, both based on much the same kind of evidence:

	London cost of living (1700 = 100)		English prices of consumer goods (1700–1 = 100)
1760	97	1760–1	94
1761	99	1761–2	94
1800	252	1800–1	228
1801	190	1801–2	174
1814	198	1814–15	191
1815	183	1815–16	172

E. W. Gilboy, 'The Cost of Living and Real Wages in Eighteenth-Century England', *Review of Economic Statistics*, XVIII (1936), and E. Boody Schumpeter, 'English Prices and Public Finance, 1660–1822', *ibid.*, xx (1938).

[37] Deane and Cole, 23.

[38] From a reprint in Mitchell and Deane, 470–1. Though the G.R.S. index is a commodity index, it is weighted heavily in favour of food and coal.

[39] A. L. Bowley, *Wages in the United Kingdom in the Nineteenth Century*, Cambridge, 1900, 70. Money wages of agricultural labourers doubled between 1790 and 1806–15; those of others increased by 60 per cent at most.

agriculture in general in the war years. For the period as a whole, the Phelps Brown index of the building craftsman's wage rate, expressed as its power to buy 'composite units of consumables', shows a steady and substantial fall[40]:

Average	1759–61	62
„	1789–91	55
„	1813–15	49

In 1800 it had been as low as 38, and in 1801 34. The London artisan's real wage, according to Tucker, similarly fell from an average of 47·2 in 1790–2 to 42·8 in 1814–16, having been as low as 33 in 1800 and 1801.[41]

Such estimates of 'real wages' are at best of limited value in this context. They might tell us something about the fate of workers staying in the same jobs, but not about those changing their jobs, nor about their total family incomes. In this period, the transfer to new jobs was likely to have had a positive result on total wages, and the gains in money wages of agricultural workers entering the coal mines, or of cottage workers entering the mills, were substantial. Against this, the contributions of wives and children did not change very much —even in the industries being transformed most rapidly, they would continue to be fully employed—and the real wages of those remaining in their old jobs, craftsmen, domestic workers and agricultural labourers, appear to have fallen like those of the building workers. In total, the trend was likely to be downwards, particularly after 1795.[42]

Further, growing specialisation, and particularly the loss of gardens and small plots by industrial workers, made all wage earners more vulnerable to fluctuations of trade, and these were aggravated by war conditions. The problem of unemployment began to take on its modern guise, and was made acute during the bad harvests and sudden price rises of the war years. Poor Law expenditure quadrupled, and, while this was partly accounted for by rising prices, McCulloch's figures (p. 186) showed that even expressed in grain, and measured against population increases, it almost doubled in the war years.[43]

From whatever angle it is approached, it seems certain that the incomes of wage-earners stagnated during this period and fell towards its end, and some particularly bad years occurred during the French wars. The distribution among the classes also seemed to work against

[40] *Economica*, N.S. XXIII (1956), 313.
[41] R. S. Tucker, 'Real Wages of Artisans in London, 1729–1935', *J. Amer. Statistical Assoc.,* XXXI (1936).
[42] Cf. also Gayer, Rostow and Schwartz, *The Growth and Fluctuation of the British Economy, 1790–1850*, Oxford, 1953, II, 657.
[43] J. R. McCulloch, *Statistical Account of the British Empire*, 2 vols, 1837, II.

	Expenditure for the relief of the poor £ million	Expressed in wheat at current prices, 000 qts	Per head qts
Average			
1775–76	1·5	680	0·09
1783–85	2·0	862	0·11
1801–03	4·1	1,500	0·17
1814–16	5·8	1,700	0·15

labour, particularly in the war period, when 'there took place a whole series of transfers of income—to landlords, farmers, houseowners, bondholders, and entrepreneurs—and these almost certainly worsened the economic status of labour'.[44] It is unlikely that profit *rates* increased in this period: the reverse may well have been true. The reason for the relative fall in wage incomes per head must rather be sought in the likelihood of a rising capital-output ratio, and an increase of the proportion of the population depending on wages.[45]

As far as the other classes are concerned, there are some signs of distinct rises of income in this period. The tax returns, once they become fairly reliable in 1802, show a steady rise in the incomes they covered: between 1803 and 1814, Schedules C and E (incomes from Government Securities and Government employment) which could be avoided least, showed a rise of over 100 per cent; Schedules A and B (landowning and farming) which could also not be hidden, showed increases of about two-thirds; and only Schedule D, the least controllable, remained constant; but only perhaps one-sixth of all families were covered by all the returns put together.[46]

It is more difficult still to combine the estimates of falling wage rates for labour and rising incomes for some other classes into national average incomes. Estimates derived from the production figures lead to a plausible growth rate of 0·6–0·9 per cent a year *per capita*[47]

[44] T. S. Ashton, 'The Standard of Life of the Workers in England, 1790–1830', *Capitalism and the Historians* (ed. F. A. Hayek), 1954, 135. Miss Deane also notes the growth of inequality between Gregory King (1688) and Patrick Colquhoun (1812), though she is not sure when this occurred—'The Industrial Revolution and Economic Growth: the Evidence of Early British National Income Estimates', *Economic Development and Cultural Change*, VI (1957), 168.

[45] For the theoretical mode of such a shift, see E. H. Phelps Brown, 'The Long-Term Movement of Real Wages', *The Theory of Wage Determination* (ed. J. T. Dunlop), 1957.

[46] P. K. O'Brien, 'British Incomes and Property in the Early Nineteenth Century', *Ec.H.R.*, XII (1959); Arthur Hope-Jones, *Income Tax in the Napoleonic Wars*, Cambridge, 1939, 74–7; also Deane, 'The Industrial Revolution and Economic Growth', 166, and R. M. Hartwell, 'The Rising Standard of Living in England, 1800–1850', *Ec.H.R.*, XIII (1961), 398.

[47] Deane and Cole, 80, 280.

before 1800, but much of this was lost in investment, wars and exports at falling prices: any remainder to raise incomes *per capita* must have been negligible. After 1800, the national product at constant prices is estimated to have risen at well over one per cent to 1821,[48] though real incomes per head were said, by the same authorities, to have fallen between 1800 and 1812 from an index of 100 to 94, to rise to 114 only by 1822.[49] It is possible to combine these diverse series into a combined picture of real consumption,[50] to reveal the following outline of developments (in £ per head at constant 1791 prices):

	Gross national income	Allowance for investment, Government expenditure and balance of trade	Private consumption
England and Wales			
1751	12·4	2·3	10·1
1761	13·5	5·2	8·3
1771	12·5	2·0	10·5
1781	13·5	3·1	10·4
1791	14·0	2·0	12·0
1801	12·2	3·5	10·2
1811	14·9	3·1	11·8

The picture is one of general stagnation over the period as a whole, whether measured in terms of total income or of consumption, with noticeable dips in the war years 1761 and 1801, but less so in 1781, and, significantly, least in 1811. There is a slight impression of a rise to the outbreak of the French War, held back in the last two decades by the war expenditure.

The middle column seems to have been affected more by wars than by the costs of investment, but there is reason to believe that the figures on which this table is based understate the growth in the rate of investment, and thus the sum that has to be subtracted from total national income or product to arrive at what was available for consumption. The gap between output and consumption was particularly wide during the war of 1793–1815; it was the first modern war to affect the creation of wealth of Britain seriously and adversely.

The withdrawal of men from productive occupations to the forces was more massive than before, though still not large by twentieth-century standards: at a maximum of perhaps 550,000, the men under

---

[48] *Ibid.*, 282–3.
[49] 'The Industrial Revolution and Economic Growth', p. 171.
[50] J. E. Williams, 'The British Standard of Living, 1750–1850', *Ec.H.R.*, XIX (1966), Tables IV and V. Figure for 1801 corrected by author after publication.

arms never exceeded the peace-time establishment by more than half a million, or 3·2 per cent of the United Kingdom population of 15·7 million in 1801,[51] and many of them, especially those from Ireland, left only positions of disguised unemployment. Casualties, at 210,000, were very small in relation to the national population increase over 22 years. The loss of their production may thus not have been serious in itself, but the war meant an interruption of the conversion to an industrial society paying for part of its food by exports, and caused a large-scale diversion of resources to agriculture which tended to slow down industrialisation before 1813, and created widespread agricultural distress thereafter. The reduction in concrete investment is well reflected in the flow of monetary funds to the Government: quite apart from the rises in taxation, some of which must have come out of capital, the expenditure raised by borrowing, averaging about £20 million a year in the American War of Independence and £30 million in the French Wars, was of the same order of magnitude as total actual capital formation.[52] Part of this, again, stimulated some industries and even financed some productive investment; but the major part was clearly wasted, and the £57 million transferred as subsidy to the Allies, in 1793–1815,[53] as well as the cost of the forces abroad, had to be earned as foreign exchange.

It is true that the isolation from Britain induced some countries, notably in North-West Europe and the U.S.A., to expand their industries without knowledge of the latest British technology, and the virtual destruction of these war-infant industries after 1815 gave an additional boost to British exports, especially to textiles and metal goods; but it does not seem plausible that this made up for the loss in the long run. Losses of ships, and the costs of the interruption of trade and production caused by financial and monetary crises were also much heavier than in peace-time. Little is to be set against this in terms of inducements to entrepreneurship or inventiveness, and while some administrative innovations, such as the income tax and the Census of Population, and the development of the capital market, may be accounted positive, other necessary administrative and taxation reforms were held up because of the war.

[51] W. W. Rostow, *The Process of Economic Growth*, Oxford, 1960, 150 *seq.* Gayer, Rostow and Schwartz, 136 (note); also Deane and Cole, 151–3, 291.
[52] Actual 'net' borrowing averaged £41 million a year in both the American War of Independence and the French wars, but part of this was transfer payments, especially the servicing of existing debt. E. B. Schumpeter, 'English Prices', 27–8, 36–7; W. Sombart, *Krieg und Kapitalismus* (Munich and Leipzig, 1913), 10; J. H. Clapham, 'Europe after the Great Wars, 1816 and 1920', *Economic Journal*, XXX (1920), 424.
[53] J. H. Clapham, 'Wars and Subsidies in Times of War 1793–1914', *Economic Journal*, XXVII (1917), 494–5.

Conclusion

The rising prosperity of the first half of the eighteenth century had provided a certain amount of slack in the economy, which could be taken up when the strain of industrialisation began to affect the following two generations. Manufacturing output increased very much faster in the second half of the century, particularly after 1780, but this improvement scarcely benefited the men and women living through this period, for a series of interconnected reasons. Instead of benefiting the producers, the enlarged output, much of it produced by new methods which required much readjustment on the part of the industrial population, was almost wholly absorbed by the need for exports to pay for raw materials and for food, to meet the gap in home food supplies, as well as for capital repatriation and some foreign investment; by the need to provide capital and consumer goods for a growing population; by the need for large-scale investment, especially in providing the infrastructure for an industrial country with a national market; and by long, increasingly costly wars.

As a result, total incomes per head, if they rose at all, rose only slightly to the 1790s, and then stagnated, most of the war years thereafter being well below the levels attained in the previous years of peace. Similarly, wage incomes stagnated, or at best rose but slightly, to the mid-1790s, with growing differentials between London wages and urban industrial wages, which had to rise relatively to attract labour,[54] and rural wages, which certainly fell even then. In 1795–1815, all real wages declined, and the fall in real standards of living was greater still because of the greater needs of urban living, the loss of domestic food production and the growing incidence of periodic unemployment.

The war years, and possibly the period before, saw a transfer of income to landlords, farmers, rentiers, and capital owners, but it is doubtful if much of this found its way to higher consumption. Instead of building bigger country houses,[55] or spending more on finer carriages or better furniture, even the upper and middle classes invested in drainage schemes, roads, canals or workmen's cottages. Whereas the people of Britain before 1760 had consumed most of the growing wealth, the next two generations spent it in laying the foundations of an industrial state, and safeguarding their commercial and colonial supremacy by costly wars.

[54] 'Buildings were always better where there were industries'—C. E. Fussell and C. Goodman, 'The Housing of the Rural Population in the Eighteenth Century', *Economic History*, II (1930), 75; also Deane and Cole, chapter 3.
[55] 'The building cycle we have just examined (i.e. the French War years) was probably coloured more by working-class houses and less by luxurious architecture than any (since 1700)', J. Parry Lewis, 28.

Chapter seven

The Triumph of Industrialism, 1815–1873

The Long Peace

The battle of Waterloo ended a period of major wars. There followed, for Britain, a century of peaceful development, interrupted only by minor excursions such as the Crimean War and the Boer War, which affected the economy only marginally. This long period of peace was one favourable factor; the virtual absence of effective foreign competition until the 1870s was another; and thus favoured, Britain was able to develop the firm industrial basis laid by 1815, backed up as it was by commercial supremacy and a large Colonial Empire, into a flourishing modern economy.

In some ways, the previous period had seen the more fundamental structural changes, since they set going a new development which now merely remained to be extended to an ever-growing area. But the area actually covered before 1815 was small. Measured in tons or square yards, measured in the sheer size of the output of the new industries, the expansion of the 60 years after 1815 was incomparably greater than of any similar period before. The table on p. 191 will give an indication of some of the quantities involved.[1]

There were other industries, it is true, which did not grow as fast as the old 'staples', and in many of them there had been no real change to factory- or mass-production even by 1873—cutlery, furniture making or tailoring, for example. Yet, there too, the craftsman at the end of the period was able to make use of mass-produced machinery, tools or components, imported or mass-produced raw materials, perhaps, or he had more mechanical horsepower at his command: fixed steam power has been estimated at 350,000 h.p. in 1840, 700,000 h.p. in 1860 and 2,000,000 h.p. in 1880.[2]

The shift of employment towards manufacturing industry and transport and commerce continued, creating the typical structure of a fully

---

[1] Mitchell and Deane, 8–9, 115, 131–2, 179, 190–2, 271; Deane and Cole, chapter 6.

[2] M. G. Mulhall, *Dictionary of Statistics*, 4th edn, 1899, 546. Steam power in locomotives and steamships grew much faster, from 250,000 h.p. in 1840 to 5,600,000 in 1880.

	Raw cotton consumption U.K. mn. lbs	Raw wool consumption U.K. mn. lbs	Index of real net output of textiles (1800 = 100)	Coal U.K. mn. T.	Pig iron G.B. 000T.	Hoffmann index all industrial production ex. building (1913 = 100)	Population G.B. mn.
Average							
1814–16	81	113[a]	127[c]	15·9[f]	325[h]	7·12	12·94
1845–7	554	188[a]	632[d]	45·9[g]	2,000[d]	21·4	19·71
1872–4	1,234	453[b]	1,481[e]	126·5[a]	6,433	48·9	26·85
Factors of increase, 1814/16 to 1872/4	15	4	12	18	20	7	2·1

[a] Estimated [b] 1870–4 [c] 1815 [d] 1847 [e] 1872 [f] 1816 [g] 1845 [h] 1818

developed industrial society at the end, as shown in the following statistics relating to the British labour force[3]:

| | Mining, manufacturing, building | | Trade and transport | | Total occupied population |
	% of labour Force	Millions	% of Labour Force	Millions	Millions
1811	30·2	1·7	11·6	0·6	5·5
1841	40·5	3·3	14·2	1·2	8·4
1871	43·1	5·3	19·6	2·3	12·0

At the same time, the proportion of people living in towns also increased sharply. Eighteenth-century industries, including mining and textiles, were still largely rural occupations, and so, of course, was the largest occupational group of all, agriculture. But while in 1801 only one quarter at most, and probably much less, lived in towns with more than 10,000 inhabitants, by 1831 one quarter lived in towns of over 20,000, by 1841 it was over one third, by 1851 one half, and by 1881 over two-thirds.[4] At the same time, even many nominally rural parishes were, particularly after 1851, to be found increasingly in what were properly urban overspill areas.[5] This population was being bound much closer together by the railway system, built up mainly in the 1830s and 1840s, which allowed a division of labour undreamt-of in earlier centuries, and with it, a rapid growth in productivity.

There was a price to pay for this concentration, and the development of a capital-intensive system of production. It created social problems of urban living, which will be discussed further below; but it also required a staggeringly large effort of investment at home and abroad, to which we must now turn.

The growth of capital

The creation of capital in this period may be usefully thought of as proceeding along three parallel routes. The first was the building of houses, of streets, of waterworks and municipal buildings, made necessary simply by the growth of the population and its urbanisation, without implying any consequent rise in productivity or wealth. The second was the building of factories, of blast furnaces, of railways and

---

[3] Deane and Cole, 142–3.
[4] Deane and Cole, 9, 120; S. G. Checkland, *The Rise of Industrial Society in England 1815–1885*, 1964, 33; J. H. Clapham, *An Economic History of Modern Britain*, 3 vols, 1964 edn, 67; A. K. Cairncross, *Home and Foreign Investment 1870–1913*, Cambridge, 1953, 68–70; John Saville, *Rural Depopulation in England and Wales, 1851–1951*, Routledge, 1957, ch. 1.
[5] A. L. Bowley, 'Rural Population in England and Wales', *J. R. Stat. S.*, 77 (1914), 609.

docks, and of machinery and equipment, or in other words, the creation of those means of production on which the progress of an industrial society was ultimately based. The third was the investment of British capital abroad. Though for the purpose of exposition, these may be kept apart, in practice the interest lies in the close way in which they were all interconnected.

We have seen that, to 1815, total building only just kept pace with population growth, which implied, in view of the growth of industrial building, a decline in housing standards. After 1815, the position improved somewhat: according to Shannon's statistics, the annual rate of growth in 1817–1849 inclusive was 1·366 per cent for the population, and 1·796 per cent for the brick index[6]; but the production of bricks and of other materials for which we have no records had to carry the vast amount of new railway building and urban development as well. If we limit ourselves to housing alone, it seems that over the period 1815–1873, building probably just about kept pace with population increase. Between 1815 and 1851 there was probably some deterioration, but there was a marginal improvement between 1851 and 1871, when the number of people per 'house' decreased from 5·22 to 5·02 in England and Wales, at least.[7] Such estimates of house building as exist show a similar development. In Great Britain, between 1856 and 1865, a new house was built for every 4·4 additional population, and in 1866–73, one for every 3·9. The *net* increases in the housing stock in England and Wales, compared with the net increase in the population, showed the following rates[8]:

1831–41	3·9
1841–51	6·4
1851–61	4·3
1861–71	4·4
1871–81	4·6

The marginal rate thus being below the average was bound to have improved the total number of housing 'units' to a given number of people.

As a proportion of the national income, or as a burden on the economy, domestic building also did not change much in this period. In 1855, when usable estimates begin, total residential building

---

[6] H. A. Shannon, 'Bricks, a Trade Index, 1785–1849', *Economica*, N.S. I (1934).

[7] Census of Population, etc.

[8] I.e. additional people divided by additional houses. B. Weber, 'A New Index of Residential Construction and Long Cycles in House Building in Great Britain, 1838–1950', *Scottish J. of Political Economy*, II (1955), Tables II and VII

accounted for just under 1·5 per cent of net national income of the U.K.; the peak of one of the periodic building cycles which were a prominent feature of the century[9] was reached in 1875–7, when it amounted to 2·4 per cent.[10] Over the period as a whole, it is likely to have fluctuated around 1½ per cent to 2 per cent, seldom diverging far from it. Yet this apparent secular stability hides an actual relative decline of the provision of housing and related facilities. Technical change and the increase in output per man largely passed the building industry by, and any gains from slight improvements and techniques of lower costs of materials were offset by the reduction in working hours of building labour; while the relative fall in the costs of materials was partly due to reduced taxation, and represents a transfer rather than a real saving in cost.[11] Therefore house building, to keep its relative share, should have shown an increase in its share of national production.

But further, and more significantly, the conglomeration of houses into ever larger towns itself reduced the amenities of living, and would require large-scale investment in sewerage, water supply, street paving, the provision of parks etc. to counteract this effect. It is clear that investment in those utilities did not keep pace with urban growth. Instead, urban residential construction, by terrace building, multi-storey apartments and back-to-backs, sought to gain reductions in cost from the herding together of populations, and thus reduced the real standards of housing.[12] Comparing the 1790s with 1830, the Webbs noted that

'all . . . (the) nuisances were found in undiminished intensity with the important difference that, instead of one such street or group of underground dwellings or lodging houses there were in 1830, literally thousands in the same awful state. This meant that the wretched inhabitants of these cellars and tenements had become, not only more densely crowded together, but also increasingly hemmed in, so that their whole lives were passed in the slums. The growth of Manchester, together with the corresponding transformation of Salford, Stockport, Stalybridge, Hyde, Ashton and

[9] Parry Lewis, *Building Cycles and Britain's Growth*, Macmillan, 1965. Figures in App. 4, 316–17.
[10] Figures based on C. H. Feinstein, 'Income and Investment in the United Kingdom, 1856–1914', *Econ. J.*, 1961, expanded in Mitchell and Deane, 367 and 373. This section owes much to this work, as also to Deane and Cole, ch. 8 and App. 3.
[11] K. Maiwald, 'An Index of Building Costs in the United Kingdom', *Ec.H.R.*, VII (1954).
[12] See the discussion in Asa Briggs, *Victorian Cities*, Odhams, 1963, esp. chapters 1 and 2.

other townships, had, for miles in every direction, defiled the atmosphere, polluted the streams, and destroyed the vegetation.'[13]

The horrors revealed by the Reports on the Sanitary Condition of the Labouring Population (1842), on the Health of Towns (1840), and on the State of Large Towns (1844–5), we have constantly to remind ourselves, were not exceptional: they represented the normal environment of the poorer sections of all urban residents. And just as, in the 1790s, Eden found the workhouse diet better than that of many labourers outside, Chadwick, in 1842, found conditions in the towns worse than in the prisons:

'The prisons', he wrote, 'were formerly distinguished for their filth and their bad ventilation; but the description given by Howard of the worst prisons he visited in England (which he states were among the worst he had seen in Europe) were exceeded in every wynd in Edinburgh and Glasgow, inspected by Dr. Arnott and myself. . . . More filth, worse physical suffering and moral disorder than Howard describes . . . are to be found amongst the cellar population of the working people of Liverpool, Manchester, or Leeds, and in large portions of the metropolis. . . . At Edinburgh, there were instances of poor persons in a state of disease committed from motives of humanity to the prison, that they might be taken care of and cured.'[14]

This was, indeed, the one major field of social life in which conditions seriously deteriorated. Unlike the old, smaller market town, the new industrial town isolated the middle classes from 'the conditions of the slums on the other side of the town [which] when revealed to them, they regarded with much the same kind of incredulous horror that was aroused by travellers' tales of savage Africa'.[15] This revelation came in the last quarter of the century, and was summarised by the Royal Commission of 1884–5:

'At the very outset of their inquiry Your Majesty's Commissioners had testimony proving two important facts: first, that though there was a great improvement, described by Lord Shaftesbury as "enormous" in the condition of the housing of the poor compared to that of 30 years ago, yet the evils of overcrowding, especially in London, were still a public scandal, and were becoming in certain localities more serious than ever they were; second, that there was much legislation designed to meet these evils, yet that the existing laws were not put into force, some of them having remained a

[13] S. and B. Webb, *English Local Government: Statutory Authorities for Special Purposes*, 1922, 401.
[14] Quoted in J. H. Clapham, *Economic History of Modern Britain*, 3 vols, Cambridge, 1964 edn, I, 537–8.
[15] W. J. Reader, *Life in Victorian England*, Batsford, 1964, 68.

dead letter from the date when they first found a place in the statute book. . . .

The conditions in provincial towns . . . is less unfavourable than that of the poorer districts of the Metropolis . . . but the evil is not confined to London. . . .

What is called "jerry building" is too well known to need evidence. . . . The old houses are rotten from age and neglect. The new houses often commence where the old ones leave off, and are rotten from the first. It is quite certain that the working classes are largely housed in dwellings which would be unsuitable even if they were not overcrowded.'[16]

While the evidence from which these conclusions were drawn referred largely to city centres and the East End of London, conditions in industrial towns and in agricultural cottages were no better in the 1880s. The main reason for the survival of these conditions was that the poor could not have afforded the rent for better dwellings.[17] Farmers' houses, by contrast, had been much improved, and the top ranks of the skilled artisans moved into new four-roomed terrace houses which, though equally drab, were less dangerous to health.[18]

Most of the building and most of the population increase in this period were necessarily concentrated in the urban areas. Yet it is significant that the slight improvement in the number of persons per house noted before was mainly to be found in the rural areas, owing, in part, to emigration from them: in the urban registration districts (taking into account changes in boundaries), the population increased by 69 per cent between 1841 and 1871 in Great Britain, and the housing stock in those areas, in England and Wales, by 72 per cent, a barely noticeable improvement; but in the rural areas the increases were 12 per cent and 19 per cent, respectively.[19] The failure of house building to meet adequately the challenge of rapid urbanisation of the majority of the population—let alone its failure to match general productivity increases—was one of the most potent factors holding down general living standards in this period.

If house building fell short of needs, the creation of productive capital equipment in this period was its outstanding achievement. From 1856, when the best estimates begin,[20] there was a relatively stable long-term rate of gross domestic fixed capital formation around

---

[16] R.C. on the Housing of the Working Classes, Report, Parl. Papers, 1884–1885, XXX, Cd. 4402, 4, 8, 12.

[17] Marian Bowley, The British Building Industry, Cambridge, 1966, 360.

[18] J. H. Clapham, An Economic History of Modern Britain, 3 vols, Cambridge, 1926–30, II, 49 seq.

[19] Based on Tables 1, 2 and 3 (pp. 328, 332) of App. 7 of J. Parry Lewis, Building Cycles and Britain's Growth, Macmillan, 1965.

[20] Feinstein, and Deane and Cole, Table 82, 308.

seven to eight per cent of national expenditure. Recent evidence would support the view that such a rate has been maintained since about 1830, and probably since 1820. This is confirmed by Robert Giffen, who found a cumulative annual growth rate of 'property' of only 1·1 per cent (1·7 per cent in Scotland) between 1815 and 1845, as against 2·6 per cent (2·8 per cent) in 1845–75, while population growth, if anything, slowed down from 1·4 per cent to 1·25 per cent per annum; but, when changes in prices are taken into consideration, the rate of progress was not dissimilar in the two periods.[21] At the same time, the same kind of proportionate investment had a much greater power of increasing the real wealth and income of the country after the turning point of the mid-1840s than before. The reasons for this bear closer examination.

In the first place, let us remember that we measure a proportion of the national income or product. As incomes per head (and the number of people) rise, so does the real equipment represented by such a figure. Secondly, this investment, in concrete terms, did not necessarily go into the same kinds of things. The cotton industry, for example, was wholly mechanised in the 1820s and 1830s, and the woollen in the 1850s and 1860s, but in both the investment, in real terms, accelerated. The largest single factor, however, was the creation of the railway network in 1830–50, employing perhaps three to four per cent of the national income, or one half of the total productive investment, in those years.[22] It is true that much railway investment continued in the second half of the nineteenth century, but it was an ever lighter burden on the economy. With the railways, the ironmaking and engineering capacity was expanded, and with them, in turn, investment in coal mines. This was the period when British coal output exceeded that of the rest of the world put together, and when the country thought of itself as the 'workshop of the world', exemplified by the triumph of the 1851 Exhibition.[23] But many of these are investments of 'long gestation', eating up vast sums of capital for little immediate increases in output,[24] meanwhile raising the capital-output ratio, until the fruits of these efforts show themselves in the long run, rather like the somewhat different adverse conversion conditions of the eighteenth century, noted above.

[21] Robert Giffen, *The Growth of Capital*, 1889, 59, 155.
[22] Actual gross investment averaged £5 million in the late 1830s, and £15 million 10 years later, with a peak of £30 million in 1847—A. G. Kenwood, 'Railway Investment in Britain, 1825–1875', *Economica*, N.S. XXXII (1965), 322.
[23] J. D. Chambers, *The Workshop of the World*, London, O.U.P., 1961.
[24] This seems a more reasonable explanation than that in W. W. Rostow, *British Economy of the Nineteenth Century*, Oxford, 1947, 17, which leaves unresolved the contradiction with p. 19, where the low consumption levels are being stressed.

Finally, it was only with these investments, particularly in engineering and transport, that the industrialisation of the country was, in a sense, completed, and a single economy created. In the early stages, new methods spring up here and there, but are not necessarily inter-related: spinning machinery may have become efficient, but not yet the making of it[25]; or the making may have been mechanised, and steel could still be expensive: yet steel-making or machine building could not be developed until a large-scale spinning industry (among others) had created the demand for them. There comes a point in economic development when the mutual interaction of several improvements create 'external economies' beyond those available to different sectors individually. These depend very much on a transport network, and seem to have been particularly effective about the middle of the century.

Thereafter, from c. 1850 onwards, the effects on lowering costs and rising incomes are both swift and powerful, and while the increase in the total national product will make any constant proportion of its increase worth more and more in real terms, the efforts of setting aside that percentage in savings and investment themselves become easier to bear.

In a century with a growing population, the cumulative effects of a growth rate exceeding the population increase can be quite startling: on Giffen's figures, 'personal property' in Britain amounted to £1,200 million in 1814 and £1,300 million in 1819, compared with £3,500 million in 1865 and £5,000 million in 1875, so that the *increase* in the last 10 years exceeded the total at the beginning of the period, only half a century earlier.[26]

Behind it all was continuous technical progress, cost-reducing and cumulative despite trade cycles and the fluctuating direction taken by investment. It was affecting the production of final consumer goods, though more slowly, as well as the production of capital goods and intermediate products, and it had even begun to affect agriculture, where for the first time output per acre rose sharply after 1820, and output per man after about 1850.[27]

[25] For a striking testimony of the effectiveness of such growing confluence of technical factors, see the evidence given to the *Select Committee on Artisans and Machinery*, 1825, and on *Manufactures, Commerce and Shipping*, 1833.

[26] This was not, on the whole, affected by changes in the price level, and 'we can only ascribe [it] to the accumulated effects of mechanical and chemical discoveries, so that year by year the industrial machine is more and more productive in proportion to the labourers employed'—R. Giffen, 'Recent Accumulation of Capital in the United Kingdom', 1878, reprinted in *Essays in Finance, First Series*, 5th edn, 1890, 185.

[27] J. R. Healey and E. L. Jones, 'Wheat Yields in England, 1815–59', *J.R. Stat. S.*, Series A, 125 (1962), Table I, 578; David Grigg, *Agricultural Revolution in South Lincolnshire*, Cambridge, 1966, 117, 152–3, 192; Leo Drescher, 'The

Finally, part of the investment was made abroad. This was a relatively new departure. Until the later eighteenth century, Britain was probably a net creditor, largely to the Dutch, and even by 1815 the net credit balance abroad has been estimated at an almost negligible figure of £10 million.[28] Exports of capital by Britain were among the most changeable of her activities, fluctuating violently and reflecting the delicate and complex inter-relationship between her own economy and that of the rest of the world, but there was a clear long-term upward trend in the figures. In the 40 years from 1816 to 1855, a net total of about £240 million was so invested, or £6 million a year; in the 20 years 1856–75, the total was £816 million, or £41 million a year, seven times as much. By that time, it was not only large enough to affect the total British economy: it was, in peak years, of an order of magnitude comparable with that of the whole of productive investment at home.

This surplus in the foreign balance of payment was not achieved by commodity exports: commodity trade, year by year, showed a heavy deficit. It was financed by 'invisible earnings' from shipping and financial services, and from the dividend and interest payments of the earlier investments themselves. Thus, insofar as this export of capital abroad was helping to raise British wealth and incomes, it was achieved largely by technical improvements in shipping, which thus became as important as those, for example, in cotton spinning and iron making, and by the efficiency of the City of London, achieved less by technical improvements as such, as by the 'external economies' of being at the centre of the most advanced industrial country and trading nation.

In concrete terms, these investments took numerous forms. Many were merely loans to Governments, forming perhaps 'a mere prop for military despotism' or at best creating political stability in a region for the furtherance of British trade and the supply of raw materials, as in South America after its liberation. For other investors, 'it was not enough that the money they invested be spent in one way or another for the products of British workshops ... they had calculated the unearned increment of progress and were seeking its appropriation ... the application of their capital should be reproductive. It should assume the form of what modern economists have called "producer's goods". The capital should be so used as to create the means for its

Development of Agricultural Production in Great Britain and Ireland from the early Nineteenth Century', *Manchester School*, 1955, 168.
    [28] Albert H. Imlah, *Economic Elements in the Pax Britannica*, Cambridge, Mass., 1958, Table 4, on which much of the following is based. This is a notional figure and may well be too low.

repayment'.[29] Thus a large proportion went into docks, canals, and railways abroad, or into civic loans used to underwrite such enterprises. Other sums went to foreign banks and merchant houses that were intermediaries in developing mines or financing cotton crops abroad—though some also went into industries that were to compete ultimately with those of Britain. After 1850 a much greater effort went into financing, and building, railways abroad, in Europe, India and North America, than in building out the British system, and other public utilities as well as mines overseas, were also financed from Britain and at times built or developed by British engineers.

Throughout this period, the export of capital was heaviest when building at home was slack—the 'inverse building cycle'[30] was evening out total investment, which was thus more steady than either home or overseas investment alone. Further, foreign investment was, to a considerable extent, a necessary complement to the home economy which required overseas supplies of raw materials, overseas markets and, increasingly, overseas food to extend its own industrial specialisation. For a time, the world, or at least the Atlantic economy, consisted of a single industrial complex, in Great Britain, having close mutual links with the non-industrial world. From the middle of the century onwards, other industrial regions came into being, but the international exchanges of goods continued to expand. No doubt foreign supplies of minerals, raw cotton or food would have expanded in any case. But in order to maintain the growth rate of which the British industrial economy was then capable, Britain had to transfer to the rest of the world some of the capital accumulation, and some of the capital goods, she created out of her own resources. At home and abroad, growing wealth and growing productivity were based on the intelligent use of capital.

The standard of living, 1815–1845

The conditions of life of the industrial population in the first half of the nineteenth century have been among the most hotly debated questions in economic history, both among contemporaries, who presumably based their views at least partly on direct personal impressions, and among historians since.[31] At first sight, this must appear puzzling

[29] L. H. Jenks, *The Migration of British Capital to 1875*, Nelson, 1963; 1st edn, 1927, 71.

[30] Brinley Thomas, *Migration and Economic Growth*, Cambridge, 1954, chapter XI.

[31] For a recent summary of the controversy, see E. J. Hobsbawm and R. M. Hartwell, 'The Standard of Living during the Industrial Revolution: A Discussion', *Ec.H.R.*, XVI (1963), and for a bibliography, W. H. Chaloner, 'Labour Conditions during the Industrial Revolutions: A Select Bibliography, 1953–1963', *Bulletin of the Society for the Study of Labour History*, 8 (1964).

in view of the substantial increase in the national productive potential and in output and income per head. The best recent estimates put the increase of the real product at 2·9 per cent per annum, compound, or 1·5 per cent per annum and *per capita*.[32] There is no reason to doubt the general order to magnitude of these figures and their breakdown also seems plausible: manufacturing, mining and building rose from 20·8 per cent of the total in 1811 to 34·4 per cent in 1841, or from £62·5 million to £155·5 million, while the product of agriculture, forestry and fishing correspondingly fell from 35·7 per cent to 22·1 per cent, the rest remaining constant, at 43·5 per cent.[33] The Hoffmann index of industrial production (including building) which is probably more reliable for this period than for some others, rose from an average 9·01 in 1814–16 to 23·7 in 1844–6, an increase broadly in line with these estimates.

This, by any standard, even that of the preceding decades, is very rapid increase indeed. It ought to have been clearly evident to contemporary observers, for a compound rate of 1·5 per cent gives the 'average' British citizen an increase, over 30 years, of around 56 per cent; concretely, national product per head at constant prices was computed at £13·2 in 1811 and £21·3 in 1841, after an unbroken progression.

It is, of course, possible that the distribution between different sectors of the population was uneven, and turned against the low income earners. But, in view of the relatively small class of rent and profit receivers, the growth in their share would have had to have been enormous to make much impact on a growth of that magnitude among the rest of the population, but, in fact, everything but a minor shift seems unlikely *a priori*. Prices, on the whole, were falling in this period,[34] and this, while it might benefit rent incomes, tends in general to work against profits and in favour of such workers as keep in employment. Despite the Ricardian forecasts, evolving at that time,

[32] These figures are over the period 1811–21 to 1841–51 for Great Britain— Deane and Cole, Table 73, 283. Also cf. Deane, 'The Industrial Revolution and Economic Growth: the Evidence of Early British National Income Estimates', *Economic Development and Cultural Change*, V (1957), Table 3, 171; and J. C. Stamp, *British Incomes and Property*, 1916, 427.

[33] *Ibid.*, Tables 37 and 76. These figures treat housing as a capital good, and income from housing as a 'product'.

[34]

	Gayer–Rostow–Schwartz commodity prices	Rousseaux
Average prices 1814–16	134	170
1829–31	95	110
1844–46	83	109

Gayer, Rostow and Schwartz, *op. cit.*; P. Rousseaux, *Les Mouvements de Fond de l'Economie Anglaise 1800–1913*, Brussels, 1938; Mitchell and Deane, 470–1.

which expected the rent receivers in any growing economy to gain disproportionate benefits, there were other causes to reduce the level and the share of rents for most of this period,[35] and only urban rents are likely to have increased substantially. As for interest rates, the yield on Consols was firmly downward, from $4\frac{1}{2}$ to five per cent at the end of the war, to about $3\frac{1}{2}$ per cent around 1830 and just over three per cent in the mid-forties. Thus, only urban rents could be expected to show a disproportionate rise.

For profits, the story is more complex. The increase in the quantity of capital was clearly exceeding the rate of increase of capitalists. In an age of partnerships, when few industries were as yet covered by joint-stock enterprises, and those that did, like the railways, were still unable to distinguish capital from revenue,[36] high profit rates were hidden by a heavy rate of investment which as yet escaped taxation, or even the taxation returns, and in this context the striking growth of home and foreign capital investment is proof of the relative prosperity of capital owners, at a time when price falls were accompanied by falls in costs, including labour costs.

No useful statistics exist, and the orders of magnitude cannot even be estimated. Some redistribution against the labouring population occurred, but it could not have been large enough to wipe out a potential rise of over one half in incomes.

There are three other possibilities. One is that the price fall has been exaggerated, particularly in the case of prices of goods bought by the poorer classes. The price indices used are, indeed, open to much doubt on that score, and if the real falls in prices were less, then the total rise in real *per capita* incomes was also less[37] and the hands of those who doubt any rise in living standards are strengthened. Secondly, since the terms of trade worsened, part of the increased output was 'lost' in conversion to consumption goods by foreign trade.[38]

The third consideration is one that affects all comparisons of industrialised and traditional economies, and the transition between them. Such comparison tends to exaggerate the growth by counting in some productive activities at the advanced stage, because they have entered the market, but ignoring exactly parallel value creations in the first stage, since they are carried on domestically. Thus home-brewing or baking, the produce of kitchen gardens, the gathering of

[35] Deane and Cole, Table 80.
[36] H. Pollins, 'Aspects of Railway Financing Before 1868', *Studies in the History of Accounting* (ed. A. C. Littleton and B. S. Yamey), 1956.
[37] This is also true of the discussion on wage levels, below (p. 204).
[38] A. J. Taylor, 'Progress and Poverty in Britain, 1780–1850. A Reappraisal', *History*, N.S. 45 (1960).

firewood or home-dressmaking will be ignored in the early stage; but the products of the brewing and baking industry, market gardening, coal production or the dressmaking industry will appear in the later total, suggesting a fictitious rise in real incomes.[39] Where technical and organisational change was rapid, as in 1815–1845, this could make a substantial difference.

Further, much of the new output, appearing as an increase in the total national product, was used in the productive process rather than by consumers. It should therefore properly be counted as a *cost*, to be set *against* the benefits of more complex methods of production, and not as an increase in the total product. Thus the railway system, except when it was used for pleasure, represented a cost to be offset against the specialisation and concentration of industry it made possible, and not an increase in welfare itself. The same was true of much of the other capital goods sector, e.g. large parts of the engineering or shipping industry. In terms of a real increase in the welfare of consumers, a large part of the increase in the national product was irrelevant.

The effect of these factors, in total, was substantial, so that real wages can be shown to have increased far less than the average 'product' per head.[40] A collation of Bowley's and Wood's statistics produces the following changes in average real wages[41]:

1816	94
1831	108
1840	100
1850	110

The maximum improvement, therefore, is only of the order of 16 points, or about 18 per cent. Among these, the agricultural labourer probably fared worst until the mid-1830s, when much unemployment, particularly over the winter, robbed him of the advantages he had gained in the war boom, without the compensations of many former payments in kind: it was only the rise in farm prices and profits,[42] and the demands of labour for navvying after about 1836 which permitted

---

[39] S. Kuznets, 'Economic Change', 145 *seq.*

[40] This appears to be denied by R. M. Hartwell, who argues for a low capital-income ratio, and a higher conversion rate of output into actual income. Despite a well-argued case, however, the evidence seems to be against him in this respect—'The Rising Standard of Living in England, 1800–1850', *Ec.H.R.*, XIII (1961), 398 *seq.*

[41] S. G. Checkland, *The Rise of Industrial Society in England, 1815–1885*, Longmans, 1964, 228. This section is much indebted to this excellent summary. See also G. H. Wood, 'The Course of Average Wages between 1790 and 1860', *Econ. J.*, IX (1899), A. L. Bowley, *Wages in the United Kingdom in the Nineteenth Century*, Cambridge, 1900, 70.

[42] N. Gash. 'Rural Unemployment, 1815–34', *Ec.H.R.*, VI (1935). L. P. Adams, *Agricultural Depression and Farm Relief in England, 1813–1852*, Cassell, 1965, 165 *seq.*

his wages to rise in proportion to others, despite a temporary set-back during the potato blight and the depression of 1845–6. The older type of craftsman also did much worse than the average, particularly to the early 1830s. By contrast, if Bowley's figures are to be believed, it was the newer crafts, the factory labourer, and the miner, as well as the navvy in boom times whose gains exceeded the average given above. This was but a reflection of the need of manufacturing and mining to attract labour from elsewhere in a technically free labour market.

But there were great differences, not only in the rate of change, but also in the absolute levels of wages of these groups, as the skilled urban craftsman and the miner and iron worker earned perhaps double the wage of an urban labourer, and the latter, in turn, brought home perhaps a third more than the farm worker. This opened up the possibility of moving from a lower-paid to a higher-paid occupation, a path taken by many, which would give them considerable benefits without affecting the wage level statistics. In this period, the agricultural labourer who entered the mines, the Irish peasant who took to navvying, or the village craftsman who migrated to the towns, were representative of large numbers who enjoyed improvements of real wages well above those shown by changes in wage rates. Bearing in mind these important shifts between jobs, increases in real wages as a whole might well have reached 15–25 per cent over the period, though they were not as great as the 50–60 per cent suggested by national output figures.

Why then, the persistent belief in stagnation or decline, and the fact that the years between 1816 and 1848 formed the most rebellious period in the history of the British working class? The answer lies essentially in the fact that in a period of a rapidly changing social and industrial structure wage indices do not tell the whole story.

For one thing, money wages still have to be translated into spending, and it was here that serious deterioration faced the new industrial proletariat.[43] There was the deterioration of food brought from a distance; there was increasing efficiency in adulteration[44]; there was the extension of truck, especially in the coal and iron districts. Services obtainable free or cheaply in the traditional village community, like sewage removal, funerals, or a minimum of education, might become

---

[43] This paragraph owes much to Checkland, 232–44, which should be consulted for further details and references.
[44] The author of an early exposure, the noted chemist F. Accum, *Treatise on the Adulteration of Food and Culinary Poisons*, 1820, was hounded out of his job and out of the country by the enraged brewers and others—J. C. Drummond and Anne Wilbraham, *The Englishman's Food*, 1939; 1957 edn, 290–1.

outrageously expensive in the towns. Drunkenness changed from the bucolic celebration of set feast days, which ultimately might have raised morale, to the demoralising daily drinking to escape the slum surroundings: the Beerhouse Act of 1830 greatly worsened the evil. Female labour outside the home, instead of within the domestic surroundings, was bound to play havoc both with domestic economy and domestic comfort. What Hobsbawm, in his penetrating study, has called the 'secondary poverty', arose out of the inability of this new and displaced proletariat to adapt quickly enough to the food and culinary revolution which town living and industrial work had imposed.[45]

Above all, it was the deterioration of housing amenities, even if not necessarily of individual houses, which reduced the quality of life, and kept up death rates in the towns and even created new scourges, like the cholera epidemics, despite a growing awareness of the connection between filth, overcrowding and disease. Protective legislation was constantly overtaken by new growth, and the infantile mortality rate, perhaps the most sensitive indicator, did not decline at all, in spite of all medical progress, between 1838, when registration first began, and 1900.[46] This throws, incidentally, an interesting light on McKeown's belief that, since therapy did not improve in the course of the nineteenth century, it must have been the social environment (rising standards of living and sanitary improvements) which was responsible for the fall in the general death-rate.[47]

Consumption statistics show a much less clear-cut rise than the nominal wage figures. There was little rise in the retained imports *per capita* of tea, tobacco and sugar, until the 1840s, at least[48]; such indications as there are show a decline in the quantity of wheat

[45] E. J. Hobsbawm, 'En Angleterre: Révolution Industrielle et Vie Matérielle des Classes Populaires, *Annales*, Nov.–Dec. 1962, 1050–1.
[46] The Registrar General's figures for the deaths of infants under one year per 1,000 live births in England and Wales averaged 150 in 1839–41 and 156 in 1899–1901, never departing far from those levels. Urban rates were always much worse than rural, and Ireland, despite her poverty, averaged only 97 in 1864–6, when figures began, and 106 in 1899–1901—Mitchell and Deane, 36–7.
[47] Thomas McKeown, *Medicine in Modern Society*, Allen and Unwin, 1965, esp. 56–8.
[48]

Per capita consumption in lbs:

	Coffee (G.B.)	Tea (U.K.)	Sugar (U.K.)	Tobacco (U.K.)
1814–16	0·51	1·27	15·5	0·92
1829–31	0·91	1·25	18·5	0·81
1844–46	1·22	1·59	19·1	0·93

Mitchell and Deane, 355–6, also 358. These figures are affected, in their short-term fluctuations, by changes in taxation and not necessarily by the general state of prosperity. The following summary is from G. R. Porter, *Progress of the Nation*, 1847, 551 *seq.*

available *per capita*, matched by a rise in the quantity of potatoes; the consumption of milk and cheese fell, and that of butter, in joint demand with bread or potatoes, rose; meat consumption was declining in London, judging by the Smithfield market slaughterings, and was not rising elsewhere, but may have been made up by bacon, ham and pork, and imports from Ireland. It might also be argued that the quantities of fish, fruit and vegetables consumed may have risen, but such estimates are extremely doubtful, and in any case the quantities involved in popular diet were small or insignificant.[49] In concrete terms, 'the diet of the poor people in the towns was bad. The greater part of their nourishment came from bread, potatoes and strong tea': certainly, the rise in the tea consumption was the most consistent of all the available series.[50] A rather optimistic household budget of the 1820s showed a family of four, earning 21s. a week, spending 12s. 6d. on food, of which 4s. went on bread and 3s. on meat,[51] but a more normal income, or larger number of children, would at once reduce the meat consumption. An estimate of 1834, showing a family of four on an income of 21s. spending only 10s. 6d. on food, added:

> 'though every reader must be conscious that thousands or millions are compelled to live on a very much reduced rate, yet he will be utterly at a loss to know how it is accomplished'.[52]

Even more significant, an employer taking the budgets of 23 families

[48]—*continued*

Per capita consumption

	Sugar (G.B.) lb	Coffee (G.B.) lb	Tea (U.K.) lb	Malt (U.K.) bushel	Spirits (E.&W.) gal.	Beer (E.&W.) gal.	Tobacco (G.B.) oz.	Paper (G.B.) lb	Soap (G.B.) lb
1811	29·27	0·51	1·07	1·60	0·33	25·19	18·95	2·06	5·83
1831	20·11	1·34	1·24	1·63	0·53	21·10	14·84	2·54	6·23
1841	17·65	1·47	1·37	1·35	0·51	—	15·52	3·58	9·20
1845	20·33	—	—	1·30	—	—	—	—	9·65

Per capita tax

1811	5·29	0·33	4·02	6·83	3·42	5·77	2·71	0·54	1·10
1831	5·01	0·67	2·75	4·17	3·98	4·75[a]	2·82	0·60	1·56
1846	6·06	0·88	2·92	3·48	4·83	—	2·93	0·45	1·11

a = 1829

The tax burden on these items alone, averaging around 22 shillings a head or, say, £6.10.0. for an average family of six, should be compared with an annual income of perhaps £25 for agricultural labourers, £35 for urban labourers and £55 for town artisans.

[49] E. J. Hobsbawm, 'The British Standard of Living 1790–1850', *Ec.H.R.*, X (1957); also Hartwell, 'Rising Standard of Living', and T. S. Ashton, 'The Standard of Life of the Workers in England, 1790–1830', *J. Econ. Hist.*, Suppl. IX, 1949.

[50] J. C. Drummond and Anne Wilbraham, *The Englishman's Food*, 1939; 1957 ed., 329. Also E. J. Hobsbawm, 'En Angleterre: Révolution Industrielle et Vie Matérielle des Classes Populaires', *Annales*, Nov.-Dec. 1962, 1056.

[51] Drummond and Wilbraham, 337.

[52] Quoted in Mrs C. S. Peel, *op. cit.*, 131.

in 1841, selected from 'the respectable and steady workmen [who] obtain rather better wages than unsteady operatives', found the average family to contain six persons, with an expenditure of 5s. 3d. a head, or 31s. 6d. a family. 1s. 6d. a head was spent on bread and flour, another 1s. 6d. on milk, butter, cheese and potatoes and about two-thirds on food as a whole, but there is no mention of meat whatever.[53] An interesting attempt to apply the Rowntree-Bowley standards of 'poverty' of the early twentieth century to the Oldham of the 1840s shows 41 per cent of the *total* Oldham population to have been in primary poverty in the bad year of 1847, and 15·5 per cent in the good year of 1849, compared with 5–17 per cent in four towns in the good year of 1913.[54]

Agricultural workers, with wages around the 10–14s. level, clearly did worse, and Robert Giffen, intent on showing the improvement to the 1880s, had no difficulty in disposing of G. R. Porter's misleadingly optimistic interpretation in the 1830s that meat formed any substantial part of their diet. He showed that, in 1843, an agricultural family with an income of 13s. 9d. spent 9s. on bread and 1s. on potatoes, but nothing on meat.[55] Cheap cotton, cheaper cutlery and earthenware, must, however, have increased material standards somewhat.

Legislative action did not on the whole favour the poorer classes. The end of the war saw the immediate repeal of the income tax and the tightening up of the Corn Law, both actions favouring large property owners, while a National Debt of £848 million represented a substantial shift, year by year, from the poor to the rich, particularly those who had profiteered during the war; Cobbett, though he was despised by the middle classes, was right to attack the 'tax eaters', and to stress the importance of domestic economy. In 1842, it is true, the income tax was reimposed and the gradual relaxation of the protective tariff favoured the consumer, but, against this, the drastic revision of the Poor Law in 1834 was intended to, and did, hit the working classes hard. Protective legislation on health, factory hours, or education did not have any major effects until after the 1840s.

Over and above the simple comparison of incomes and expenditure, another factor had entered the material conditions of life: the factor of insecurity. It has been said[56] that the dislocations of the age were not entirely negative in their effects, and that opportunities to move,

---

[53] *S.C. on Exportation of Machinery, 2nd Report*, Parl. Papers, 1841, VII, 400. Evidence J. P. Westhead, Q.3864; also Burnett, 45–8.

[54] John O. Foster, *Capitalism and Class Consciousness in Early Nineteenth Century Oldham*, unpublished Cambridge D.Phil. thesis, App. 2, Table 6, p. 342.

[55] Giffen, *Essays in Finance*, 2 vols, 3rd edn, 1890, 450; Burnett, 26.

[56] E.g. Hartwell, *loc. cit.*

to change, and to rise, represented a human gain of great significance in the process of industrialisation. It is true that the social and geographical mobility thus created was eagerly used by some, and, insofar as it led to transfers to better-paid jobs, we have already taken account of this in our wage analysis. Yet for most men insecurity is not a gain and, above all, the new phenomenon of periodic mass unemployment, at a time when traditional stand-bys like kitchen gardens were being lost, represented a serious deterioration in men's condition of life.[57] While some 10 per cent of the population was permanently pauperised, every major crisis rendered perhaps a third of the working classes unemployed, making it entirely dependent on charity and the Poor Law.[58] We know now that fear and uncertainty affect even those fortunate enough to remain in employment, and this adverse side of the new industrialism, particularly bad in building and in the crafts and industries in transition, especially the doomed domestic industries, in this period had therefore a far more pernicious effect than might appear merely by counting the loss in wages. Besides, the pawning of persons' possessions, the indebtedness, the need to move one or more families to a house, the losses of skills and changes of jobs had consequences outlasting the duration of the depression itself.

Finally, and beyond all the factors enumerated so far, there was the intangible loss and break-up of an old society without as yet the creation of a new to which the lower classes could feel they belonged. This aspect, stressed particularly by the Hammonds,[59] is difficult to quantify, but was nonetheless real to those affected. Even the extent of the rootlessness is difficult to grasp: in 1851, in the 62 largest towns in England and Wales, three out of five persons, or two million altogether, were immigrants, and only in three towns had more than half the inhabitants actually been born there.[60] Deprived of political or social influence, living in towns which had come 'into being almost by inadvertence: they were merely the places where factories, offices, depots and warehouses were built and to which the new industrial

[57] Stressed, e.g., by Hobsbawm and Taylor. See the graphic example of the effect of hard times on workers at the Styal Mill in 1825–31—Frances Collier, *The Family Economy of the Working Classes in the Cotton Industry, 1784–1833*, Manchester, Chetham Society, 3rd ser., 12, 1965, 40.
[58] The average number of paupers in receipt of Poor Relief amounted to 13 per cent *of the whole population* (not the adults) in 1818, about 10 per cent in 1831–2, and even after the Reform, it rose to around six per cent, or over one million, in the late 1840s. This was much higher than anything seen in the eighteenth century—S. and B. Webb, *English Poor Law History*, part II, vol. 2, 1929, 1040–1.
[59] E.g., J. L. Hammond, 'The Industrial Revolution and Discontent', *Ec.H.R.*, II (1930); J. L. and B. Hammond, *The Rise of Modern Industry*, 1925, esp. part III and chapter XIII—'The Curse of Midas'.
[60] J. H. Clapham, *An Economic History of Modern Britain*, 3 vols, Cambridge, 1925–30; 1964 edn, I, 536–7.

population was attracted',[61] the common people of Britain were restless not merely because new opportunities taught them to ask for still greater ones: they were genuinely deploring the passing of the old bases of their existence, the family in its old form as a work unit, the land, local associations, the old skills and identification with job or product, the established social balance, and the personal relationships. It was not only later nostalgic historians who deplored the passing of a golden age: even though the past had not been golden, the men affected were themselves found to be petitioning, protesting and rioting again and again for its retention, when faced with the alternative of the new. In due course, in the second half of the century, they were to build up their new associations, their new culture and a greater social influence, but in the interim they had existed as a generation of social orphans.

A summary is difficult, not least because the fate of different sections of the population varied so greatly. At one extreme there were the craftsmen with scarce new skills, the mechanics, toolmakers, masons or miners, able to eat well, to form trade unions or friendly societies,[62] and to make use of savings banks or Mechanics' Institutes. At the other extreme were the displaced cottagers, the casual labourers in the towns, the handloom weavers and stocking-knitters, and the surprisingly large population of street vendors, scavengers, petty thieves and prostitutes whom Mayhew described with such a skilful pen.[63] In between was the great mass of the population, buffeted by the winds of change and ignorant and fearful of their destiny. If there was tangible improvement for them, it could not have been very great, but in their own eyes it was often more than swallowed up by the worsening social conditions in which their lives were spent.

The standard of living, 1845–1873

There is no visible break in the growth of production in our period, yet its effects on standards of life changed remarkably from the end of the 1840s onward. Perhaps the most startling proof of this change is the difference in the response to working-class demands for freedom of association and for the vote: what had been cause for imprisonment or deportation, and had made martyrs out of the Dorchester Labourers in 1834, became in 1871 and 1875 legally favoured and

[61] Checkland, 251.
[62] It is interesting that the membership of Friendly Societies in the late 1840s (which included, however, many middle-class members), was at about the same order of magnitude as the members relieved by the Poor Law, one-and-a-half million—*Workshop of the World*, 209–10.
[63] Henry Mayhew, *London Labour and the London Poor*, 4 vols, 1861 edn; J. L. and B. Hammond, *The Skilled Labourer, 1760–1832*, 1920.

protected; and the main plank of the Chartist demands, treated almost as treason and a cause of civil war in 1839 and 1848, was granted by the consent of both parties in 1867. Working-class movements themselves seem to have changed from fears of disaster to hopes for improvement.[64] What had happened in between was that the bulk of the working classes, and particularly the factory workers and the skilled workers, were at last beginning to get some of the benefits of industrialisation.

As late as 1848, John Stuart Mill was able to declare, in a famous passage:

> 'Hitherto it is questionable if all the mechanical inventions yet made have lightened the day's toil of any human being. They have enabled a greater proportion to live the same life of drudgery and imprisonment and an increased number of manufacturers and others to make fortunes. They have increased the comforts of the middle classes. But they have not yet begun to effect those great changes in human destiny, which it is in their nature and their futurity to accomplish.'[65]

His views were shared by Lord John Russell in 1844:

> 'The general feeling was that the toil which (the working classes) were obliged to undergo in order to obtain the bare necessities of life was more than the people of any country ought to be called upon to submit to.'[66]

Two generations of men had been sacrificed to the creation of an industrial base, which was completed by about 1845–50. Thereafter, the population of Great Britain (though not yet of Ireland) was lifted, for the first time in human history, by a clear margin above a subsistence standard, while at the same time hours of work were cut and protective Factory Acts began to affect the working conditions of a growing proportion of the occupied population.[67]

The cornucopia of the new means of production did not limit its fruits to the wage earners alone. Growing investments abroad opened up vast new territories overseas, and helped the industrialisation of Europe, offering further profitable openings for British investors and exporters. Exports, running at 21–22 per cent of national income by

---

[64] E. J. Hobsbawm, 'Economic Fluctuations and some Social Movements since 1800', *Ec.H.R.*, V (1952).

[65] *Principles of Political Economy*, quoted by T. S. Ashton, 'The Standard of Life of the Workers in England, 1790–1830', in F. A. Hayek (ed.), *Capitalism and the Historians*, 1954, 129.

[66] *Hansard, Parl. Debates*, 1844, vol. 73, col. 1260.

[67] J. T. Ward, *The Factory Movement 1830–1855*, 1962; W. M. Thomas, *The Early Factory Legislation*, 1948; B. L. Hutchins and A. Harrison, *A History of Factory Legislation*, 1903.

1870, had never been higher.[68] Owners of land and of capital expanded their real incomes probably even faster than the recipients of wages.

It should be stressed that there was no acceleration in the rate of growth of the national production: on the contrary, all indications show that the rate slowed down slightly, though this was almost made up by the fact that population growth had also slightly decreased.[69] In this total, the manufacturing industries were still dominated by the old staples; but the rate of growth of industrial production had also slowed down, from well over 40 per cent per decade to the mid-forties, to around 35 per cent in 1845–75.[70] Against this, however, trade and transport and personal service expanded much faster. Thus between 1851 and 1881 in Great Britain, while agriculture lost 460,000 of the occupied population, manufacturing and mining gained 1,433,000, building 377,000, trade and transport 980,000, domestic service 762,000, and other occupations, mostly professional, 524,000.[71] In percentages, commerce and domestic service grew fastest. The first was the most tangible proof of the prosperity of the middle classes and even the best-paid artisans, who can, in the Census returns, be found to have servants living in.[72] At the same time, the expansion in the trade and transport figures hint at the benefit which Britain began to derive from local and international specialisation: the deterioration in the terms of trade was arrested by 1855, and the improvements thereafter could be looked on in part as a return on the overseas investments made in the first half of the century, which lowered the real costs of many imports that were particularly sensitive to transport costs.[73]

Thus Feinstein's figures of net national income per head, at constant (1900) prices, show a steady improvement from £18·3 in 1855, when the series begins, to £26·6 in 1873,[74] or by 45 per cent in 18 years; from the mid-forties, the increase could not have been less than 60 per cent. This is not dissimilar from the growth of 1815–1845, but in the second period, unlike the first, the population received the full benefit, together with some delayed benefits from the earlier

[68] Deane, 'The Industrial Revolution and Economic Growth', Table 5, 171.
[69] Deane and Cole, Tables 37–9, 72–3.
[70] Ibid., Table 77, based on Hoffmann, and Table 9.
[71] Charles Booth, 'Occupations of the People of the United Kingdom, 1801–1881', J. R. Statistical S., 49 (1886), App. C, 426–9. 'Industrial Service' has been split in our summary among Trade and Transport ('Commercial') and Manufacturing ('General Labour'), according to App. A(1) and A(2).
[72] Incomes generally in manufacturing, mining and building increased by £240 million between 1841 and 1881, or by 155 per cent; in trade and transport, they grew by £159 million, or by 190 per cent—Deane and Cole, Table 37.
[73] Imlah, op. cit., 94–8.
[74] Reported in Mitchell and Deane, 367.

investments, and an increase of this order of magnitude in one generation could not fail to be impressive.

For the first time, we have a fairly reliable series for middle-class incomes in Stamp's series of taxable income for the United Kingdom, which starts with the financial year 1842–3.[75] On certain assumptions, these incomes averaged £203·5 million in the three years ending in 1844–6; £252·2 million in 1859–61; and £450·6 million in 1873–5. The large increases came in the last years before the boom of 1872–3, perhaps the most powerful boom in the century, at least in the heavy and the capital goods industries. Deflated by the Rousseaux price index, real taxable incomes then averaged as follows (index):

Average of tax-years ending in:	1844–6	100
	1859–61	116
	1873–5	190

It is not possible to establish with any accuracy the numbers among whom this income was shared: the best estimates show that the number between 1860–1 and 1874–5 increased faster than the total population.[76] In any case, the accession to the tax-paying class from below, as rising incomes brought new families into the tax-paying range, might have helped to lower the averages, while yet allowing all families within the range to register substantial increases[77]; and it was one of the signs of prosperity that, while middle-class families became richer, there were also more of them. But the growth of taxable incomes (at current prices) by 121 per cent between 1843–5 and 1872–4 (United Kingdom) may be compared with the growth of total national income (Great Britain) by 103 per cent between 1841 and 1871, so that middle-class and upper-class incomes, despite the relative fall in land rents, appear to have held more than their share.

There were tangible indications to show that the prosperity of the Mid-Victorian middle classes was no myth. Starting from a position of relative comfort in the 1840s, there were no striking new fields of expenditure which were opened to them, though some particular developments stand out. One was the remarkable growth in the number of domestic servants, noted above—a sign not only of new wealth, but also of the fact that prosperity was not evenly distributed among the working classes, and the fate of the woman was still to earn her own wages, at least until marriage, in the lowest-paid occupations.

[75] J. C. Stamp, *British Incomes and Property*, 1916, reproduced in Mitchell and Deane, 369.
[76] J. C. Stamp, 448. The numbers of incomes over £150 for the United Kingdom were: 1860–1, 306,700–319,500 and 1874–5, 518,200–539,800, on certain assumptions.
[77] This effect is neglected by Giffen in his concern to belittle the rise of middle-class wealth—*Essays in Finance*, II, 394–404.

Another was the ability of growing numbers of the merchants and industrialists to seal their rise to economic power by the age-old stamp of success, the purchase of estates and marriage into the landed classes.

Agricultural rent incomes were growing much more slowly than other incomes from property. A representative sample of estates yielded 20s. 6d. an acre in 1844–6 and 25s. 2d. in 1872–4, and the index of rents of a similar set of estates stood at 83 in 1846–8 and 101 in 1872–4, exactly in step with the yield on Schedule A tax for England and Wales, which rose from 82 in 1843 to 101 in 1872–4.[78] Even these increases were achieved only by heavy investments, which rarely yielded more than investments in the Funds would have done.[79] But such concentration on agricultural values was misleading. 'Men spoke still of the land, but more and more the land was coming to mean house property or industrial sites.'[80] The common interests of moneyed men ambitious to become landed gentry, and landowners wishing to cash in on rising property values because of industry, mining or housing, were cemented by intermarriage, and, while Parliament still consisted largely of nobility and gentry even after the Reform Act of 1832, the voters who pulled the puppets' strings were increasingly the middle classes.[81]

Those who had not quite reached the height of buying landed estates, settled in large suburban villas, in which sheer size and ornate, if incongruous, decoration were to bear witness to wealth, and large gardens and large fireplaces showed part of its origin in the cheap labour of gardeners, slaveys and coal-miners.

> 'The greatest change, and one that affected the whole concept of civilisation during the period, was the growth of suburbs which housed the respectable middle classes, with their delicately adjusted social levels, and their sincere support for the rigid edifice of snobbery, erected and maintained by their betters. United by a sense of superiority to the "lower orders", segregated from the congestion of slums, they were proud of being householders.'[82]

[78] Robert J. Thompson, 'An Inquiry into the Rent of Agricultural Land in England and Wales during the Nineteenth Century', *J.R. Stat. Soc.*, 70 (1907), 598–9, 613, 614.
[79] David Spring, *The English Landed Estate in the Nineteenth Century: Its Administration*, Baltimore, 1963; F. M. L. Thompson, *English Landed Society in the Nineteenth Century*, 1963, 247 *seq.*
[80] G. M. Young, *Victorian England, Portrait of an Age*, 2nd ed., Paperback, 1964, 147.
[81] F. M. L. Thompson, 277–8; W. O. Aydelotte, 'Business Interests of the Gentry in the Parliament of 1841–7', *The Making of Victorian England* (ed. G. Kitson Clark), 1962.
[82] John Gloag, *Victorian Comfort, A Social History of Design from 1830–1900*, Black, 1961, 22.

'All through our period and beyond we can trace a definite ten-dency to standardize the house on the lines of the great house in miniature', commented one historian.

A French observer put it more unkindly:

'From Baker Street to St George's in the East the height of the houses and of their floors is sharply reduced, but it is still every-where that sad, square box with holes which represents the total effort of English architectural genius. The squares are replaced by narrow courts entered by dark passages. . . .'[83]

Thus,

'the middle class villa became the badge of prosperity—yearly more crowded with more ornate furniture in ever worse taste, though all of the finest materials and solidest construction'.[84]

The jewels and the gold, the spices and rich silks of the East, once the prerogative of the few, now became available to broad strata of the middle classes, by dint of the efficiency of the British export in-dustries whose produce paid for them. Tropical fruits and fibres, piled high in British holds and along the new docks, were brought within their easy reach, and the richness of overseas soils, helped by reduced costs of transport and by the repeal of taxation, was soon to augment even the fruits of British agriculture: wool from the 1860s, grain from the 1870s, meat in refrigerated ships from the 1880s. Victorian in-genuity in factories and workshops permitted not so much the mass-production of consumer goods, which had been achieved earlier, but the mass-production of heavy ornamentation: in furniture and pianos, in locks and gas lamps, in print and in china ware.[85] Where the machine failed, as in clothing, there was still room, in sweated work-shops and by cheap female labour, to produce over-ornateness, costly in man-hours and eyesight, if not in pounds, shillings and pence.

Beyond the middle classes, the new conditions of industry and trade also began to call forth a new social stratum, of white-collar workers or lower middle classes, for the offices, the shops, the teach-ing posts and others. It was not yet large by the 1870s, but it was growing more rapidly than any other group,[86] and while its services, together with that of the growing professions, represented a new form

[83] Mrs C. S. Peel, 'Homes and Habits', *Early Victorian England* (ed. G. M. Young), 2 vols, 1934, I, 79; Charles Gavard, *Un Diplomate à Londres, Lettres et Notes, 1871–1877*, Paris, 1895, 78.
[84] Roy Lewis and Angus Maude, *The English Middle Classes*, 1949, 58.
[85] E.g. George Dodd, *Days at the Factories*, 1843.
[86] 'Clerks' alone were calculated to number, in England and Wales 95,000 in 1851 and 318,000 in 1881, nearly all male—F. D. Klingender, *The Condition of Clerical Labour in Britain*, 1935, 108–9.

of consuming the growing wealth of Britain, it formed itself an important group to which members of the labouring classes could rise, or professional and wealthier people decline. At its best, it could reach comfortable incomes comparable with those of the professions, which were themselves in flux; at its worst, it fell below the earnings of skilled artisans,[87] and forced to 'keep up appearances', to dress well, to maintain at least one servant, the men in those growing occupations paid dearly for their cherished social status.

All in all, the wage-earners, though they shared in the wealth, did not do quite so well as their betters. Even taking into account the incidence of unemployment, which exaggerated the rise to the exceptional boom year of 1873, the increase in average real wages between 1850 and 1872–4 was only 31 or 32 per cent; nearly all this growth occurred in the last 10 years of the period. There are fewer reliable statistics for the years 1845–50, but since money wages remained constant in those years, while prices fell by 10–15 per cent, we may assume a total increase in 1845–73 of about 50 per cent. In many respects, this overstates the rise, because of the greater costs of living in towns, to which many workers migrated, and because of the greater rise among the unionised trades, from which most figures are taken and for other reasons[88]; at the same time, the strong counter-effect of the transfer from lower-paid to higher-paid occupations has been calculated for the first time with some accuracy for the period: for 1850–1870, this factor would raise the average wage-increase from 23 to 34 per cent.[89] On balance, therefore, it is likely that the averaged-out increases in real wage rates should be raised, to around the same figure of 55–60 per cent increase as we noted for national *per capita* incomes as a whole. This fact, together with a marked fall in hours, of perhaps one sixth, concentrated mainly in two periods, 1847–51 and 1871–3, basically accounts for the feeling of rising prosperity in this period among sections of the working classes also.

This rise was not uniform among all groups of workers. Two main trends can be noted, both of which may in part be due to the growing power of trade unions. One was the tendency among skilled trades for the better-paid occupations to rise less than the others, allowing a

---

[87] Samuel Smiles, *Thrift*, 1877, 324, discusses artisans 'earning from two to three pounds a week—or more than the average pay of curates and bankers' clerks'.
[88] See the summary in J. Kuczynski, *Die Geschichte der Lage der Arbeiter unter dem Kapitalismus*, vol. 24, Berlin, 1965, App., 237–40.
[89] Virtually all published wage statistics for this period are based on the path-breaking work of A. L. Bowley and C. H. Wood at the turn of the century—cf. Deane and Cole, 22–3; Mitchell and Deane, 343–4; J. Kuczynski, *A Short History of Labour Conditions in Great Britain 1750 to the Present Day*, 1942.

certain amount of levelling-up among them. Thus, between 1850 and 1873, the cotton and building workers' wages rose faster than the, on the whole, better-paid printers, engineers, and shipbuilders.[90] At the same time, the difference between the skilled men and the unskilled labourers remained large and may even have increased somewhat, though the wages of the latter fluctuated more, and were therefore particularly high in the boom years of 1872–4.[91] Apart from their lack of union organisation, the unskilled suffered from a relative deterioration of their concrete economic role in society. Much of the growth and superiority of Victorian industry was due to the unmatched skill of the skilled artisan, who sooner or later exacted the appropriate pay for it. By contrast, the labourer remained, or became, a mere helper, often still employed or paid by the skilled man, and he was easily replaceable. As a result, quite apart from his low wage, his employment was also less secure, partly because in slumps in such industries as shipbuilding or iron and steel the employers kept their skilled labour force on longer, and partly because much unskilled work, as in the docks and road transport, was in any case casual.[92] Dudley Baxter put the differential as follows for 1867[93]:

	Ratio	Annual wage	Numbers
Highly skilled	5·0	£60–73	1·3 million
Semi-skilled	3·3	46–52	5·0 million
Unskilled and agricultural	2·4	20–41	4·5 million

It is too often forgotten how large was this submerged group of unskilled and casual labour, and how little it had raised itself above the subsistence level. The lack of reserves at times of unemployment was here particularly disastrous, and a bad spell meant, inevitably, the pawning of furniture and clothing, the moving together of several families into one house, lack of food and near-starvation, and indebtedness remaining as a burden into better days. A particular exception were the agricultural workers, whose flight from the land began to outpace the decline in their employment opportunities from the late 1840s onward, so that their wages show not only the typical break about the mid-century, but go beyond the average to begin to close the gap with the better-paid urban workers by the early 1870s.[94]

[90] Kuczynski, *Geschichte*, 120–1.
[91] Kuczynski, *Short History*, 55–6.
[92] Kuczynski's summary of the statistics, *Short History*, 76–7, does not show this difference, for the figures are derived largely from the organised men, whereas it was the unorganised who suffered most—cf. Charles Booth, *Life and Labour of the People of London*, 17 vols, 1902–4, and *Report of the Industrial Remuneration Conference*, 1885.
[93] Quoted in Checkland, 232.
[94] E. L. Jones, 'The Agricultural Labour Market in England, 1793–1872', *Ec. H.R.*, XVII (1964).

At much the same time the vicious bias of the taxation system against the poor was relaxed. As large sections of them were, in effect, exempt from rates, the legislation of 1848–52, providing for public health measures, public baths, common lodging houses and public libraries, among others, represented almost pure gain which gradually became effective in the following 30 years. National taxation was still regressive: even on optimistic assumptions, the working classes paid 14 per cent of their incomes in taxes in 1858 against 11½–12 per cent for the upper and middle classes, but this still represented an improvement. The average burden on a working-class family fell from 16 per cent in 1842 to 7½ per cent in 1882, while total tax revenue per head had fallen only slightly. Most of the benefit, shared by all classes, arose from the rise in total incomes, out of which the taxes were paid.[95] Particularly notable was the fall of the taxes on necessities from 31·5 per cent of total revenue in 1842 to 22·4 per cent in 1862 and 6·9 per cent in 1882, while taxes on 'luxuries', which, however, included tobacco and alcohol, widely consumed by the poorer classes, rose from 26 per cent to 38·7 per cent and 52·7 per cent in the same years.[96]

The effect of the repeal of taxes on food, following the 'hungry forties' and symbolised by the repeal of the Corn Laws, was thus no myth, as has occasionally been suggested. It is true that the price of bread did not fall dramatically at once, though the fall was more pronounced in the 1870s and 1880s. The average price of a four-pound loaf in London was 9d. in the trade cycle 1840–47 and 8·1d. in the trade cycle 1868–77.[97] But the significance of this fall is increased if we consider that this was in a period of rising prices, and it affected by far the largest item of expenditure in a working-class household, so that even a marginal gain was significant. At the same time, the fall in excise and customs duties on other consumption goods had a much more dramatic impact on their prices: sugar, for example, fell from 68s. 8d. a cwt in 1839–40 to 21s. 9d. in 1883.[98]

The comparison of two budgets of 1834 and 1859, both referring to a mechanic's household, makes the change clear.[99]

[95] Total tax revenue per head was calculated at:

1821–30	£2 8. 1.
1851–60	£2 2. 11.
1871–80	£2 0. 0.

Leons Levi, 'Statistics of the Revenue of the United Kingdom for 1859–82, in Relation to the Distribution of Taxation', *J. R. Statistical S.*, 47 (1884), 5; *ibid.*, 23 (1860), 45; Clapham, *Economic History*, II, 462–3.
[96] *J. R. Statistical Soc.*, 1884, 10.
[97] *18th Abstract of Labour Statistics of the U.K.*, 1926, Cd. 2740, 143. For variations of London prices from those of Edinburgh and Dublin, see *15th Abstract*, 1912, Cd. 6228, 153.
[98] Giffen, II, 380.
[99] From Mrs C. S. Peel, 134.

	1834	1859
Food	16s. 11d.	18s. 6½d.
Coal and light	2s. 5½d.	1s. 6d.
Clothes	5s. 6d.	3s. 0d.
Rent	3s. 6d.	4s. 0d.
Sundries	1s. 10½d.	2s. 11½d.
	30s. 3d.	30s. 0d.

In view of the general rise in wages, the later budget is, in fact, the poorer one. Yet apart from the important effect of drastic falls in the prices of coal, gas and clothing, and the slight increase in elbow room in the 'sundries' the food consumed in the first budget was based on a total of 24 lbs of bread; that of the second, on 32 lbs of bread *plus* half a peck of meal a week.

Thus food still accounted for 50–60 per cent of household expenditure, but now it was beginning to be adequate. Prices of meat were rising, but no faster than money wages; all other important foodstuffs were falling in price, as low-cost imports were added to home production, carrying an ever-increasing burden of taxes and transport costs. The cattle plague of the mid-1860s caused a setback, but its long-term effects were to accelerate the import of canned and preserved food, including bacon, and soon after of refrigerated food. The Census Statistics show a rapid rise of the food processing industries as well as of employment in retailing in 1851–81, and while some of the processing developed by the end of the period, like factory-made jam or the manufacture of margarine, produced inferior foods, these were consumed by the poor in addition to, not in place of, their earlier diet.

The rise in consumption per head can be traced in all the retained import figures. Others are still only estimates, but Mulhall's statistics, even if they are not entirely reliable, show at least the development that appeared reasonable at the time. What is notable is not only the rise after 1850, but the stagnation before.[100]

United Kingdom, average annual consumption per head

	Wheat (lb)	Meat (lb)	Sugar (lb)	Tea (oz.)	Salt (lb)	Beer (gal.)	Rice (lb)	Eggs (No.)
1811–30	270	80	19	18	16	22	1	40
1831–50	255	87	20	23	25	24	1	48
1851–70	320	90	35	44	45	28	3	60
1871–80	354	93	60	67	72	29	11	65

[100] M. G. Mulhall, *Dictionary of Statistics*, 4th edn, 1899, 286, 288.

Total expenditure per head on wheat, meat, tea, and sugar

	£	s.	d.
1831–40	3	12	0
1841–50	3	7	0
1851–60	4	2	0
1861–70	4	15	0
1871–80	5	5	0

Again, it must be emphasised that even these improvements gave little grounds for satisfaction with absolute levels. Adulteration, exposed by *The Lancet* in 1851, was curbed only slowly after the Health Act of 1872 by the patient work of local analysts and Medical Officers; in the earlier reports, all the samples of bread, all the samples of butter, all the samples of tea (the basic ingredients of the poor's diet) and about half of the milk were found to be impure.[101] Rickets, the 'English disease' of urban poverty, was even in 1870 found to affect one third of the poor children in large towns; the state of teeth deteriorated over the nineteenth century; and vitamin A deficiency was still prevalent. Milk not only remained a common source of tuberculosis infection—the early decades of the railways, which allowed urban cowsheds to be closed and milk to be brought in from a distance, led to a further deterioration of the quality of milk supplied.[102] Even in the late 1870s there was still a frightening gap between the average weights of middle-class and working-class children.[103]

Though death-rates were falling in this period, no doubt in part due to better nutrition, sanitary improvements were still not keeping pace with the growing need for them until the legislation of the 1870s. It was the devoted and uphill struggle of civil servants at the centre, particularly of Sir John Simon, and of local officials, which gained the upper hand over the death and disease-dealing environment at the end of the period. Leeds appointed its first Medical Officer of Health in 1866, Manchester in 1868, Birmingham only in 1872, and Newcastle in 1873.[104] Restrictions on dangerous trades (other than coal mines) also only began in the 1860s.

Beside the national improvements from the 1840s on, the mass of the population now also found itself on an upward curve in the

[101] J. Mitchell, *Treatise on the Falsification of Food*, 1848; A. H. Hassall, *Food and its Adulteration*, 1855; *Adulterations Detected*, 1861; Viscount Goderich, 'On the Adulteration of Food and its Remedies', *Meliora* (ed. Viscount Ingestre), 1852; John Burnett, *op. cit.*

[102] Drummond and Wilbraham, 379 *seq.*; E. M. Whetham, 'The London Milk Trade, 1860–1900', *Ec.H.R.*, XVII (1964), 370.

[103] Details in Hobsbawm, 'En Angleterre', 2, 1060.

[104] G. Kitson Clark, *The Making of Victorian England*, 1962, 103; Sir John Simon, *English Sanitary Institutions*, 1890; W. H. Frazer, *A History of Public Health*, 1951.

general quality of its life, as important in this positive era as it had been in the dark days before. Several factors contributed to this. One was the reduction in hours, enforced in the factories in 1847 and 1850, but spreading, by trade union action and others means, to most other trades. From 1851 to 1871 the 'ten-hour day' became the norm, and it was coupled with the valuable concession of an earlier closing of firms on Saturdays, though this meant in effect that 10½ hours were worked on weekdays. The beneficial effects on the shopping and cash-payment habits of housewives, and on the leisure habits of their menfolk, were incalculable.[105] In the boom year of 1871, the engineers on the north-east coast made the first break-through to the 'nine-hour day' (i.e. 9½ hours), which again spread quickly elsewhere in the next two years.

There was greater ease also in the ability of the labouring family to save. The largest membership was to be found in the Friendly Societies, put on a legal basis in 1793. By 1850 there were perhaps 1½ million members, scattered over a mass of small units as well as a few giant ones, but the average subscription was only 4d. a week, and out-payments were also of the order of under £1 per member per year. The majority of the membership came from working-class families, though there were also professional and tradespeople among them. Even by 1860, however, it had become clear that not only the more ephemeral dividing clubs but also many nominally permanent societies had become financially unsound, and, while the Act of 1875 enforced some sounder rules, by the end of the century even the great societies numbering hundreds of thousands were fundamentally bankrupt, and were saved from disaster only by the skill with which they moulded the national scheme for their own purposes.[106] The main weakness had become the unwillingness of younger members to join and finance the ageing majority. While they lasted, however, they gave both status and some security to broadly based groups.

Depositors in the Savings Banks, which were legalised in 1817, exceeded a million in number by 1845, and nearly reached a million and a half by 1873; the Post Office Savings Bank, set up in 1861, just topped the 1½ million mark by that date. The average holding in the former was £25–30, in the latter about £12, and about one third of the depositors might have belonged to the artisan, operative and labourers' classes.[107] Trade unionists only numbered perhaps 100,000

[105] Clapham, 'Work and Wages', in *Early Victorian England*, I, 31, and *Economic History*, II, 448.

[106] B. B. Gilbert, 'The Decay of Provident Institutions and the Coming of Old-Age Pensions in Great Britain', *Ec.H.R.*, XVII (1965); Samuel Smiles, *Thrift*, 1877, 116–19.

[107] H. O. Horne, *A History of Savings Banks*, 1947, 97, 231–2, 386–92.

in the mid-forties, and co-operative societies, founded on a new basis after the example of the Rochdale Pioneers in 1844, received legal security by the Act of 1852 and were also numerically still small, but their savings were used more effectively to raise the economic power of their members.

Many of the sums involved were only small, yet for people living on the margin of subsistence the accession of human dignity and of family resilience, given by small savings or rights to benefit, compared with their loss by indebtedness, was enormous. They were part of a wider, and in the end, a decisive achievement—the ability of second- and third-generation proletarians to cope with the new environment, and surmount it. By forming their own organisations, by learning to use the products of industrialism, by slow and patient economic gains, the feeling of degradation or catastrophe gave way to one of normality, of self-confidence and some contentment with their lot. We have seen that this was no fatalistic acceptance: it was based on solid realities.

It would be too much to say that there was easy comfort for the masses in the third quarter of the century, nor were they fully 'respectable' in the current sense, but they had survived, and they were beginning to see better times in the future. The railways made day-outings to the sea coast possible, to take the place, after a gap of years, of the earlier easy access to the countryside.[108] The worst aspects of child labour (though not women's labour) had been abolished, bringing a greater understanding of the human needs of children, even of the poorer classes. Pauperism and crime were said to have declined, though useful figures are hard to come by; drunkenness was certainly less destructive an evil. Sports, music halls, widely sold cheap printed matter, home music and singing showed, in their development, the ability to rise above the despair of the generation before.[109] The flourishing optimistic literature of the day agreed that 'manners' had improved; there was, perhaps, less violence in the working-class quarters and blood sports were increasingly limited to the upper classes. Working men, when they got the vote in 1867, voted obediently for Liberal or Conservative candidates. Self-respect might mean no more than a deliberate creation of a gap between oneself and the paupers, but it offered something positive that had been lacking in the earlier decades of the century.

---

[108] Reader, *Life in Victorian England*, 67. Trevelyan is mistaken in speaking of weeks by the seaside for any but the middle classes at that time—G. M. Trevelyan, *English Social History*, 1955 edn, 560.
[109] E.g., Checkland, 236–7, 265–6.

Summary

In the course of the nineteenth century, the industrialisation which had affected certain key sectors before 1815 triumphed in the country as a whole. It brought in its wake a vastly increased flow of goods, it created a national market and a national transport system, and it allowed Britain to tap the wealth of other regions of the globe much more effectively than ever before. At the same time, the needs of the new system, such as the crowding together of population in closely built towns and in large factories and workshops, destroyed the known environment and the conditions of life of millions of people, and set social problems which for a time British society was unable, and in part unwilling, to solve.

Up to the middle of the century, the costs of industrialisation, including particularly the costs of investment, limited the benefits which the population could hope to derive from the new wealth while the novelty of many of the social problems it faced made adequate defence impossible. As a result, while physical wealth grew visibly and measurably, the enjoyment of it diminished, and those years are rightly remembered as dark, grim, rebellious ones; years of poor health, of high death-rates and of economic uncertainty and material stagnation.

From the 1840s onwards the picture began to change. While in some respects overcrowding in ever-larger towns and its attendant evils got worse, the measures taken to deal with it became increasingly effective, and by the 1870s had begun to gain the upper hand. At the same time, the population itself had had time to develop new attitudes, to adapt itself to the new conditions, to create its own defence organisations and in the process to gain its confidence and self-respect. But behind it all was the fact that incomes rose, consumption became more varied, manufactured goods and public utilities like water, gas, railways, became available to most, and those living from hand to mouth at the subsistence level were limited to a minority only of paupers and casual labourers.

Though some of the disastrous crises of the first half of the century were not repeated, the uncertainties of economic life for the majority of the population could still be highly destructive. Periodic depressions, a continuing high death-rate, especially for children, and the effects of dangerous trades were not even beginning to come under control. But for these contingencies, also, the margin available allowed some provision by organised savings, and a more humane Poor Law than the authors of the 1834 Act had envisaged. Life in Britain had become distinctly more civilised, and the growing wealth flowing into virtually every household must take a large share of the credit.

Chapter eight

The Hey-day of Empire, 1873–1914

The end of an epoch

There is a certain unity in the last 40 years of the long peace, and they have often been treated as a single phase of development. Industrialisation was now complete, agriculture was declining to an ever less significant share in national productive resources, and a highly complex and specialised commercial and financial system had made Britain, and London in particular, the centre of a much enlarged world-wide network of commodity exchange, and of an 'international economy'.[1]

The structure of the economy had now become remarkably stable. The share of manufacturing industry, in particular, did not change any further, and the growth in the services, in the professions, and the Government services was largely balanced by the decline in domestic service. Only agriculture continued to decline significantly, and trade and commerce to rise, but otherwise the major structural transformation of industrialisation was now over[2]:

	% of Labour force, G.B.			% of National product, G.B.		
	1871	*1891*	*1911*	*1871*	*1901*	*1924*
Agriculture, forestry, fishing	15·1	10·1	8·3	14·2	6·1	4·2
Manufacturing, mining	43·1	43·0	46·4	38·1	40·2	40·0
Trade, transport	19·6	22·6	21·5	26·3[a]	29·8[a]	35·0[a]
Domestic, personal services	15·3	15·8	13·9 ⎫			
Professional, government services, etc.	6·8	7·1	9·9 ⎭	13·9	15·5	14·4
Housing	—	—	—	—	—	—
	100	100	100	100	100	100

[a] Incl. income from abroad

[1] W. Ashworth, *A Short History of the International Economy, 1850–1950,* 1952.
[2] Deane and Cole, Tables 30, 76 and 81; also, cf. Tables 34, 37, 70 and 71.

The capital structure showed a similar basic stability, in this case the relative decline in agriculture being matched by the phenomenal rise of overseas assets:

| | % of Reproducible capital in G.B. | | |
	1865	1885	1913
Buildings	28	26	25
Farm capital	16	7	2
Overseas assets	10	18	25
Industrial-commercial-financial (inc. railways)	39	43	41
Public property	8	7	7
	100	100	100

After a century of industrial leadership, the predominant mood of the business community was one of pride, not to say complacency. British wealth was the envy of the world; the rest of the world came to these shores to learn its technology, and to sell its ideas to be matched with British capital and initiative. Whatever nation might be in the struggle for second place, it had come to be accepted that the place in the sun was reserved for Britons, and while other Great Powers spent enormous efforts in gaining a foothold in Africa or Asia for the foundation of colonial empires, Britain enlarged her Empire, almost absent-mindedly, by an addition much greater than the total possessions of others.

At the same time, the period was also a turning point—some historians have spoken of a 'climacteric'. There were at least two aspects to this. On the one hand, the rate of expansion of the basic staple industries on which British prosperity had been based seemed to be slowing down, and new industries were not rising fast enough to take their place. On the other, there were some manufacturers in the advanced countries abroad who used techniques of production and marketing superior to those applied in Britain, and were not only disputing their own or other foreign markets with British exporters, but even beginning to invade the British home market itself. These two developments were not entirely independent; moreover, they reinforced each other to create the conviction among later historians that a distinct period of history had ended, and a new one was opening—quite apart from the World War, which was in any case to shatter much of the foundation on which the wealth of Britain was built up.

Some of this was sensed also by contemporaries, many of whom were deeply troubled by the prevailing sentiments of self-satisfaction and jingoism. The poor provisions for the social services came increasingly under attack, and the growing political and economic power of labour ensured that a beginning was made towards their enlargement into a comprehensive system. The ideas of Free Trade were also coming to be questioned, another sign of unease, and Imperialism found its accusers as well as its devoted or self-interested protagonists. But at the time these weaknesses were seen, not as signs of economic decline, but as a failure to use the growing wealth more fairly and more effectively. It was in this period that the first conscious steps were taken towards using the State power, and the budget in particular, for the purpose of adjusting incomes in favour of the poorer families.

The interest of later historians in this period and its growing social awareness of itself have ensured that it is much better documented statistically than any earlier age. At the same time, readers should be warned that the accuracy which seems to be achieved by some of the series on wealth and income is still spurious, and that many of them give, at best, but a general indication of direction or quantity involved.

The slowing-down of economic growth

No matter how it was measured, it is evident that the rate of economic growth slowed down in the last quarter of the century, though opinion is still divided as to whether the critical date is to be found after the boom of 1873, or in the 1890s.[3] Of course, output per head, and even more clearly the total national product, continued to expand, but the *rate* of growth was now less than earlier in the century, and it was substantially less also than among the other leading industrial nations in those years. In view of the subsequent history of the British economy, it has even been possible to view this period as a turning point, in which the original momentum of the industrial revolution was finally lost and in which Britain also lost permanently

---

[3] Among the voluminous literature on the subject, the following stand out: E. H. Phelps Brown and S. J. Handfield-Jones, 'The Climacteric of the 1890s: A Study in the Expanding Economy', *Oxford Economic Papers*, IV, 1952; D. J. Coppock, 'The Climacteric of the 1890s: A Critical Note', *Manchester School*, 26, 1956, and 'British Industrial Growth during the "Great Depression" (1873–1896): A Pessimist's View', *Ec.H.R.*, XVII (1964); A. E. Musson, 'The Great Depression in Britain, 1873–1896: A Reappraisal', *J. Econ. Hist.*, 19 (1959), 'British Industrial Growth during the "Great Depression" (1873–1896): Some Comments', *Ec.H.R.*, XV (1963) and 'British Industrial Growth, 1873–96: A Balanced View', *ibid.*, XVII (1964); Derek H. Aldcroft, 'The Entrepreneur in the British Economy, 1870–1914', *ibid.*, XVII (1964); H. W. Richardson, 'Retardation in Britain's Industrial Growth, 1870–1913', *Scottish J. of Political Economy*, XII (1965).

her industrial supremacy and her role as the main supplier of manufactured goods to the rest of the world.

There were, however, significant differences in the movement of
output and income figures, if our statistics are to be believed, and it
was production and productivity which showed the sharpest decline.
Here, most authors base themselves on the Hoffmann index of industrial production, which shows the following startling changes:

**Average annual growth rates of industrial productivity, corrected for
unemployment, from cycle to cycle**

1861/5–1866/74	2·2%
1866/74–1875/83	1·0
1875/83–1884/9	0·5
1884/9–1890/9	0·1
1890/9–1900/07	0·2
1900/07–1908/13	−0·1

In decades, the decline was equally sharp:

Rate of increase per decade	
1860s–1870s	33·2%
1870s–1880s	20·8
1880s–1890s	17·4
1890s–1900s	17·9
1895/1904–1904/5	18·0[4]

It should be stressed that the first line, the growth before 1873, was
not exceptional, but on the contrary was typical of the whole of the
preceding period of rapid growth.

The Hoffmann production index has been called into question from
time to time as being unrepresentative or misleading, but it is difficult
to escape the fact that it includes a large proportion, somewhere
around two-thirds, of British industry, and that no matter what reasonable allowances are made, the main picture remains unchanged.[5]
Further, a glance at individual industries will demonstrate the slowing-
down concretely, particularly in such staples as coal, iron and steel,
machinery, cotton, wool and transport.[6] It should also be observed
that the volume of exports, which can be measured with a much
greater degree of reliability and on which there can be little dispute,

[4] W. G. Hoffmann, *British Industry 1700–1850*, Oxford, 1955; Coppock,
'Climacteric', 7; Deane and Cole, 297.
[5] W. Ashworth, 'Changes in the Industrial Structure: 1870–1914', *Yorkshire
Bulletin of Economic and Social Research*, 17 (1965).
[6] Coppock, 'Climacteric', 28; Deane and Cole, chapter 6.

shows the same characteristic slowing-down. The cumulative annual growth rate in U.K. exports was 4·9 per cent in 1841–70, but only 2·3 per cent in 1871–1901 and 2·7 per cent in 1881–1911.[7]

It was one of the peculiar characteristics of this period that in many fields the former almost automatically long-run falling cost curves ceased to function in this desirable way: growing output and new technology seemed to bring a lesser immediate return than before. In some cases, as in coal-mining, this was the natural result of working out easy deposit in a primary industry. In other cases, British entrepreneurs seemed to be unable to match the real cost reductions of other countries at similar stages of technological progress, and fell behind the then maximum possible technical efficiency. In what is perhaps the outstanding example, the iron and steel industry, they neglected to work the low-grade home ore deposits which should have provided them with cheaper pig than they were then able to obtain from abroad; but even in one of the most successful industries, shipbuilding, where the large home market and early specialisation still provided strong competitive advantages, the technical equipment was increasingly obsolescent compared with the best practice abroad.[8]

It was inevitable that the rate of growth of old-established industries should at some stage slow down, as otherwise they would grow to infinite size, but in a progressive economy this is more than balanced by new industries in their earliest and fastest growth stages. Unfortunately, it was precisely in the new developments, in machine tools and motor cars, in electrical engineering and chemicals, that Britain was farthest behind her leading competitors.

The maturity and high stage of development of industrialisation in Britain cannot therefore be made responsible for the slowing-down: other countries were passing similar stages at a faster rate, and a faster growth, indeed, was resumed here also later on in the twentieth century. A number of other causes have been suggested, including failure in entrepreneurship, lack of adequate technical education, the 'exhaustion' of the innovational drive coming from steam and iron, or steam and steel, the sharp decline in exports and the inability of the London Money Market to channel sufficient capital into home industries.[9] There are good grounds for all these suggestions, though it is

[7] Deane and Cole, 313.

[8] Thomas J. Orsagh, 'Progress in Iron and Steel: 1870–1913', *Comparative Studies in Society and History*, III (1960–1); S. Pollard, 'British and World Shipbuilding 1890–1914', *J. Econ. Hist.*, XVII (1957); and, in general, G. T. Jones, *Increasing Return*, 1933.

[9] In addition to the literature already cited, see also J. Saville, 'Mr Coppock and the Great Depression: a critical note', *Manchester School*, 31 (1963), and the reply; Alfred H. Conrad and John R. Meyer, *Studies in Economic History*, 1965, chapter 5; D. S. Landes, 'Entrepreneurship in Advanced Industrial Coun-

difficult to pinpoint the primary one, if there was one; what is beyond question is that they all reinforced each other.

Since the capital-output ratio did not change noticeably in this period at a time when both capital and output grew by perhaps two-thirds, it follows that capital investment showed the same abrupt acceleration as output. Increases of physical capital invested in industry, per head of population, compared as follows over the decades[10]:

1865–75	39%
1875–85	14
1885–95	6
1895–1905	7

Two important points, however, should be noted here. The first is that there were two important building booms in this period, in the late 1870s and around 1900, and the latter in particular added greatly to national welfare by adding large middle-class and working-class suburbs to all the major cities, built more generously and healthier than before owing to the mobility given to the industrial population by the cheap electric tramway service. This investment, though it did not add directly to 'productivity', clearly added to wealth.[11]

Secondly, this period, particularly in its later years, saw an immense increase in foreign investment. Over the years 1874–1914 as a whole, while domestic gross fixed capital formation amounted to just over £5,000 million, net foreign investment exceeded £3,000 million, and in the years 1905–14 it was considerably larger than the home figure.[12] The effect of this investment on home incomes was twofold. On the one hand, the interest and dividends derived from it provided

tries: The Anglo-German Rivalry', in *Entrepreneurship and Economic Growth*, Cambridge, Mass., 1954; W. A. Lewis, 'International Competition in Manufactures', *Amer. Econ. Rev.*, 1957; C. P. Kindleberger, 'Foreign Trade and Economic Growth: Lessons from Britain and France, 1850 to 1913', *Ec.H.R.*, XIV (1961); J. Saville, 'Some Retarding Factors in the British Economy before 1914', *Yorkshire Bulletin*, XIII (1961); E. Rothbarth, 'Causes of the Superior Efficiency of U.S.A. Industry compared with British Industry', *Econ. J.*, 56 (1946).

[10] Based on P. H. Douglas, 'An Estimate of the Growth of Capital in the United Kingdom, 1865–1909', *J. of Econ. and Business History*, II (1929–30); Hoffmann, 207–8; E. H. Phelps Brown and B. Weber, 'Accumulation, Productivity and Distribution in the British Economy, 1870–1938', *Econ. J.*, 63 (1953). See also p. 236 below.

[11] See J. Parry Lewis, *Building Cycles and Britain's Growth*, 1965, 194–210; A. K. Cairncross, *Home and Foreign Investment, 1870–1913*, Cambridge, 1953; E. M. Sigsworth and J. Blackman, 'The Home Boom of the 1890s', *Yorkshire Bulletin*, 17 (1965).

[12] C. H. Feinstein, 'Income and Investment in the United Kingdom, 1856–1914', *Econ. J.*, 71 (1961); Imlah, *op. cit.*, Cairncross, 2 *seq.*; Deane and Cole, 266, 308; S. B. Saul, *Studies in British Overseas Trade 1870–1914*, Liverpool, 1960, 66.

a large and growing part of incomes in Britain, by the end of the period reaching perhaps one tenth of total national income. On the other hand, by the development of transport facilities, estates, mines and other cost-reducing investments among the overseas suppliers of the British markets, it helped to reduce the real costs of imports to the British consumer, and to impart a favourable direction to the terms of trade in this period, which played such a large part in the raising of the standard of living between 1873 and 1900.

There is also a further consideration. Concentration on the obvious indices of production may neglect the fact that the process of growth may be accompanied by external economies which allow better use of existing facilities: 'It is one of the features of the process of industrialisation that it makes some forms of existing capital more productive than at the time of their creation.'[13] In this period this seems to have been particularly applicable to the public utilities, the railways, docks, urban street systems, and gas and waterworks.

Finally, it has been argued that much of the ingenuity and entrepreneurial initiative in those years had been concentrated on the services and on the refinement of consumer goods, which were both causes and signs of rising wealth and incomes for large sections of society.[14] After the basic wants of the majority of the population had been met, it was to be expected that the goods and services on which people would choose to spend the marginal surpluses of incomes should be more and more diversified. In the past, this had been relevant to a small privileged minority only. In the years after 1873, it became increasingly relevant to broad groups of wage-earners also, and ultimately to a majority, to all but the lowest paid. It is to the new phenomenon of mass consumption that we must now turn.

The rise of mass consumption

W. W. Rostow gave the name of the 'age of high mass consumption' to the latest stage in his scheme of economic development, but while noting that it followed at once on the preceding stage of full industrialisation, or the 'drive to maturity' in the case of the U.S.A. and Germany, he found it hard to explain the long interval which elapsed in Britain before the onset of this higher stage.[15] He may have been

---

[13] Deane and Cole, 277.

[14] Charles Wilson, in his paper on 'Economy and Society in Late Victorian Britain', *Econ. Hist. Br.*, XVIII (1965), suggests that this was enough to outweigh the slackening elsewhere. It seems unlikely, for even according to his own showing, the fast growth sectors covered by him accounted for only one third of the Census of Production of 1907 totals, and in any case leave the technical obsolescence of other industries, and the crass failures of the 'new' manufactures unexplained. But his emphasis is important.

[15] W. W. Rostow, *The Stages of Economic Growth*, Cambridge, 1960, 68–70.

misled by the fact that here this stage, beginning earlier and differing from the others in that so many of Britain's consumption goods were imported from abroad, did not at once show all the features he had expected from the example of the U.S.A. In fact, there are good reasons for thinking that the delay before the onset of the latest stage was not as long as he suggests; and there are distinct signs that the new age of high mass consumption began in Britain in the late Victorian era.

As far as the domestic supply was concerned, one important indication is the substantial growth in new types of employment, particularly the services. Domestic service declined, showing a similar flight from the lowest-regarded and lowest-paid occupation on the part of females,[16] as was shown by men in the flight from agricultural labour, and simultaneously other opportunities were opened up: teaching, clerical work, retail distribution. Each of these, in turn, implied a rise in the standard of the wants of society, and the implementation of the Education Act of 1870, in particular, offered to the mass of the population in elementary education both a new consumption good and a means of obtaining more highly qualified, and therefore better paid, employment. Persons in 'commercial' occupations rose from a census figure of 217,000 in 1871 to 896,000 in 1911, or by 313 per cent, while the total numbers occupied rose by only 63 per cent.

The growth in retail distribution is also interesting as a reflection of the greater quantity of commodities now on sale to the public, and of the new mass-production, and the transference of the place of production from the 'craftsmen of village or town' to 'the factory stage of production'.[17] It was in this period that the first chain stores arose, concentrating, significantly, on newly mass-produced footwear, clothing, books and stationery, and chemists' goods, as well as on imported foods.[18] It was this period that first saw widespread advertising, packaging—and price maintenance[19] of advertised goods—and J. K. Galbraith has taught us to associate the effectiveness of advertising with the 'affluent society'. Each campaign presupposed a substantial enlargement of the number of people able to afford such purchases.

In part, of course, the new shops retailed goods formerly made at

---

[16] 'The young working-girl of today', Mrs C. S. Peel wrote in 1902, 'prefers to become a Board School Mistress, a post-office clerk, a type-writer, a shop girl, or a worker in a factory—anything rather than enter domestic service'—noted in Marghanita Laski, 'Domestic Life', 143, *Edwardian England 1901–1914* (ed. S. Nowell-Smith), 1964.

[17] Wilson, 191. Much of this section is based on this article.

[18] J. B. Jefferys, *Retail Trading in Britain 1850–1950*, 1954.

[19] B. S. Yamey, *The Economies of Resale Price Maintenance*, 1954; R. Harris and A. Seldon, *Advertising in a Free Society*, 1959.

home or by bespoke tailors, shoemakers and similar craftsmen, but the main reason for their establishment was the new ranges of commodities that had now become available. There were canned and bottled foods, sauces and drinks, food extracts, new products like margarine, cheap clothes, cheaper soap, toothpaste and cosmetics, shoe polish and patent medicines. The press began to cater for the new mass market. *Tit-Bits* and *Answers* were developed for working-class readers, and in 1896 the new popular *Daily Mail*, selling at a halfpenny, created a true mass readership for a daily newspaper. Sheet music for pianos, for cheaper instruments, found increasingly in clerks' or skilled workers' homes, were sold as well as postcards at seaside resorts during day trips. Cheap glass and pottery appeared in village stores or in specialist town shops. Every industrial town of any size saw its first department store raise its three or four floors in the three decades after 1880—usually a store owned by the local co-operative society, or in other words by the skilled artisans themselves. In London and the largest cities, department stores aimed at higher social classes, but they had, by their nature, to attract large numbers, and they saw to it that white-collar workers and their wives were not entirely excluded in a line of development that began with Whiteley's and achieved its epitome with the creation of Selfridge's, a child of the American mass-consumption society, in 1909. Others, like Lewis's at Liverpool, catered from the beginning for the average shopper as 'friends of the people'.[20]

Their importance, together with the services, commerce and the new industries, is brought out in the following summary (on p. 232) of the Census of Production of 1907, the first comprehensive survey of the British economy.[21]

Many of the new commodities were, however, brought in their cheaper form from abroad. Besides the traditional staple imports of wheat, tea and sugar, there was also now frozen meat, canned meat or tropical fruit imported in temperature-controlled vessels, and produced on the wide, cheap acres of new worlds overseas. Bacon and butter from Europe, wool from Australia, palm kernels from the tropics—the list could be extended. In the long run, their production was bound to be eased and cheapened by British investment and by native development, but in the short run also, the years after 1881 saw a remarkable lowering of import prices, turning the terms of

[20] Asa Briggs, *Friends of the People: the Century History of Lewis's*, 1956; J. W. Ferry, *History of the Department Store*, N.Y., 1960.
[21] Based on Deane and Cole, 175. The total of 102·0 per cent is in the original.

Output as percentage of national income, gross of depreciation

Agriculture, forestry, fishing	6·0	6·0
Mines, quarries	6·0	
Engineering and metal manufacture	8·2	
Textiles and clothing	8·0 } 25·7	} 37·0
All other manufactures	9·5	
Gas, electricity, water	1·6	
Building, contracting	3·7	
Commerce	18·0	} 27·5
Transport	9·5	
Government and defence	3·0	
Professions, miscellaneous services	10·1 } 16·9	} 24·3
Domestic service	3·8	
Rents of dwellings	7·4	
Income from abroad	7·2	7·2

trade sharply in Britain's favour.[22] Though the latter declined again temporarily in the early twentieth century, and this decline was material in preventing a further rise in popular living standards in 1900–1913, yet for the last two decades of the nineteenth century low prices were of basic importance in raising the consumption of many imported commodities. Between 1870–4 and 1910–14, the *per capita* consumption of tea rose from 4·02 lbs to 6·59 lbs, of sugar from 49·1 lbs to 80·2 lbs, and of tobacco from 1·38 lbs to 2·08 lbs. The consumption of wheat, significantly, had ceased to rise, while the consumption of potatoes, an inferior commodity, as well as, more surprisingly, of coffee, actually fell.[23]

Last, but not least, the two building booms and the greatly enlarged municipal expenditure on street improvements and sanitary works, together with improvements in medicine and the provision of hospitals, as well as tighter building by-laws, greatly eased the housing position and began at last to overtake the problems created by continuous urbanisation. The number of people per house fell sharply, especially between the censuses of 1891 and 1911, and the most sensitive index of all, infantile mortality, also fell drastically, while the general mortality rate continued its downward trend. There were bad

[22] W. W. Rostow, *The Process of Economic Growth*, Oxford, 1953, chapters 8 and 9, and 274–5; and *British Economy of the Nineteenth Century*, Oxford, 1948, 101; R. E. Baldwin, 'Britain's Foreign Balance and Terms of Trade', *Explorations in Entrepreneurial History*, V, 1953; Cairncross, 206–7; and see p. 229 above.
[23] Mitchell and Deane, 257–8; John Burnett, *Plenty and Want*, 1966, 98 *seq.*; Barker, McKenzie, Yudkin, *Our Changing Fare*, 1966, esp. 40–1, 80–90, 115 *seq.*

patches of overcrowding and insanitary areas, particularly in Scotland, in the ports and in purely industrial towns. The central slums were not cleared, but filled by ever larger numbers of ever lower income-groups. The actual provision of municipal housing or housing by non-profit-making organisations like the Peabody Trust, or by firms paying special attention to their workers' needs like Cadbury's, Rowntree's or Lever Brothers were still minute when measured against national needs. Nevertheless, urban by-laws were restricting the worst features of cheap housing, low interest rates reduced building costs to private owners for letting, and suburban estates allowed those with a growing margin of incomes available for higher rent and for tram fares, to begin to solve the most intractable of social problems.[24] The recent housing booms had created 'one type of dwelling' in particular, 'found to be more or less prevalent through all the urban aggregations. That is, the small four- or five-roomed cottage, containing on the ground floor a front parlour, a kitchen and scullery built as an addition to the main part of the house; and on the upper floor the bedrooms, the third bedroom in the five-roomed house being built over the scullery.'[25]

Over the period as a whole, the increase in total consumption continued as fast as it had done since the 1840s; real expenditure on goods and services per head grew by nearly 50 per cent in 40 years. It should be noted, however, that virtually all this gain was made in the first 25 years, to about 1900. In the 14 years of the new century, the advance was negligible[26]:

Flow of goods and services per capita, at constant (1912–13) prices

Decade averages, £

1870–1879	30·1
1880–1889	34·5
1890–1899	40·7
1895–1904	42·7
1905–1914	43·8

Within this total, there was a substantial shift to services, including housing. There was also a striking rise in the proportion of imported

[24] Clapham, *Economic History*, III, Cambridge, 1963, 452–60; W. Ashworth, *An Economic History of England 1870–1939*, 1960, 190, and *The Genesis of Modern British Town Planning*, 1954, chapter 6.
[25] C. F. G. Masterman, *The Condition of England*, 1909, 100–1.
[26] J. B. Jefferys and D. Walters, 'National Income and Expenditure of the United Kingdom, 1870–1952', *Income and Wealth*, series V (1956), 15; also G. H. Wood, 'Real Wages and the Standard of Comfort since 1850', reprinted in E. M. Carus-Wilson (ed.), *Essays in Economic History*, III (1962), 141; A. R. Prest and A. A. Adams, *Consumer Expenditure in the United Kingdom, 1900–1919*, Cambridge, 1954.

goods[27] encouraged by more favourable terms of trade and rising purchasing power, to the 1890s. The result was a fall in the share of consumption drawn from home manufactures, though this trend was to
some extent reversed to 1913, when terms of trade deteriorated again.

Here is seen part of the mechanism by which sharply rising incomes
could be sustained by production that was rising much more slowly.
Further, it should be noted that not all these substantial gains in real
incomes were made at the same speed, nor did they affect all classes
of the community equally. The improvements due to the reductions in
real costs tended to spread their effects widely, but there were also
important shifts in relative incomes in this period, which greatly
affected the share-out of the benefits.

Incomes and their distribution

While consumers' expenditure in the period 1873-1914 increased as
fast as in the preceding period (most of the increase occurring before
1900), actual incomes probably increased faster still. At constant
(1913-14) prices, income per head, measured conventionally, rose
from £28·81 in 1873 to £44·51 in 1895 and to £50·27 in 1914 (it had
been higher still, nearly £52 in 1913), or by 74 per cent over 42 years.
Again, the rise was faster in the first half of the period than the
second: the average increase *per decade* in the 20 years 1870-79 to
1890-99 was 25 per cent, while in the period 1885-94 to 1905-14 it
had dropped back to 13 per cent.[28] This was as fast a growth as had
ever been recorded, and for the 'Great Depression', 1873-96, probably
the fastest rate of growth of incomes to that date. This rise was associated with a similar, and more precisely measurable, rise in the
volume of exports and the volume of trade in general.[29]

The increase in the stock of capital was equally striking, and probably unprecedented[30] (see p. 235).

In addition, on the same basis, total net overseas investments made
at 1912-13 prices between 1875 and 1913 added up to £2,537 million,
or £56 a head of the 1913 population. Total capital formation, as a
proportion of current incomes, fluctuated violently in this period and

---

[27] Including all alcoholic drinks and motor-cars, some of which were imported.
[28] Deane and Cole, Table 74, 284, and Table 90, 329-30. Also E. H. Phelps
Brown and S. V. Hopkins, 'The Course of Wage-Rates in Five Countries,
1860-1939', *Oxford Economic Papers*, II, 1950.
[29] Deane and Cole, 311; Conrad and Meyer, *op. cit.*
[30] E. H. Phelps Brown and B. Weber, 'Accumulation, Productivity and Distribution in the British Economy 1870-1939', *Econ. J.*, 63 (1953), 286; J. H.
Lenfant, 'Great Britain's Capital Formation 1865-1914', *Economica*, 1951;
also C. H. Feinstein, 'Income and Investment in the United Kingdom, 1856-
1914', *Economic Journal*, 71 (1961), and Mitchell and Deane, 373-4.

	Stock of revenue-yielding buildings (1912–13 prices) £ mn., U.K.	Stock of capital goods other than buildings, at replacement cost (1912–13 prices), £ mn., U.K.	Total of first two columns, £ mn.	Per head (1912–13) price) £
Averages				
1872–1874	1,668	1,723	3,391	105
1894–1896	2,481	2,924	5,405	138
1910–1912	3,309	4,669	7,978	175

was highest at its beginning and at its end, but it showed no slowing-down in the twentieth century.

The share of wage-earners in this total remained surprisingly constant between the beginning and the end of the period at around 40 per cent of national income, or 55 per cent if salary earners are also included.[31] This stability, however, was the result of two contrary movements. During the 'Great Depression', up to the mid-nineties, there was a substantial shift of incomes to wage earners, and against the incomes from property; in the second half of the period the movement was reversed, and, since real wages then virtually remained constant, almost the whole of the *per capita* increase went to the owners of capital. Since the rate of investment remained high throughout, the origins of the feeling of 'depression' in 1873–96 become clear: it was a period when a high rate of investment was sustained out of shrinking profits.[32] The average rate of return on *real* capital, while fluctuating, showed no secular trend to change; but the yield on industrial equities fell sharply to the 1890s, and was only very partially restored in 1897–1913. Even the switch to overseas investment with its higher returns on capital, which was one of the significant features of 1905–13, did not raise the percentage yield on capital back to its boom level of 1870–73.[33]

[31] On slightly different definitions, wages and salaries remained closely around the 48 per cent mark, varying only between a maximum of 49·8 per cent in 1890–9 and a minimum of 47·2 per cent in 1905–14 in this period; Deane and Cole, 247.

[32] H. L. Beales, 'The Great Depression in Industry and Trade', *Ec.H.R.*, V (1934), reprinted in Carus-Wilson, *Essays*, I (1954).

[33] Phelps Brown and Weber, *loc. cit.*; E. H. Phelps Brown and P. E. Hart, 'The Share of Wages in National Income', *Econ. J.*, 62 (1952); E. H. Phelps Brown, 'Long-Term Movement of Real Wages', *The Theory of Wage Determination* (ed. J. T. Dunlop), 1957; A. G. Ford, 'The Transfer of British Foreign Lending, 1870–1913', *Ec.H.R.*, XI (1958) and 'Overseas Lending and Internal Fluctuations: 1870–1914', *Yorkshire Bulletin*, 17 (1965); A. L. Bowley, *The Change in the Distribution of the National Income, 1880–1913*, Oxford, 1920, 18, and *Wages and Income since 1860*, Cambridge, 1937, 94.

Thus, while the richer sections of the population appropriated nearly all the increments after 1896, they did so not because they earned more on their investments, but because they had more of them, while the wage earners failed to benefit from increasing production. Taking 1870–78 as 100, output per occupied person rose by 32 per cent in 1886–94 and wages rose by 32 per cent; but by 1905–13, output had risen by 55 per cent, i.e. they stood at 155, while a distributive shift of 23 per cent had occurred against labour, so that wages still stood at 132. According to Bowley and Wood, the annual average change in real wages, allowing for unemployment, was +1·85 per cent in 1874–1900 and −0·71 per cent in 1901–14.[34]

The rapid accumulation of capital was still largely confined to the wealthy; the savings of the working classes remained insignificant. Thus this period saw a widening differentiation between the poor and the rich in terms of property which greatly exceeded their differentiation in terms of income. According to the calculations of Chiozza Money, made mainly for 1903–4, the top five million incomes had rather less than half of the total national income, and earned £166 per head, compared with £23 per head for the rest of the population, or about seven times as much; the top 4·4 million of property owners owned about 110 times as much, on average, as the rest of the population. Seven per cent of income-earners owned seven-eighths of the national wealth. There had been some slight spreading of share-ownership by the end of the period, and some companies were now issuing shares of very small denomination, but the typical capitalist was still a very wealthy capitalist. For the period 1911–12 to 1913–14 only 20 per cent of property was left by persons owning less than £5,000, and only eight per cent by those under £1,000, while the proportions of stocks, funds and shares etc. were only 10 per cent and two per cent respectively—i.e. 90 per cent of shares etc. were held by the very rich.[35] With the passage of time and the enormous growth of capital, it merely seemed that the rich were getting richer, without any notable spread of property other than personal possessions among the poor. 'Class divisions were never so acutely felt as by the Edwardians.'[36]

Wage incomes, as we have seen, rose sharply to the mid-nineties,

[34] Phelps Brown, 'Long-Term Movement'; W. W. Rostow, *British Economy of the Nineteenth Century*, 91.
[35] L. G. Chiozza Money, *Riches and Poverty*, 1st edn, 1905; 3rd edn, 1906, 30, 34, 66 *seq.*, 127. There seems to be an error in the last line of the relevant Table 7 of Deane and Cole, p. 25, which shows real wages rising by 10 points while money wages rose only by two points between 1900 and 1906, when prices were rising rather than falling; Cairncross, 84–8.
[36] A. J. Taylor, 'The Economy', *Edwardian England 1901–1914* (ed S. Nowell-Smith), 1964, 134.

and then dropped again, the levels in 1912–14 remaining below the peak levels of 1899–1901. Wage rates in the United Kingdom, taking into account changes in the cost of living, moved as follows[37]:

	Real wages of employed workers (Kuczynski) (1900 = 100)	Real wages, taking into account unem- ployment (Kuczynski) (1900 = 100)	Real wages, U.K. (Bowley) (1914 = 100)
Averages			
1872–1874	72	74	66
1894–1896	98	95	99
1899–1901	103	103	103
1912–1914	95	95	98

A separate study for London showed real wages to have dropped by six per cent between 1900–1 and 1911–12.[38] Again, these figures do not fully represent the gain of the working classes as a whole, because they neglect the shift from lower-paid to better-paid occupations. According to Wood, the real wage index of workers in unchanged occupations (and including losses by unemployment) with 1850=100, rose from 113 in 1870–4 to 147 in 1900–2, or by 30 per cent; but taking into account the shift in employment, it rose from 122 to 174, or by 43 per cent. There was no change between 1899–1901 and 1913, the money wages on both assumptions rising by about 12 per cent, or rather less than the cost of living.[39] This is likely to be the most accurate measure of the improvement in working-class standards of living in the period as a whole.

Not every trade fared equally well. Miners and builders did rather better than the average up to 1900, and worse later; agricultural labourers and textile workers did worse before 1900 and better after-wards. Engineers did fairly well throughout.[40] Differentials between the skilled and unskilled, already very high, probably expanded even further in this period, particularly up to 1900; what was to become a secular decline in the differential may have set in by 1900, though it made but little difference before 1914. On the other hand, it may have

[37] J. Kuczynski, *A Short History of Labour Conditions in Great Britain 1750 to the Present Day*, 1942, 75–6, 120 (U.K.); G. H. Wood, 'Real Wages and the Standard of Comfort since 1850', *J.R. Stat. S.*, 1909, reprinted in Carus-Wilson, *Essays*, III; A. L. Bowley, *Wages and Income in the United Kingdom since 1860*, Cambridge, 1937.
[38] Frances Wood, 'The Course of Real Wages in London, 1900–1912', *J.R. Stat. S.*, 77 (1913–14), 37.
[39] *Loc. cit.*, III, 138; A. L. Bowley, *The Change in the Distribution of the National Income 1880–1913*, Oxford, 1920, 15.
[40] Wood, *loc. cit.*; Clapham, III, 466–7.

merely been the case that in a period of falling real wages the incomes of the low-paid workers could not be squeezed any further, and all the pressure fell on the better-paid men. Indices of gross money wages moved as follows as between Kuczynski's two groups of the 'labour aristocracy' and the 'great mass of the workers' (recalculated on 1895–1903 = 100)[41]:

| | Gross money wages index | | Real wage Index | |
| | 'Aristocracy' | 'Great mass' | (Bowley cost of living 1914 = 100) | |
			'Aristocracy'	'Great mass'
1870–1874	85	100	73	86
1894–1896	96	96	115	116
1899–1900	100	98	112	111
1904–1914	92	96	93	97

According to another calculation, the (unweighted) average of unskilled wages as a proportion of skilled in coal, cotton, engineering, buildings and railways was 60 per cent in 1886 and 58·5 per cent in 1913.[42] The wage census of 1906 showed the actual average weekly earnings of adult males, including overtime and short time, to have lain between 26s. 8d. and 28s. 3d. a week, or only just above the nominal labourer's rates, in such diverse industries as railways, public utilities, earthenware and chemicals, textiles and clothing, and food and drink. The three higher-paid trade groups were building and woodwork (30s. 8d), metals, engineering, shipbuilding (32s. 3d.) and paper and printing (34s. 2d.).[43]

In these changes, truck payments and the abuses of long pays and of indirect, sub-contract pay were becoming insignificant, except in a few limited 'sweated trades',[44] which began to be treated as a special problem. There was a sharp fall in the numbers of children at work, and a slight fall in the proportions of women working. Factory legislation spread to a widening range of trades, including those considered 'dangerous', and Workmen's Compensation Acts helped to improve safety and health conditions in the majority of firms. Hours of work

[41] Kuczynski, 76–7, 93; see also Ashworth, *Economic History*, 201, note 1.
[42] K. G. J. C. Knowles and D. J. Robertson, 'Differences Between the Wages of Skilled and Unskilled Workers, 1880–1950', *Bull. Oxford Inst. of Statistics*, 13 (1951), III.
[43] A. L. Bowley, *The Division of the Product of Industry*, Oxford, 1919, 29, Table V.
[44] The House of Lords Committee on Sweating (1890) defined sweating as 'earnings barely sufficient to sustain existence; hours of labour such as to make the lives of the workers periods of almost ceaseless toil; sanitary conditions injurious to the health of the persons employed and dangerous to the public'—S. and B. Webb, *The Prevention of Destitution*, 1911, 88.

did not change much, though the tendency was downwards, and while some isolated firms instituted a normal 48-hour week instead of the 54 hours worked in the 1870s, the miners won their legal (and nominal) eight-hour day in 1908. The incidence of unemployment fluctuated widely, but did not worsen during the period as a whole. In a whole range of industries, in transport and in mining, a remarkable growth of trade unionism helped to improve actual working conditions in detail, and gave the workers more security, a higher status and more influence over their working conditions. Against this, the indications are that work may have been speeded up or become more intense in many industries.[45] Altogether, working conditions were undoubtedly improving, particularly by cutting out the worst practices.

As long as wages continued to rise satisfactorily, that is to say until the end of the century, the pressure to make at least the privileged section of the working classes 'respectable', and to imbue them with the same ideals and the same pattern of consumption as the classes above them continued to be remarkably successful. Their voting behaviour remained largely unchanged, the Liberals, in particular, having some of their staunchest support in the working-class quarters. Better housing in the suburbs, one of the most difficult barriers to cross, but also one of the most powerful influences in this direction, was accessible to growing numbers. Small savings, another important ingredient of 'respectability', continued to increase: by 1910, the last year before compulsory insurance, the friendly societies had 6·6 million members, with average holdings of £5.4.9., and the collecting societies had over seven million, averaging 14s., though most of them were unsound.[46] By 1914 the co-operative societies had three million members and the trade unions, 3¼ million members, with funds of £2 a head. Including the Post Office Savings Banks (£182 million) and the Trustee Savings Banks (£54 million), small savings were totalling well over £400 million.[47] In smaller matters, also, the late Victorian working man, with his best Sunday suit, his watch and gold chain, a family photograph on his upright piano and a Landseer reproduction on his front room wall, had moved a long way towards the bourgeois ideal anxiously presented to him by middle-class well-wishers.

This consensus began to falter after 1900, though in some instances, like the beginning of independent labour politics or the unwillingness to suffer sharp unemployment as acts of God, signs of dissatisfaction had not been wanting from the 1880s onwards. The pressure on

[45] Ashworth, 192 *seq.*; Clapham, II, 469 *seq.*
[46] Cf. p. 220 above.
[47] Cairncross, 88 *seq.*; Clapham, III, 504–5.

living standards in the new century intensified the protest and widened this divergence. Just as the respectable Liberals or 'Lib-Labs' were challenged by a younger generation of Socialists within the trade unions and the new Labour Party, so the population at large was disturbed to see not only the formerly meek and lowly 'unskilled men', the dockers and carters and railwaymen, organise strikes which led to violence, but even the skilled engineers, boilermakers, and cotton spinners, and above all the miners, conduct their industrial bargaining with a new militancy. In part, this was the result of general education and of the experience in politics and organisation which accompanied it.[48] In part, it was frustration over price rises which cancelled out any hard-won wage gains. But, in part, it also arose from the fact that a large minority of the population remained at a level of stark poverty, apparently untouched by the general progress. In this class there were some who seemed permanently condemned to a life of need: widows, labourers, casual workers, workers in the 'sweated trades'; but no working man, no matter how privileged, could be sure of avoiding falling into this class when struck by the twin scourges of working-class life: unemployment and old age. The dreaded Poor Law institutions, in particular, had become a refuge for those who had worked as long as they were able, but had survived into an age when they could no longer earn their own keep. 'On the whole people are poor because they are old', Charles Booth wrote in 1894, and, while about one-third of the aged were on relief, 'if a division of classes could be made, it would probably be found that amongst the working class and small traders the rate of pauperism for all over 65 is not less than 40 to 45 per cent'.[49] The failure to abolish real poverty at the bottom of the social pyramid was still a grim reality affecting the welfare, actual or potential, of a large majority of the population.

The survival of poverty

In 1901, B. Seebohm Rowntree published his *Poverty, a Study of Town Life*, the result of two years' detailed enquiry in York. This was not a city distinguished by exceptional poverty (nor by exceptionally high wages); nevertheless, he found that 10 per cent of the population lived in 'primary poverty', unable to sustain efficient life owing to low incomes, and a further 18 per cent, despite somewhat higher incomes, also in fact lived in poverty similarly defined. Rowntree's findings bore out the result of the less systematic, but more impressive study by Booth, made some years before into London life, who found 30·7

---

[48] E. H. Phelps Brown, *Growth of British Industrial Relations*, 1959.
[49] Charles Booth, *The Aged Poor in England and Wales*, 1894, 420.

per cent of the population living in actual poverty,[50] and were in line with the results of a study of four provincial towns in 1912–13.[51]

It was characteristic that Booth, dividing London's population into eight classes, of whom four were below the poverty line, should begin with a first group (A), composed of 'the lowest class of occasional labourers, loafers and semi-criminals', the other three being those dependent on (B) casual earnings, (C) intermittent earnings and (D) small regular earnings. Today we might be less inclined to connect poverty with moral failings, and would look rather at the social circumstances that have brought it about.

From this point of view, poverty might also be held to have four separate sets of causes. First, there were the natural calamities of prolonged illness, widowhood, orphanage and there was old age. The persons affected were the 'deserving' poor for whom the Victorian Poor Law and Victorian charities were set up and whose problems were illuminated by the monumental researches and reports of the Poor Law Commission of 1909. Both the Majority and the Minority Reports advocated the separate treatment of each of these classes, but it was the Minority Report alone which regarded destitution as a social, rather than a personal, defect, and wanted it tackled by collective action.

The second great cause was unemployment, striking at workers in most industries in periodic slumps and depressions. Trade union funds and the Poor Law were the common resort of those affected, and in 1886, Chamberlain's famous circular[52] urged local authorities to make employment available in public works in times of poor trade. This approach received legal sanction by the Unemployed Workmen Act of 1905, which obliged authorities of towns of over 50,000 to set up Distress Committees for helping the unemployed to find work. In 1909, Labour Exchanges were set up to coordinate the placing of workers on a national scale. None of this was intended to tackle the original problem, unemployment itself.

Thirdly, there were those in casual and irregular employment, Booth's categories B and C. Some were the victims of a system of employment which seemed to require this, like the dockers; others had never acquired a trade, and depended on seasonal, or temporary, jobs. Elsewhere again, as in building, continuous employment seemed impossible to ensure by the nature of the work. Lastly, and representing the greatest failure of society, there were those who even when fully

[50] Charles Booth, *Life and Labour of the People in London*, 2 vols, 1889, and 17 vols, 1903.
[51] A. L. Bowley and A. R. Burnett-Hurst, *Livelihood and Poverty*, 1915.
[52] Reprinted in W. H. B. Court, *English Economic History 1870–1914, Commentary and Documents*, Cambridge, 1965, 402–5.

employed and paid did not take home enough to live on. The most important groups amongst them were those in unskilled jobs and in domestic trades, and those with large families. To some extent, the Trade Boards Act of 1909 was a belated effort to deal with one aspect of this, but it went not much further than the narrowly conceived 'sweated trades'. Ultimately, the labour shortage of the war, extended Trade Boards Acts and strong trade-union action were to reduce this cause of poverty, but before 1914 it was a vivid reminder that a rising national income did not necessarily ensure a share of its benefits to all those who contributed to it.

In practice, these categories overlapped in numerous cases. Thus, Dudley Baxter estimated in 1868 that 20 per cent of average working time was lost by illness, unemployment or other mishaps by ordinary workers, 33 per cent by women and boys and 10 per cent by agricultural workers[53]; this hit the lower-paid workers much harder than the others. Again, the Census of 1901 showed that more than one third of the paupers (and probably nearly one half) had been labourers or other unskilled workers.[54]

The strongest link between them, however, appeared to be the frightening fact that the large minority living in poverty was actually and seriously suffering in health for lack of nourishment, and, since large families were an important contributory factor to 'poverty', the proportion of children so suffering was invariably much greater than that of adults. The Medical Congress Report, published in 1889, for example, described the strikingly high incidence of rickets, a deficiency disease, among children.

> 'In some areas, such as the Clyde district, almost every child was found to be affected. A map of its distribution over the whole of England was a map showing the density of the industrial population.'[55]

Declining standards of teeth were another sign of lack of calcium, and vitamin A deficiency affected children also more than adults. The British Association Enquiry of 1873–83, covering 53,000 persons, found boys aged 11–12 in public schools five inches taller than boys of similar age in industrial schools; the differences between the averages of adults of the middle and working classes being $3\frac{1}{2}$ inches.

If the findings of Booth and Rowntree might be held, in some quarters, to have been biased by an exceptional social conscience, the

[53] Dudley Baxter, *National Income. The United Kingdom*, 1868, 49; Ashworth, *Economic History*, 23.
[54] Money, 271.
[55] J. C. Drummond and Anne Wilbraham, *The Englishman's Food*, 1939; 1957 edn, 381.

reports of the Inspection of Recruiting and the Director General of the Army Medical Service were not. In the Boer War, it was found that 40 per cent of the recruits had to be rejected—in some areas up to 60 per cent—because of physical disabilities. In 1917, when conscription was introduced, the figures were found to be similar: 36 per cent of the conscripts were in good health, and 22·5 per cent were subject to 'partial disabilities'—a total of 58·06 per cent; but 31·5 per cent had 'marked disabilities' and 10 per cent were totally unfit for service.[56] The minimum height for infantry soldiers had to be lowered twice, in 1883 and 1902. The Inter-Departmental Committee on Physical Deterioration, reporting in 1904, confirmed all that the social reformers and medical observers had conveyed earlier, listing as causes of poor health and physique, poverty, bad housing, insanitary employment conditions, alcohol and insufficient or badly assorted diet.[57]

These factors, together with inadequate clothing and heating and poor medical care, all had to take part of the blame, but an inadequate diet, badly balanced because of concentration on cheap or adulterated food, was the main cause of the small stature of many working-class children, their deformities, and their proneness to disease. If the general death-rate was declining, this merely helped to underline the fact that the rise in general health had by-passed an important section of the people; in any case, a large part of the cause for the falling death-rate was the 'reduction, in most cases almost to vanishing point, of the more serious infectious diseases such as typhus, cholera, enteric and smallpox' in this period,[58] because of general medical and sanitary advances.

What was it like to live on 'round about a pound a week'[59] in the late Victorian and Edwardian period? Among the 2½ million men who received less than 25s. if in regular work, some two million must have been married, and their families must have numbered eight million altogether. They were bound to be 'underfed, under-housed and insufficiently clothed. The children among them suffer more than the adults. Their growth is stunted, their mental powers are cramped, their health is undermined.'[60]

These numbers are likely to be conservative. Philip Snowden, basing himself on Bowley's statistics of May 1911 showing 32 per cent of male adult workers, even in regular work, getting less than 25s.,

[56] J. C. M. McGonigle and J. Kirby, *Poverty and Public Health*, 1937, 26–37, quoted in E. J. Hobsbawm, 'Révolution Industrielle et Vie Matérielle des Classes Popularies', *Annales*, Nov.–Dec. 1962.
[57] *Ibid.*
[58] W. M. Frazer, *A History of English Public Health 1834–1939*, 1950, 285.
[59] Mrs Pember Reeves, *Round About a Pound a Week*, 1913.
[60] *Ibid.*, 214.

and on the official statistics, showing that virtually all agricultural workers and general labourers, 40 per cent of cotton workers etc. were in that category, estimated the numbers at nearly one half of the wage-earning class.[61] Taking into account the incomes of other members of their family on one side, and the short time and unemployment on the other, the likely proportion of the *total* population with that inadequate income would approximate very closely to the 30 per cent established by the social enquirers.

The official survey of nearly 2,000 working-class households in 1904 showed that those earning under 25s. a week spent 67 per cent on food, and even all those up to 40s. spent well over 60 per cent, a standard reached and even exceeded in the mid-eighteenth century. Only the fortunate minority (30 per cent of the sample) earning over £2 a week spent less—57 per cent.[62]

Again, in a survey, Bowley estimated the median (wage earner's) family with three children to have experienced the following changes in its budget[63]:

	1860	1880	1914
Total income	20s. 6d.	26s. 6d.	35s. 6d.
Percentage spent on bread	26%	17%	15%
,, ,, ,, meat	8%	9%	20%
,, ,, ,, all food	67%	61%	63%
Calories per full man— equivalent per day	3,240	3,470	3,900

Although the decline in bread consumption and the increase in meat, as well as caloric, intake speaks of a substantial improvement by current standard, the total food expenditure, even of the average workers was, as late as 1914, still above the tell-tale poverty level of 60 per cent.[64]

A survey of agricultural labourers' budgets in the Midlands in 1893 showed them as spending 55 per cent on food (18½ per cent on bread and flour alone), a diet without butcher's meat, though some additional proportion was stated to have been spent on meat and milk.[65] This was a group with a steady income which lived largely on cabbage

[61] Philip Snowden, *The Living Wage*, 1912, 28-35.
[62] Cd. 2337 and Money, *op. cit.*, 140.
[63] A. L. Bowley, *Wages and Income in the United Kingdom since 1860*, Cambridge, 1937, 36.
[64] For a discussion of Engels' law on this question, see C. C. Zimmermann, *Consumption and Standard of Living*, 1936, ch. 5, and R. G. D. Allen and A. L. Bowley, *Family Expenditure*, 1935.
[65] Joseph Ashby and Bolton King, 'Statistics of Some Midland Villages', *Econ. J.*, III (1893), reprinted in Court, *op. cit.*, 297.

and lard and in the 1870s had a bit of cheese, with 'suet pudding with scraps of bacon rolled in it and mushrooms, too, once or twice a year, and then it was the richest of dishes'.[66]

At the other extreme, there were casual workers like the Liverpool dockers, described by a Committee to the Liverpool Economic and Statistical Society in 1909.[67] Of 27 budgets kept over any length of time, only three had average incomes of over 30s., 12 of 20s. to 30s., and 12 under 20s. The husbands' earnings alone were much lower, only five averaging over 20s. and 10 below 15s. a week, and the incomes were made up by the women, who went out 'charing, washing, sewing or hawking', or kept lodgers, on top of looking after their children. The important factor, however, was the irregularity of the earnings from week to week, and the consequent inability to plan. For many, 'the week forms a sort of cycle, the fare being particularly generous on Sunday and decreasing through the week till Saturday when pay day brings sufficiency again'. In bad periods, debts were incurred, and even a comparatively well-off and steady family, earning 28s. 6d. a week fairly regularly, was found in 1908 to have debts of over £8, requiring payments of over 10s. a week, together with 7s. a week rent. Clothes were pawned on Monday and redeemed on Saturday, adding another weekly interest burden.

In such families, only the most fortunate spent 60 per cent, or even 50 per cent, on food; most of them spent *less*, not because of their affluence, but because the total income was so small that the fixed element took much more than half. Rent was 4s. 6d. to 7s. a week for a two-roomed dwelling in London, 6s. to 9s. for three rooms (about two-thirds of this in the provinces[68]; clothing (clubs) took 2s. 3d., coal 1s. 10d. and household sundries 10d.; not even this much and the minimal 13s. 9d. a week for food for a family of five, established by Rowntree on the basis of absurdly ideal purchasing and management, could be reached. Even then,

'it must be allowed that this sum (for non-food expenditure) allows nothing for sick-clubs and trade unions, or beer or tobacco, or trams or travelling, or amusements or newspapers, or writing materials and stamps; and if an evening paper is bought, or the children have coppers given to them to go and see the "moving pictures", physical efficiency suffers'.[69]

[66] M. K. Ashby, 'Joseph Ashby of Tysoe', Cambridge, 1961, reprinted in *ibid.,* 299.
[67] *Ibid.,* 304 seq.; also *Round About a Pound a Week,* chapter 14.
[68] Masterman, 100; Board of Trade, *Report on Working-Class Rents and Retail Prices,* 1908, Cd. 2864, xiv; 1913, Cd. 6955, xvi–xvii.
[69] B. S. Rowntree, 'The Industrial Unrest', *Contemporary Review,* Oct. 1911, 455.

For that class, nearly a third of the population, the new mass-produced wealth was not a boon, but, since it did lure the pennies from their pockets, a curse which destroyed their chance of a reasonable diet. What was left was as bad as, if not worse than, the poorest budget of earlier centuries: bread, potatoes, butter, tea, sugar and, perhaps, tinned milk, in inadequate quantities, and almost nothing else.[70] The wage statistics and the social investigations agreed on this point: the population subsisting temporarily and permanently on such a standard, formed nearly one third of the nation.

Conclusion

To most contemporaries, the last 40 years of the long peace appeared as a happy age of uninterrupted progress at home and abroad. At home, not only were incomes and wealth demonstrably rising, but the mere accumulation of wealth had allowed society to deal, for the first time, with such formerly intractable evils as overcrowding, lack of sanitation, disease and a high rate of infantile mortality. Abroad, the expansion of trade, investment, British naval power and the Empire seemed to underline a supremacy which had not been challenged since the Industrial Revolution.

Yet there were some, and they have received much support from historians since, who not only saw this period as a turning point, an age in which progress slowed down and international leadership was lost, but also insisted that society had failed to deal with its own urgent problems of social injustice and of poverty. No doubt it could be said of this, as of other ages, that protest and the roused conscience were merely the results of progress, the result of the fact that men who had received some education, the power to vote, and the power of choice in their spending and leisure habits for the first time, had inevitably learned to ask for more, and there is a grain of truth in this. But it is a more serious criticism of a wealthy than of an impoverished society that it tolerates so much grinding poverty, poverty that inhibits health and a full human development, poverty above all among the aged and among children.

A wealthy society, depending on its world trading network for food and other necessities, may be a much safer society than a traditional one, for its resources allow it to lay in stores to cushion any shocks, and to escape the ill-effects of bad harvests as of the dwindling minerals within its borders. At the same time it is also a more vulnerable society, for its poor are further away from the land with its food, its space, and its healthy air. Many, probably most, of the British population benefited by the technical and commercial progress which

---

[70] *Round About a Pound a Week*, 108 *seq.*

had made it all possible, though even they suffered from the uncertainties of the trade cycle and the overcrowding and ugliness of the towns and cities. A substantial minority, however, suffered all the losses, and shared very few of the gains.

If the 'poverty line' of contemporary observers is to be taken as a guide, that minority amounted to about 30 per cent of the population and nearly half the working classes, with a much higher proportion of children included in it. They also had some of the benefits of the new civilisation, cheap imported foods, cheap newspapers and entertainments, an elementary education, and a medical practice (if they could afford it) that was no longer lethal. But, still living at the margin of subsistence, they suffered more than they might have done in other ages, because of the vision of the wealth around them, the vast and crushing size of their cities, the cutting-off of the last contacts with the land and their rural ancestors, the pitiless pervasion of new methods, of factory competition, of booms and slumps, of the obsolescence of old skills. Contemporaries might well feel that it was a high price to pay for the apotheosis of Empire.

Chapter nine

The Last Half-Century, 1914–1966

The unquiet years

The last five decades have seen more drastic and more violent changes in the political and social framework of the British economy than perhaps any other in recent history, the Industrial Revolution not excluded. They have seen two World Wars, both of them 'total wars', particularly in the economic sphere, the most severe and most persistent world slump on record in the 1930s, a reversal of the traditional role of Britain as a net foreign lender and, since the Second World War, a rate of growth which (though it is much lower than that of other European countries) is yet faster than anything in the past and implies a more rapid change of attitudes, skills and institutions.

Wealth and income per head have grown more rapidly than ever before, and have now reached a level which could not have been imagined even a few decades ago. But a price had to be paid for this rise, a price which includes the wars, and the years of economic warfare that separated them. These upheavals are indeed impossible to exclude from this history, and we shall, in fact, divide our account of the creation of wealth for purposes of exposition, into the period 1914–38, the First World War and the depression period which followed, and 1939–66, the Second World War and the recovery and growth that have succeeded it.

The economic effects of the wars were many, and are not easily summarised. Both wars had much in common. In both, resources were used more fully than in peacetime, and new ones emerged, like sections of female labour that had not been considered before, but in both the output of consumption goods dropped sharply, since so much of the manpower was in uniform, or engaged in the production of armaments. Both saw major diversions of industries—the expansion of steel production, ships, vehicles, agriculture, for example, and the forced decline of others like textiles or the service trades, as well as a frightening running-down of capital goods (including housing) and postponement of replacements and even of repairs. All these left permanent effects, in the greatly expanded scope for women's labour, for instance, or in the enlarged capacity of heavy industries.

Again, both wars, like former conflicts, saw inflations, though in the Second World War the supply of funds was better controlled than in the First, and both saw sharp rises in taxation, implying a redistribution of incomes, and these were not entirely reversed in peacetime. In the Second World War the forced sale of foreign investment and the contracting of foreign loans to pay for imports unmatched by exports went much farther than in the First. While the First World War saw the widespread adoption of collective bargaining on a national scale, so that wages in any industry moved together all over the country, and the immediate postwar period saw the extension of unemployment insurance to virtually all wage-earners, the Second saw the implanting of Keynsian-type economic regulatory control, and the setting up of the more comprehensive 'Welfare State'.

Both accelerated some changes that were in preparation in any case; and both, therefore, may have contributed to the ability of the British economy to accept more rapid change and growth in the future. But the physical losses and the destruction of assets, quite apart from the human losses and sufferings, slowed down the total advance, for a considerable term. In both wars it took about 10 years from the beginning of the conflict, that is to say, until 1924 and 1950 respectively, to restore the country to that level of output and income which it had reached in the last year of peace.

Production and productivity, 1914–1938

Official statistics were not as developed in the 1914–18 war as they were to become in 1939–45, and the dislocations, such as the replacement of male labour by female, drawn from the home, the neglect of

Industrial production in the U.K. (1924 = 100)[1]

	Excluding building	*Including building*
Average		
1910–13	86·3	84·6
(1913)	(92·6)	(90·5)
1914–18	84·3	80·6
1919–23	85·6	84·0
(1923)	(92·5)	(90·0)
1924–9	104·3	107·0
1930–4	107·7	109·8
1935–8	139·7	142·3

[1] K. S. Lomax, 'Production and Productivity Movements in the United Kingdom since 1900', *J.R. Stat. S.*, 1959, 122, ser. A, 196. See also T. M. Ridley, 'Industrial Production in the U.K., 1900–1953', *Economica*, 1955, 22, and W. G. Hoffmann, *op. cit.*

investment, the falling-away of exports, the encouragement of import-saving industries, like agriculture, were so substantial that most statistical series of the early century prudently omit the war years and begin again in 1920 or later.

Industrial production figures (p. 249), however, have been hazarded and show a relatively mild fall, particularly if the exceptional level of the 1913 boom year is borne in mind.

Though production declined steadily in the war years, the lowest point being reached in 1918, that absolute decline was less important than the growing share of armaments in it, leaving less for consumption. Thus, while the index for chemicals rose from 86·6 to 93·3 between 1914 and 1918, of metals from 94·7 to 98·0 and of engineering from 95·3 to 118·5, textiles fell from 102·6 to 94·4, clothing from 114·6 to 70·9 and food, drink and tobacco from 92·5 to 72·7.[2] Really drastic falls in output and consumption were prevented by the rapid cutting of investment. Economically speaking, the war was above all a period of capital consumption. Exact measurement is not possible, but it is significant that in building and contracting the production index fell from 64·0 in 1913 to 20·8 in 1918, or by two-thirds, and for house building alone, in 34 towns, from 41·5 to 2·2 or by nearly 95 per cent,[3] while the railways also had cause to complain of the neglect of their permanent way. Seven and threequarter million tons of shipping were lost, 38 per cent of the tonnage at the outbreak of the war, and despite vigorous building the fleet was smaller by 18 per cent or by over three million tons, in 1918 than in 1914. In agriculture, the ploughing-up of grasslands with its short-term advantages and the mass slaughter in the winter of 1917–18 also represented some capital consumption, and stocks were run down everywhere. Overseas investments to the tune of some £550 million gross and £300 million net (after deducting new investments made in the period) had to be sold, and the Government borrowed some £1,365 million abroad, but this went not to meet import bills, but to make loans to Allies totalling £1,741 million, many of which were never repaid.[4] Last, but not least, there were the losses in manpower. About three-quarters of a million men (nine per cent of the men aged 20–45) were killed and 1,700,000 wounded, a figure proportionally much larger than in any previous war in historic times.[5]

[2] Lomax, 192–3.
[3] B. Weber, 'A New Index of Residential Construction and Long Cycles in House Building in Great Britain, 1838–1950', *Scottish J. of Political Economy*, 2 (1955), 131. (1900–1909=100).
[4] E. V. Morgan, *Studies in British Financial Policy 1914–1925*, 341; J. A. Salter, *Allied Shipping Control*, Oxford, 1921, 362.
[5] 210,000 casualties, out of a population one third as large as in 1914–18,

At the same time, however, there was much useful and productive investment in such industries as iron and steelmaking, engineering and shipbuilding and chemicals. It is true that in the changed conditions of the postwar world markets could not be found for all of this new capacity, so that it contributed to the high level of unemployment besetting the economy, but in terms of its productive equipment, its capital and skilled labour, the British economy emerged from the war with relatively small losses both at home and abroad. The worst that one could say was that it had lost the growth which might otherwise have occurred in four peacetime years.

Output, however, was distorted by the violent postwar boom to 1920 and the severe depression which followed it, and did not reach the prewar *per capita* levels until 1923–4.[6] By 1924, not only had the prewar peak of production been exceeded, but in view of the widespread reduction of the normal 'working day' from nine hours to eight in 1919–20, productivity in the sense of output per operative-hour had increased by the substantial margin of 1·6 per cent per year for all industries between 1907 and 1924, and two per cent per year for manufacturing industries alone. Most industries, it is important to note, had grown in productivity at very near the average rate, only vehicles (5·1 per cent) and paper and printing (3·2 per cent) being much above, and textiles (0·7 per cent) and precision instruments (0·6 per cent) being much below, while in mining and quarrying productivity had actually *decreased* by 0·8 per cent per annum, a telling result of diminishing returns and overexpanded capacity in coalmining.[7]

This rate of growth of productivity compared well with that of the preceding period, 1870–1913, which has been estimated at 1·5 per cent per annum, and, for that matter, it compared well with growth in other countries.[8] By 1924 Britain had, therefore, succeeded in making good the loss in growth momentum of the war years, and at the same time allowed her working population to take out some of the benefit in increased leisure. In terms of absolute production, of course, growth had almost come to a halt, the growth rate for the period 1905–14— 1915–24 being less than one half per cent a year, compared with over

---

were almost as high in the French Wars of 1793–1815, but were spread over 22 years, not 4¼. Mobilisation reached a maximum of 3·2 per cent of the population in the earlier war, 13·2 per cent in 1914–18—W. W. Rostow, *The Process of Economic Growth*, Oxford, 1960, 150; W. Ashworth, *An Economic History of England, 1870–1939*, 1960, 285 *seq.*

[6] See Table on p. 249 above.

[7] Lomax, *loc. cit.*, 203.

[8] Angus Maddison, *Economic Growth in the West*, N.Y. and London, 1964, 37; H. W. Richardson, *Economic Recovery in Britain, 1932–1939*, 1937.

three per cent in the middle of the nineteenth century, and $1\frac{1}{2}$ per cent just before the war.[9]

Between 1924 and the outbreak of war output was less a function of capacity—for much capacity was idle over long periods—than of the general prosperity of the country. Thus production fell from 1924–6, rose to a minor peak in 1929, fell again to a point hardly above 1924 in the depression years of 1931–2 and only then began to rise substantially, slowly at first and then very rapidly in 1934–8. Most of the increase for this period as a whole was, in fact, concentrated in those last five years of peace, when industrial output, including the booming building industries, reached a level just half as high again as in 1924. The rate of growth of industrial production was again about $2\frac{1}{2}$ per cent per annum, or better than it had been since the 1870s, and output per man-hour had risen by 63 per cent since 1913, or by an annual compound rate of 2·03 per cent.

The 1920s, in fact, had been a period of fundamental, and painful, readjustment to new conditions, when overseas markets lost much of their capacity and willingness to absorb British goods,[10] and the buoyant market was formed among the relatively prosperous, and increasingly protected, customers at home. Adaptation to this new situation involved the drastic reduction in size of some old staple and export industries, including cotton, coal and shipbuilding, the stagnation of others such as agriculture, and the rapid expansion of a few, such as building, vehicles, electrical engineering and chemicals. At the same time, the prewar tendency for service industries to expand, including retail distribution, commerce and finance generally, teaching and entertainment, accelerated spectacularly. Between about 1920 and 1938, over two million were added to employment in these 'tertiary' industries, while employment in the extractive industries, mainly agriculture and mining, fell drastically, and employment in manufacturing grew much more slowly.[11] There was an equally sharp increase in the number of 'white-collar' workers in all industries, and both these tendencies were symbols of a rising prosperity among consumers, and a growing sophistication in production.

A comparison of the three censuses of production in 1907, 1924 and 1935 shows the same sharp decline in the share of agriculture (from six per cent to 3·9 per cent) and mining (from six per cent to 3·1 per cent), as well as of textiles, with a corresponding relative

[9] Deane and Cole, 297.
[10] Export *volume* fell from an index number 173 in 1913 to 132 in 1924 and 100 in 1938—G. C. Allen, *British Industries and their Organisation*, 4th edn, 1959, 48.
[11] S. Pollard, *The Development of the British Economy, 1914–1950*, 1962, 287–8.

growth of manufacturing, building and the services, though the shifts
were perhaps less drastic than might have been expected.

Distribution of gross national product in %[12]

	G.B. 1907	G.B. and N.I. 1924	G.B. and N.I. 1935
Agriculture and mining	12·0	9·6	7·0
Textiles and clothing	8·0	7·7	5·6
'Growth' manufactures[a]	17·7	22·1	22·7
Building and contracting	3·7	3·1	4·1
Commerce and transport	27·5	29·8	30·3
All others (including services)	31·1	27·7	30·3
	100·0	100·0	100·0

[a] Including 'Miscellaneous manufactures'

It is clear that a switch of this magnitude, and the continuous
rise of output and productivity, rested on substantial capital investments. Home investment was, in fact, higher than in the years before
the war, though this high rate was achieved only at the cost of the
virtual abandonment of overseas investment. Much of it, in the 1930s,

	Gross domestic fixed capital formation, % of G.N.P.	Net foreign investment, % of G.N.P.
Average of Years[13]		
1913–14	6·0	7·8
1920–24	8·6	3·0
1925–29	8·8	2·1
1930–34	8·1	−0·6
1935–39	10·6	−1·2

consisted of housing which improved consumption rather than productive performance. Indeed, at constant (1912–13) prices, and at
replacement cost, 'revenue-yielding buildings' increased in value by
over £1,000 million between 1924 and 1938, while the stock of all
other capital goods increased by only £660 million.[14]

A second reason for this satisfactory growth in the face of periodic
severe depressions, which might be thought to be inhibiting to innovation, was the new opportunities provided by accelerating technical

[12] Deane and Cole, Tables 40, 41 and 79.
[13] Deane and Cole, Table 91, 333.
[14] E. H. Phelps Brown and B. Weber, 'Accumulation, Productivity and Distribution in the British Economy, 1870–1938', *Econ. J.*, 63 (1953), 287.

change. Science and technology, fostered by growing numbers of researchers and experimenters who increasingly developed new techniques and opportunities quite independently of the immediate demands of industrialists, added a new momentum to economic progress. This quasi-autonomous force for innovation has been immeasurably strengthened since, and has become one of the outstanding characteristics of the twentieth century. Moreover, Britain was no longer in a position of technical leadership. The U.S.A.—and other countries in certain fields—was well ahead, so that at any given time the gap between an existing British technique and the best-known method was often very wide, allowing rapid gains to be made whenever the market encouraged new investments. This was particularly true of the 'new industries', which, together with building, did carry much of the rising productivity in the years to 1938.

Production and productivity, 1939–1966

The Second World War cost fewer British casualties than the First, and the extent of mobilisation was less also, assembling a maximum of 10·5 per cent of the population in the forces compared with 13·2 per cent in 1914–18,[15] but the economic dislocation went much deeper, and the resources devoted to the war effort were considerably larger. Little more than half of an enlarged output (compared with threequarters in peacetime) went into civilian consumption, and the other half was devoted to the war effort. To achieve this degree of economic mobilisation, capital was run down to an unprecedented extent, and net foreign investments were virtually wiped out, the remaining assets abroad being balanced by almost equally large debts to foreign countries, run up because of the war.

% of Gross national product at market prices[16]

	Consumers' expenditure	Public authorities' expenditure	Gross domestic capital formation	Net foreign investment
Average of years				
1935–9	77·6	13·0	10·6	−1·2
1940–4	56·1	49·9	2·2	−8·2
1945–9	69·3	22·8	10·4	−2·6
1950–4	68·2	17·3	13·6	0·8
1955–9	66·9	16·8	15·5	0·7
1960–4	66·7	16·8	16·8	−0·4

[15] Rostow, *loc. cit.*
[16] Deane and Cole, Table 91, 333; *National Income Blue Books.*

This astonishing performance was possible only by means of very tight Government control, over production as well as foreign trade, prices and incomes, which ensured, among other things, that the cut in consumption was limited largely to luxuries, leaving the supply of necessities at a satisfactory level. It did, however, mortgage the future in at least three ways. First, the loss of foreign investments meant that after the war more of home production would have to be used to pay for the same quantity of imports—a problem which was further aggravated by the move of the terms of trade against Britain in the postwar years. Secondly, capital equipment was drastically weakened by the virtual suspension of maintenance and replacement, and much of the postwar productive effort had to be diverted to make good the backlog of necessary work on the railways, roads and canals, on buildings, machinery and vehicles, and on human skills. Thirdly, the war effort had not only led to the neglect of some sectors, but to the over-development or distortion of others. Armaments works, shipyards, farms, had after 1945 to be reconverted to peacetime uses, men who had spent years in the Forces had to be reintegrated, both professionally and psychologically, into productive work, and, on a different plane, the postwar 'bulge' in births needed adjustment in the housing and school building plans, among others.

On the credit side were the hothouse developments of certain key industries with up-to-date technology, such as vehicles and aircraft, electrical and electronic engineering, and chemicals including plastics and man-made fibres. There was also a much more positive attitude towards the development of new techniques, a much enlarged role, and increased resources, awarded to scientists, and a greater willingness to take their advice.[17]

In total, industrial production had exceeded its highest prewar level by 1946,[18] and thereafter continued to grow faster than before the war,

Total output[19] **(Volume of gross domestic product at factor cost 1913 = 100)**

1935–8	153·8
1948–9	180·0
1950–4	199·6
1955–9	226·6
1960–4	261·3
1965	280·2

[17] S. Pollard, *Development of the British Economy*, 310–18.
[18] Lomax, 192–3.
[19] Pollard, 377–8; G. D. N. Worswick and P. H. Ady, *The British Economy in the Nineteenth-Fifties*, 1962, 75; Maddison, 201; *National Income Blue Books* (in volumes for the 1960s, Table 14).

and the product of other sectors of the economy also increased faster than before, though not as fast as in most other advanced countries. Since the labour force grew only slowly and hours remained virtually unchanged, productivity *per man hour* also increased satisfactorily. According to Maddison, it rose by 1·5 per cent (compound) per annum in 1870–1913 and 1·7 per cent between 1913 and 1950, when it was slowed up by two war periods, but increased to 2·0 per cent a year between 1950 and 1960.[20] From 1950 to 1965, productivity *per worker* rose by the slightly faster compound rate of 2·2 per cent a year.[21]

In this total, agriculture, whose share had risen sharply in wartime, dropped back again to its prewar level of under four per cent, and mining continued to decline.[22] Commerce and transport took a sharp downward dip from which they did not recover in the postwar years,

Distribution of gross national product, in %[23]

	1935	1949	1955	1964
Agriculture and mining	7·0	9·9	8·1	6·1
Manufacturing	28·3	33·7	36·6	35·0
Building and construction	4·1	5·5	5·7	6·8
Commerce and transport	30·3	24·7	23·9	23·5
All others	30·3	26·2	25·7	28·6

and 'others', including the services, also fell, but have expanded again in recent years. The important increases were recorded in building and construction, reflecting the growing diversion of resources to capital investments, and above all in manufacturing, now by far the largest sector. Within manufacture, the decline of textiles and clothing continued, from 5·6 per cent in 1835 to 4·8 per cent in 1955 and 3·85 per cent in 1964, but engineering and vehicles continued their striking advance, from six per cent to 13·4 per cent and 13·0 per cent in those three years, and metal manufactures from 3·4 per cent to 5·4 per cent and 5·1 per cent. While the volume of production of all industries and services grew by 47 per cent between 1950 and 1965, that of industry grew by 59 per cent, and of manufacturing industry alone, faster still.[24]

Thus the former staples of textiles and coal are receding into the background, and little further expansion can be expected from the already highly mechanised agriculture, so that Britain has become, to a

[20] *Op. cit.,* 37.
[21] Min. of Labour, *Statistics on Incomes, Prices, Employment and Production.*
[22] Compare Table on p. 253 above.
[23] Deane and Cole, Table 41 and *N.I. Blue Book,* used as described in *ibid.,* note 2 for breakdown in text.
[24] *Statistics on Incomes,* etc.

greater extent than ever before, dependent on her machines and motors for her continuous prosperity and growth. The secular expansion of commerce and communications has also been brought to a halt. The real growth points were among the more complex products requiring science and skill, though the heavy investment programme at home and abroad, in power stations, roads and buildings, also helped to expand some of the bulk goods industries. With them, the 'professional and scientific services', have expanded at an equally fast rate, and so has the employment of non-manual workers.[25]

The changing statistics reflect real changes in the economic position of the country in recent years. The 'invisible earnings' of the City of London, of shipowners and insurance companies, have been drastically cut in importance, partly because London has ceased to be the sole monetary centre of the world, partly because client countries have developed their own banks, insurance companies and shipping lines, and in part, because Great Britain is no longer the main supplier of international short-term or long-term capital. The pound sterling is still a widely used international currency, but Britain is now a major borrower as well as a lender, and the earnings from these activities are little more than marginal. Because food and raw materials from abroad are needed as much as ever, and have to be paid for by exports, Britain will have to remain a major trading country, but her role as the international shipping centre and trading depot for other countries, so important in the nineteenth century, is inevitably declining.

By contrast, more and more of her welfare has come to depend on the productive effort at home, both to meet home demands and for exports. It is on her manufacturing industry, on the transport and distributive network, on the intelligence with which her own limited natural resources and her skilled manpower are being used, that her wealth is, almost exclusively, coming to be based.

Incomes and their distribution

Real national income per head probably grew faster in this period than in any comparable period in the past, in spite of the set-backs of the two World Wars. Its rate of progress closely paralleled that of production and productivity (p. 258).

The effects of the two wars and of postwar reconstruction are evident, as also is the fact that the growth periods were concentrated into a few years in the later 1930s, and the years since 1950. These

[25] In manufacturing industries alone, their proportion has been estimated to have risen from 12·9 per cent in 1935 to 17·2 per cent in 1951 and 22·6 per cent in 1962. P. Galambos, 'On the Growth of the Employment of Non-Manual Workers in the British Manufacturing Industries, 1948-1962', *Bull. Oxford Inst. Statistics*, 26 (1964), 369.

Net national income per head
at factor cost, at constant
(1913–14) prices, index [26]

Average of years

1913–14	100
1920–24	88·4
1925–29	97·0
1930–34	98·0
1935–39	115·0
1940–44	134·8
1945–49	117·6
1950–54	126·8
1955–59	146·9
1960–64	171·2
1965	182·8

irregular movements confirm the impression of these years as an uncertain, unquiet period, in spite of the strong upward trend of production. The growth of incomes, at a compound rate of 1·19 per cent
between 1913–14 and 1964–5, was slightly slower than that of output;
for this 'loss', the increase in necessary investment and the unfavourable overseas factors, the loss of overseas investments and the adverse
terms of trade, are largely responsible. The proportion of the actual
working population and average working hours per week did not
change materially after 1920.   There was one period, however, in the
1930s, when the terms of trade turned sharply in Britain's favour and
when incomes were rising faster than productivity, allowing a marked
enjoyment of prosperity at least in the households of those in work.

The wars caused important shifts in the distribution of this income:
in both, wages and salaries gained considerably, largely at the expense
of incomes from capital and 'mixed incomes', and these gains were
held in the period that followed. Rents meanwhile continued their
long-term decline, the steep growth of incomes from city centre properties being unable to stem the relative decline of agriculture, and the
effects of rent control on incomes and 'imputed incomes' from dwellings.

The figures, presented thus baldly, are misleading. Some of this
apparent relative gain of wages and salaries is genuine, and includes
a sharp rise in insurance contributions from 0·8 per cent in 1920–29 to
4·6 per cent in 1950–9 and 5·4 per cent in 1960–5 and a further transfer
of workers from lower to higher occupations. Much of it, however, is

[26] Deane and Cole, Table 90, 330–1; *National Income Blue Books.*

Distribution of the national income, U.K. %[27]

	Wages and salaries	Rents	Profits, interest and mixed incomes
Average of years			
1905–14	47·2	10·8	42·0
1920–29	59·7	6·6	33·7
1930–39	62·0	8·7	29·2
1940–49	68·8	4·9	26·3
1950–59	72·4	4·9	22·7
1960–65	74·0	6·0	20·0

illusory, accounted for by the conversion of even the smallest businesses into joint-stock enterprises, and by other changes induced largely by the taxation laws, which moved incomes from the 'mixed' or profits category into 'salaries': the proportion of the population classified as wage and salary earners among the 'gainfully occupied' has increased in like manner from 87 per cent in 1911 to 93 per cent in 1965.[28]

Such real wage and salary gains as there were at the expense of incomes from property, have occurred in the two World Wars, which have had a levelling effect such as no peace years can parallel. It was only then that society summoned the means to raise the lowest incomes and limited some of the highest by high taxation and direct controls. Between the wars, however, the share of wages fell again from 41·9 per cent in 1924–6 to 38·9 per cent in 1937–9 (while the proportion of wage-earners in the population dropped from about 73 per cent to 71·5 per cent),[29] and only salaries kept their high levels. After the Second World War, however, it was wages which held their gains and even moved ahead by much overtime working, while salaries fell behind badly. Most of the rise in real wages over this half-century is concentrated in the last 20 years of full employment.

As far as real wage *rates* were concerned, the war years saw a substantial decline, and by July 1918 they stood at about 85 (July 1914 = 100); actual wages fared slightly better, because of full employment, and had probably fallen by about 12 per cent only.[30] By 1920 the real

[27] Deane and Cole, Table 65; 247; *N. I. Blue Books*.
[28] Deane and Cole, 245–7; *Census of Population*, 1961; *Annual Abstract of Statistics*.
[29] E. H. Phelps Brown and P. E. Hart, 'The Share of Wages in National Income', *Economic Journal*, 62 (1952), 277.
[30] Jurgen Kuczynski, *A Short History of Labour Conditions Under Industrial Capitalism, 1/1, Great Britain 1750 to the Present Day*, 3rd edn, 1947, 120, 137; A. L. Bowley, *Prices and Wages in the United Kingdom 1914–1920*, Oxford, 1921; S. J. Hurwitz, *State Intervention in Britain. A Study of Economic Control and Social Response, 1914–1919*, New York, 1949, esp. chapter 7.

wage level had exceeded the immediate prewar figure and was back at the peak of 1900. There was a drop again in the mid-twenties, and thereafter real wages began a steady rise which took them to a level estimated variously at some 6–12 per cent above the 1920 peak in the last peace years of 1935–8; actual earnings were considerably less because of the high level of unemployment.[31] Up to the outbreak of the Second World War, therefore, wages had failed to keep pace with productivity, and the rising share of earned incomes was due to the rise in 'salaries' and to the transfer from lower-paid occupations to higher ones.

The Second World War saw a very different development from the First. Wage rates, it is true, rose only with the cost of living. But real earnings, largely because of full employment and longer hours, increased steadily and substantially by some 20 per cent by the end of the war; even if higher taxes and contributions are taken into account,[32] a rise remains at a time when national income left to the personal sector was substantially cut. This does not mean that total consumption of wage-earners' families increased, since they also contributed to the savings which permitted the high degree of economic mobilisation; nevertheless, it represented the most striking shift of incomes to wage-earners in any comparable period.

After the war full employment and the increased power of trade unions ensured that the gains were held, and that workers shared the benefits of rising productivity. With 1938=100, real wages stood at 104 in 1945, 107 in 1950, 121 in 1960 and 124 in 1965; earnings, however, had moved to 122, 130, 170 and 191 in 1965.[33] The appropriate progress of real earnings of those in full employment may, therefore, be summarised as follows:

$$1900 = 100$$
$$1914 = 97$$
$$1918 = 84$$
$$1920 = 100$$
$$1938 = 110$$
$$1945 = 134$$
$$1960 = 187$$
$$1965 = 210$$

In these selected years the total wage bill was seriously affected by unemployment only in 1938.

[31] Kuczynski, *loc. cit.*, A. L. Bowley, *Wages and Incomes Since 1860*, Cambridge, 1937, 30; Mitchell and Deane, 344–5; S. Pollard, 290.
[32] Kuczynski, 135–6.
[33] Worswick and Ady, *The British Economy 1945–1950*, Oxford, 1952, 326, and *The British Economy in the Nineteen Fifties*, Oxford, 1962, 536; Min. of Labour, *Statistics on Income, Prices, Employment and Production.*

The levelling-up process went on equally clearly within the field of wages alone, and again it was the two wars which were largely responsible for this. In four important industries, the time-rates of unskilled men as a proportion of skilled ranged between 50 per cent and 66 per cent in 1913–14; by 1919, it was 74–83 per cent and, after a relapse in the peace years, the gap was narrowed still further to 76–82 per cent in 1945 and 77–84 per cent in 1950.[34] By April 1966, it was close to 85 per cent in all of a similar group of industries. By contrast, in weekly *earnings*, the gap was still rather wider: in four representative industries, among time workers, the average labourers' pay varied between 71 per cent and 87 per cent of that of the craftsmen.[35] At the same time, casual labour among such groups as dockers and carters has been gradually eliminated or safeguarded by a minimum fall-back wage; 'sweated trades' have been raised from their lowly position by legislation, unionisation and the effects of full employment; and labour shortages have also ended the irregular and low weekly earnings of such groups as unskilled building labourers.

The net effect of these changes was to reduce progressively from the 1920s, and virtually to abolish by the 1940s, that large submerged minority that had existed 'round about a pound a week' before 1914 while nominally in work. We have shown that the improvement in real wages was exceptionally slow in the 1920s, and could not have made such tangible difference to wage-earners' families until the mid-thirties. Much of the improvement, however, was concentrated on the point of its greatest effectiveness, among this low-wage group.

Unfortunately, primary poverty was not thereby abolished between the wars. If the scandal of starvation wages was about to be abolished, two other groups which had always been among 'the poor' increased very much in numbers during this period: one consisted of the old age pensioners, rising numerically because of greater longevity and the rising numbers of births 60–70 years earlier; the other consisted of the unemployed. The proportion of people of 65 and over increased from 5·3 per cent in 1911 to 8·9 per cent in 1939, 10·6 per cent in 1947 and 12·1 per cent in 1966.[36] The registered unemployed alone never fell below one million, and at times topped three million. At its worst, actual unemployment reached $3\frac{3}{4}$ million, representing some six or seven million people altogether living entirely by relief.

For both these groups (as well as for the sick, the injured, the

[34] J. G. C. J. Knowles and D. J. Robertson, 'Differences Between the Wages of Skilled and Unskilled Workers, 1880–1950', *Bull. Oxford Inst. Statistics*, 13 (1951), 111.

[35] Min. of Labour, *Statistics on Incomes*. The Industries in 1966 were general engineering, shipbuilding, chemicals and construction.

[36] *R.C. on Population, Report*, 1949, Cmd. 7695; *Annual Abstract of Statistics*.

widows and orphans), insurance and relief provisions were more generous than before 1914, but their weight on society was now much greater. Also, large families with low incomes still remained below the poverty line, however that is defined. In the only town in which a direct comparison is possible, in York, 'primary poverty' fell from 15·5 per cent of the working classes in 1899 to 6·8 per cent in 1936; but if the reasonable assumption was made that families required more than the bare minimum of food, shelter and clothing, and would spend some of their incomes on such items as newspapers, fares or tobacco, about one sixth of the working-class population was still found to live in poverty in the 1930s in several large towns in which surveys were made. Among the unemployed, the proportion was one third; and among those living on old-age pensions or other relief, the proportion may have been higher still. In each case large families fared worse, so that the proportion of children in poverty was much greater than those figures would suggest. One study showed that at least one half of the population had a deficient diet even in the most prosperous years of the 1930s.[37]

After 1945, unemployment was held in check, and its effects were less than at any time since industrialisation, but with the further increase in the number of the aged they, together with the large families of low-wage earners, have become the major sufferers from real poverty.[38] Their numbers are still much too large in a society which prides itself on its affluence, but the kind of low income at which there is bound to be a deficiency of food and of fuel and clothing is now much rarer than before the war. For those in work, and for many of those depending on the State welfare services, the evils of hunger and cold have at last been banished. B. S. Rowntree, returning to York for yet a third time, found only three per cent of the working class in primary poverty, mostly among the old.[39] The frustration of their human development, the indignity and the feeling of injustice, still remain, but it is important not to forget the immense steps forward taken in the last half-century.

It is evident that most of this improvement was the result of a rising national income per head—a larger cake to be shared out. How far it was also due to a redistribution from the rich to the poor is a much more uncertain matter. In our period, the State was the major agency

---

[37] J. Boyd Orr, *Food, Health and Income*, 1936; John Hilton, *Rich Man, Poor Man*, 1944; B. S. Rowntree, *Poverty and Progress*, 1941. For a brief *résumé* of the statistics and a list of the main surveys, see S. Pollard, 295–6.

[38] Peter Townsend, *The Family Life of Old People*, 1954, ch. 12; Dorothy Wedderburn, 'Poverty in Britain Today. The Evidence', *Sociological Review*, 10 (1962).

[39] B. S. Rowntree and G. R. Lavers, *Poverty and the Welfare State*, 1951.

of such redistribution, and many of the bitterest political battles of the last half-century have been fought over the actions of the State in this issue, and in its levying of taxes, and spending on welfare services, in particular, as the most powerful levelling instruments.

It was the wars, again, which had the most egalitarian effects, while the peace years saw relapses. Taxes on income and capital, hitting mostly the rich, increased from about a third of the revenue in 1913 to one half, and then fell to about 45 per cent in the interwar years; they jumped again to about 60 per cent in the Second World War, only to drop back to around 45 per cent in the 1950s.[40] In other ways, also, the movement was not all one way. The high, and rising, absolute level of indirect taxes, or taxes on outlay, hit poor families hard. The growing sums collected in insurance contributions since 1911, forming now, as shown above, a substantial proportion of national income, are a particularly regressive form of poll tax that hit the low incomes directly in proportion to their poverty. Many of the highest tax rates are avoided by skilful manipulation, and the payment of full estate duties on very large estates has become a rarity. At the same time, some welfare provisions like higher education are used more by the middle classes than the poorer groups, and tax provisions have permitted much of middle-class spending on housing, pensions, even education and child allowances, to come out of the public purse.[41] The total tax burden is still heavier for the lower incomes than for the higher, even in percentage terms, and only the very largest (admitted) incomes pay higher proportional rates than low-wage families.

There has, undoubtedly, been some change. While it has been calculated that in 1913–14 the working classes paid one-fifth *more* in taxes than they received in social benefits, by 1925–6 they contributed only 85 per cent of their cost and, by 1935–6, 79 per cent, gaining £45 million from the other classes in the former year, and £97 million in the latter.[42]

For 1937 and 1948–9 more sophisticated calculations exist. For the first year, it was calculated that the taxation and welfare system was responsible for a net transfer of £386 million from the rich to the poor, or 8·8 per cent of the national income; for the latter, though incomes were more evenly spread, the transfer was around £1,260 million, or 13·1 per cent of the national income. In detailed groups, the poor received more, and the rich lost more, in the second year

[40] U. K. Hicks, *British Public Finances. Their Structure and Development 1880–1952*, 1954, 75.
[41] R. M. Titmuss, *Income Distribution and Social Change*, 1962, and 'The Social Division of Welfare', in *Essays on 'The Welfare State'*, 2nd edn, 1964, 45 *seq.*
[42] Colin Clark, *National Income and Outlay*, 1937, 145–8.

than the first.[43] This, however, was immediately after the extreme economic democracy of the war years. In the years since, these effects have been progressively reduced. The relationship of indirect to direct taxes has not been greatly changed, though capital taxes have declined because of the greater evasion of death duties: the capital gains tax of 1965 may in future redress the balance. Direct taxes bore more heavily on the poorer consumers, and the reduction in food subsidies hit them most. Perhaps the most drastic change in favour of the rich, apart from the gradual lowering of the standard rate of income tax, was the surtax concession of 1961.[44] In total, most of the war and postwar gains have been lost, and the taxation-plus-expenditure system of the mid-1960s is probably no more egalitarian than that of 1937, in spite of the great social, legislative and political effort that has gone into the creation of the Welfare State. Most of the redistribution has been *within* the classes, from those in work to those temporarily or permanently out of employment.

The combined effects of these complex factors, including the variable shares of different types of incomes arising in the 'free market', the changing numbers of people receiving them, and the doubtful direct and indirect influence of public authorities, are extremely hard to evaluate. The main sources of direct evidence, the tax returns, are also doubtful and hard to interpret, and, while few would deny that incomes are more fairly distributed in the 1960s than before 1914, it is by no means certain that any relative gains have been made by the poorer sections of the people since the 1920s or 1930s. Indeed, one detailed study appeared to show that there was 'little increase in the amount of vertical distribution between 1937 and 1959', and since then the movement has certainly been the other way.[45] If full employment, the action of powerful trade unions, and the political struggles of this century have been unable to effect the share-out of incomes since 1920, the main reason lies in the power of one factor working the other way, the uneven distribution of property.

There are calculations which purport to show that the inequality of property (or capital) holdings has also been lessened. Thus the hold-

---

[43] A. M. Carter, *The Redistribution of Income in Post-War Britain*, New Haven, 1955, esp. 66–7; T. Barna, *The Redistribution of Incomes Through Public Finance in 1937*, Oxford, 1945, 229–30; Dudley Seers, *The Levelling of Incomes since 1938*, Oxford, 1951; H. F. Lydall, *British Incomes and Savings*, Oxford, 1955.

[44] I. M. D. Little, 'Fiscal Policy', in Worswick and Ady (ed.), *The British Economy in the Nineteen-Fifties*, 285–91.

[45] Titmuss, *op. cit.*, J. S. Nicholson, 'Redistribution of Income in the U.K. in 1959, 1957 and 1953', reprinted from *Income and Wealth Series*, X (1964), 61. A positive view will be found in H. F. Lydall, 'The Long-Term Trend in the Size Distribution of Income', *J. Royal Statistical Soc.*, 122 (1959), 1–37.

ings of the top one per cent of owners have been stated to have dropped as follows[46]:

1911–13	65–70% of total personal wealth
1924–30	60
1936–38	55
1946–48	50
1951–56	42
1960	42

The inequality is still strikingly great, much greater, for example, than in the U.S.A.,[47] and, since rich people receive higher rates on their capital than poorer people, the income derived from this wealth was even more unequal; but at least it appears to be declining. Yet, even on this showing, there was no progress in the 1950s, and it should be noted that, according to the same calculations, the share of the top five per cent has fallen much more slowly, from 87 per cent in 1911–13 to 79 per cent in 1936–8 and to 75 per cent in 1960. However, the main criticism against these estimates is that, with a greater or lesser degree of sophistication, they depend on the returns of estate duties, and therefore neglect the growing efficiency with which large estates avoid these payments.[48] Further, they ignore the increasingly valuable pension rights on the one hand, and personal liabilities, to building or mortgage societies for example, on the other, and they neglect the weight and indirect influence of corporate holdings of property.[49] Taking all of these factors into account, it may well be that the years since the Second World War have seen a change in the other direction, a growing inequality of property.[50]

Although the poorer classes in the 1960s possess much more personal property and small savings than their counterparts 50 years earlier, the distribution of capital is still as highly concentrated in the hands of a tiny proportion of the population as ever. It is the buoyancy of this capital, its ability to emerge from every attack and every crisis

[46] Kathleen M. Langley, 'The Distribution of Capital in Private Hands in 1936–8 and 1946–7', *Bull. Oxford Inst. of Statistics*, 13 (1951); H. F. Lydall and D. G. Tipping, 'The Distribution of Personal Wealth in Britain', *ibid.*, 23 (1961), 92; J. E. Meade, *Efficiency, Equality and the Ownership of Property*, 1964, 27.
[47] Harold Lydall and John B. Lansing, 'A Comparison of the Distribution of Personal Income and Wealth in the United States and Great Britain', *Amer. Econ. Rev.*, 49 (1959).
[48] The crude estate duty returns, indeed, show a further substantial fall for the top one per cent of estates, from 20·7 per cent (top 1·03 per cent) in 1950–1 to 12 per cent (top 0·94 per cent) in 1964–5, taking estates over £2,000 in the first year, and over £4,000 in the second—Commissioners of Inland Revenue, *Annual Reports*.
[49] John Saville, 'Labour and Income Redistribution', *The Socialist Register, 1965* (ed. R. Miliband and J. Saville), 1965, 147–62.
[50] See e.g. E. Victor Morgan, *The Structure of Property Ownership in Great Britain*, Oxford, 1960.

with as high an income-generating power as before, which has been largely responsible for keeping up the inequality of incomes, in spite of all the attempts made by Government and others to modify it.

Changes in pattern of consumption

The rising incomes and wealth per head accruing in the past half-century have, for the first time, been superimposed on a society in which the majority was well above the subsistence level, and the minority still on that level was becoming very small indeed. The way in which the extra was spent was, therefore, no longer dictated by necessity, and the bulk of the population has been able to do what in the past has been a privilege of the small upper classes only; they have been able to exercise some choice. As a result, significant new patterns of expenditure have emerged.

One of the most striking changes took place in the provision of housing, in which, as we have had occasion to note before, improvement for individual families tends to occur in big jumps rather than by slow stages. This was accentuated by the World Wars, in both of which new building virtually ceased, and by changing legislation and movements of interest rates. The net result of these developments was that large numbers of subsidised (council) houses for the working classes were built in the 1920s, houses for private-owner-occupancy in the 1930s and council houses again after 1945, with a rapidly growing proportion of private houses from the mid-fifties on.

In quantity of units completed, the private housing boom of the 1930s was unprecedented. Whereas, even in the great boom of the turn of the century, the building rate did not exceed 160,000 dwellings a year, in 1935–8 it topped 350,000. After the war, the annual rate of building averaged around 200,000 in 1946–51, and then quickly rose to 350,000 in 1954; since then it has generally kept well above the 300,000 mark, largely by the high rate of private building.[51]

This new housing was both a symbol and a determinant of the way in which much of the new income was spent. Nearly all of it, except for some deliberate and isolated city centre developments by local authorities since 1945, was well away from earlier urban concentrations, either along the main roads into the country, in 'ribbon development', or in suburban estates up to 1939, and in new suburbs or entirely 'New Towns' after 1945. The owner-occupied houses were largely for the fast growing numbers of lower-middle-class, 'white-collar' workers, for whom the move to the new suburbs set the seal

[51] B. Weber, 'A New Index of Residential Construction, 1838–1950', 132; Worswick and Ady, *British Economy in the Nineteen-Fifties*, 25–7; *Annual Abstract of Statistics.*

on their rise from their working-class origins. Others left large town houses which were then turned into offices or sank into the twilight zone of flats and lodgings. The workers in council estates generally came from slum terraces which were either pulled down, or, if they were still inhabitable, became the refuge for people vacating still worse slums. Much of the local authority housing programme in the 1930s was for slum clearance, and by 1939 only a small proportion of 'slums' were said to have remained, and might have been cleared in a few more years but for the war; the overall housing shortage, acute since 1918, had allegedly almost been met.[52] At the end of the Second World War a fresh housing shortage had been incubated, which even by 1966 had not been entirely overcome, but both after 1918 and after 1945 the 'shortage' was largely a reflection of the sharply rising levels of expectation. Similarly, the standards applied to condemned housing or to 'slums' rose significantly over this period, so that many even of the houses built around 1900, and certainly those built in the 1860s, might be considered marginal today because of lack of room or of facilities. Great strides have been made in these respects in recent years, and there are now virtually no households without indoor water taps, and hardly any without water closets (6·9 per cent in England and Wales, and 2·6 per cent in Scotland, in 1961), but about one fifth still had no hot-water tap, and nearly one quarter no fixed baths in 1961.[53]

In the middle-class estates, and more so in those for the working-classes, the new plan of building meant a certain social loss, a loss of contact with neighbours and a splitting-up of families, with the consequent need to rely more on the inner resources of the small household. There were gains, in health and sanitation, in having a garden, and in pride of the home, and it was this which determined much of the direction of the new expenditure.

Apart from those who had to rent uncontrolled accommodation, the proportion of incomes spent on rent was low, and was falling during this period, because of low interest rates (after 1931), reasonable building-society terms helped by large tax concessions, rent restrictions and subsidised council houses. But better housing also demanded expenditure on furniture, furnishings, kitchen equipment, electrical gadgets, china and glassware. It was these 'consumer durables' which formed an ever-larger share of personal expenditure, and it was these, in turn, together with the supply of gas and electricity, in which growing demand and methods of mass production permitted the most striking reductions in real unit costs and the most tangible proofs of rising

[52] S. Pollard, 254–61; Ministry of Health, *Report on the Overcrowding Survey in England and Wales*, 1936; R. Stone *et al.*, *Consumer Expenditure and Behaviour in the United Kingdom, 1920–1938*, Cambridge, 1954, I, 196–200.
[53] *Census of 1961*, England and Wales, and Scotland.

standards of comfort. This development was noticeable even between the wars; it has become particularly significant since 1945. By 1963, 76 per cent of households possessed a radio, 82 per cent a T.V. set, 78 per cent an electric vacuum cleaner, 45 per cent a washing machine, 30 per cent a refrigerator, and 46 per cent a sewing machine.[54]

In the actual share-out of expenditure, however, the change was less than might be expected, since the consumer durables of which more were bought were falling in unit price, while this was less true for perishables, which also happened to bear the brunt of important outlay tax increases. Thus the share of tobacco alone rose from under two per cent of *total* flow of goods and services to consumers before 1914 to over eight per cent in the 1940s, largely because of taxation, and there were similar rises in the taxation of alcoholic drinks and liquid fuels. The share of services fell only slightly: the losses of domestic service being made good by growing services in shops, laundries, transport, etc.[55]

Percentage distribution of the total flow of goods and services to consumers, current prices, U.K.

| *Averages* | | *Commodities*[56] | | *Services* | |
	Perishable	*Semi-durable*	*Durable*	*Rents*	*Other*
1900–09	53·0	9·5	4·9	11·5	21·1
1920–29	52·5	12·2	7·2	8·7	19·5
1930–39	49·0	10·8	8·0	10·9	21·3
1940–49	56·3	9·8	5·2	8·9	19·8
1950–52	55·8	11·3	7·6	7·1	18·2

The table shows the changes between 1900 and 1952. In the years since the war, between 1945 and 1965, while the quantity of food consumed rose by only 57·4 per cent and of clothing by 97·9 per cent, furniture, household goods, radio, electrical goods, etc., rose by 177·6 per cent, electricity by 412·9 per cent and motor cars by no less than 1,287·9 per cent. Yet, again, the changes in the shares of total expenditure were scarcely significant. Thus food fell only from 28·5 per cent

[54] Reader's Digest, *Products and People*, 1963, Table 1.
[55] J. B. Jefferys and Dorothy Walters, 'National Income and Expenditure of the United Kingdom, 1870–1952', *Income and Wealth*, series V, 20–21, Tables IX and X. See also A. R. Prest and A. A. Adams, *Consumer Expenditure in the United Kingdom, 1900–1919*, Cambridge, 1954, and R. Stone, *et. al.*, *The Measurement of Consumer Expenditure and Behaviour in the United Kingdom, 1920–1938*, vol. I, Cambridge, 1954.
[56] 'Perishable'—lasting not more than six months, e.g. food, drink, paper, fuel. 'Semi-durable'—six months to three years, e.g. clothes, fancy goods, toys. 'Durable'—over three years, e.g. furniture, furnishings, jewellery, books, motor vehicles.

to 26·1 per cent of the total between those years, housing and maintenance rose from 10 per cent to 10·5 per cent; clothing fell from 9·4 per cent to 9·2 per cent, durable household goods rose from 4·7 per cent to 6·7 per cent, and only motor vehicles and fuel rose significantly from 1·7 per cent to 7·6 per cent, but this item was affected by the serious restrictions and rationing in the earlier year.[57]

The apparently constant share of different commodities and services should not be allowed to hide the boon to consumers of having made available to them the output of the mass-production industries, the furniture, electrical goods, watches and clocks, chemists' goods, table ware and textiles, and the new and often better materials of which they were made. Occasionally, there was a loss in quality: but on the whole, the immensely greater variety of goods, the technical inventions they incorporated, and the versatility of new materials, e.g., of plastics and man-made fibres, represented pure consumers' gain. Much of it was based on the enormous increase of the supply and coverage of the public utilities, particularly electricity, gas, water and street lighting. The boon of gas lighting was Victorian, and by 1885 there were over two million consumers, rising to $7\frac{1}{2}$ million by 1920. Since then the growth has been slow, to 11 million in 1937 and just under 13 million in 1965, of whom over 12 million were domestic, but it marked the general conversion to gas cooking. Electricity in the home, however, was an interwar phenomenon. There were only one million consumers in 1920, but 10 million in 1939. By 1965 this had risen to 17 million, of whom 15 million were domestic, including virtually all the households within reach of mains in the country. The sales of electricity rose from 3·7 milliard units in 1920 to 34·0 milliard in 1946 and 138·9 milliard in 1964–5, and of gas from 1,189 million therms in 1921 to 2,240 million in 1946 and 3,220 million in 1964–5.[58]

Apart from changes in prices, however, there was a second factor at work to limit the growth of expenditure on 'luxuries' as against 'necessities'. It was found that beyond a certain low level, consumers do not merely seek new goods as their incomes go up, but also better quality in their original shopping lists. Thus after a satisfactory level of nutrition is reached, more is spent on 'better', more varied or more exotic food, and ultimately, also on food bought in a higher stage of preparation, or consumed outside the home. Put differently, food itself is turned from a necessity into a 'luxury'. Conversely, the consumption of 'inferior' foods declines, even as the total food bill

[57] Expenditure at constant (1958) prices. Based on *National Income Blue Books*.
[58] *Annual Reports* of British Electricity Authority, Central Electricity Generating Board, General Electricity Council, and Gas Council. Also *P.E.P. Report on the Gas Industry in Great Britain*, 1939, 47.

goes up—interrupted only by the temporarily enforced austerity of the war years.

Consumption per head in lbs, U.K.[59]

	1909–13	1934–8	1944	1962
Liquid milk	219	217	308	325
Meat (incl. bacon, ham, poultry, game)	136	138	114	157
Eggs	16	28	27	34
Butter	16	25	8	20
Lard, etc.	4	19	19	24
Sugar	79	96	71	111
Vegetables, fruit and nuts	146	231	192	235
'Inferior goods':				
Margarine	6	9	18	11
Potatoes	243	190	275	214
Wheat flour	211	195	234	161
Other cereals	26	16	19	16
Fish	41	26	20	21

The case of margarine is particularly enlightening. At a time of widespread poverty, before 1914, its growing consumption represented a rise in welfare over the alternative of dry bread, but at the next stage rising incomes led to a decline in favour of butter—which itself begins to decline as bread and butter is replaced by meat dishes. Exactly the same development occurred rather earlier in the case of wheaten bread: an improvement on oats or barley in the eighteenth century, it gives way to meat in the twentieth. The consumption of fish is even more interesting. At first it may have grown as an improvement on a poor diet; greater prosperity led to its replacement by meat and eggs; but it may well be that the refinement of a higher stage may bring it back into favour, though perhaps in different kinds of fish, and differently prepared.

The end of this development is not yet, for current family expenditure surveys[60] show that wealthier families will spend much more on food than poorer families, and they spend it on better food, combined with better services. At the same time it is clear that the vast differences between Victorian middle-class gluttony and working-class starvation or even the differences of the 1930s,[61] have now shrunk to a

[59] J. C. McKenzie, 'Past Dietary Trends as an Aid to Prediction', in T. C. Barker, et. al., Our Changing Fare, 1966, 136.
[60] Ministry of Labour, Family Expenditure Survey for 1963.
[61] John Burnett, Plenty and Want, 1966, esp. part II, and 245–55.

very much narrower gap between the food of the rich and that of the poor. Something similar occurred also in every other kind of expenditure.

The change has been significant only since 1939, first because of rationing, and later also because of full employment. Even in the middle and late 1930s, the poverty of a large minority, noted above, brought it about that a substantial proportion of the population, estimated at between one third and one half, was inadequately fed for physical efficiency; in districts particularly affected by unemployment, such as the Rhondda Valley, a high rate of maternal mortality could be directly linked with undernourishment. Whereas in the First World War, 41 per cent of volunteers were rejected as medically unfit, in 1935 (out of a rather different sample) no fewer than 62 per cent were below the physique required by the army.[62]

In the years of the Second World War and the years since, the last strongholds of this primary poverty were attacked with great vigour. Special allowances to children, to pregnant and nursing mothers, and later, family allowances, dealt with some of the worst effects of maldistribution. Rising incomes and more regular employment have maintained the momentum. Pockets of distress remain, among the aged, and among large families or young, homeless families, but it is not impossible that the next decade will see their elimination also.

The total effect of all these changes on the chances of survival has been striking. General death-rates on a standardised population in England and Wales fell from 204 in 1911–13 to 91 in 1960–2 (1950–2= 100), and actual infantile mortality per 1,000 live births fell from 111 to 22 in the same years.[63] That further progress is possible is shown by the fact that the rates for the rich are still below those of the poor, and the country districts well below those of the industrial areas.

Conclusion

The history of changes in consumption becomes infinitely more complex as we leave a society in which large sections live near the subsistence level, and enter a stage when freedom to spend is widespread. In Britain, as in other advanced countries, this stage, which was reached only little more than half a century ago, was accompanied inevitably by a levelling-up, a narrowing of the gap between the poorest and the richest in the community, though this evening-out process has gone less far even today than is commonly assumed.

It is only at that point that the fruits of civilisation, the work of artists and doctors, of scientists and engineers, hitherto limited to a

[62] *Ibid.*, 239–43.
[63] *Registrar General Reports.*

narrow privileged class, become fully available to the population at large. It is at that point that workers demand more leisure as well as more money, and education to enjoy it, and that this demand is echoed by their womenfolk too.

We, as a nation, have only begun to deal with the problems set by rising affluence.[64] A society with high incomes must be one with a high output, and this can only be achieved by a growing complexity and interdependence of economic life. Such a society is more vulnerable to disturbances, as well as offering greater opportunities for human growth. Already, in this century, our society has been subject to more violent shocks than could have been dreamed of by earlier generations, and it is by no means certain that it will develop sufficient wisdom to avoid even worse ones in the future. Man's social skills may not develop as fast as his mastery over his physical environment.

In this long survey over eight centuries, the upward trend of progress has not always been very clear. In the earlier periods, the rise in wealth and incomes, achieved by technical gains, by greater political security, by social systems better adapted to growth, and by the opening-up of new parts of the world to European influence, was so slow that it could be reversed often for long periods, by the major scourges of disease, war, civil commotion and natural disaster. Economic growth becomes persistent enough to overtake any possible hostile influences and show its effects on popular living standards only in the last hundred years; it had a major effect only in the last 50 years, and accelerated sharply only in the last 20. We cannot even be sure now that this progress will be permitted to continue.

The gains, within the limited range of economic goods and services, have been immense. It is true that, even in this sphere, there have been some losses, like the spoliation of the countryside, the overcrowding of roads and beaches, the poisoning by chemicals and tobacco, the insecurity and competitiveness of man's personal environment. Nevertheless, the full measure of the achievement of the conquest of disease. starvation, cold, damp, flood and drought can, perhaps, be taken only by those who have experienced them and been rescued from them. Men soon forget the evils of the past, they are often more concerned with the gaps remaining than with those overcome, and this is part of their humanity. Besides, there are other things in life beyond those treated in this study. Whether the gains recorded here have made men really happier, we have no means of knowing.

[64] See, e.g. George Katona, *The Mass Consumption Society*, New York, 1964.

Appendix

In this book we have been wary of the inclination to erect some comprehensive yardstick with which to judge individual wealth over the centuries. The problems of preparing a meaningful index for so lengthy a period are numerous, not the least being the great changes in the sources of income at all points in the social scale.

This is not, however, to question the value of the published index of real wages of building workers over seven centuries for establishing changes in the standards of living of wage-earners (see figure on p. 275). But it does become increasingly clear how wise its compilers were to stress the pitfalls of such an approach.[1] For our purposes here it is perhaps fair to suggest that a real-wage index for such a group of crafts is of more value for short rather than long-term comparisons. At this level of society an outstanding long-term change has been the increasing part played by money-wages in a craftsman's income. In the medieval period these might be comparatively unimportant, but in the last 200 years they have come to be the exclusive source. In the shorter term, perhaps in comparisons between adjacent centuries, this kind of index can be most effective; we see clearly, for instance, the contrast between the fifteenth century, with workmen in comparatively short supply, and the later sixteenth century, their position in the labour market reversed. Or in the still shorter term we may contrast the tight real-wage levels of the Napoleonic War decades with those before and after. But even in the short run there are problems. Was one particular group of workers typical in its reliance on wages? Can seventeenth-century builders, continuously employed until a job was completed, be compared with men such as miners, voluntarily underemployed with time to tend stock and land, or textile workers, their assessed wage-rates offset by trade recessions?

The choice of a sample of products to whose prices money-wages may be related also presents problems; changes in consumption patterns governed by the changing availability of the foodstuffs on which this particular index is based can largely be taken care of, by varying the composition of the sample from century to century, but the authors warn us of other, less tractable problems; an example is the difficulty

---

[1] E. H. Phelps Brown and S. V. Hopkins, 'Seven Centuries of the Prices of Consumables, Compared with Builders' Wage-Rates', *Economica*, N.S. 23 (1956), 303–5.

in the early modern period involved in using a basket of largely un-processed goods at a time when the prices of manufactured articles and foods were rising less rapidly.[2] This must, at the risk of stating the obvious, lead us to a further warning over the use of the chosen group of goods as an indication of actual consumption patterns. Apart from periods when manufactured goods might be more attractive, there have clearly been times when although real incomes in terms of certain goods have been high, saving and voluntary limitation of consumption have been widely adopted. The late fourteenth-century labourer or peasant, anxious to take on newly available cheap rents, or the six-teenth-century husbandman or yeoman, amassing the entry-fine for a lease, are clear examples. But it is probably safe to say that the groups of goods chosen, as near-necessities, and modified over the centuries, come as close to consistency of esteem as is possible without endless complication.

[2] E. H. Phelps Brown and S. V. Hopkins, 'Wage-Rates and Prices: Evidence for Population Pressure in the Sixteenth Century', *Economica*, N.S. 24 (1957), 293.

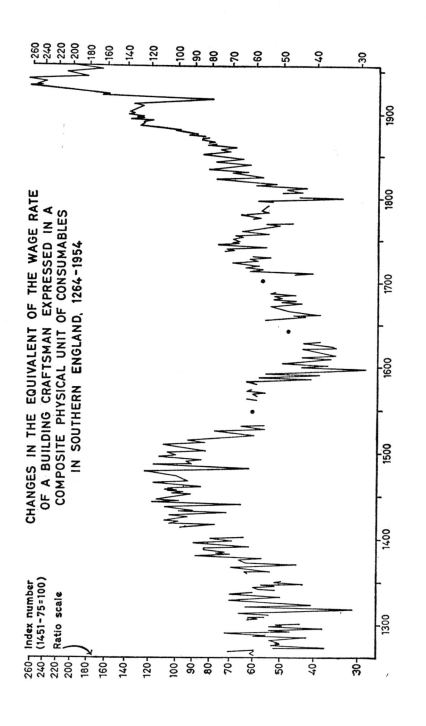

CHANGES IN THE EQUIVALENT OF THE WAGE RATE
OF A BUILDING CRAFTSMAN EXPRESSED IN A
COMPOSITE PHYSICAL UNIT OF CONSUMABLES
IN SOUTHERN ENGLAND, 1264-1954

Index number
(1451-75=100)

Ratio scale

Select Bibliography

The Bibliography is divided into the following sections:

I GENERAL ECONOMIC HISTORY

II INCOME AND WEALTH
- a General
- b Investment and Capital
- c Income and Wealth in Agriculture: General
- d Income and Wealth in Agriculture: The Landed Classes
- e Income and Wealth in Commerce
- f Income and Wealth in Industry, Mining, etc.
- g Class-distribution of Incomes
- h Wages, Working-Class Living Standards
- j Fluctuations
- k War and Wealth

III CONSUMPTION
- a General
- b Food Consumption
- c Manufactured Articles Consumption
- d Housing, Sanitation, Social Services
- e Poverty

Note Where a periodical is followed by two figures separated by an oblique stroke, the first figure represents the *series*, the second, the number of the *volume*. In other cases, the figure always represents the volume number.

I General Economic History

T. S. Ashton	*An Economic History of England: The Eighteenth Century* (1955)
W. Ashworth	*An Economic History of England, 1870–1939* (1960)
S. G. Checkland	*The Rise of Industrial Society in England, 1815–1885* (1964)
Clapham, Sir John	*A Concise Economic History of Britain, From the Earliest Times to 1750* (Cambridge, 1949)
W. H. B. Court	*A Concise Economic History of Britain, From 1750 to Recent Times* (Cambridge, 1954)
J. Hales	*A Discourse of the Common Weal of this Realm of England* (1549) (ed.) E. Lamond, 1893
R. H. Hilton	*A Medieval Society* (1966)
H. R. Loyn	*Anglo-Saxon England and the Norman Conquest* (1962)
P. Mantoux	*The Industrial Revolution in the Eighteenth Century* (1928, also paperback)
E. Miller	'The English Economy in the Thirteenth Century', *Past and Present* 28 (1964)
M. M. Postan	'The Fifteenth Century', *Econ. Hist. R.* 9 (1938)
S. Pollard	*The Development of the British Economy, 1914–1950* (1962)
P. Ramsay	*Tudor Economic Problems* (1965)
E. M. Carus-Wilson (ed.)	*Essays in Economic History* (3 vols, 1954–1962)
C. Wilson	*England's Apprenticeship, 1603–1763* (1965)

II Income and Wealth (a) General

D. Baxter	*National Income of the United Kingdom* (1868)
H. Beeke	*Observations on the Produce of the Income Tax and its Proportion to the Whole Income of Great Britain* (1800)
M. W. Beresford and J. K. St. Joseph	*Medieval England* (Cambridge, 1958)
A. L. Bowley	*Wages and Incomes since 1860* (Cambridge, 1937)

Y. S. Brenner	'The Inflation of Prices in Early Sixteenth-Century England', *Econ. Hist. R.* 2/14 (1961); '. . . 1551–60', *ibid.* 2/15 (1962)
E. J. Buckatzsch	'The Geographical Distribution of Wealth in England, 1086–1843', *Econ. Hist. R.* 2/3 (1951)
H. Campion	*Public and Private Property in Great Britain* (1939)
Central Statistical Office	*National Income and Expenditure* (Annual)
G. Chalmers	*An Estimate of the Comparative Strength of Great Britain* (1794)
C. Clark	*The National Income, 1924–1931* (1932)
C. Clark	*National Income and Outlay* (1937)
P. Colquhoun	*Treatise on the Wealth, Power and Resources of the British Empire* (1812)
H. C. Darby (ed.)	*The Domesday Geography of Eastern England* (Cambridge, 1952)
H. C. Darby and I. S. Terrett (ed.)	*The Domesday Geography of Midland England* (Cambridge, 1954)
H. C. Darby and E. M. Campbell (ed.)	*The Domesday Geography of South-East England* (Cambridge, 1962)
H. C. Darby and I. S. Maxwell (ed.)	*The Domesday Geography of Northern England* (Cambridge, 1962)
H. C. Darby and R. W. Finn (ed.)	*The Domesday Geography of South-West England* (Cambridge, 1967)
P. Deane and W. A. Cole	*British Economic Growth, 1688–1959* (2nd edn., Cambridge, 1967)
P. Deane	'The Implications of Early National Income Estimates', *Economic Development and Cultural Change* 4 (1955)
P. Deane	'The Industrial Revolution and Economic Growth', *ibid.* 6 (1957)
P. Deane	'Contemporary Estimates of National Income in the First Half of the 19th Century', *Econ. Hist. R.* 2/8 (1956)
P. Deane	'Contemporary Estimates of National Income in the Second Half of the 19th Century', *ibid.* 2/9 (1957)
C. H. Feinstein	'Income and Investment in the United Kingdom, 1856–1914', *Econ. J.* 71 (1961)
H. E. Hallam	*Settlement and Society* (Cambridge, 1965)

W. G. Hoskins (ed.)	*Essays in Leicestershire History* (Liverpool, 1950)
W. G. Hoskins	*Provincial England* (1963)
W. G. Hoskins	'The Wealth of Medieval Devon' in *Devonshire Studies*, ed. Hoskins and Finberg, 1952
W. G. Hoskins	'Harvest Fluctuations and English Economic History, 1480–1619', *Agric. Hist. R.* 12 (1964)
J. B. Jefferys and D. Walters	'National Income and Expenditure of the United Kingdom', *Income and Wealth Series* V (1955)
A. H. John	'Aspects of English Economic Growth in the First Half of the Eighteenth Century', *Economica* 28 (1961)
G. King	*Two Tracts by Gregory King* (ed. Geo. E. Barnett, Baltimore, 1936)
James, Earl Lauderdale	*An Inquiry into the Nature and Origins of Public Wealth* (1804)
R. Lennard	*Rural England, 1066–1135* (Oxford, 1959)
E. Kerridge	'The Movement of Rent, 1540–1640', *Econ. Hist. R.* 2/6 (1953–4)
P. Mathias	'The Social Structure of the Eighteenth Century', *Econ. Hist. R.* 2/10 (1957)
J. R. McCulloch	*A Statistical Account of the British Empire* (1837)
B. R. Mitchell and P. Deane	*Abstract of British Historical Statistics* (Cambridge, 1962)
M. G. Mulhall	*Fifty Years of National Progress, 1837–1887* (1887)
P. K. O'Brien	'British Income and Property in the Early Nineteenth Century', *Econ. Hist. R.* 2/12 (1959)
P. Pebrer	*Taxation, Expenditure, Power, Statistics and Debt of the Whole British Empire* (1833)
A. R. Prest	'National Income of the United Kingdom, 1870–1946', *Econ. J.* 58 (1948)
P. Rousseaux	*Les Mouvements de Fond de l'Economie Anglaise 1800–1913* (Louvain, 1938)
P. H. Sawyer	'The Wealth of England in the Eleventh Century', *Trans. Roy. Hist. Soc.* 5th ser., XV (1965)
J. C. Stamp	*British Incomes and Property* (1916)

L. Stone	'State Control in Sixteenth-Century England', *Econ. Hist. R.* 17 (1947)
J. E. Williams	'The British Standard of Living', *Econ. Hist. R.* 2/19 (1966)
T. Wilson	*The State of England* (ed. F. J. Fisher), Camden Misc. 16 (1936)
A. Young	*Political Arithmetic* (2 vols, 1774–9)

II (b)   Investment, Capital

M. Blaug	'The Productivity of Capital in the Lancashire Cotton Industry During the Nineteenth Century', *Econ. Hist. R.* 2/13 (1961)
A. K. Cairncross	*Home and Foreign Investment, 1870–1913* (Cambridge, 1953)
A. K. Cairncross and B. Weber	'Fluctuations in Building in Great Britain, 1785–1849', *Econ. Hist. R.* 2/9 (1956)
A. Carter	'Dutch Investment 1738–1800', *Economica* 20 (1953)
D. C. Coleman	*Sir John Banks, Baronet and Businessman* (Oxford, 1963)
E. W. Cooney	'Capital Exports and Investment in Building in Britain and the U.S.A., 1856–1914', *Economica* 17 (1950)
E. W. Cooney	'Long Waves in Building in the British Economy of the Nineteenth Century', *Econ. Hist. R.* 2/13 (1960)
G. W. Daniels and H. Campion	*The Distribution of the National Capital* (Manchester, 1936)
K. G. Davies	'Joint-Stock Investment in the Late Seventeenth Century', *Econ. Hist. R.* 2/4 (1952)
P. Deane	'Capital Formation in Britain before the Railway Age', *Economic Development and Cultural Change* (1961)
P. G. M. Dickson	*The Financial Revolution in England* (1967)
P. H. Douglas	'An Estimate of the Growth of Capital in the United Kingdom, 1865–1909, *J. Economic and Business History* 2 (1930)
C. H. Feinstein	*Domestic Capital Formation in the United Kingdom, 1920–1938* (Cambridge, 1965)
H. Feis	*Europe, the World's Banker, 1870–1914* (New Haven, 1930)
R. Giffen	*The Growth of Capital* (1889)

H. J. Habakkuk	'The Long-Term Rate of Interest and the Price of Land', *Econ. Hist. R.* 2/2 (1952)
R. H. Hilton	'Rent and Capital Formation in Feudal Society', *Internat. Ec. Hist. Conf.* 1962 (1965)
C. K. Hobson	*The Export of Capital* (1914)
J. K. Horsefield	*British Monetary Experiments, 1650–1710* (1960)
L. H. Jenks	*The Migration of British Capital to 1875* (N.Y., 1927)
A. G. Kenwood	'Railway Investment in Britain', *Economica* 32 (1965)
K. Langley	'An Analysis of the Asset Structure of Estates, 1900–1949', *Bull. Oxford Univ. Institute of Statistics* 13 (1951)
K. Langley	'The Distribution of Capital in Private Hands in 1936–8 and 1946–7', *Bull. Oxford University Institute of Statistics* 13 (1951)
J. H. Lenfant	'Great Britain's Capital Formation, 1865–1914', *Economica* 18 (1951)
K. Maiwald	'Fire Insurance and the Capital Co-efficient in Great Britain, 1866–1952', *Econ. Hist. R.* 2/7 (1954)
K. Maiwald	'An Index of Building Costs in the United Kingdom', *Econ. Hist. R.* 2/9 (1956)
V. Morgan	*The Structure of Property Ownership in Great Britain* (Oxford, 1960)
G. Paish	'Great Britain's Capital Investments in Individual Colonial and Foreign Countries', *J. R. Statistical Society* 34 (1911)
H. Pollins	'A Note on Railway Constructional Costs', *Economica* 19 (1952)
M. M. Postan	'Credit in Medieval Trade', *Econ. Hist. R.* 1 (1928)
T. K. Rabb	'Investment in English Overseas Enterprise 1575–1630', *Econ. Hist. R.* 2/19 (1966)
P. Redfern	'Net Investment in Fixed Assets in the U.K., 1938–1953', *J. R. Statistical Society* 118 (1955)
R. D. Richards	'The Pioneers of Banking in England', *Ec. Hist.* 1 (1929)
R. de Roover	*Gresham on Foreign Exchange* (Cambridge Mass., 1949)
H. A. Shannon	'Bricks—A Trade Index, 1785–1849', *Economica* 1 (1934)

| R. H. Tawney (ed.) | *Thomas Wilson's Discourse on Usury* (*1572*) (1925) |
| B. Weber | 'A New Index of Residential Construction, 1838–1950', *Scottish J. Political Economy* 2 (1955) |

II (c) Income and Wealth in Agriculture—General

K. J. Allison	'Flock Management in the Sixteenth and Seventeenth Centuries', *Econ. Hist. R.* 2/11 (1959)
A. R. H. Baker	'Evidence in the Nonarum Inquisitions of Contrasting Arable Land in England in the Early Fourteenth Century', *Econ. Hist. R.* 2/19 (1966)
D. C. Barnett	'Allotments and the Problem of Rural Poverty, 1780–1840', in Jones and Mingay (ed.), *Land, Labour and Population in the Industrial Revolution* (1967)
M. K. Bennet	'Britain's Wheat Yield for Seven Centuries', *Economic History* 3 (1934)
H. S. Bennett	*Life on the English Manor* (Cambridge, 1937)
J. R. Bellerby	*Agriculture and Industry: Relative Income* (1956)
J. R. Bellerby	'Distribution of Farm Income in the United Kingdom, 1867–1938', *J. Agricultural Economics Society* (1953)
J. R. Bellerby	'Gross and Net Farm Rent in the United Kingdom, 1867–1938', *ibid.* (1954)
M. W. Beresford	*The Lost Villages of England* (1954)
Cambridge Economic History of Europe, I: The Agrarian Life of the Middle Ages (1966)	
B. E. Cracknell	*Canvey Island: The History of a Marshland Community* (Leicester, 1959)
H. C. Darby	*The Medieval Fenland* (Cambridge, 1940)
L. Drescher	'The Development of Agricultural Production in Great Britain and Ireland from the Early Nineteenth Century', *Manchester School* 23 (1955)
H. P. R. Finberg	*Tavistock Abbey* (Cambridge, 1951)
M. W. Flinn	'Agricultural Productivity and Economic Growth in England, 1700–1760: A Comment', *J. Econ. Hist.* 26 (1966)

G. E. Fussell and C. Goodman	'Eighteenth-Century Estimates of British Sheep and Wool Production', *Agricultural History* (1930)
G. E. Fussell	'Population and Wheat Production in the Eighteenth Century', *History Teacher's Miscellany* (1939)
G. E. Fussell	*The Old English Farming Books from Fitzherbert to Tull* (1947)
G. E. Fussell	'The Low Countries' Influence on English Farming', *Eng. Hist. R.* 74 (1959)
G. E. Fussell	'Crop Nutrition in Tudor and Stuart England', *Agric. Hist. R.* 3 (1955)
G. E. Fussell (ed.)	*Robert Loder's Farm Accounts*, Camden 3rd ser. 53 (1936)
N. S. B. Gras	*The Economic and Social History of an English Village* (Cambridge, Mass., 1930)
E. M. Halcrow	'The Decline of Demesne-Farming on the Estates of Durham Cathedral Priory', *Econ. Hist. R.* 2/7 (1954–5)
P. D. A. Harvey	*A Medieval Oxfordshire Village* (Oxford, 1965)
J. R. Healey and E. L. Jones	'Wheat Yields in England, 1815–1859', *J. R. Statistical Society* 125 (1962)
R. H. Hilton	'Winchcombe Abbey and the Manor of Sherborne', in *Gloucestershire Studies*, ed. Finberg (1957)
R. H. Hilton	*The Economic Development of some Leicestershire Estates in the Fourteenth and Fifteenth Centuries* (Oxford, 1947)
G. C. Homans	*English Villagers of the Thirteenth Century* (Cambridge, Mass., 1942)
W. G. Hoskins	*The Making of the English Landscape* (1955)
W. G. Hoskins	*The Midland Peasant* (1957)
W. G. Hoskins (ed.)	*Studies in Leicestershire Agrarian History* (Leicester, 1949)
W. G. Hoskins	'The Leicestershire Farmer in the Seventeenth Century', *Agric. Hist.* 25 (1951)
A. H. John	'The Course of Agricultural Change, 1660–1760', in *Studies in the Industrial Revolution*, ed. L. S. Pressnell (1960)
A. H. Johnson	*The Disappearance of the Small Landowner* (1909)

J. B. Laws and J. H. Gilbert	'Home Produce, Imports, Consumption and Price of Wheat', *J. R. Agricultural Society* (1893)
E. Miller	*The Abbey and Bishopric of Ely* (Cambridge, 1951)
G. E. Mingay	'The Agricultural Depression, 1730–1750', *Econ. Hist. R.* 2/8 (1956)
G. E. Mingay	'The Size of Farms in the Eighteenth Century', *Econ. Hist. R.* 2/14 (1961)
E. K. O. Ojala	*Agriculture and Economic Progress* (1952)
F. M. Page	*The Estates of Crowland Abbey* (Cambridge, 1934)
M. M. Postan	'The Chronology of Labour Services', *Trans. Roy. Hist. Soc.* 4/20 (1937)
M. M. Postan	'Village Livestock in the Thirteenth Century', *Econ. Hist. R.* 2/15 (1962)
J. A. Raftis	*The Estates of Ramsey Abbey* (Toronto, 1957)
H. A. Rhee	*The Rent of Agricultural Land in England and Wales, 1870–1946* (1949)
B. H. Slicher van Bath	*The Agrarian History of Western Europe, 500–1800* (1963)
C. Smith	*Three Tracts on the Corn Trade* (1766)
R. A. L. Smith	*Canterbury Cathedral Priory* (Cambridge, 1943)
M. Spufford	*A Cambridgeshire Community* (Leicester, 1965)
S. G. Sturmey	'Owner-Farming in England and Wales, 1900–1950', *Manchester School* 23 (1955)
R. H. Tawney	*The Agrarian Problem in the Sixteenth Century* (1912)
J. Thirsk (ed.)	*The Agrarian History of England and Wales IV* (Cambridge, 1967)
J. Thirsk	*English Peasant Farming* (1957)
R. J. Thompson	'An Enquiry into the Rent of Agricultural Land in England and Wales during the Nineteenth Century', *J. R. Statistical Society* 70 (1907)

II (d)   Income and Wealth in Agriculture—The Landed Classes

J. M. W. Bean	*The Estates of the Percy Family, 1416–1537* (Oxford, 1958)

D. C. Coleman	'The Gentry Controversy and the Aristocracy in Crisis, 1558–1641', *History* 51 (1966)
M. E. Finch	*The Wealth of Five Northamptonshire Families* (Northants. Rec. Soc. XIX 1956)
H. J. Habakkuk	'English Landownership 1680–1740', *Econ. Hist. R.* 10 (1940)
G. A. Holmes	*The Estates of the Higher Nobility in 14th-Century England* (Cambridge, 1957)
G. E. Mingay	*English Landed Society in the Eighteenth Century* (1963)
S. Painter	*Studies in the History of the English Feudal Barony* (Baltimore, 1943)
J. T. Rosenthal	'The Estates and Finances of Richard Duke of York, 1411–60', *Studies in Medieval and Renaissance History* II (1965)
C. D. Ross	'The Estates and Finances of Richard Beauchamp, Earl of Warwick', *Dugdale Soc.* 12 (1956)
C. D. Ross and T. B. Pugh	'Materials for the Study of Baronial Incomes in Fifteenth-Century England', *Econ. Hist. R.* 2/6 (1953)
L. F. Salzman	'The Property of the Earl of Arundel 1397', *Sx Arch. Colls* 91 (1953)
A. Simpson	*The Wealth of the Gentry* (Cambridge, 1963)
L. Stone	*The Crisis of the Aristocracy, 1558–1641* (Oxford, 1965)
F. M. L. Thompson	*English Landed Society in the Nineteenth Century* (1963)

II (e) Income and Wealth in Commerce

J. N. Bartlett	'The Expansion and Decline of York in the Later Middle Ages', *Econ. Hist. R.* 2/12 (1965)
M. W. Beresford	*New Towns of the Middle Ages* (1967)
P. J. Bowden	*The Wool Trade in Tudor and Stuart England* (1962)
E. M. Carus-Wilson	'The Medieval Trade of the Ports of the Wash', *Medieval Archaeol.* 6–7 (1962–3)
E. M. Carus-Wilson	'The First Half-Century of the Borough of Stratford-upon-Avon', *Econ. Hist. R.* 2/18 (1965)
D. Charman	'Wealth and Trade in Leicester in the Early Sixteenth Century', *Trans. Leics. Archaeol. Soc.* 25 (1949)

G. N. Clark	*Guide to English Commercial Statistics 1696–1782* (1938)
K. G. Davies	'Empire and Capital', *Econ. Hist. R.* 2/13 (1960)
R. Davis	'Earnings of Capital in the English Shipping Industry, 1670–1730', *J. Econ. Hist.* 17 (1957)
R. Davis	'England and the Mediterranean', in *Essays on the Economic and Social History of Tudor and Stuart England*, ed. F. J. Fisher (1961)
R. Davis	'English Overseas Trade, 1660–1760', *Econ. Hist. R.* 2/7 (1954)
D. A. Farnie	'The Commercial Empire of the Atlantic, 1607–1785', *Econ. Hist. R.* 2/15 (1962)
J. W. F. Hill	*Medieval Lincoln* (Cambridge, 1948)
G. A. Holmes	'Florentine Merchants in England, 1346–1436', *Econ. Hist R.* 2/13 (1960)
J. M. Holzman	*The Nabobs in England* (New York, 1926)
W. G. Hoskins	'English Provincial Towns in the Early 16th Century', *Trans. Roy. Hist. Soc.* 5/6 (1956)
F. E. Hyde, B. B. Parkinson and S. Marriner	'The Nature and Profitability of the Liverpool Slave Trade', *Econ. Hist. R.* 2/5 (1953)
A. H. Imlah	*Economic Elements in the Pax Britannica* (Cambridge, Mass., 1958)
W. J. MacCaffery	*Exeter, 1540–1640* (Cambridge, Mass., 1956)
K. Maiwald	'The Construction Costs and the Value of the Merchant Fleet 1850–1938', *Scottish J. of Pol. Econ.* 3 (1956)
E. Power and M. Postan	*Studies in English Trade in the Fifteenth Century* (1933)
E. Power	*The Wool Trade in English Medieval History* (Oxford, 1941)
G. D. Ramsay	*John Isham's Accounts* (Northants. Rec. Soc., 21, 1962)
G. D. Ramsay	*English Overseas Trade in the Centuries of Emergence* (1957)
A. A. Ruddock	*Italian Merchants and Shipping in Southampton, 1270–1600* (Southampton, 1951)
A. A. Ruddock	'London Capitalists and the Decline of Southampton in the Early Tudor Period', *Econ. Hist. R.* 2/2 (1949)

R. B. Sheridan	'The Wealth of Jamaica in the Eighteenth Century', *Econ. Hist. R.* 2/18 (1965)
W. Schlote	*British Overseas Trade from 1700 to the 1930s* (Oxford, 1952)
E. B. Schumpeter	*English Overseas Trade Statistics, 1697–1808* (Oxford, 1960)
L. Stone	'Elizabethan Overseas Trade', *Econ. Hist. R.* 2/2 (1949)
B. E. Supple	*Commercial Crisis and Change in England, 1600–1642* (Cambridge, 1959)
G. V. Scammell	'Shipowning in England, 1450–1550', *Trans. Roy. Hist. Soc.* 5/12 (1962)
S. L. Thrupp	*The Merchant Class of Medieval London* (Chicago, 1948)
E. M. Veale	*The English Fur Trade in the Later Middle Ages* (Oxford, 1966)
J. Webb	*Great Tooley of Ipswich* (Ipswich, 1962)
R. B. Westerfield	*Middlemen in English Business, 1660–1760* (New Haven, 1915)
T. S. Willan	*The English Coasting Trade, 1600–1750* (Manchester, 1938)
T. S. Willan	*River Navigation in England 1600–1750* (Oxford, 1936)
T. S. Willan	*The Muscovy Merchants of 1555* (Manchester, 1953)
T. S. Willan	*Studies in Elizabethan Foreign Trade* (Manchester, 1959)
C. Wilson	'Treasure and Trade Balances', *Econ. Hist. R.* 2/2 (1949)
C. Wilson	*Profit and Power* (1957)
G. A. Williams	*Medieval London, from Commune to Capital* (1963)

II (f)   Income and Wealth in Industry, Mining, etc.

K. J. Allison	'The Norfolk Worsted Industry in the Sixteenth and Seventeenth Centuries', *Yorks. Bull.* 12 (1960) and 13 (1961)
A. Birch	*The Economic History of the British Iron and Steel Industry, 1784–1879* (1967)
E. M. Carus-Wilson	'The English Cloth Industry in the Late Twelfth and Early Thirteenth Centuries', *Econ. Hist. R.* 14 (1944)
E. M. Carus-Wilson	'An Industrial Revolution of the Thirteenth Century', *Econ. Hist. R.* 11 (1941)

E. M. Carus-Wilson   'Evidence of Industrial Growth on some Fifteenth-century Manors', *Econ. Hist. R.* 2/12 (1959)

W. H. B. Court   *The Rise of the Midland Industries, 1600–1878* (Oxford, 1938)

D. W. Crossley   'The Management of a Sixteenth-Century Ironworks', *Econ. Hist. R.* 2/19 (1966)

M. B. Donald   *Elizabethan Monopolies* (Edinburgh, 1961)

M. W. Flinn   *Men of Iron: The Crowleys in the Early Iron Industry* (Edinburgh, 1962)

M. W. Flinn   'The Growth of the English Iron Industry, 1660–1760', *Econ. Hist. R.* 2/11 (1958–9)

H. Heaton   *The Yorkshire Woollen and Worsted Industries*, 2nd ed. (1965)

W. G. Hoffmann   *British Industry 1700–1950* (Oxford, 1955)

G. T. Lapsley   'The Account-Roll of a Fifteenth-Century Ironmaster', *Eng. Hist. R.* 14 (1899)

H. Leak   'Statistics of the Census of Production and Distribution', *J. R. Statistical Society* 112 (1949)

G. R. Lewis   *The Stannaries* (1907)

K. S. Lomax   'Production and Productivity Movements in the United Kingdom since 1900', *J. R. Statistical Society* 122 (1959)

B. McClenaghan   *The Springs of Lavenham* (Ipswich, 1924)

E. Miller   'The Fortunes of the English Textile Industry in the Thirteenth Century', *Econ. Hist. R.* 2/18 (1965)

B. R. Mitchell   'The Coming of the Railway Age and United Kingdom Economic Growth', *J. of Econ. History*, 24 (1964)

J. U. Nef (ed.)   *The Rise of the British Coal Industry*, 2 vols (1932)

R. A. Pelham   'The Cloth Markets of Warwickshire during the Late Middle Ages', *Trans. Birm. Arch. Soc.* 66 (1950)

J. E. Pilgrim   'The Rise of the New Draperies in Essex', *Univ. Birm. Hist. Jnl* 7 (1961)

W. H. Price   *The English Patents of Monopoly* (Boston, 1906)

A. Raistrick and E. Allen   'The South Yorkshire Ironmasters, 1690–1750', *Econ. Hist. R.* 9 (1938–9)

A. Raistrick   *Dynasty of Ironfounders: The Darbys of Coalbrookdale* (1953)

G. D. Ramsay	*The Wiltshire Woollen Industry in the Sixteenth and Seventeenth Centuries* (1965 edn)
T. M. Ridley	'Industrial Production in the U.K., 1900–1953', *Economica* 22 (1955)
L. F. Salzman	*English Industries of the Middle Ages* (1923)
L. F. Salzman	*Building in England down to 1540* (1952)
H. R. Schubert	*A History of the British Iron and Steel Industry to 1755* (1957)
W. R. Scott	*The Constitution and Finance of English Joint-Stock Companies to 1700*, 3 vols (Cambridge, 1910–12)
L. Stone	'An Elizabethan Coalmine', *Econ. Hist. R.* 2/3 (1950–1)
A. J. Taylor	'Labour Productivity and Technological Innovation in the British Coal Industry, 1850–1914', *Econ. Hist. R.* 2/14 (1961)
J. Thirsk	'Industries in the Countryside' in *Essays in the Economic and Social History of Tudor and Stuart England*, ed. F. J. Fisher (1961)
G. Unwin	*Studies in Economic History* (1927)

Victoria County History: Wiltshire, vol. 4 (1959)

| A. P. Wadsworth and J. De L. Mann | *The Cotton Trade and Industrial Lancashire, 1600–1780* (1931) |

II (g)   Class-distribution of Incomes

T. Barna	*The Redistribution of Incomes Through Public Finance in 1937* (Oxford, 1945)
P. T. Baver and B. S. Yamey	'Economic Progress and Occupational Distribution', *Econ. J.* 61 (1951)
A. L. Bowley	*The Change in the Distribution of the National Income, 1880–1913* (Oxford, 1920)
A. L. Bowley	*The Division of the Product of Industry* (Oxford, 1919)
A. M. Carter	*The Redistribution of Income in Post-War Britain* (New Haven, 1955)
E. A. Kosminsky	*Studies in the Agrarian History of England* (Oxford, 1956)
H. F. Lydall	*British Incomes and Savings* (Oxford, 1955)
H. F. Lydall	'The Long-Term Trend in the Size Distribution of Income', *J. R. Statistical Society* 122 (1959)

H. Lydall and J. B. Lansing	'Distribution of Personal Income and Wealth in the United States and Great Britain', *Amer. Economic R.* 49 (1959)
H. F. Lydall and D. G. Tipping	'The Distribution of Personal Wealth in Britain', *Bull. Oxford Institute of Statistics* 23 (1961)
J. G. Marley and H. Campion	'Changes in Salaries in Great Britain, 1924–1939', *J. R. Statistical Society* 103 (1940)
J. S. Nicolson	'Redistribution of Income in the U.K. in 1959, 1957 and 1953', *Income and Wealth* Series 10 (1964)
E. H. Phelps Brown and P. E. Hart	'The Share of Wages in National Income', *Econ. J.* 62 (1952)
E. H. Phelps Brown and B. Weber	'Accumulation, Productivity and Distribution in the British Economy, 1870–1938', *Econ. J.* 63 (1953)
E. H. Phelps Brown	'The Long-Term Movement of Real Wages', in J. T. Dunlop (ed.), *The Theory of Wage Determination* (1957)
G. Routh	'Civil Service Pay, 1875–1950', *Economica* 21 (1954)
J. Saville	'Labour and Income Redistribution', in R. Miliband and J. Saville (ed.), *Socialist Register* (1965)
D. Seers	*The Levelling of Incomes Since 1938* (Oxford, 1951)
R. M. Titmuss	*Income Distribution and Social Change* (1962)

II (h)   *Wages, Working-Class Living Standards*

T. S. Ashton	'The Standard of Life of the Workers in England, 1790–1830', *J. Econ. Hist.* 9 (1949)
Beveridge, Sir William (Lord), *et al.*	*Prices and Wages in England from the Twelfth to the Nineteenth Century* vol. 1 (1939)
W. H. Beveridge	'Wages on the Winchester Manors', *Econ. Hist. R.* 7 (1936)

W. H. Beveridge 'Westminster Wages in the Manorial Era', *Econ. Hist. R.* 2/8 (1955–6)

A. L. Bowley 'The Statistics of Wages in the U.K. during the Nineteenth Century', *J. R. Statistical Society* (several issues, 1898–1902)

A. L. Bowley and
  G. H. Wood 'The Statistics of Wages in the U.K. during the Nineteenth Century: Engineering and Shipbuilding', *J. R. Statistical Society* 69 (1905–6)

A. L. Bowley *Wages in the United Kingdom in the Nineteenth Century* (Cambridge, 1900)

A. L. Bowley 'Index Numbers of Wage Rates and Cost of Living', *J. R. Statistical Society* 115 (1952)

A. L. Bowley *Prices and Wages in the United Kingdom, 1914-1920* (Oxford, 1921)

A. L. Bowley *Studies in the National Income, 1924–1938* (Cambridge, 1944)

A. L. Chapman *Wages and Salaries in the United Kingdom, 1920–1938* (Cambridge, 1952)

D. C. Coleman 'Labour in the English Economy of the Seventeenth Century', *Econ. Hist. R.* 2/8 (1956)

F. Collier *The Family Economy of the Working Classes in the Cotton Industry, 1784–1833* (Manchester, 1965)

A. Fox 'Agricultural Wages in England and Wales during the Last Fifty Years', *J. R. Statistical Society* 66 (1903)

R. Giffen *Economic Inquiries and Studies* (2 vols, 1904)

E. W. Gilboy 'The Cost of Living and Real Wages in the Eighteenth Century', *Rev. of Economic Statistics* 18 (1936)

E. W. Gilboy *Wages in Eighteenth-Century England* (1934)

R. M. Hartwell 'The Rising Standard of Living of England, 1800–1850', *Econ. Hist. R.* 2/13 (1961)

R. H. Hilton 'Peasant Movements before 1381', *Econ. Hist. R.* 2/2 (1949)

R. H. Hilton 'Freedom and Villeinage in England', *Past and Present* 31 (1965)

R. H. Hilton 'The Social Structure of Rural Warwickshire in the Middle Ages', *Dugdale Soc. Occ. paper* 9 (1950)

E. J. Hobsbawm	'The British Standard of Living, 1790–1850', *Econ. Hist. R.* 2/10 (1957)
E. J. Hobsbawm	'Révolution Industrielle et Vie Matérielle des Classes Populaires', *Annales* (1962)
E. J. Hobsbawm and R. M. Hartwell	'The Standard of Living During the Industrial Revolution: A Discussion', *Econ. Hist. R.* 2/16 (1963)
E. L. Jones	'The Agricultural Labour Market in England, 1793–1872', *Econ. Hist. R.* 17 (1965)
R. K. Kelsall	*Wage Regulation under the Statute of Artificers* (1938)
K. G. J. C. Knowles and D. J. Robertson	'Differences between the Wages of Skilled and Unskilled Workers, 1880–1950', *Bull. Oxford University Institute of Statistics* 13 (1951)
J. Kuczynski	*Die Geschichte der Lage der Arbeiter unter dem Kapitalismus*, vol. 24 (Berlin, 1965)
J. Kuczynski	*A Short History of Labour Conditions in Great Britain 1750 to the Present Day* (1942)
L. Levi	*Wages and Earnings of the Working Classes* (1885)
W. I. Leyton	'Changes in the Wages of Domestic Servants during Fifty Years', *J. R. Statistical Society* 71 (1908)
W. A. Mackenzie	'Changes in the Standard of Living in the U.K., 1860–1914', *Economica* 1 (1921)
R. Millond and G. Evans	'Scottish Farm Wages from 1870–1900', *J. R. Statistical Society* 113 (1950)
E. H. Phelps Brown and S. V. Hopkins	'Seven Centuries of Building Wages', *Economica* N.S. 22 (1955)
E. H. Phelps Brown and S. V. Hopkins	'Seven Centuries of the Prices of Consumables, Compared with Builders' Wage Rates', *Economica* 23 (1956)
E. H. Phelps Brown and S. V. Hopkins	'Wage Rates and Prices: Evidence for Population Pressure in the Sixteenth Century', *Economica* 24 (1957)
I. Pinchbeck	*Woman Workers in the Industrial Revolution, 1750–1850* (1930)
M. M. Postan and J. Z. Titow	'Heriots and Prices on Winchester Manors', *Econ. Hist. R.* 2/11 (1959)
E. C. Ramsbottom	'The Course of Wage Rates in the U.K., 1921–1934', *J. R. Statistical Society* 98 (1935)

E. C. Ramsbottom	'The Course of Wage Rates in the U.K., 1934–1937', *ibid.* 101 (1938)
E. C. Ramsbottom	'The Course of Wage Rates in the U.K., 1938', *ibid.* 102 (1939)
J. E. T. Rogers	*Six Centuries of Work and Wages* (1906)
J. F. W. Rowe	*Wages in Practice and Theory* (1928)
G. F. Steffen	*Studien zur Geschichte der Englischen Lohnarbeiter* (3 vols, Stuttgart, 1901)
A. J. Taylor	'Progress and Poverty in Britain, 1780–1850: A Reappraisal', *History* 45 (1960)
J. Z. Titow	'Some Differences between Manors and Their Effects on the Condition of the Peasant in the Thirteenth Century', *Agric. Hist. R.* 10 (1962)
R. S. Tucker	'The Real Wages of Artisans in London, 1729–1935', *J. American Statistical Assoc.* 31 (1936)
C. Wilson	'The Other Face of Mercantilism', *Trans. Roy. Hist. Soc.* 5/9 (1959)
F. Wood	'The Course of Real Wages in London, 1900–1912', *J. R. Statistical Society* 77 (1913–14)
G. H. Wood	'The Course of Average Wages between 1790 and 1860', *Econ. J.* 9 (1899)
G. H. Wood	'Real Wages and the Standard of Comfort since 1850', *J. R. Statistical Society* 72 (1909)
G. H. Wood	'The Statistics of Wages in the United Kingdom during the Nineteenth Century: the Cotton Industry', *ibid.* 73 (1910).

II (j) Fluctuations

T. S. Ashton	*Economic Fluctuations in England 1700–1800* (1959)
T. S. Ashton	'Economic Fluctuations, 1790–1850', *Econ. Hist. R.* 7 (1955)
H. L. Beales	'The Great Depression in Industry and Trade', *Econ. Hist. R.* 5 (1934)
Beveridge, Sir William	'Unemployment in the Trade Cycle', *Econ. J.* 49 (1939)
D. J. Coppock	'The Climacteric of the 1890s', *Manchester School* 26 (1956)
A. Gayer, W. W. Rostow and A. J. Schwartz	*The Growth and Fluctuations of the British Economy, 1790–1850* (2 vols, Oxford, 1953)

E. J. Hobsbawm	'Economic Fluctuations and Some Social Movements since 1800', *Econ. Hist. R.* 2/5 (1952)
J. Parry Lewis	*Building Cycles and Britain's Growth* (1965)
R. C. O. Matthews	'The Trade Cycle in Britain, 1790–1850', *Oxford Economic Papers* N.S.6 (1954)
A. E. Musson	'The Great Depression in Britain, 1873–1896: A Reappraisal', *J. Econ. Hist.* 19 (1959)
A. E. Musson	'British Industrial Growth, 1873–96: A Balanced View', *Econ. Hist. R.* 2/17 (1964)
H. W. Richardson	*Economic Recovery in Britain, 1932–1939* (1967)
W. W. Rostow	*British Economy of the Nineteenth Century* (Oxford, 1948)
B. Thomas	*Migration and Economic Growth* (Cambridge, 1954)

II (k)   War and Wealth

J. H. Clapham	'Europe after the Great Wars, 1816 and 1920', *Economic J.* 30 (1920)
J. H. Clapham	'Wars and Subsidies in Times of War, 1793–1914', *Economic J.* 27 (1917)
G. N. Clark	'War Trade and Trade War 1701–1713', *Econ. Hist. R.* 1 (1927)
J. G. Edwards	'The Building of Edward I's Castles in Wales', *Proc. Brit. Acad.* 32 (1946)
G. E. Fussell and M. Compton	'Agricultural Adjustment after the Napoleonic Wars', *Econ. History* 4 (1939)
W. K. Hancock and M. M. Gowing	*British War Economy* (1949)
A. Hope-Jones	*Income Tax in the Napoleonic Wars* (Cambridge, 1939)
A. H. John	'War and the English Economy, 1700–1763', *Econ. Hist. R.* 2/7 (1955)
A. H. John	'Farming in Wartime: 1793–1815', *Land, Labour and Population in the Industrial Revolution* (ed. Jones and Mingay, 1967)
C. L. Kingsford	*Prejudice and Promise in Fifteenth-Century England* (1925)
J. H. Kirk	'The Output of British Agriculture during the War', *J. Agricultural Economics* (1945)
K. B. Macfarlane	'Bastard Feudalism', *Bull. Inst. Hist. Res.* 20 (1945)

K. B. Macfarlane	'England and the Hundred Years' War', *Past and Present* 22 (1962)
K. B. Macfarlane	'The Investment of Sir John Fastolf's Profits in War', *Trans. Roy. Hist. Soc.* 5/7 (1957)
Mancur Olson Jr.	*The Economics of Wartime Shortage* (Durham, N.C., 1963)
J. U. Nef	*War and Human Progress* (Cambridge, Mass., 1950)
R. Pares	*War and Trade in the West Indies* (1936)
M. M. Postan	'Some Social Consequences of the Hundred Years' War', *Econ. Hist. R.* 12 (1942)
M. M. Postan	'The Costs of the Hundred Years' War', *Past and Present* 27 (1964)

III Consumption (a) General

T. S. Ashton	'Changes in the Standards of Comfort in Eighteenth-Century England', *Proc. British Academy* 41 (1955)
M. Campbell	*The English Yeoman* (New Haven, 1942)
J. B. Jefferys	*Retail Trading in Britain, 1850–1950* (Cambridge, 1954)
S. Nowell-Smith (ed.)	*Edwardian England 1901–1914* (1964)
A. R. Prest and A. A. Adams	*Consumers' Expenditure in the United Kingdom, 1900–1919* (Cambridge, 1954)
A. Rive	'The Consumption of Tobacco since 1600', *Economic History* I (1926)
J. R. N. Stone and D. Rowe	*The Measurement of Consumers' Expenditure and Behaviour in the United Kingdom, 1920–1938* (2 vols, Cambridge, 1954, 1966)
G. M. Young (ed.)	*Early Victorian England* (2 vols, 1934)
G. M. Young (ed.)	*Victorian England* (Oxford, 1937)

III (b) Food Consumption

F. Accum	*Treatise on the Adulteration of Food and Culinary Poisons* (1820)
W. J. Ashley	*The Bread of our Forefathers* (1928)
T. C. Barker, J. C. McKenzie and J. Yudkin (ed.)	*Our Changing Fare* (1966)
J. Burnett	*Plenty and Want* (1966)

G. Dodd	*The Food of London* (1956)
J. C. Drummond and A. Wilbraham	*The Englishman's Food* (1939)
D. L. Farmer	'Some Grain-Price Movements in Thirteenth-Century England', *Econ. Hist. R.* 2/10 (1957)
F. J. Fisher	'The Development of the London Food Market, 1540–1640', *Econ. Hist. R.* 2 (1935)
W. F. Galpin	*The Grain Supply of England during the Napoleonic Period* (N.Y., 1925)
N. S. B. Gras	*The Evolution of the English Corn Market* (Cambridge, Mass., 1915)
A. H. Hassall	*Food and its Adulteration* (1855)
C. L. Kingsford (ed.)	*Stonor Letters and Papers* (Camden 3rd Ser. 29, 30, 1919)
Min. of Agriculture and Fisheries	*The Agricultural Output and Food Supplies of Great Britain* (1929)
J. Mitchell	*Treatise on the Falsification of Food* (1848)
J. Boyd Orr	*Food, Health and Income* (1936)
V. B. Redstone (ed.)	*The Household Book of Dame Alice de Bryene* (Suffolk Inst. of Archaeol. and Nat. Hist., Ipswich, 1931)
R. H. Rew	'An Inquiry into the Statistics of the Production and Consumption of Milk and Milk Products in Great Britain', *J. R. Statistical Society* 55 (1892)
R. N. Salaman	*The History and Social Influence of the Potato* (1949)
W. M. Stern	'The Bread Crisis in Britain 1795–96', *Economica* 31 (1964)
E. M. Whetham	'The London Milk Trade, 1860–1900', *Econ. Hist. R.* 2/17 (1964)
K. L. Wood-Leigh	*A Small Household in the Fifteenth Century* (Manchester, 1956)

III (c) Manufactured Articles Consumption

D. E. C. Eversley	'The Home Market and Economic Growth in England, 1750–80', in Jones and Mingay (ed.), *Land, Labour and Population in the Industrial Revolution* (1967)
F. J. Fisher	'The Growth of London as a Centre of Conspicuous Consumption', *Trans. Roy. Hist. Soc.* 4/30 (1948)

C. H. Wilson   'Economy and Society in Late Victorian Britain', *Econ. Hist. R.* 2/18 (1965)

III (d) Housing, Sanitation, Social Services

M. W. Barley   *The English Farmhouse and Cottage* (1961)

M. Biddle   'The Deserted Medieval Village of Seacourt, Berkshire', *Oxoniensia* 26/7 (1961–2)

M. Bowley   *Housing and the State, 1919–1944* (1945)

M. C. Buer   *Health, Wealth and Population in the Early Days of the Industrial Revolution* (1926)

R. K. Field   'Worcestershire Peasant Buildings, Household Goods and Farming Equipment', *Medieval Archaeol.* 9 (1965)

W. M. Frazer   *A History of Public Health* (1951)

G. E. Fussell and C. Goodman   'The Housing of the Rural Population in the Eighteenth Century', *Economic History* 2 (1930)

G. Talbot Griffith   *Population Problems of the Age of Malthus* (Cambridge, 1926)

B. Hammond   'Urban Death Rates in the Early Nineteenth Century', *Econ. Hist.* 1 (1928)

B. Harvey   'The Population Trend in England, 1300–48', *Trans. Roy. Hist. Soc.* 5/16 (1966)

M. A. Havinden   *Household and Farm Inventories in Oxfordshire* (1965)

R. H. Hilton and P. A. Rahtz   'Upton, Gloucestershire, 1959–64', *Trans. Bristol and Glos. Archaeol. Soc.* 85 (1966)

W. G. Hoskins   'The Rebuilding of Rural England', *Past and Present* 4 (1953)

J. G. Hurst   'The Medieval Peasant House', *4th Viking Congress York, 1961* (Aberdeen, 1965)

A. E. Levett   'The Black Death on the St Albans Manors' in *Studies in Manorial History* (Oxford, 1938)

A. E. Levett   *The Black Death on the Estates of the See of Winchester* (Oxford, 1916)

T. McKeown and R. G. Brown   'Medical Evidence Relating to English Population Changes in the Eighteenth Century', *Population Studies* 9 (1955)

M. M. Postan   'Some Economic Evidence of Declining Population in the Later Middle Ages', *Econ. Hist. R.* 2/2 (1950)

J. C. Russell   *British Medieval Population* (Albuquerque, 1948)

Simon, Sir John   *English Sanitary Institutions* (1890)

S. Thrupp   'The Problem of Replacement Rates in Late Medieval English Population', *Econ. Hist. R.* 2/18 (1965)

G. S. L. Tucker   'English Pre-Industrial Population Trends', *Econ. Hist. R.* 2/12 (1963)

III (e) Poverty

L. P. Adams   *Agricultural Depression and Farm Relief in England 1813–1852* (1965)

C. Booth   *Life and Labour of the People of London* (17 vols, 1902–4)

C. Booth and A. R. Burnett-Hurst   *Livelihood and Poverty* (1915)

P. Colquhoun   *Treatise on Indigence* (1806)

Eden, Sir F. M.   *State of the Poor* (3 vols, 1797)

N. Gash   'Rural Unemployment, 1815–34', *Econ. Hist. R.* 6 (1935)

J. Hilton   *Rich Man, Poor Man* (1944)

W. K. Jordan   *Philanthropy in England, 1480–1660* (1959)

E. M. Leonard   *The Early History of English Poor Relief* (1900)

J. C. M. McGonigle and J. Kirby   *Poverty and Public Health* (1937)

L. Money   *Riches and Poverty* (1905)

F. W. Purdy   'Statistics of the English Poor Rate before and since the Passing of the Poor Law Amendment Act', *J. R. Statistical Society* 23 (1860)

H. Mayhew   *London Labour and the Poor* (4 vols, 1961 ed.)

Reeves, Mrs Pember   *Round About a Pound a Week* (1913)

B. S. Rowntree   *Poverty and Progress* (1941)

B. S. Rowntree and B. R. Lavers   *Poverty and the Welfare State* (1951)

S. and B. Webb   *English Local Government: vol. 7 English Poor Law History, 1. The Old Poor Law* (1927)

Index